A *Jerry Baker* Health Book

HOMEMADE
HEALTH

www.jerrybaker.com

A *Jerry Baker* Health Book

HOMEMADE HEALTH

Over 415 Remarkable Recipes with the Magical Power to Heal!

Colleen Pierre, M.S., R.D.

Published by American Master Products, Inc. / Jerry Baker
Kim Adam Gasior, Publisher

A Jerry Baker Health Book and A Blackberry Cottage Production
Editorial: Ellen Michaud, Blackberry Cottage Productions
Design: Nest Publishing Resources
Editor: Carol Keough
Book Composition: Wayne Michaud
Illustrator: Wayne Michaud
Copy Editor: Jane Sherman
Assistant Managing Editor: Carol Spennachio

Printed in the United States of America

Illustrations copyright © 2003 by Wayne Michaud

Publisher's Cataloging-in-Publication
(*Provided by Quality Books, Inc.*)

Pierre, Colleen.
    Homemade Health: over 415 remarkable recipes with the magical power to
        heal / by Colleen Pierre.
        p. cm.
    Includes index.
    "A Jerry Baker health book."
    ISBN: 0-922433-47-X
        1. Cookery for the sick.   2. Diet therapy.
3. Functional foods.
    I. Baker, Jerry. II. Title.

    RM219.P54 2003   613.2
                       QBI02-200918

           6 8 10 9 7 5 hardcover

FOREWORD

When I was invited to dinner at my son's house last week, I got there a bit early, as I usually do. But instead of watching the Dolphins destroy the Lions, I hung around the kitchen, watching my daughter-in-law, Laurie, whose cooking could put Julia Child to shame. She was busier than a beaver, running from oven to counter to sink to table and back again. Tonight's menu? Eggplant lasagna, fresh green beans, and a salad overflowing with the freshest veggies this side of my garden.

As I helped Laurie set the table, I couldn't help but marvel. By day, she works at our family publishing company; by night, she's a healthy-dinner-preparing, bill-paying, homework-helping, advice-giving wonder. It made me stop and think: Just how does she do it?

Well, that's a good question: Just how does *any* woman do it today?

When I was growing up, times sure were different. Simpler. Less hectic. More relaxed. My Grandma Putt spent hours preparing our nightly meals—precious hours that today's wives and mothers simply don't have. Women worked hard back then, sure, but the pressures on women today—they're something else! Gone are the days when the men hunted to provide food for the family. Health care costs and college tuition for a couple of kids now means a couple of incomes. And while taking care of the family is still a full-time job, so is a full-time job— which means something has to give.

Or, in this case, someone. Watching Laurie started me thinking. So I called my friend Colleen, a registered dietitian and nutrition editor at *Child* magazine, who prepared the recipes for my first health book, *Kitchen Counter Cures*. I decided to ask for her help once again. I told her about Laurie, and while I had her on the phone, I also told her about my old friend George, a seed-swapping buddy who had so many fat balls running around in his arteries that his triglyceride levels were about to do him in.

I wanted to do something to help George lower his triglyc-erides and get Laurie out of the kitchen faster, I told Colleen. In short, I wanted her to put together a book chock-full of quick and easy recipes with an emphasis on raising strong, healthy families. And I wanted those recipes to combat the all-too-common ail-ments of my friends and neigh-bors—diabetes, high cholesterol, indi-gestion (I swear, sometimes my tummy feels like a weed-eater's running amuck in there!)—and, of course, triglycerides. And finally, the recipes just had to taste good!

Of course, Colleen came through like a champ, just as she always does. *Homemade Health* is jam-packed with recipes that promote good health and are absolutely delicious—so much so that you won't even miss those personal pizzas and jumbo fries at the mall! In addition, it will help you and your family prevent the health hazards that are all too prevalent today, plus give you some practical pointers, such as:

♥ How to give your body an "oil change" to reduce your risk of heart attack and stroke.

♥ How to DASH away high blood pressure with an *amazing* system.

♥ How to cut fat and boost flavor with quick dishes to keep your heart happy and healthy.

♥ How to build better bones and tickle your taste buds without having a cow about drinking milk.

♥ How to use our Quick Tricks to cut kitchen prep time by more than *half*!

♥ How to stave off strokes, deter diabetes, pump up your heart, and save your sight with the Staff of Life.

♥ How to flavorize the cabbage clan with a little clever cooking for tasty cancer-preventing dishes your whole family will love.

I'm happy to report that Laurie loves these recipes—partly because her family thinks they taste so good, but mostly because now that she's started using them, she has time to exercise in the evenings after work!

And George? Well, let's just say that he's no longer on a first-name basis with the kids at the local fast-food joint. As a result, his triglyceride count is steadily decreasing, and I expect that we'll be trading our heirloom tomato seeds for a long time to come.

So read on, my friends! The Table of Contents, Health Finder, and Index will help you find what you need, and the label at the bottom of each recipe will tell you whether it's an appetizer, soup, salad, dressing, breakfast, lunch, main dish, marinade, sauce, side dish, snack, beverage, or dessert. *Homemade Health* will help make your family as strong as Grandma Putt made mine! And in half the time!

CONTENTS

INTRODUCTION

When I was a young wife and mother with a freshly
minted degree in dietetics, I spent a lot of time in the kitchen,
cooking from scratch. Not any more! Oh, I still cook from
scratch, but I don't spend a lot of time doing it. Over the years,
I've learned enough shortcuts and time trimmers to fill a pretty
big book, and I'm going to share them all with you.

If you're like me, your days are packed with a million things to
do, so you can't spend hours preparing a meal. But cooking and
sharing healthy, delicious meals have always been the golden
threads that tie me to the people I love. I cherish that, don't you?

Think back with me. I can still see my daughter Bobbi at four
years old, standing on a chair, helping me knead dough to make
bread. To this day, she can recite the rhythm—turn, fold,
push…turn, fold, push. Oh, the taste of that bread, hot from the

oven! I love to watch her face when she talks about it. Her eyes shine with pleasure; she feels connected, secure, safe—and loved.

While I admit that I'm not likely to make bread all that often these days, it wouldn't be surprising to see me cooking up buckwheat pancakes like my dad did on Sunday mornings, or crumb-coating a tray of my mom's oven-fried chicken. Faster still, I pan-grill pork chops with savory leeks—in 10 minutes or less. My son, Mike, taught me that.

On any given Sunday, you might find my husband, Ted, and me in the kitchen, turning out a delicious dinner of filet mignon, oven-roasted potatoes, lemony broccoli, and a hearty, veggie-packed salad, all in about 20 minutes! We never get over how close we feel when we sit down together to eat a meal like that.

Given the number of times folks eat away from home these days, it seems to me that they're missing out on some of life's best moments—and it's so unnecessary. Most of my cooking is faster than a pizza delivery—plus, it's dynamite when it comes to flavor and nutrition.

Why not experience the closeness, comfort, and good health that home cooking provides? Turning out delicious meals is probably easier than you think. Our need for speed has jam-packed grocery stores with healthy ingredients that allow us to make homemade meals in minutes. We have the means to liberate ourselves from some of the pretty awful stuff that passes for food out there. Even better, we can escape the heavy toll it takes in heart disease, obesity, diabetes, and high blood pressure.

Those homemade meals are more powerful than we ever imagined. In recent years, food and nutrition scientists have teased out some of Mother Nature's most closely guarded kitchen secrets. My college professors would be floored to learn about the sight-saving power of spinach, the memory-boosting potential of blueberries, or the cold-curing dynamics of a little old clove of garlic. And we thought we were just eating great food!

Just for you, I've tried to weave together all the best that food has to offer—great flavor, good health, and lots of love. And you know what? It was easier than I expected. Now, if you're ready for a great taste test, gather your family and friends around the table. I think you're all going to like what this book has to offer. Enjoy!

COLLEEN

Colleen Pierre, M.S., R.D.

CHAPTER 1

BOOST EVERY HEARTBEAT

TRY MY ANTI-CHOLESTEROL CUISINE

MORE THAN 20 YEARS AGO, MY DAD HAD BYPASS surgery to replace a blocked coronary artery. Normally, he could expect that artery to clog back up in 10 to 15 years. But a recent checkup amazed his doctors, because that bypass was still as clean as a whistle!

Dad's secret? It's not really a secret at all. He did what his doctors told him to do: He lowered his cholesterol by exercising regularly and actually sticking to the low saturated fat diet prescribed for him during his recovery. (Yes, for the full 20 years!) He traded his nightly soup bowl of Häagen-Dazs for a small serving of ice milk, switched from cheeseburger lunches to peanut butter and crackers, and replaced bacon-and-egg breakfasts with oatmeal and fat-free milk. And his program of exercise and diet really worked!

Thirty years of research make it clear: Diets high in saturated fat will raise most people's bad low-density lipoprotein (LDL) cholesterol—and heart disease risk along with it. Happily, the reverse is also true. When you cut saturated fat, both cholesterol and the risk of heart disease usually plummet. And there's more good news: Unless you have diabetes or your cholesterol is very high (around 300 mg/dl), foods high in cholesterol but low in saturated fat (such as egg yolks and shrimp) have very little effect on your blood cholesterol level, so you can include them in a heart-healthy diet.

On an even more positive note, trading in some of your meat-chicken-fish meals for beans gives you a double bang for your buck. Not only do beans have no saturated fat, but they also actively work to lower your cholesterol. And here's a bonus: They deliver big doses of folate, the B vitamin that controls homocysteine, an element in your blood that can trigger a heart attack.

And the news gets even better. You don't have to abandon red meats like beef, pork, lamb, and veal; just skip the plate-size slabs! By following a few simple guidelines, you can eat them all!

♥ **Think of meat as a condiment** or flavor enhancer for other foods instead of the centerpiece of the plate, and choose smaller, 2- or 3-ounce portions. I'll show you how.

♥ **Select low fat instead of choosing Choice.** That's right, the Select grade of beef has less hidden fat than Choice.

♥ **Put an end to finish.** "Finish" is the fat that wraps around the outside of the meat. Just trim it off and throw it away.

♥ **Gird your loins for battle.** Buy cuts labeled "loin" (sirloin, tenderloin) or "round" (top round, bottom round, eye of round). They deliver the least fat.

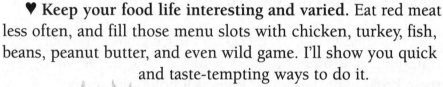

♥ **Add flavor, not fat, when cooking.** Grill, broil, or simmer lean meats with wine, herbs, onions, garlic, tomatoes, and other vegetables instead of frying. Yum, yum!

♥ **Keep your food life interesting and varied.** Eat red meat less often, and fill those menu slots with chicken, turkey, fish, beans, peanut butter, and even wild game. I'll show you quick and taste-tempting ways to do it.

These suggestions are just the tip of the iceberg lettuce! You can do lots more good things to keep your heart happy. This chapter (and the remainder of this book, too!) is jam-packed with healthy ideas and delicious recipes for you to try. Bet you never had Snow Soup before. And have you ever prepared a Passionate Chicken? No? Well, you're about to begin a delightful adventure in cooking right for your heart.

Learning to eat healthier is easier and more delicious than you think. Come on out to the kitchen, and I'll show you how it's done!

Sausage-Stuffed Mushroom Caps

I'm always looking for simple appetizers that leave my guests hungry for the dinner I've slaved over. This one is so simple that I can do it ahead, then relax and have a drink with my friends instead of working myself into a frenzy. And I always feel better knowing that something so sinful-tasting is, when prepared this way, heart smart, too!

1 pound very low fat smoked beef sausage
16 large mushrooms, cleaned and stems removed

Cut the sausage into 16 pieces and place a piece in each mushroom cap. Broil for about 5 minutes, or until the sausage starts to brown but the mushrooms still hold their shape.

Yield: 16 servings

Nutritional data per serving: Calories, 41; protein, 5 g; carbohydrate, 4 g; dietary fiber, 0 g; total fat, <1 g; saturated fat, 0 g; cholesterol, 10 mg; sodium, 244 mg; vitamin A, 0% of Daily Value; vitamin C, 3%; calcium, 0%; iron, 2%; vitamin B$_2$ (riboflavin), 6%; vitamin B$_3$ (niacin), 5%.

The
P·E·R·F·E·C·T
Companion

Put some sparkle in your cocktail hour. Fill a tall glass with ice, add a squeeze of fresh lime juice, and fill with tonic. It's cold, fizzy, and refreshing!

Curried Hummus Spread

My kids have learned to love hummus as an appetizer, especially since I started whipping up my own in the blender. Every now and then, I change the spices just to keep their taste buds tuned up.

1 can (15½ ounces) chickpeas, rinsed and drained
2 tablespoons chopped garlic (from a jar)
2 tablespoons peanut oil
2 tablespoons fresh lemon juice
1 teaspoon curry powder
1 tablespoon dried chives
3 tablespoons water

In a blender, combine the chickpeas, garlic, oil, lemon juice, curry powder, chives, and water. Blend until smooth. Serve with toasted whole wheat pita wedges.

Yield: 15 servings

Nutritional data per serving: Calories, 50; protein, 1 g; carbohydrate, 7 g; dietary fiber, 1 g; total fat, 2 g; saturated fat, 0 g; cholesterol, 0 mg; sodium, 70 mg; vitamin A, 0% of Daily Value; vitamin C, 4%; calcium, 1%; iron, 2%; vitamin B$_6$, 7%; folate, 5%; zinc, 2%.

Lovely Leftovers Store leftovers in a see-through container in the front of the fridge. Keep washed and cut-up veggies nearby. Your refrigerator raiders will have a field day!

Snow Soup

When snowflakes started to fall, my Aunt Narcie would head for the kitchen and put a pot of this soup on to simmer. By the time her kids were finished shoveling the walks, the soup was ready, and the kitchen was warm and cozy. Boy, that was a long time ago, but the soup is as good as ever!

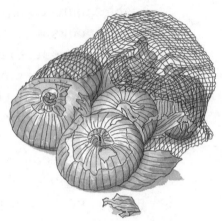

8 ounces very lean ground beef
1 large onion, chopped
2 large ribs celery, sliced
2 large carrots, sliced
1 cup pearled barley, rinsed
1 can (15 ounces) crushed tomatoes
¼ cup parsley flakes
2 beef bouillon cubes
Freshly ground black pepper to taste
8 cups water

In a large nonstick soup pot or Dutch oven over medium-high heat, brown the beef and onion. Pour off the fat. Add the celery, carrots, barley, tomatoes (with juice), parsley, bouillon, pepper, and water. Stir and bring to a boil. Reduce the heat, cover, and simmer for about 1 hour, or until the barley is tender. Serve hot with crusty bread and a green salad.

Yield: 8 servings

Nutritional data per serving: Calories, 201; protein, 12 g; carbohydrate, 27 g; dietary fiber, 6 g; total fat, 5 g; saturated fat, 2 g; cholesterol, 28 mg; sodium, 420 mg; vitamin A, 38% of Daily Value; vitamin C, 17%; calcium, 5%; iron, 15%; vitamin B$_3$ (niacin), 15%; zinc, 16%.

Mighty Minestrone

This is not your grandmother's soup, stewing around all day long. Nope. Although it is warm and zesty, this bean-filled beauty is packed with all the "hearty" ingredients your body could ever hope for. And it takes less than 30 minutes to make! Just add a green salad and a slice of 7-grain bread for healthy perfection.

1 tablespoon dehydrated onions
4 ounces gemelli pasta
6 cups water
2 cups frozen mixed vegetables
1 can (4½ ounces) Del Monte Fresh Cut diced tomatoes with garlic, oregano, and basil
1 can (15½ ounces) red kidney beans, rinsed and drained
1 can (15½ ounces) chickpeas, rinsed and drained
1 tablespoon olive oil

In a large pot, combine the onions, pasta, and 4 cups of the water. Bring to a boil, reduce the heat, and simmer for 8 minutes. Add the mixed vegetables, return to a simmer, and cook for 5 minutes. Add the tomatoes (with juice), kidney beans, chickpeas, oil, and the remaining 2 cups water. Simmer for 15 minutes.

Yield: 14 servings

Nutritional data per serving: Calories, 124; protein, 5 g; carbohydrate, 23 g; dietary fiber, 5 g; total fat, 2 g; saturated fat, 0 g; cholesterol, 0 mg; sodium, 365 mg; vitamin A, 9% of Daily Value; vitamin C, 10%; calcium, 4%; iron, 9%; folate, 14%.

DOUBLE DUTY

Not only does olive oil replace saturated fat in this soup, it also helps your body absorb cancer-fighting lycopene from the tomatoes.

Chicken Winter Waldorf Salad

My friend Carol was coming for lunch, and I wanted something yummy. I thought of Waldorf salad to use up some leftover chicken, but I was missing the rest of the classic ingredients—apples, raisins, and walnuts. So I made some quick substitutions, and we had a great lunch!

4 ounces cooked chicken breast
1 Anjou pear, cored and cut into chunks
½ cup diced celery
2 tablespoons coarsely chopped hazelnuts
2 tablespoons dried cranberries
¼ teaspoon salt
Freshly ground black pepper to taste
1 teaspoon balsamic vinegar
¼ cup low-fat mayonnaise
2 leaves red lettuce

Cut the chicken into bite-size pieces. In a medium bowl, combine the chicken, pear, celery, nuts, and cranberries. Toss well. In a small bowl, combine the salt, pepper, vinegar, and mayonnaise. Blend well with a small wire whisk. Pour the dressing over the chicken mixture and toss again. Place a lettuce leaf on each of two plates and arrange half of the chicken mixture on each.

Yield: 2 servings

Nutritional data per serving: Calories, 253; protein, 18 g; carbohydrate, 30 g; dietary fiber, 5 g; total fat, 8 g; saturated fat, <1 g; cholesterol, 44 mg; sodium, 503 mg; vitamin A, 8% of Daily Value; vitamin C, 14%; calcium, 5%; iron, 7%; vitamin B$_3$ (niacin), 26%; folate, 6%; potassium, 13%.

Turkey-in-the-Straw Mushrooms

Every time I see straw mushrooms, I have to chuckle because they remind me of Walt Disney's movie Fantasia. I hear that music and see those cute little mushrooms dancing around, and I feel like a kid again. And this salad will help keep you feeling like a kid, too, packed as it is with heart-smart vitamin E and folate, as well as plenty of lean protein.

2 cups mixed salad greens
2 tablespoons light Catalina dressing
3 ounces cooked turkey breast, cut into strips
½ cup canned straw mushrooms, rinsed and drained
1 tablespoon unsalted dry-roasted hulled
    sunflower seeds

In a medium bowl, combine the greens and dressing and toss until well coated. Place on a dinner plate and arrange the turkey and mushrooms on top. Garnish with the sunflower seeds.

Yield: 1 serving

Nutritional data per serving: Calories, 289; protein, 32 g; carbohydrate, 18 g; dietary fiber, 6 g; total fat, 10 g; saturated fat, 1 g; cholesterol, 70 mg; sodium, 721 mg; vitamin A, 40% of Daily Value; vitamin C, 30%; calcium, 9%; iron, 24%; vitamin E, 24%; folate, 46%.

Passionate Chicken

Home alone? Whip out your "storm supplies," put on some tropical music, and take a mind-mellowing trip to an exotic island!

2 cups mixed salad greens
1 can (8 ounces) tropical fruit salad in light syrup and
    passionfruit juice
1 can (5 ounces) flaked white-meat chicken
1 tablespoon toasted pine nuts

In a medium bowl, toss the greens with the fruit, then pile the mixture on a plate. Top with the chicken and sprinkle with the pine nuts. Serve with a hot roll or some crackers.

Yield: 1 serving

Nutritional data per serving: Calories, 361; protein, 35 g; carbohydrate, 20 g; dietary fiber, 4 g; total fat, 16 g; saturated fat, 4 g; cholesterol, 88 mg; sodium, 757 mg; vitamin A, 35% of Daily Value; vitamin C, 85%; calcium, 12%; iron, 29%; vitamin B$_3$ (niacin), 49%; folate, 34%; potassium, 17%; zinc, 19%.

The P·E·R·F·E·C·T Companion

Relax by the fire with a soothing cup of chamomile-mango tea. Ahhhh, your trip to the tropics is complete!

Take-Flight Buffalo Salad

If you love the taste of fiery hot chicken wings, do your body a favor and try this zesty salad instead. It tastes just as savory and flavory as ordinary hot wings but skips the greasy fat.

5 Morningstar Farms veggie Buffalo wings
2 cups Bordeaux blended red salad greens
½ cup sliced celery
½ cup sliced cucumbers
½ cup red bell pepper strips
2 tablespoons light blue cheese dressing

On a microwave-safe plate, microwave the wings on high for 1 to 1½ minutes. Place on a tray in the toaster oven and toast until crisp.

Meanwhile, in a salad bowl, combine the greens, celery, cucumbers, peppers, and dressing and toss until well coated. Top with the hot wings. ZOWIE!

Yield: 1 serving

Nutritional data per serving: Calories, 334; protein, 16 g; carbohydrate, 31 g; dietary fiber, 7 g; total fat, 16 g; saturated fat, 3 g; cholesterol, 0 mg; sodium, 1,064 mg; vitamin A, 44% of Daily Value; vitamin C, 258%; calcium, 13%; iron, 24%; vitamin B_1 (thiamin), 76%; vitamin B_3 (niacin), 158%; potassium, 22%.

SUPER SUB

1 CUP

Morningstar Farms Buffalo wings are made of soy instead of chicken with skin, so you cut saturated fat and get soy's special cholesterol-lowering effect.

Bean Burrito with Avocado

I tend to make vegetarian lunches for myself when I'm home alone. This one is really yummy and bursting with heart-healthy stuff.

1 large corn tortilla
1/8 avocado
1/3 cup cooked black beans
2 tablespoons Mexican-style corn
1 tablespoon sliced black olives
2 teaspoons mild chipotle taco sauce

On a paper plate, microwave the tortilla on high for 20 to 30 seconds, or until warm. Mash the avocado in the center of the top half of the tortilla. Top with the beans, corn, olives, and sauce. Fold the bottom half of the tortilla over the top half. Fold in the sides, then fold in half.

Yield: 1 serving

SUPER SUB

Using straight avocado instead of guacamole (avocado and mayonnaise) gives you more of the heart-healthy fat of the avocado and none of the hip-hugging fat of mayo.

Nutritional data per serving: Calories, 305; protein, 11 g; carbohydrate, 48 g; dietary fiber, 7 g; total fat, 9 g; saturated fat, 1.5 g; cholesterol, 0 mg; sodium, 679 mg; vitamin A, 2% of Daily Value; vitamin C, 5%; calcium, 12%; iron, 16%; folate, 26%; omega-3 fatty acids, 12%.

Chicken and Black Olive Wrap

Leftovers from last night's dinner usually make the best lunches, so whenever I cook chicken, I always make extra. Here's one of my favorites.

2 ounces cooked chicken breast, cut into strips or chunks
1/2 cup shredded romaine lettuce
2 tablespoons sliced black olives
2 tablespoons pico de gallo*
1/4 cup shredded reduced-fat cheddar cheese
1 large corn tortilla

Place the chicken, lettuce, olives, pico de gallo, and cheese on the top half of the tortilla. Fold the bottom half over the top half, then roll into a wrap.

Yield: 1 serving

Nutritional data per serving: Calories, 410; protein, 31 g; carbohydrate, 44 g; dietary fiber, 4 g; total fat, 3.5 g; saturated fat, <1 g; cholesterol, 111 mg; sodium, 992 mg; vitamin A, 5% of Daily Value; vitamin C, 71%; calcium, 10%; iron, 22%; vitamin B_3 (niacin), 38%; vitamin B_6, 28%.

*Available in Mexican markets and many large supermarkets.

Pizza Muffin

Sometimes, I just want the taste of pizza without having to deal with that whole big thing (and all the calories), so I crank up my trusty toaster oven and make my own personal pizza. The Canadian bacon-anise-red pepper combo creates zesty sausage flavor without the fat. Sneaky, huh?

1 whole wheat English muffin
1/4 cup roasted-garlic pasta sauce
1/4 teaspoon aniseeds
Dash of crushed red pepper
2 slices Canadian bacon
1 ounce shredded reduced-fat mozzarella cheese

Split the English muffin. Top each half with 2 tablespoons of the sauce and sprinkle with the aniseeds and red pepper. Add the Canadian bacon, then the mozzarella. Place in the toaster oven and toast until the bottom is crisp and the cheese is melted.

Yield: 1 serving

SUPER SUB

A whole wheat muffin delivers more heart-smart vitamin E than its white counterpart, and it delivers enough fiber to help keep your bowels moving.

Nutritional data per serving: Calories, 322; protein, 26 g; carbohydrate, 34 g; dietary fiber, 6 g; total fat, 10 g; saturated fat, 4 g; cholesterol, 45 mg; sodium, 1,546 mg; vitamin A, 6% of Daily Value; vitamin C, 5%; calcium, 38%; iron, 14%; vitamin B_1 (thiamin), 42%; vitamin B_3 (niacin), 29%; zinc, 18%.

Turkey Pesto Wrap

Fans of Kitchen Counter Cures *may remember that I'm just crazy about pesto over pasta, but it's way too rich and calorie-packed to eat regularly. One way I get that yummy taste year 'round and keep the calories under control is to use it as a sandwich spread. Here's a sample.*

1 large flour tortilla
1 tablespoon pesto sauce (from a jar)
3 ounces cooked turkey breast, diced
1/4 baby zucchini, diced
1/4 cup diced red bell peppers
Salt and freshly ground black pepper to taste

On a paper plate, microwave the tortilla on high for 20 to 30 seconds, or until warm. Spread the pesto down the center of the tortilla. Pile the turkey, zucchini, and peppers on top of the sauce on the top half of the tortilla. Fold the bottom half over the top half, then fold in one side and roll into a wrap.

Yield: 1 serving

Nutritional data per serving: Calories, 437; protein, 35 g; carbohydrate, 44 g; dietary fiber, 4 g; total fat, 13 g; saturated fat, 3 g; cholesterol, 76 mg; sodium, 508 mg; vitamin A, 24% of Daily Value; vitamin C, 122%; vitamin E, 9%; calcium, 21%; iron, 25%; vitamin B_3 (niacin), 46%; folate, 27%.

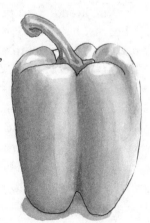

"Wing It" Buffalo Burger

Buffalo meat is super-lean, so you can squeeze in just a little real blue cheese. Add wing sauce for a fiery kick. Then pile on the salad to cool things down. Your taste buds will be flying!

1 buffalo burger (4 ounces)
1 Kaiser roll
1 leaf romaine lettuce
2 slices tomato
1 ring green bell pepper
2 tablespoons hot-wing sauce
1 tablespoon crumbled blue cheese

Grill or broil the burger just until cooked through. Place it in the roll and top with the lettuce, tomato, pepper, sauce, and cheese.

Yield: 1 serving

Nutritional data per serving: Calories, 456; protein, 34 g; carbohydrate, 50 g; dietary fiber, 3 g; total fat, 13 g; saturated fat, 5 g; cholesterol, 61 mg; sodium, 939 mg; vitamin A, 12% of Daily Value; vitamin C, 36%; calcium, 13%; iron, 29%; zinc, 27%.

The Inside Skinny: Buffalo wings were invented in Buffalo, New York. They have nothing at all to do with buffalo meat…except in this recipe!

Italian Sausage Sandwich with Peppers and Onions

I'll bet you never expected to find this heart stopper in a book on healthy cooking, and neither did I. The secret is soy! Nothing tastes quite like Italian sausage, but the Boca folks got it right. The texture isn't quite the same, but the sausage is exquisitely spicy.

1/2 cup water
1 frozen Boca Italian sausage
1 teaspoon olive oil
1/2 cup sliced onions
1 cup green and red bell pepper strips
1 hot dog bun

Place the water and sausage in a small nonstick skillet. Bring the water to a boil, then reduce the heat, cover, and simmer for about 5 minutes, or until the sausage is thawed. Add the oil and brown the sausage over medium-high heat. Add the onions and peppers and sauté until soft. Fill the bun, and go to town!

Yield: 1 serving

Nutritional data per serving: Calories, 357; protein, 17 g; carbohydrate, 44 g; dietary fiber, 10 g; total fat, 14 g; saturated fat, 1 g; cholesterol, 0 mg; sodium, 1,219 mg; vitamin A, 30% of Daily Value; vitamin C, 289%; calcium, 18%; iron, 27%; folate, 20%; potassium, 12%.

> **QUICK TRICK:** Replace fresh peppers with a mixture of frozen red, green, and yellow peppers. Replace fresh onions with frozen diced onions.

Talkin' Turkey Tacos

My son-in-law Paul is a big, handsome guy who really loves meat. So, in the interest of protecting his heart, my daughter Bobbi has started talking turkey to him. Ground turkey breast is nearly fat-free.

1 pound ground turkey breast
1 small onion, chopped
1 teaspoon olive oil
¾ cup Taco Bell Pour 'n Simmer Taco Seasoning Sauce
4 ounces shredded reduced-fat four-cheese blend
2 medium tomatoes, chopped
2½ cups shredded iceberg and romaine lettuce
1 avocado, chopped
10 soft taco shells (small tortillas)

In a large nonstick skillet over medium-high heat, brown the turkey and onion in the oil. Stir in the sauce and simmer for about 3 minutes. Place in a serving bowl and keep warm.

Meanwhile, place the cheese, tomatoes, lettuce, and avocado in individual serving bowls. Wrap the taco shells in plastic wrap and microwave on high for 1 minute, or until warm. Place on a serving platter, then step back and let everyone create their own special tacos.

Yield: 10 servings

Nutritional data per serving: Calories, 204; protein, 19 g; carbohydrate, 18 g; dietary fiber, 4 g; total fat, 6 g; saturated fat, 2 g; cholesterol, 42 mg; sodium, 351 mg; vitamin A, 4% of Daily Value; vitamin C, 15%; calcium, 14%; iron, 10%; vitamin B$_3$ (niacin), 20%; vitamin B$_6$, 17%; folate, 12%; potassium, 10%.

Ham and Chutney Sandwich

Do you remember ham with raisin gravy? It tastes kind of salty, sweet, and spicy at the same time. This sandwich has a similar flavor—plus, it's way lower in cholesterol than ham and cheese.

2 ounces lean low-salt ham
2 tablespoons chutney (from a jar)
½ teaspoon Dijon mustard
2 slices pumpernickel bread
1 leaf romaine lettuce

Cut the ham into small cubes and place in a small bowl. Add the chutney and mustard and stir until blended. Pile the mixture on one slice of the bread, top with the lettuce, and add the remaining slice of bread. Cut the sandwich diagonally, wrap it up, and toss it in your lunch bag. You're out of here!

Yield: 1 serving
Nutritional data per serving: Calories, 268; protein, 17 g; carbohydrate, 39 g; dietary fiber, 4 g; total fat, 5 g; saturated fat, 1 g; cholesterol, 30 mg; sodium, 966 mg; vitamin A, 5% of Daily Value; vitamin C, 17%; calcium, 5%; iron, 16%; zinc, 17%; vitamin B_1 (thiamin), 42%.

 **The
P·E·R·F·E·C·T
Companion**

Add a foil-wrapped Earl Grey tea bag and a lemon honey straw to your lunch bag. At lunchtime, put the tea bag in your favorite cup, fill with boiling water, and steep for 3 minutes. Remove the tea bag and sweeten with the honey straw.

Romanian Sausage Bake

Okay, you probably won't find any Romanian sausage around, but my own imported husband, Ted, relies on Polish sausage to fill the bill. He's even willing to use the very low fat kind, so that his wonderfully happy heart remains healthy, too.

4 medium red-skin potatoes, scrubbed
2 pounds low-sodium sauerkraut, well rinsed
$^1/_2$ cup frozen chopped onions
1 teaspoon caraway seeds
1 pound Healthy Choice Polish sausage
$^1/_2$ cup water

Pierce the potatoes and microwave on high for 10 minutes, turning once.

Meanwhile, combine the sauerkraut, onions, and caraway seeds in an $11^3/_4$ x $7^3/_4$ x $1^3/_4$-inch baking dish. Cut the cooked potatoes into quarters and bury them in the sauerkraut. Cut the sausage into 2-inch pieces and place on top of the sauerkraut. Pour the water over all. Bake at 350°F for about 20 minutes, or until the sausage browns.

Yield: 4 servings

Nutritional data per serving: Calories, 307; protein, 21 g; carbohydrate, 50 g; dietary fiber, 9 g; total fat, 3.5 g; saturated fat, 1 g; cholesterol, 41 mg; sodium, 1,680 mg; vitamin A, 1% of Daily Value; vitamin C, 81%; calcium, 9%; iron, 26%; copper, 26%.

Friday Night Sausage Bowl

I was thinking recently about how Friday nights have changed from "date nights" to "crash nights." One thing that hasn't changed is that I still want a quick, tasty meal.

2 frozen Boca Italian sausages
1 teaspoon olive oil
2 cups frozen bell pepper strips
1 cup frozen diced onions
2 cups drained canned diced tomatoes
1/4 teaspoon dried oregano
1/2 teaspoon dried basil
1/4 teaspoon aniseeds
1 tablespoon chopped garlic (from a jar)
1 can (7 ounces) button mushrooms, rinsed and drained
2 tablespoons Parmesan cheese

On a microwave-safe plate, microwave the sausage on high for 1 minute, or until thawed. Slice into 1/2-inch rounds. In a medium nonstick skillet over medium-high heat, brown the sausage in the oil. Stir in the peppers, onions, tomatoes, oregano, basil, aniseeds, garlic, and mushrooms. Reduce the heat and simmer for about 5 minutes, or until the sauce thickens. Divide between two soup bowls and sprinkle each serving with 1 tablespoon of the cheese. Serve with crusty rolls, salad, and red wine.

Yield: 2 servings

Nutritional data per serving: Calories, 294; protein, 21 g; carbohydrate, 31 g; dietary fiber, 12 g; total fat, 10 g; saturated fat, 1.5 g; cholesterol, 5 mg; sodium, 1,738 mg; vitamin A, 12% of Daily Value; vitamin C, 62%; calcium, 24%; iron, 33%; vitamin E, 2%.

Pork Loin Chops with Mangoes and Lemon Curd

Pork is now bred to have 30 percent less fat than it had in 1940, creating a valid claim to being "the other white meat." That claim applies only to the lean cuts, of course, not to stuff like spareribs, sausage, or bacon. But now that the lean is sooooo lean, it tends to be a bit dry, and that means it needs a little sauce. Here's a very fruity yet simple one.

2 boneless loin pork chops (4 ounces each), trimmed of all fat
2 teaspoons walnut oil
1/2 teaspoon garlic powder
1/4 teaspoon salt
Freshly ground black pepper to taste
1/2 fresh mango, diced
1 teaspoon lemon curd

> **DOUBLE DUTY**
>
> Walnut oil not only replaces butter's saturated fat, it also adds heart-healthy omega-3 fatty acids—the kind of fat you usually get only from fish.

Brush the pork chops with the oil and sprinkle with the garlic powder, salt, and pepper. Broil or grill just until barely pink inside and still juicy.

Meanwhile, in a small bowl, combine the mango and lemon curd. Place each chop on a plate and top with half of the sauce.

Yield: 2 servings

Nutritional data per serving: Calories, 284; protein, 30 g; carbohydrate, 10 g; dietary fiber, 1 g; total fat, 13 g; saturated fat, 3.5 g; cholesterol, 81 mg; sodium, 351 mg; vitamin A, 20% of Daily Value; vitamin C, 25%; calcium, 4%; iron, 5%; vitamin B_1 (thiamin), 78%; vitamin B_2 (riboflavin), 20%; vitamin B_3 (niacin), 29%; vitamin B_6, 27%; zinc, 15%; omega-3 fatty acids, 51%.

Three-Pound Goulash

This zesty recipe is a favorite of my husband, Ted. One pound each of beef, potatoes, and carrots give this dish its funny name!

2 beef bouillon cubes
1 cup boiling water
1 pound lean stew beef cubes, trimmed of all fat
1 pound tiny red-skin potatoes, scrubbed and halved
1 pound baby carrots
1 small onion, sliced
2 tablespoons minced garlic
3 tablespoons paprika
Salt and pepper to taste

In a small bowl, dissolve the bouillon in the water. In a slow cooker, combine the beef, potatoes, carrots, onion, garlic, paprika, salt, and pepper. Stir well and add the bouillon. Cover and simmer on low for about 8 hours. Serve with Oyster Mushroom and Spinach Salad (page 352) and crusty bread.

Yield: 4 servings

Nutritional data per serving: Calories, 261; protein, 24 g; carbohydrate, 35 g; dietary fiber, 5 g; total fat, 4 g; saturated fat, 1 g; cholesterol, 49 mg; sodium, 139 mg; vitamin A, 202% of Daily Value; vitamin B_6, 27%; vitamin C, 31%; calcium, 5%; iron, 20%; potassium, 22%.

> **QUICK TRICK:** Faced with a morning rush? Pile all the ingredients in the slow cooker the night before and refrigerate the whole thing. In the morning, just plug in the pot and go!

Beef Stew Sauvignon

I've always wanted a wife. You know, someone who has my dinner ready when I come through the door at night. But since I do enjoy being a woman, I often settle for a slow cooker meal. This one just lights me up with its rich flavors and heady fragrance. Now, if I can just get someone else to make the salad...

1 pound beef round, trimmed of all fat and cubed
2 cups cubed peeled potatoes
2 cups sliced carrots
$1/2$ cup sliced celery
1 cup pearl onions
2 cups Cabernet Sauvignon wine (box wine is fine)
2 cups water
1 envelope mushroom-onion soup mix
3 tablespoons cornstarch
$1/2$ cup water

In a slow cooker, combine the beef, potatoes, carrots, celery, onions, wine, water, and soup mix. Cover and simmer on low for about 8 hours. Just before serving, in a small bowl, add the cornstarch to the water and stir until smooth. Pour into the stew and stir. Simmer for 10 minutes, or until the stew thickens. Serve in soup bowls, with pumpernickel bread and a green salad.

Yield: 4 servings

Nutritional data per serving: Calories, 426; protein, 37 g; carbohydrate, 39 g; dietary fiber, 6 g; total fat, 5 g; saturated fat, 2 g; cholesterol, 79 mg; sodium, 1,024 mg; vitamin A, 192% of Daily Value; vitamin B_6, 47%; vitamin C, 33%; calcium, 7%; iron, 23%; potassium, 38%; zinc, 41%.

(Not) Your Mother's Meat Loaf

Mmmmmeat loaf. Nothing beats that homey fragrance wafting from your oven for drawing family and friends around the table. This time, make your meat loaf heart-smart as well as warm and loving.

1 pound very lean (8% fat) ground beef
3/4 cup old-fashioned or instant oats
1 egg
1/2 cup fat-free evaporated milk
1/2 cup grated carrots
1/2 cup minced onions
1 teaspoon garlic powder
1/2 teaspoon salt
1/8 teaspoon ground black pepper

Preheat the oven to 350°F. Lightly coat a loaf pan with nonstick spray. In a large bowl, combine the beef, oats, egg, milk, carrots, onions, garlic powder, salt, and pepper. Use a large spoon to stir until well mixed.

Pile the mixture into the pan and gently smooth into an even shape, without packing too hard. Bake for 50 minutes, or until the meat loaf is cooked through and the top is brown. Pour off any liquid, then use a spatula to loosen the meat loaf from the pan. Place a serving plate on top of the pan and quickly invert it, turning the meat loaf onto the plate. Garnish with a squirt of ketchup.

Yield: 8 servings

Nutritional data per serving: Calories, 138; protein, 14 g; carbohydrate, 9 g; dietary fiber, 1 g; total fat, 6 g; saturated fat, 2 g; cholesterol, 54 mg; sodium, 209 mg; vitamin A, 22% of Daily Value; vitamin C, 3%; calcium, 6%; iron, 13%.

Pepper Steak with Tomatoes and Onions

I really don't grill many steaks any more. To make a small portion go a long way, I cook it with plenty of veggies and serve it over rice, noodles, or a plain potato. That eliminates the need for a baked potato loaded with butter and sour cream. And it makes a big plateful of rich-tasting, tummy-satisfying food. Life is good!

8 ounces lean round steak, trimmed of all fat
1 tablespoon canola oil
1 medium onion, thinly sliced
1 large green bell pepper, coarsely chopped
8 Roma (plum) tomatoes, cut into rounds
1/2 teaspoon salt
Freshly ground black pepper to taste

Slice the steak into strips about 1/4 inch thick. In a medium nonstick skillet over high heat, sear the steak in the oil. Deglaze the pan with water. Reduce the heat, add the onion, and cook, stirring, until the onion browns and softens. Add the green pepper, then layer the tomatoes on top. Sprinkle with the salt and black pepper. Cover and cook over low heat for 1 hour, or until the steak is tender. For each serving, spoon over a baked potato, brown rice, or noodles.

Yield: 2 servings

Nutritional data per serving: Calories, 296; protein, 28 g; carbohydrate, 24 g; dietary fiber, 6 g; total fat, 11 g; saturated fat, 2 g; cholesterol, 59 mg; sodium, 661 mg; vitamin A, 21% of Daily Value; vitamin C, 211%; calcium, 4%; iron, 19%; folate, 15%; potassium, 33%; zinc, 29%.

Your Goose Is Cooked

It's true, domestic goose is really, really fatty! Wild goose, on the other hand, is super-lean. My friend Carolyn Howe gave me this recipe many years ago, and I pass it on to you.

1 wild goose, cleaned, all feathers and shot removed
1 cup flour
1/2 teaspoon salt
1 teaspoon dried thyme
2 tablespoons butter
2 tablespoons olive oil
1/4 cup chopped shallots
1/2 cup sliced mushrooms
1/4 cup white wine
3/4 cup canned tomatoes
2 tablespoons parsley flakes
1/4 teaspoon tarragon

> **The P·E·R·F·E·C·T Companion**
>
> Although this dish is cooked with white wine, pour yourself a glass of red (maybe Merlot?) when you're ready to dine. Its bolder flavor brings out the best in this recipe.

Cut the goose into serving-size pieces.
In a shallow bowl, combine the flour, salt, and thyme. Dredge the pieces in the flour mixture. In a large nonstick skillet over medium-high heat, sauté the goose in the butter and oil. Add the shallots, mushrooms, wine, tomatoes (with juice), parsley, and tarragon. Cook over low heat for 2 to 3 hours, or until the goose is tender. Serve over cooked wild rice.

Yield: 6 servings

Nutritional data per serving: Calories, 236; protein, 21 g; carbohydrate, 11 g; dietary fiber, 1 g; total fat, 12 g; saturated fat, 3 g; cholesterol, 131 mg; sodium, 286 mg; vitamin A, 6% of Daily Value; vitamin C, 8%; calcium, 3%; iron, 8%.

Meat and Mushroom Pasta Sauce

After years of trying to make do with beef substitutes, I had to admit that sometimes, I really love the taste of ground beef with my pasta. Here's my slimmer, trimmer version that delivers the taste (but not the saturated fat!) I crave.

4 ounces ground chuck
1/2 cup chopped onions
6 ounces fresh mushrooms, sliced
1 large clove garlic, minced
1 jar (28 ounces) roasted-garlic and onion pasta sauce

Crumble the meat in a deep nonstick skillet and brown over medium-high heat. Stir in the onions and cook, stirring, for about 5 minutes, or until the onions soften. Stir in the mushrooms and garlic. Cook, stirring, for about 5 minutes, or until the mushrooms begin to give up their liquid. Stir in the sauce and cook until heated through.

Yield: 6 servings

Nutritional data per serving: Calories, 74; protein, 7 g; carbohydrate, 11 g; dietary fiber, 3 g; total fat, <1 g; saturated fat, 0 g; cholesterol, 10 mg; sodium, 401 mg; vitamin A, 3% of Daily Value; vitamin C, 12%; calcium, 4%; iron, 9%; zinc, 5%.

> **QUICK TRICK:** Stop peeling and mincing garlic. Get yourself a Zyliss garlic press (available at most kitchenware stores) and instantly mince the unpeeled cloves. My kids are experienced cooks, and they are amazed at how well this tool works.

Mom's Oven-Fried Chicken

Here is the fried chicken recipe I grew up on.

8 boneless, skinless chicken breasts (3 ounces each)
1 medium egg
2 tablespoons fat-free milk
2 tablespoons canola oil
1 cup Italian-style bread crumbs
1/2 cup whole yellow cornmeal
1/2 cup toasted wheat germ
1 tablespoon onion powder
1 tablespoon garlic powder
1 tablespoon parsley flakes
1 tablespoon sesame seeds
1 tablespoon celery salt
1/4 teaspoon freshly ground black pepper

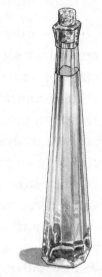

Wash the chicken and pat dry. In a small bowl, combine the egg, milk, and oil. Beat with a fork until blended. In a medium bowl, combine the bread crumbs, cornmeal, wheat germ, and spices. Lightly coat a baking sheet with nonstick spray. Dip each breast in the egg mixture, then in the crumb mixture, coating evenly. Place on the baking sheet and bake at 350°F for 30 minutes, or until cooked through and crisp.

Yield: 8 servings

Nutritional data per serving: Calories, 259; protein, 26 g; carbohydrate, 21 g; dietary fiber, 2 g; total fat, 7 g; saturated fat, <1 g; cholesterol, 77 mg; sodium, 837 mg; vitamin A, 3% of Daily Value; vitamin C, 4%; calcium, 5%; iron, 23%; vitamin B$_3$ (niacin), 52%; vitamin B$_6$, 28%; folate, 9%; potassium, 10%; zinc, 13%.

Green Chicken Chili

There are as many ways to make chili as there are people who make it. This recipe does a right-angle away from the classic beef-and-beans fare.

12 ounces unbreaded chicken tenders
1 cup thinly sliced onions
1/2 tablespoon olive oil
1 tablespoon minced garlic
1 teaspoon ground cumin
1/2 teaspoon dried oregano
1 cup bottled salsa verde
   (green salsa)
1 can (15 1/2 ounces) chickpeas,
   rinsed and drained

Wash the chicken and pat dry. Cut into 1-inch pieces. In a nonstick skillet over medium-high heat, brown the chicken and onions in the oil. Stir in the garlic, cumin, oregano, and salsa verde. Reduce the heat, cover, and simmer for 5 minutes. Stir in the chickpeas and cook just until heated through. Serve over cooked rice.

Yield: 4 servings

Nutritional data per serving: Calories, 275; protein, 32 g; carbohydrate, 21 g; dietary fiber, 4 g; total fat, 6 g; saturated fat, 1 g; cholesterol, 72 mg; sodium, 533 mg; vitamin A, 1% of Daily Value; vitamin C, 5%; calcium, 6%; iron, 13%; vitamin B_3 (niacin), 58%.

DOUBLE DUTY

The soluble fiber in chickpeas boosts protein and helps lower cholesterol.

CHAPTER 2

LOWER YOUR BLOOD PRESSURE

A DASH-ING DIET RIDES TO YOUR RESCUE

WHEN I FIRST MET MY FRIEND BILL BROWN, HE described himself as a man who never missed a meal. His favorite breakfast was scrapple and eggs or pancakes drowning in syrup and melted butter. As with many Americans, fruit was a stranger to his lips, and vegetables were a "sometimes" thing. He had high blood pressure, sleep apnea, elevated cholesterol, and soaring triglycerides. He needed help. Badly. So badly, in fact, that he agreed to give the DASH diet a try.

One month later, his blood pressure had dropped 20 points—enough so that his doctor cut his medication in half. A month after that, he was off meds altogether. Can this miracle diet be for real?

Absolutely!

DASH (Dietary Approaches to Stopping Hypertension) was developed and scientifically tested on nearly 500 men and women, about one-third of them with high blood pressure. Some ate a typical American diet. (Their blood pressure readings didn't budge.) Others ate the American diet, but with extra fruits and vegetables. (Their readings nudged down a little.) And the last group ate a diet low in saturated fat and cholesterol and rich in fruits, vegetables, and low-fat dairy foods. Their blood pressure dropped like a stone—as much as if they had taken medication—in just two weeks! Now that's a powerful diet! And a follow-up study showed that cutting down on sodium could lower blood pressure even more.

Why the magic? Researchers think the combination of calcium, magnesium, potassium, and fiber delivered by food did the trick. *Delivered by food* is the key here. All those nutrients had been tested in pill form—and failed. Only when they arrived in food, glorious food, did they succeed. Thanks, Mother Nature!

Tempted to give it a try? Here's what you will eat each day.

♥ 4–5 servings of vegetables (such as 1 cup cooked vegetables or 1/2 cup raw vegetables)

♥ 4–5 servings of fruit (such as 1 medium whole fruit or 1/2 cup fresh, frozen, or canned fruit)

♥ 2–3 servings of low-fat or fat-free dairy foods (such as 8 ounces milk or yogurt or 1 1/2 ounces cheese)

♥ 2 or fewer servings (3 ounces each) of lean meat, poultry, or fish

♥ 7–8 servings of grains (such as 1 slice bread or ¹/₂ cup cooked rice or pasta)

♥ 2–3 servings of fat (such as 1 tablespoon soft margarine or 1 teaspoon olive or canola oil)

Each week, you can have:

♥ 4–5 servings of nuts, seeds, or dried beans (such as 1¹/₂ ounces nuts or seeds or ¹/₂ cup cooked beans)

I know, I know. The thought of eating all those fruits and vegetables is mind-boggling. But you can do it. And you can do it simply and deliciously. You won't miss the salt too much, because we'll season with garlic, onions, basil, cumin, and other spices. We'll ditch the saturated fat and add flavor with olive oil, walnuts, sunflower seeds, and avocados. We'll do it fast, and we'll do it easy. And it'll be so good, you'll wonder what you ever saw in french fries!

To round out your DASH diet, you can get ideas for eating more dairy foods from chapter 6. Chapter 1 is packed with lean meat and poultry recipes, and you can catch a lot of fish in chapter 3. Then beat a path to chapter 5 for whole grain goodies. And for the healthiest fats, make an appointment with chapter 4 for an oil change. Once you've gotten the hang of cooking vegetables, you'll find even more in chapters 7, 8, 9, 10, 12, and 14.

Now grab a basket, and let's head for the produce department. I have some delicious surprises in store for you!

Marinated Vegetable Antipasto

If you're looking for a quick appetizer, try the Italian foods section in your local supermarket. You'll find all sorts of vegetables to make a pretty party platter.

Curly red leaf lettuce
1 jar (12 ounces) fire-roasted peppers
1 jar (12 ounces) marinated artichoke
    hearts
1 jar (12 ounces) marinated mushrooms
1 can (15 ounces) hearts of palm
1 can (16 ounces) jumbo black olives

Place the lettuce on a serving platter and arrange the peppers, artichokes, mushrooms, hearts of palm, and olives on top. Then stand back and let the party begin!

Yield: 10 servings

Nutritional data per serving: Calories, 81; protein, 3 g; carbohydrate, 12 g; total fat, 4 g; saturated fat, 0 g; cholesterol, 0 mg; sodium, 705 mg; vitamin A, 9% of Daily Value; vitamin C, 24%; calcium, 6%; iron, 13%; vitamin E, 6%; potassium, 2%.

Lovely Leftovers Toss the surplus into tomorrow's salad, drizzle with Italian dressing, and top with grilled chicken. It's superb!

Shoppers' Minestrone

My daughters, Bobbi and Cathy, and I can shop 'til we drop on this stuff!

4 cans (14½ ounces each) reduced-sodium chicken broth
2 cloves garlic, minced or pressed
2 medium potatoes, scrubbed and diced
½ teaspoon dried thyme
¼ teaspoon ground white pepper
2 ounces very small pasta (such as orzo)
1 can (15½ ounces) white cannellini beans,
   rinsed and drained
1 small zucchini, quartered lengthwise and sliced
2 tomatoes, diced
1 cup sliced red Swiss chard stems
2 cups sliced Swiss chard leaves
2 ounces freshly grated Parmesan cheese

In a 4-quart pot, combine the broth, garlic, potatoes, thyme, and pepper. Bring to a boil, reduce the heat, and simmer until the potatoes are tender and the broth is reduced by half. Stir in the pasta and cook for 5 minutes. Add the beans, zucchini, tomatoes, and Swiss chard stems and leaves. Simmer for 5 minutes. Serve fresh and piping hot, garnished with the cheese.

Yield: 4 servings

Nutritional data per serving: Calories, 265; protein, 17 g; carbohydrate, 41 g; dietary fiber, 7 g; total fat, 5 g; saturated fat, 3 g; cholesterol, 14 mg; sodium, 624 mg; vitamin A, 31% of Daily Value; vitamin C, 56%; calcium, 24%; iron, 29%; folate, 21%; potassium, 32%.

Springtime Vegetable Soup

While it's true that most soups taste better when they've had a couple of days to rest and let their flavors blend, this soup isn't interested in resting. In fact, it absolutely rushes to the table. The less you cook it, the better it tastes!

4 cups fat-free chicken broth
2 ounces spiral pasta
2 green onions, thinly sliced
1/2 cup frozen petite peas
2/3 cup frozen artichoke heart quarters
4 ounces asparagus, washed and tough stems removed

Bring the broth to a simmer in a medium saucepan over medium heat. Stir in the pasta and cook for about 3 minutes (or about 5 minutes less than directed on the package). Stir in the onions, peas, and artichokes. Cut the asparagus into 1-inch pieces and add to the pan. Return to a simmer and cook for 5 minutes, or until the asparagus is crisp-tender. Serve immediately.

Yield: 4 servings

Nutritional data per serving: Calories, 94; protein, 6 g; carbohydrate, 17 g; dietary fiber, 4 g; total fat, <1 g; saturated fat, 0 g; cholesterol, 0 mg; sodium, 617 mg; vitamin A, 4% of Daily Value; vitamin C, 13%; calcium, 2%; iron, 7%; vitamin B$_1$ (thiamin), 12%; folate, 28%; potassium, 5%.

> **QUICK TRICK:** Replace the fresh asparagus with a package of frozen cut asparagus.

Mindy's Mom's Pureed Vegetable Soup

My friend Mindy told me her mom invented this rich, delicious soup to trick her grandchildren into eating their vegetables. It works! (It's also effective with husbands.)

2 large onions, chopped
1 tablespoon olive oil
8 cups cut-up vegetables (such as
    2 cups each broccoli florets
    and stalks, cauliflower florets, carrots, and potatoes)
2 cans (15½ ounces each) fat-free chicken broth
½ teaspoon dried thyme
8 ounces grated reduced-fat cheddar cheese

In a deep pot over medium-high heat, sauté the onions in the oil for about 5 minutes, or until soft. Add the vegetables, broth, and thyme. Bring to a boil, then reduce the heat and simmer for 15 to 20 minutes, or until tender.

In a food processor, puree the vegetables and broth in batches, returning each finished batch to the pot. When all the batches are pureed, reheat the soup to serving temperature. Ladle into bowls and top each serving with 1 ounce of the cheese. For a complete meal, serve with dinner rolls. (And remember Mom's best advice: Never tell the kids what they're eating!)

Yield: 8 servings

Nutritional data per serving: Calories, 161; protein, 11 g; carbohydrate, 21 g; dietary fiber, 5 g; total fat, 4 g; saturated fat, 1.5 g; cholesterol, 6 mg; sodium, 528 mg; vitamin A, 103% of Daily Value; vitamin C, 85%; calcium, 17%; iron, 6%; vitamin E, 5%; folate, 11%; vitamin K, 132%; potassium, 14%.

Jicama Fiesta Salad

Can a salad say "PARTY!"? Absolutely! I toss this amazing multicolored feast-for-your-eyes in the gigantic yellow bowl my mother gave me years ago. Sunshine should make you feel so good.

1 head red leaf lettuce
1 small jicama, shredded
1 baby zucchini, thinly sliced
1 baby yellow squash, thinly sliced
1 cup sliced red radishes
1 large orange bell pepper, cut
    into chunks
½ cup chopped fresh cilantro
¼ cup light vinaigrette dressing
8 Roma (plum) tomatoes, cut into rounds
1 avocado, thinly sliced
½ cup yellow corn
½ cup cooked black beans

Tear the lettuce into bite-size pieces. In a large salad bowl, combine the lettuce, jicama, zucchini, squash, radishes, pepper, cilantro, and dressing. Toss until well coated. Gently stir in the tomatoes. Arrange the avocado on top and garnish with the corn and beans.

Yield: 8 servings

Nutritional data per serving: Calories, 149; protein, 3 g; carbohydrate, 19 g; dietary fiber, 8 g; total fat, 8 g; saturated fat, 1 g; cholesterol, 0 mg; sodium, 197 mg; vitamin A, 13% of Daily Value; vitamin C, 132%; calcium, 5%; iron, 8%; folate, 12%; potassium, 18%.

Dad's Cucumber Salad

My father taught me how to make this marinated salad. It's a trick he learned in desperation one year when his garden was overrun with cucumbers. For years after that, he and Mom ate the same fresh-from-their-garden dinner every summer night: cucumber salad, sliced tomatoes, and freshly picked corn.

3 large cucumbers, peeled and thinly sliced
1 medium sweet onion, thinly sliced
1/2 teaspoon salt
Freshly ground black pepper to taste
1 cup apple cider vinegar
1 cup water
1 teaspoon sugar

In a narrow bowl small enough that the vegetables fill it, combine the cucumbers, onion, salt, and pepper. Place a plate on top to press down on the cucumbers, then place a book or other heavy weight on top of the plate. Let stand for 1 hour or more, or until the cucumbers give up some of their water. Drain the liquid, then add the vinegar, water, and sugar. Refrigerate until ready to serve.

Yield: 12 servings

Nutritional data per serving: Calories, 16; protein, <1 g; carbohydrate, 4 g; dietary fiber, <1 g; total fat, 0 g; saturated fat, 0 g; cholesterol, 0 mg; sodium, 99 mg; vitamin A, 0% of Daily Value; vitamin C, 5%; calcium, 1%; iron, 1%; magnesium, 3%; potassium, 4%.

QUICK TRICK: Make short work of slicing cucumbers and onions with a food processor.

Rainbow Salsa Salad

Buzzin' around all day doing this and that makes me hungry for a salad someone else has peeled and chopped. Don't worry—help is at hand!

1 package (12 ounces) Mann's Rainbow Salad
$1/2$ cup chopped fresh cilantro
$1/4$ cup sliced green onions
$1/4$ cup light ranch dressing
$1/4$ cup medium bottled salsa

In a large bowl, combine the salad mixture, cilantro, onions, dressing, and salsa. Toss well.

Yield: 8 servings

Nutritional data per serving: Calories, 41; protein, 1 g; carbohydrate, 5 g; dietary fiber, 1 g; total fat, 2 g; saturated fat, 0 g; cholesterol, 1 mg; sodium, 110 mg; vitamin A, 2% of Daily Value; vitamin C, 50%; calcium, 3%; iron, 2%; folate, 7%; potassium, 5%.

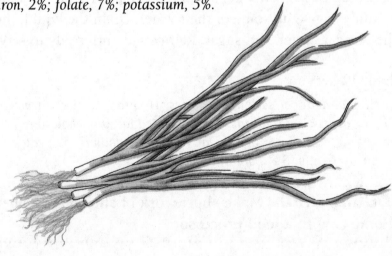

Celery Cabbage with Cashews

Have the itch to crunch? Toss up a big bowl of salad and munch away. You'll add to your potassium supply, too.

1/2 head Chinese celery cabbage, cut lengthwise, then
    crosswise into thin strips
1/4 red bell pepper, cut into thin strips
1/4 green bell pepper, cut into thin strips
1 can (8 ounces) sliced water chestnuts, drained
1 teaspoon chopped garlic (from a jar)
1 tablespoon peanut oil
1 tablespoon white rice vinegar
2 tablespoons light soy sauce
1/4 cup salted cashews, coarsely chopped

In a large bowl, combine the cabbage, red and green peppers, water chestnuts, and garlic. Drizzle with the oil, vinegar, and soy sauce and toss until well coated. Sprinkle with the cashews.

Yield: 10 servings

Nutritional data per serving: Calories, 46; protein, 1 g; carbohydrate, 5 g; dietary fiber, 2 g; total fat, 3 g; saturated fat, <1 g; cholesterol, 0 mg; sodium, 205 mg; vitamin A, 7% of Daily Value; vitamin C, 37%; calcium, 3%; iron, 2%; folate, 9%; potassium, 4%.

SUPER SUB

Power up flavor and blast away sodium by making your own salad dressing.

Yogurt-Lime Dressing

This is the simplest, most perfect dressing I've ever put on a fruit salad! It seems too easy to be true, but believe me, it is.

Grated peel of 1 lime
1 cup sugar-free, fat-free vanilla yogurt
Dash of ground cinnamon

In a small bowl, stir the lime peel into the yogurt. Place in a pretty serving dish so it looks like you've worked very hard. Dust with the cinnamon.

Yield: 8 servings

Nutritional data per serving: Calories, 28; protein, 2 g; carbohydrate, 6 g; dietary fiber, 0 g; total fat, 0 g; saturated fat, 0 g; cholesterol, 0 mg; sodium, 10 mg; vitamin A, 0% of Daily Value; vitamin C, 4%; calcium, 5%; iron, 0%; vitamin B_2 (riboflavin), 4%; potassium, 2%.

DOUBLE DUTY

True, yogurt helps lower your blood pressure. It helps build better bones, too!

Portobello-Onion Burger

If you're looking for meaty taste without the beef, try this cookout treat. My family just loves it!

½ cup sliced onions
1 clove garlic, minced
1 teaspoon olive oil
½ teaspoon Worcestershire sauce
1 large portobello mushroom
1 Kaiser roll
1 thin slice provolone cheese
   (about ½ ounce)
1 thick slice tomato
1 leaf romaine lettuce

> **The P·E·R·F·E·C·T Companion**
>
> Studies show that tea, particularly black tea, reduces blood pressure. In a tall mug, pour boiling water over a chai spice black tea bag. Steep for 3 to 5 minutes. Remove the tea bag and sweeten with 1 teaspoon tupelo honey. Hot day? Pour it over ice.

In a medium nonstick skillet over medium-high heat, sauté the onions and garlic in the oil just until the onions are soft. Stir in the Worcestershire.

Clean the mushroom and remove the stem. Coat lightly with olive oil spray and grill over medium heat until beginning to soften. Place the mushroom in the roll and fill the center with the onions. Top with the cheese, tomato, and lettuce.

Yield: 1 serving

Nutritional data per serving: Calories, 358, protein, 14 g; carbohydrate, 48 g; dietary fiber, 5 g; total fat, 14 g; saturated fat, 5 g; cholesterol, 10 mg; sodium, 484 mg; vitamin A, 8% of Daily Value; vitamin C, 34%; calcium, 21%; iron, 16%; vitamin B_2 (riboflavin), 28%; folate, 10%.

Almond Butter and Banana Sandwich

A slightly new twist on an old favorite (Elvis lives!...or he might have if he had exercised a little portion control).

2 tablespoons almond butter
1 medium banana
Freshly grated nutmeg to taste
2 slices whole wheat bread

In a microwave-safe dish, microwave the almond butter on high for 30 to 60 seconds, or until melted.

Meanwhile, slice the banana into quarters lengthwise, then into ¹/₂-inch pieces. In a small bowl, sprinkle the banana with the nutmeg. Pour in the almond butter and stir until well blended. Pile the mixture on one slice of the bread and top with the remaining slice. Cut in half and enjoy.

Yield: 1 serving

Nutritional data per serving: Calories, 449; protein, 11 g; carbohydrate, 60 g; dietary fiber, 8 g; total fat, 22 g; saturated fat, 3 g; cholesterol, 0 mg; sodium, 300 mg; vitamin A, 1% of Daily Value; vitamin C, 18%; calcium, 13%; iron, 19%; vitamin B$_2$ (riboflavin), 25%; vitamin B$_6$, 40%; vitamin E, 36%; folate, 18%; copper, 28%; magnesium, 45%; potassium, 24%; omega-3 fatty acids, 20%.

Salsa-Salmon Baked Potato

When it comes to grilled salmon, I always make "planned-overs." That bit of extra salmon gives me a chance to eat a potassium-powered potato in a delicious dish that's really low in sodium.

1 medium baked potato
¼ cup medium salsa verde (green salsa)
3 ounces grilled salmon, flaked

Split the potato and fluff the insides with a fork. Top with half of the salsa, the salmon, and the remaining salsa. *Ai, chihuahua!*

Yield: 1 serving

Nutritional data per serving: Calories: 308; protein, 24 g; carbohydrate, 35 g; dietary fiber, 3 g; total fat, 7 g; saturated fat, 1 g; cholesterol, 60 mg; sodium, 247 mg; vitamin A, 1% of Daily Value; vitamin C, 26%; calcium, 2%; iron, 14%; vitamin B_1 (thiamin), 24%; vitamin B_2 (riboflavin), 27%; vitamin B_3 (niacin), 53%; vitamin B_6, 61%; vitamin D, 60%; vitamin E, 6%; folate, 10%; potassium, 30%; omega-3 fatty acids, 195%.

SUPER SUB

Substitute rich, fatty salmon for butter and sour cream, and you'll replace 10 grams of saturated fat with the omega-3 fatty acids your heart is crying for.

Chinese Celery Cabbage Stir-Fry

When I'm hungry, I want lots to eat, but I still have to keep my calories under control. That usually means I need a big pile of vegetables. Here's a quick recipe that gets the job done and tastes just a tad spicy. Serve as a side dish or double the ingredients and top with leftover chicken or pork for a main dish.

1 tablespoon peanut oil
1/2 head Chinese celery cabbage, cut lengthwise, then crosswise into 1-inch strips
1/2 cup diced celery
1/2 cup diced onions
1/4 teaspoon Chinese five-spice powder*
1 tablespoon white rice vinegar

Heat the oil in a wok over high heat. Add the cabbage, celery, and onions. Cook, stirring, for about 5 minutes, or until soft. Turn off the heat. Add the five-spice powder and vinegar and stir well.

Yield: 6 servings

Nutritional data per serving: Calories, 37; protein, 1 g; carbohydrate, 3 g; dietary fiber, 2 g; total fat, 2 g; saturated fat, 0 g; cholesterol, 0 mg; sodium, 17 mg; vitamin A, 6% of Daily Value; vitamin C, 18%; calcium, 3%; iron, 2%; vitamin B_6, 7%; folate, 9%; potassium, 6%.

*Available in Asian markets and many large supermarkets.

QUICK TRICK: Don't chop fresh celery and onions. Instead, buy the fresh combination in the produce section of your supermarket, then just measure out what you need.

Long Beans Amandine

Green beans amandine have long been one of America's favorites. Here's a convenient (and pretty!) twist to brighten up a plain entrée.

1 bag (10 ounces) frozen baby bean mix (green beans,
    wax beans, and baby carrots)
1¹/₂ teaspoons almond oil
¹/₄ teaspoon salt
¹/₄ teaspoon dried thyme
Freshly ground black pepper to taste
1 tablespoon toasted almonds

In a medium nonstick skillet over medium heat, sauté the beans in the oil for about 5 minutes, just until thawed and beginning to soften. Sprinkle with the salt, thyme, and pepper. Garnish with the almonds and serve hot.

Yield: 4 servings

Nutritional data per serving: Calories, 49; protein, 2 g; carbohydrate, 6 g; dietary fiber, 2 g; total fat, 2.6 g; saturated fat, 0 g; cholesterol, 0 mg; sodium, 154 mg; vitamin A, 25% of Daily Value; vitamin C, 14%; vitamin E, 6%; calcium, 3%; iron, 3%; folate, 3%; magnesium, 5%; potassium, 4%.

Lovely Leftovers Toss chilled extras with a little vinegar for a cold side salad.

Snow Peas with Shiitake Mushrooms

All mushrooms are not created equal. A few, like shiitake and maitake, may fend off cancer as well as heart disease. That's good to know when you're eating a dish that tastes so delicious.

1 tablespoon sesame oil
10 ounces frozen snow peas
1 ounce (about 1/2 cup) sliced shiitake
   mushrooms
1 1/2 teaspoons House of Tsang Korean
Teriyaki Stir-Fry Sauce*

Heat the oil in a large wok over medium-high heat. Stir in the snow peas and mushrooms and cook, stirring constantly, until the peas thaw and begin to soften. Turn off the heat and add the sauce. Stir well and serve immediately.

Yield: 6 servings

Nutritional data per serving: Calories, 52; protein, 2 g; carbohydrate, 6 g; dietary fiber, 2 g; total fat, 2.5 g; saturated fat, 0 g; cholesterol, 0 mg; sodium, 79 mg; vitamin A, 1% of Daily Value; vitamin C, 17%; vitamin E, 2%; calcium, 2%; iron, 6%; folate, 5%.

*Available in Korean markets and many large supermarkets.

Dilled French Green Beans

I love the taste of fresh dill, but I've had no luck growing it. Fortunately, all the grocery stores in my neighborhood have it year 'round. Here, it makes frozen green beans taste fresh and bright, even in the middle of winter.

2 cups frozen French-style green beans
1/4 cup snipped fresh dill
2 tablespoons light country French dressing
Freshly ground black pepper to taste
1/2 teaspoon fresh lemon juice

In a colander, thaw the beans under running water for 1 minute, then drain. In a medium bowl, combine the beans, dill, dressing, pepper, and lemon juice. Refrigerate until ready to serve.

Yield: 4 servings

Nutritional data per serving: Calories, 37; protein, 1 g; carbohydrate, 8 g; dietary fiber, 2 g; total fat, <1 g; saturated fat, 0 g; cholesterol, 0 mg; sodium, 68 mg; vitamin A, 5% of Daily Value; vitamin C, 15%; calcium, 4%; iron, 5%; folate, 3%; magnesium, 5%, potassium, 4%.

Chayote Squash with Cinnamon

Sometimes, I wander through the produce section looking for new veggies and fruits. I had been eyeing the chayote squash for a long time, trying to think of something clever to do with it (besides making funny faces). Finally, I took some home to play with and discovered that when I just barely cooked it, it tasted like apples. So this simple recipe turned out to be the best.

1 chayote squash
2 teaspoons peanut oil
1/4 teaspoon ground cinnamon

Wash the squash and pat dry. On a cutting board, use a sharp knife to halve lengthwise. Place the halves flat side down, then cut lengthwise again. Remove the large seed and the seed pocket. Thinly slice the quarters.

In a heavy nonstick skillet over medium-high heat, sauté the squash in the oil until translucent but still firm. Sprinkle with the cinnamon and stir. Serve hot. It's delicious with lean ham or grilled chicken.

Yield: 4 servings

Nutritional data per serving: Calories, 30; protein, <1 g; carbohydrate, 2 g; dietary fiber, 1 g; total fat, 2 g; saturated fat, 0 g; cholesterol, 0 mg; sodium, 1 mg; vitamin A, 0% of Daily Value; vitamin C, 7%; calcium, 1%; iron, 1%; folate, 12%; potassium, 2%; omega-3 fatty acids, 2%.

Garlic Mashed Potatoes with Olive Oil

When I was growing up, potatoes, especially mashed, were my favorite food. Here's how I make them today:

1½ pounds red-skin potatoes, scrubbed and cubed
2 cloves garlic, chopped
½ teaspoon salt
⅛ teaspoon ground white pepper
2 tablespoons olive oil
⅓ cup nonfat dry milk
½ cup fat-free milk
½ cup sliced black olives

In a heavy saucepan with just enough water to cover, bring the potatoes and garlic to a boil. Reduce the heat, cover, and simmer for 15 to 20 minutes, or until tender. Drain, place in a large bowl, and sprinkle with the salt and pepper. Add the oil, dry milk, and ¼ cup of the fat-free milk.

With an electric mixer, mash the potatoes, adding more milk as needed to get a creamy texture. Gently stir in the olives and serve.

Yield: 8 servings

Nutritional data per serving: Calories, 156; protein, 6 g; carbohydrate, 24 g; dietary fiber, 2 g; total fat, 4 g; saturated fat, <1 g; cholesterol, 2 mg; sodium, 283 mg; vitamin A, 8% of Daily Value; vitamin C, 21%; calcium, 16%; iron, 3%; vitamin B$_6$, 16%; vitamin D, 12%; vitamin E, 4%; potassium, 15%.

> **QUICK TRICK:** Try Simply Potatoes, available in the refrigerated section of most supermarkets. Just heat and stir in some garlic powder, olive oil, and olives.

Mixed-Message Mushrooms

Mushrooms have an amazing way of adding flavor to foods without adding much sodium. By flavoring each mushroom a slightly different way, you can get a whole array of tastes in one simple dish.

4 portobello mushrooms, cleaned and stems removed
1 teaspoon chopped garlic
1 leaf fresh basil
1 small sprig rosemary
$\frac{1}{8}$ teaspoon dried tarragon
2 teaspoons butter
$\frac{1}{8}$ teaspoon salt
Freshly ground black pepper to taste

Preheat a grill or broiler.

Lightly coat both sides of each mushroom with olive oil spray. Place each mushroom upside down on the grill or broiler pan. Fill the stem space of one with the garlic, the second with the basil, the third with the rosemary, and the fourth with the tarragon. Grill or broil for about 5 minutes, or until the mushrooms begin to soften but still retain their shape. Remove from the heat and discard the rosemary stem. Slice the mushrooms thinly. In a medium bowl, toss with the butter, salt, and pepper. Serve over grilled meat or chicken or toss with rice or noodles.

Yield: 4 servings

Nutritional data per serving: Calories, 24; protein, <1 g; carbohydrate, 1 g; dietary fiber, <1 g; total fat, 2 g; saturated fat, 1 g; cholesterol, 5 mg; sodium, 93 mg; vitamin A, 2% of Daily Value; vitamin C, 1%; calcium, 0%; copper, 6%; iron, 2%; vitamin B$_2$ (riboflavin), 6%; vitamin B$_3$ (niacin), 5%; potassium, 3%.

Confetti Spaghetti Squash

If you're looking for a bright and colorful veggie dish to perk up a bland-looking meal, this one fills the bill.

1 tablespoon peanut oil
2 cups cooked spaghetti squash
1 teaspoon fresh lemon juice
1/8 teaspoon ground cumin
1/8 teaspoon salt
1 cup diced red, green, and yellow
    bell peppers

Warm the oil in a heavy nonstick skillet over high heat. Spread the squash evenly in the pan and cook, without stirring, for 3 to 4 minutes, or until the squash "fries" and browns on the bottom. Reduce the heat to medium. Sprinkle with the lemon juice, cumin, and salt. Spread the peppers evenly on top. Cover and steam for about 2 minutes, or just until the peppers are heated through.

Yield: 4 servings

Nutritional data per serving: Calories, 60; protein, <1 g; carbohydrate, 7 g; dietary fiber, 2 g; total fat, 4 g; saturated fat, <1 g; cholesterol, 0 mg; sodium, 22 mg; vitamin A, 8% of Daily Value; vitamin C, 84%; calcium, 2%; iron, 2%; vitamin B_6, 7%; vitamin E, 4%; folate, 3%; magnesium, 3%; potassium, 4%.

DOUBLE DUTY

Here's the funny part—although the peppers look like a garnish, they deliver a ton of vitamin C!

Garlic Potato Crisps

Okay, I don't eat french fries anymore. But that doesn't mean I don't want to! I still love their wonderful flavor. So I let my oven and a little olive oil deliver the taste I crave.

2 medium red-skin potatoes, scrubbed
1 teaspoon garlic powder, or to taste

Preheat the oven to 450°F. Coat a baking sheet with olive oil spray.

Slice the potatoes super-thin (a food processor or slicer comes in handy for this). Arrange the slices on the baking sheet, then coat lightly with olive oil spray. Sprinkle with the garlic powder. Bake for about 10 minutes, or until brown and crisp.

Yield: 2 servings

Nutritional data per serving: Calories, 144; protein, 4 g; carbohydrate, 27 g; dietary fiber, 3 g; total fat, 5 g; saturated fat, <1 g; cholesterol, 0 mg; sodium, 0 mg; vitamin A, 0% of Daily Value; vitamin C, 45%; calcium, 2%; iron, 6%; vitamin B_6, 2%; vitamin E, 3%; potassium, 21%.

Sugar Snap Peas and Baby Carrots

Pretty as a picture, this snazzy little side dish will brighten up any meal.

1 cup baby carrots
1 cup fresh sugar snap peas
1 teaspoon butter
1/8 teaspoon dried thyme
1/8 teaspoon salt
Freshly ground black pepper to taste

In a medium saucepan with just enough water to cover, bring the carrots to a boil over high heat. Reduce the heat to medium, cover, and cook for 4 minutes. Stir in the peas and cook for 2 minutes. Drain and place in a serving bowl. Add the butter, thyme, salt, and pepper. Toss lightly until coated.

Yield: 4 servings

Nutritional data per serving: Calories, 36; protein, 1 g; carbohydrate, 6 g; dietary fiber, 2 g; total fat, 1 g; saturated fat, <1 g; cholesterol, 3 mg; sodium, 186 mg; vitamin A, 20% of Daily Value; vitamin C, 14%; calcium, 3%; iron, 3%.

 ### The P·E·R·F·E·C·T Companion

Add soothing richness to your after-dinner tea by adding 1/4 cup spiced cider. Stir with a cinnamon stick.

Super K Smoothie

In chemistry, K stands for potassium (it comes from the Greek word). In fighting high blood pressure, K stands for key—it's that important. This yummy drink delivers one-third of your K for the day, so drink up. It's great for breakfast or an afternoon snack.

1 cup frozen tropical fruit chunks
1 cup calcium-fortified orange juice
1 medium banana

In a blender, combine the fruit and orange juice. Blend until smooth, pulsing if necessary. Add the banana and blend until smooth. Cheers!

Yield: 1 serving

Nutritional data per serving: Calories, 301; protein, 4 g; carbohydrate, 74 g; dietary fiber, 5 g; total fat, 1 g; saturated fat, 0 g; cholesterol, 0 mg; sodium, 5 mg; vitamin A, 18% of Daily Value; vitamin C, 296%; calcium, 38%; iron, 4%; vitamin B$_6$, 47%; vitamin E, 8%; folate, 27%; potassium, 34%.

Autumn Harvest Applesauce

I invented this warm and spicy fruit treat just to use up some left-over cranberries. Now I start with the cranberries and use the leftovers for something else! Served warm or cold, it's a delicious dose of fiber.

4 large Red Delicious apples, washed, cored,
    and cut into chunks
4 large Bosc pears, washed, cored, and thinly sliced
1 cup fresh cranberries, washed and sorted
¹/₂ cup coarsely chopped walnuts
1 teaspoon pumpkin pie spice
¹/₂ cup water

In a heavy saucepan, combine the apples, pears, cranberries, walnuts, pumpkin pie spice, and water. Cover and bring to a boil. Reduce the heat to low and simmer, stirring occasionally, for about 15 minutes, or until the apples and pears are fork-tender.

Yield: 8 servings

Nutritional data per serving: Calories, 170; protein, 2 g; carbohydrate, 32 g; dietary fiber, 6 g; total fat, 6 g; saturated fat, <1 g; cholesterol, 0 mg; sodium, 0 mg; vitamin A, 1% of Daily Value; vitamin C, 19%; calcium, 3%; iron, 4%; potassium, 8%.

Lovely Leftovers   Use a heaping spoonful as a terrific topping on pancakes or waffles.

Traffic Light Parfait

Stop the afternoon hungries dead in their tracks with this eye-popping parfait designed by the folks who grow New Zealand kiwifruit.

2 large green kiwifruit
2 large Zespri gold kiwifruit
1/2 cup orange juice
3/4 cup raspberries

Peel and slice the kiwis. In a blender, combine the green kiwi and 1 to 2 tablespoons of the orange juice. Blend just until smooth. Spoon into two tall glasses.

Wash the blender jar, then combine the gold kiwi with 3 to 4 tablespoons of the orange juice. Blend until smooth. Carefully pour over the back of a spoon on top of the green kiwi in the glasses.

Wash the blender jar, then combine the raspberries with the remaining 2 tablespoons orange juice. Blend just until smooth. Pour over the back of a spoon on top of the gold puree. *Stop* and admire the effect: three distinct layers. Now don't *Wait*. *Go* ahead and enjoy!

Yield: 2 servings

Nutritional data per serving: Calories, 134; protein, 3 g; carbohydrate, 32 g; dietary fiber, 5 g; total fat, <1 g; saturated fat, 0 g; cholesterol, 0 mg; sodium, 5 mg; vitamin A, 2% of Daily Value; vitamin C, 296%; calcium, 4%; iron, 5%; vitamin E, 12%; folate, 5%; potassium, 11%.

Casaba Melon with Raspberry Sorbet

Beautiful and luscious desserts can make your heart sing! Here's a cool sweet treat to get you through the dog days of summer.

2 cups raspberry sorbet, slightly softened
¹/₂ casaba melon, seeded
5 sprigs mint

Using the small end of a melon baller, scoop tiny balls of sorbet, place on a baking sheet, and freeze. Using the large end of the melon baller, scoop balls from the melon and place in a serving bowl. When ready to serve, mix the frozen sorbet with the melon balls. Garnish with the mint.

Yield: 10 servings

Nutritional data per serving: Calories, 69; protein, <1 g; carbohydrate, 17 g; dietary fiber, 1 g; total fat, 0 g; saturated fat, 0 g; cholesterol, 0 mg; sodium, 10 mg; vitamin A, 0% of Daily Value; vitamin C, 23%; calcium, 0%; iron, 2%; potassium, 6%.

Lovely Leftovers

Remove the rind from the other half of the melon, then cut the melon into cubes. Place strategically in the fridge where snack hunters will be tempted to dig in.

Asian Fruit Salad

Looking for a taste of the Orient to top off your Chinese takeout meal? Stir a crispy Asian pear into a handful of canned ingredients you can always have on hand, and you'll have a delicious dessert.

1 Asian pear, diced
1 can (12 ounces) water-packed mandarin
    oranges, drained
1 can (6 ounces) juice-packed crushed
pineapple
1/4 teaspoon ground ginger
6 drained canned lychees
3 tablespoons sweetened shredded
coconut, toasted

In a medium bowl, combine the pear, oranges, pineapple, and ginger and stir well. Divide among six serving dishes. Top each serving with a lychee and sprinkle with coconut.

Yield: 6 servings

Nutritional data per serving: Calories, 73; protein, <1 g; carbohydrate, 14 g; dietary fiber, 1 g; total fat, 2 g; saturated fat, 1.6 g; cholesterol, 0 mg; sodium, 4 mg; vitamin A, 3% of Daily Value; vitamin C, 29%; calcium, 1%; iron, 2%; magnesium, 1%; potassium, 2%.

> **The Inside Skinny:** Coconut is one of those rare plant foods that's packed with saturated fat. Use it gingerly to tingle your taste buds but spare your heart.

Nutty Fruit Plate

I grew up loving nuts. Add them to anything, and I'm a happy girl! And dried fruit, with its super-sweet flavor in each little bite...it's heaven! So what could be better than putting the two together when you want "just a little something" at the end of a meal? Decidedly healthy, but it sure doesn't taste like it.

6 dried whole apricots
6 walnut halves
6 dried Calimyrna figs
6 hazelnuts
6 dried pitted dates
6 almonds

Slit the side of each apricot and stuff in a walnut half. Open the side of each fig and fill it with a hazelnut. Open each date and slide in an almond. Arrange on a pretty dessert tray and serve, or wrap and refrigerate for an array of flavors that you can choose from for days to come.

Yield: 18 servings

Nutritional data per serving: Calories, 40; protein, <1 g; carbohydrate, 8 g; dietary fiber, 1 g; total fat, 1 g; saturated fat, 0 g; cholesterol, 0 mg; sodium, 1 mg; vitamin A, 2% of Daily Value; vitamin C, 0%; calcium, 1%; iron, 2%; copper, 3%; potassium, 3%; omega-3 fatty acids, 6%.

CHAPTER 3

HAVE A STROKE OF GENIUS

GET HOOKED ON FISH

WHEN I WAS GROWING UP, WE HAD LOTS AND LOTS OF "fishy" Fridays. Sometimes, my mom dished up crab cakes or shrimp, which our family loved. But other times, to my father's dismay, Mom cooked real fish. Dad and my sisters backed off, filled up on mac and cheese, and left the fish for me. I was ecstatic! Mom would put the leftover fish in the fridge, and I'd have cold flounder or rockfish sandwiches for a couple of days. Yum!

My family thought I was just a little weird, but it turns out that being a fin fanatic was very, very good for me. Fish, you see, is swimming in a special kind of fat that your body can't make but must get from food. Called omega-3 fatty acids, they've recently been revealed to net a ton of health benefits. Here's what omega-3s can do for you.

♥ Reduce excessive blood clotting, thus helping to head off strokes.

♥ Soothe the wildly irregular heartbeats that cause sudden heart attack deaths.

♥ Lighten up depression, including the postpartum kind.

♥ Reduce the pain of rheumatoid arthritis and menstrual cramps.

♥ Improve the development of babies' brain and vision.

♥ Calm asthma in both children and adults.

♥ Possibly fend off some cancers, including breast cancer.

That's a whale of a lot of benefits from those little swimmers!

Unfortunately, my dad isn't the only fish-phobic person I know. Omega-3s are in short supply across the board in the United States, because most of what we eat doesn't eat anything green. Yes, it's true; fish is "green cuisine" because it feeds on plankton. Our forebears actually got plenty of omega-3 fats because they ate wild game that ate the leaves off trees, or even beef animals that ate lots of grass. But no more. Feedlot fattening of cattle is cutting off our omega-3 supply.

But you can start angling for your share of the goodies by following the American Heart Association's recommen-

Fish-Oil Supplements Work!

The risk of sudden death is high during the first 3 months after a heart attack. But in a recent study of 11,000 Italian patients, those who took supplements of 1 gram of omega-3 fatty acids daily cut their risk of a second heart attack in half. So, on days when you're not scarfing down your favorite fish, think about taking a supplement.

dation to put fish on your menu twice a week. Fatty fish—such as salmon and anchovies—pack the most omega-3s, but water-packed white albacore tuna is a great source, too. In fact, anything that comes out of the sea will reel in more omega-3s than any land animal, although you can get a boost from flaxseed, walnut, or canola oil, as well as walnuts and dark green, leafy vegetables (you'll find more of those in chapter 12).

Now here's the fun part. Fish is amazingly quick to prepare. Whether you broil, bake, poach, or grill it, just 5 to 10 minutes gets the job done. How handy is that! Don't believe me? Just try the recipes on the following pages. You're about to experience a sea change.

Allergic to Fish?

According to the American Dietetic Association, probably not. In fact, only 1 in 50 adults, or 2%, have true food allergies of any kind. The most common reactions are to milk, eggs, peanuts and other nuts, soybeans, fish, shellfish, and wheat. If you think you have a food allergy, see a doctor rather than making a self-diagnosis. It's important to check because some reactions, especially to nuts, fish, and shellfish, can be deadly.

Salmon Lemongrass Soup

Want to pique your guests' taste buds without killing their appetites? This light, brothy soup is just what the chef ordered! And it's oh, so easy!

3½ cups fat-free chicken broth
2 stalks lemongrass (from a jar), crushed
1 baby carrot, cut into 12 rounds
1 tablespoon fish sauce*
¼ teaspoon sugar
½ teaspoon light soy sauce
2 ounces salmon filet, cut into ½-inch cubes
2 tablespoons fresh chives

Bring the broth to a boil in a 4-quart saucepan. Add the lemongrass, carrot, fish sauce, sugar, and soy sauce. Reduce the heat, cover, and simmer for 5 minutes, or until the carrots are tender. Remove the lemongrass. Add the fish and simmer for 2 to 3 minutes, or just until cooked through. Ladle into four bowls, evenly distributing the fish and carrots. Garnish with the chives.

Yield: 4 servings

Nutritional data per serving: Calories, 39; protein, 6 g; carbohydrate, <1 g; dietary fiber, 0 g; total fat, 1 g; saturated fat, 0 g; cholesterol, 10 mg; sodium, 603 mg; vitamin A, 5% of Daily Value; vitamin C, 2%; calcium, 0%; iron, 1%; vitamin D, 10%; omega-3 fatty acids, 32%.
*Available in Asian markets and many large supermarkets.

> **QUICK TRICK:** No lemongrass? Squeeze in a few drops of fresh lemon juice instead.

Grilled Shrimp Salad

Shrimp pack a lot of cholesterol, but when it comes to saturated fat, they're about as low as you can go, making them a pretty healthy treat. Combine them with lots of vegetables and spice for a savory taste sensation that delivers a full day's supply of vitamin C and omega-3 fatty acids.

1 pound very large shrimp
1 teaspoon Old Bay seafood
   seasoning
1/4 cup low-fat mayonnaise
1/2 cup diced cucumbers
1/2 cup diced red bell peppers
1 tablespoon diced garlic (from a jar)

Peel and devein the shrimp, then mist with olive oil spray. In a nonstick grill basket, grill the shrimp over a medium fire until they curl and turn pink (be careful not to overcook). Cut about one-third of the shrimp into small pieces; leave the remaining shrimp whole.

In a medium bowl, combine the shrimp, seafood seasoning, mayonnaise, cucumbers, peppers, and garlic. Toss well. Serve on lettuce as a main course, or stuff into a pita pocket.

Yield: 2 servings

Nutritional data per serving: Calories, 310; protein, 47 g; carbohydrate, 15 g; dietary fiber, 1 g; total fat, 6 g; saturated fat, <1 g; cholesterol, 345 mg; sodium, 938 mg; vitamin A, 34% of Daily Value; vitamin C, 129%; calcium, 13%; iron, 32%; vitamin D, 86%; vitamin E, 11%; potassium, 16%; zinc, 18%; omega-3 fatty acids, 100%.

Anchovy Salad

Back when I was writing Kitchen Counter Cures, I became so enthralled with olives that I started growing an olive tree in a pot on my deck. True, Maryland isn't what you'd think of as its ideal climate, but the tree is now bigger than I am, and it shades me while I'm enjoying very Italian treats like this salad. It's cool!

1 bag (10 ounces) frozen California vegetables
2 cups cooked radiatore or other pasta
1 can (2 ounces) anchovy filets, coarsely chopped
2 tablespoons olive oil
1 tablespoon garlic (from a jar)
1/4 teaspoon salt
1/4 teaspoon crushed red pepper

Pour 1 inch of water into a deep saucepan and insert a steamer basket. Place the vegetables in the basket, cover, and bring to a boil. Reduce the heat to medium and steam for 2 to 3 minutes, or until their colors brighten. Place in a large salad bowl with the pasta and anchovies. Add the oil, garlic, salt, and pepper and toss gently.

Yield: 8 servings

Nutritional data per serving: Calories, 109; protein, 5 g; carbohydrate, 13 g; dietary fiber, 1 g; total fat, 4 g; saturated fat, <1 g; cholesterol, 6 mg; sodium, 346 mg; vitamin A, 6% of Daily Value; vitamin C, 15%; calcium, 3%; iron, 6%; vitamin B_1 (thiamin), 10%; vitamin B_2 (riboflavin), 12%; vitamin E, 4%; folate, 8%; omega-3 fatty acids, 17%.

DOUBLE DUTY

True, anchovies deliver those fishy fats your arteries crave. But they also add incredibly rich, complex flavors with very little work on your part!

Fiesta (Mock) Crab Salad

Forget about "truth in advertising." Lots of folks who turn their noses up at cold fish salad will dive right in if they think it's crab salad. So lie a little. Trust me—it's for a good cause!

6 ounces cold broiled fish
1/2 cup diced red and green bell peppers
1/4 cup low-fat mayonnaise
1 teaspoon Old Bay seafood seasoning
2 leaves red leaf lettuce
2 small tomatoes
2 sprigs parsley
2 wedges lemon

In a medium bowl, flake the fish until fluffy. Add the peppers, mayonnaise, and seafood seasoning and stir until well blended. Place each lettuce leaf on a plate, then place a tomato, stem side down, on each. Without cutting all the way through, cut the tomatoes into wedges. Stuff with equal portions of the fish salad. Garnish each with a parsley sprig and a lemon wedge. Serve with dinner rolls and white wine.

Yield: 2 servings

Nutritional data per serving: Calories, 207; protein, 22 g; carbohydrate, 13 g; dietary fiber, 2 g; total fat, 8 g; saturated fat, 1 g; cholesterol, 65 mg; sodium, 572 mg; vitamin A, 24% of Daily Value; vitamin C, 131%; calcium, 3%; iron, 6%; vitamin D, 13%; vitamin E, 21%; folate, 10%; potassium, 19%; omega-3 fatty acids, 93%.

DOUBLE DUTY

Sure, the tomato serves as a colorful cup for your "crab" salad. But it's also a rich source of that powerful prostate cancer preventer, lycopene.

Blue Caesar Salad

I was serving lamb for a recent family feast and trying to figure out how to squeeze in the benefits of fish without cooking two entrées. This elegant first course blew everyone away.

1 teaspoon anchovy paste
1 tablespoon walnut oil
1 tablespoon minced garlic
2 tablespoons balsamic vinegar
1/8 teaspoon salt
4 cups chopped romaine lettuce
1 tablespoon chopped toasted walnuts
2 tablespoons crumbled blue cheese

In a small bowl, combine the anchovy paste, oil, garlic, vinegar, and salt. With a wire whisk, blend until smooth. In a large salad bowl, combine the lettuce and dressing and toss until well coated. Divide between two salad plates and top each with 1/2 tablespoon of the walnuts and 1 tablespoon of the cheese.

Yield: 2 servings

Nutritional data per serving: Calories, 177; protein, 6 g; carbohydrate, 8 g; dietary fiber, 3 g; total fat, 15 g; saturated fat, 3 g; cholesterol, 9 mg; sodium, 256 mg; vitamin A, 31% of Daily Value; vitamin C, 47%; calcium, 11%; iron, 10%; vitamin E, 6%; folate, 41%; potassium, 12%; omega-3 fatty acids, 156%.

SUPER SUB

Caesar salad's secret ingredient is anchovy paste, which, of course, is also the secret ingredient for a healthy heart. Walnuts and walnut oil add to the drama and kick up the omega-3s.

Tuna with Water Chestnuts and Cashews

*Don't you get tired of the same old tuna with mayo? I do. So some-
times, I just rummage around in my kitchen to see what I can come up
with. Here's what I found one day.*

2 leaves butterhead lettuce
1 can (8 ounces) sliced water chestnuts,
    rinsed and drained
1 green onion, thinly sliced
1 clementine, peeled and sectioned
1 can (6 ounces) water-packed white albacore tuna, drained
6 cashews, coarsely chopped
1/4 cup light Catalina dressing

Place each lettuce leaf on a plate. In a small bowl, combine
the water chestnuts, onion, and clementine. Place an equal portion on each lettuce leaf. Flake the tuna and divide between the
plates. Sprinkle each with half of the cashews and drizzle with
the dressing.

Yield: 2 servings

*Nutritional data per serving: Calories, 265;
protein, 23 g; carbohydrate, 29 g; dietary fiber,
4 g; total fat, 6 g; saturated fat, 1 g; cholesterol,
236 mg; sodium, 744 mg; vitamin A, 17% of
Daily Value; vitamin C, 11%; calcium, 4%; iron,
14%; vitamin B$_3$ (niacin), 28%; vitamin D, 34%;
potassium, 14%; omega-3 fatty acids, 82%.*

The P·E·R·F·E·C·T Companion

To warm up a cold
meal, have a steaming
mug of Campbell's
Healthy Request veg-
etable soup.

Flaxseed-Oil Dressing

Here's a tasty little dressing you can keep in your fridge. On days when you're too pooped to pop, pour a little over some bagged salad and consider yourself a kitchen wizard!

2 tablespoons flaxseed oil
2 tablespoons apple cider vinegar
2 tablespoons water
1/2 teaspoon sugar
1/4 teaspoon salt
1/2 teaspoon dried tarragon
Freshly ground multicolored pepper to taste

In a small bowl, combine the oil, vinegar, water, sugar, salt, tarragon, and pepper. With a small wire whisk, beat until well blended. Spoon over your choice of salad and toss well.

Yield: 6 servings

Nutritional data per serving: Calories, 43; protein, 0 g; carbohydrate, <1 g; dietary fiber, 0 g; total fat, 5 g; saturated fat, 0 g; cholesterol, 0 mg; sodium, 97 mg; vitamin A, 0% of Daily Value; vitamin C, 0%; calcium, 0%; iron, 0%; omega-3 fatty acids, 251%.

SUPER SUB

1 CUP

Just 1 tablespoon of this dressing on your salad feeds your need for fish for 2 1/2 days! That's a nutritional bargain on days when you'd rather eat chicken.

FlaxBerry Waffles

There's more than one way to scale a fish, and if you're looking for tasty but different ways to get your omega-3s, these crisp and flavorful breakfast waffles will get you in the swim of things. You'll find them in natural foods stores.

2 Flax Plus waffles
¼ cup reduced-fat ricotta cheese
1 cup mixed fresh berries
Dash of ground cinnamon

Thaw the waffles at room temperature for about 5 minutes, then toast on the light setting. Spread each waffle with ⅛ cup of the ricotta, then top with ½ cup of the berries. Dust with the cinnamon.

Yield: 1 serving

Nutritional data per serving: Calories, 422; protein, 12 g; carbohydrate, 59 g; dietary fiber, 10 g; total fat, 16 g; saturated fat, 6 g; cholesterol, 35 mg; sodium, 692 mg; vitamin A, 10% of Daily Value; vitamin C, 42%; calcium, 33%; iron, 15%; folate, 7%; magnesium, 5%; potassium, 5%; omega-3 fatty acids, 112%.

Walnut Corn Muffins

What could be better on a cold, rainy day than hot corn muffins fresh from the oven? They're warm, comforting, and good news for your body!

1 package (7 ounces) corn muffin mix
1 egg
½ cup water
1 tablespoon walnut oil
¼ cup chopped walnuts

Preheat the oven to 400°F. Lightly coat a six-cup muffin pan with nonstick spray.

In a small bowl, combine the muffin mix, egg, water, oil, and walnuts. Stir with a fork just until blended, then spoon into the pan. Bake for 20 minutes, or until a toothpick inserted in the center of a muffin comes out clean. Remove from the pan and cool on a rack (if they last that long). Enjoy with a cup of tea.

Yield: 6 servings

Nutritional data per serving: Calories, 190; protein, 3 g; carbohydrate, 25 g; dietary fiber, 1 g; total fat, 9 g; saturated fat, 1.5 g; cholesterol, 31 mg; sodium, 230 mg; vitamin A, 1% of Daily Value; vitamin C, 1%; calcium, 7%; iron, 6%; omega-3 fatty acids, 70%.

Lovely Leftovers Great with a glass of milk and a piece of fruit for breakfast or with a grilled chicken salad for lunch.

Keen Little Fish Sandwich

Oily, "fishy" fish turn a lot of people off, but when I bring home a can of sardines, my husband's eyes light up. Ted really loves them. That makes me love them, too, because they're packed with omega-3 fatty acids that are so good for his heart—and I'm fishing for a long life with him.

1 can (3¾ ounces) water-packed
   brisling sardines, well drained
1 tablespoon Dijon mustard
1 tablespoon diced red onions
¼ teaspoon dried basil
Freshly ground black pepper to taste
2 slices rye bread
2 slices tomato
1 leaf romaine lettuce

DOUBLE DUTY

The healthy fat in sardines protects your heart and blood vessels and helps you absorb the tomatoes' lycopene—a powerful weapon against prostate cancer.

Cut the sardines into chunks and place in a medium bowl. Add the mustard, onions, basil, and pepper. Stir until blended. Pile the mixture on one slice of the bread and top with the tomatoes and lettuce, then the remaining slice of bread. Cut the sandwich in half, then kick back and enjoy with a handful of baby carrots and an ice-cold light beer.

Yield: 1 serving

Nutritional data per serving: Calories, 376; protein, 27 g; carbohydrate, 36 g; dietary fiber, 5 g; total fat, 12 g; saturated fat, 2 g; cholesterol, 116 mg; sodium, 1,202 mg; vitamin A, 11% of Daily Value; vitamin C, 21%; calcium, 37%; iron, 25%; vitamin B$_1$ (thiamin), 26%; vitamin B$_2$ (riboflavin), 26%; vitamin B$_3$ (niacin), 35%; vitamin D, 56%; folate, 23%; magnesium, 17%; potassium, 18%; omega-3 fatty acids, 126%.

Riviera Salmon Wrap

Get lost, Peter Pan! This recipe doesn't contain a single food that I ate before the age of 30. This is a great comfort to me, because it suggests that there are big benefits to growing up!

1 tablespoon light ranch dressing
1 large flour tortilla
3 ounces cold cooked salmon, flaked
1 teaspoon capers
1 thin slice red onion, separated into rings
Salt and freshly ground black pepper to taste
1 cup Royal Blend or other mixed salad greens

Spread the dressing down the center of the tortilla. Pile the fish on the dressing on the top half of the tortilla. Add the capers, onion, salt, pepper, and greens. Fold the bottom half of the tortilla over the top half, fold in one side, and roll into a wrap. Then indulge yourself!

Yield: 1 serving

Nutritional data per serving: Calories, 365; protein, 27 g; carbohydrate, 37 g; dietary fiber, 3 g; total fat, 12 g; saturated fat, 1 g; cholesterol, 65 mg; sodium, 675 mg; vitamin A, 1% of Daily Value; vitamin C, 16%; calcium, 13%; iron, 15%; vitamin B_2 (riboflavin), 25%; vitamin B_3 (niacin), 43%; vitamin B_6, 42%; vitamin D, 60%; potassium, 18%; omega-3 fatty acids, 189%.

QUICK TRICK: Add richness and depth of flavor to many dishes by sprinkling on a few capers. These pickled tree buds make your taste buds say "Howdy!"

Shrimp Cremini

Fast, simple, and unbelievably delicious. And here, just a kiss of butter gives fabulous flavor, while total cholesterol hits the daily average. And it's packed with heart-healthy omega-3 fatty acids, plus calcium and vitamin D for better bones.

1 pound large shrimp
1 tablespoon butter
6 ounces cremini mushrooms,
    cleaned and thinly sliced
1 clove garlic, minced or pressed
1/2 teaspoon Old Bay seafood
    seasoning
1/8 teaspoon salt

Peel and devein the shrimp. Melt the butter in a deep, heavy nonstick skillet. Add the shrimp, mushrooms, garlic, and seafood seasoning. Cook, stirring often, over medium-high heat, until the shrimp curl and turn pink and the mushrooms give up some of their liquid. Sprinkle with the salt. Serve over cooked brown rice to soak up every drop of the luscious liquid.

Yield: 2 servings

Nutritional data per serving: Calories, 270; protein, 50 g; carbohydrate, 5 g, dietary fiber, 2 g; total fat, 4 g; saturated fat, <1 g; cholesterol, 345 mg; sodium, 674 mg; vitamin A, 12% of Daily Value; vitamin C, 8%; calcium, 12%; iron, 34%; vitamin D, 86%; omega-3 fatty acids, 112%.

QUICK TRICK: Use frozen peeled and deveined shrimp and presliced mushrooms.

Michael's Mediterranean Monkfish

My hairdresser, Michael Salconi, expresses his Italian heritage with food. He says the secret of all great Italian cooks is this: Choose good ingredients and simple preparation. You gotta love this guy!

4 ounces monkfish filet
1/8 teaspoon salt
1 tablespoon olive oil
1 wedge lemon
1/4 cup white wine
Freshly ground black pepper
    to taste
1 tablespoon capers

Wash the fish and pat dry. Sprinkle with the salt. In a heavy nonstick skillet over medium heat, sauté the fish in the oil for about 5 minutes, gently turning once, until the segments separate easily with a fork. Place on a dinner plate and squeeze the lemon over the fish. Deglaze the pan with the wine and pour the liquid over the fish. Add the pepper and top with the capers. Serve with Village Salad (page 192) and Italian bread.

Yield: 1 serving

Nutritional data per serving: Calories, 200; protein, 19 g; carbohydrate, 2 g; dietary fiber, 0 g; total fat, 9 g; saturated fat, 1.5 g; cholesterol, 32 mg; sodium, 572 mg; vitamin A, 2% of Daily Value; vitamin C, 8%; calcium, 2%; iron, 4%; vitamin B$_6$, 15%; potassium, 16%; zinc, 4%.

Walnut-Encrusted Rockfish

In my husband, Ted's, family tradition, the Christmas Eve meal is a gathering where the focus is on seafood. Together, we came up with a main dish fish that was astonishingly good but didn't keep us locked up in the kitchen all night. That's because we did all the preparation early in the day and refrigerated the fish right on the baking sheet.

4 tablespoons melted butter
2 eggs, beaten
1 cup Italian-style bread crumbs
4 pounds rockfish (sea bass) or other thick white fish filet
Salt and freshly ground black pepper to taste
4 tablespoons ground walnuts

Lightly brush a baking sheet with 2 tablespoons of the butter. Place the eggs in a medium bowl and the bread crumbs in a shallow dish.

Wash the fish and pat dry. Trim out eight thick pieces, about 6 ounces each. (Freeze the trimmings for later use.) Sprinkle with the salt and pepper. Dip each filet in the egg, roll in the bread crumbs, and place on the baking sheet. Sprinkle 1/2 tablespoon of the walnuts on each filet and drizzle 1 teaspoon of the remaining butter over each. Bake at 400°F for 10 to 15 minutes, or until the filets are brown and flake easily with a fork.

Yield: 8 servings

Nutritional data per serving: Calories, 255; protein, 34 g; carbohydrate, 6 g; dietary fiber, <1 g; total fat, 10 g; saturated fat, 3.5 g; cholesterol, 96 mg; sodium, 257 mg; vitamin A, 14% of Daily Value; vitamin C, 0%; calcium, 3%; iron, 7%; potassium, 20%; omega-3 fatty acids, 102%.

Blue Crab with Butter

Every now and then, when I want an absolutely luscious and outrageous treat for my family, I stop by my local seafood store and pick up a can of jumbo lump crabmeat.

1 pound jumbo lump blue crab or other crabmeat
4 leaves butterhead lettuce
2 tablespoons melted butter
2 tablespoons walnut oil
1/2 teaspoon Old Bay seafood seasoning
8 cherry tomatoes
4 wedges lemon

Without disturbing the crab lumps, remove any shell you can find. Place a lettuce leaf on each of four plates and divide the crabmeat among them. In a small bowl, combine the butter and oil. Drizzle 1 tablespoon over each serving of crab and dust with the seafood seasoning. Garnish each with two tomatoes and a lemon wedge. Serve with Oven-Crisp Sweet Potatoes (page 238), Long Beans Amandine (page 47), and white wine.

Yield: 4 servings

Nutritional data per serving: Calories, 231; protein, 24 g; carbohydrate, 2 g; dietary fiber, <1 g; total fat, 14 g; saturated fat, 5 g; cholesterol, 116 mg; sodium, 520 mg; vitamin A, 8% of Daily Value; vitamin C, 12%; calcium, 12%; iron, 6%; folate, 15%; copper, 44%; potassium, 15%; zinc, 31%; omega-3 fatty acids, 121%.

SUPER SUB

By controlling the butter portion and substituting walnut oil for half of it, you'll cut saturated fat and increase the omega-3 fatty acids.

Linguine with White Clam Sauce

Keep your emergency shelf stocked with the right ingredients, and folks will think you planned for days for this gourmet treat.

4 ounces linguine
2 tablespoons olive oil
1 tablespoon chopped garlic (from a jar)
4 ounces white wine
2 tablespoons parsley flakes
1 tablespoon dried basil
Freshly ground black pepper to taste
1 can (6½ ounces) chopped clams in juice, drained and
　　juice reserved
4 ounces bottled clam juice
2 tablespoons Parmesan cheese

Bring 4 quarts water to a boil in a large saucepan. Add the pasta and cook for about 11 minutes, or according to package directions.

Meanwhile, in a medium heavy saucepan, combine the oil, garlic, wine, parsley, basil, pepper, and the reserved and bottled clam juice. Bring to a boil, then reduce the heat and simmer.

Remove the pasta from the heat but do not drain. Stir the clams into the clam juice mixture and simmer until heated through. Drain the pasta and divide between two pasta bowls. Top each portion with half of the clam sauce and sprinkle each with 1 tablespoon of the cheese. Serve with a salad and crusty rolls.

Yield: 2 servings

Nutritional data per serving: Calories, 428; protein, 17 g; carbohydrate, 44 g; dietary fiber, 3 g; total fat, 16 g; saturated fat, 3 g; cholesterol, 23 mg; sodium, 852 mg; vitamin A, 6% of Daily Value; vitamin C, 4%; calcium, 16%; iron, 31%; magnesium, 11%; potassium, 8%; omega-3 fatty acids, 14%.

Beer-Steamed Shrimp

When I'm in the mood for a big pile of high-protein food (not often, I'll admit, but it does happen), I go for a pound of shrimp to share. It's so low in fat that you can eat a ton for just a few calories. And getting up to my elbows in all that peeling and eating restores that old "down home" feeling, especially when I'm sitting on my deck on a hot August night.

1 cup beer
1 pound large shrimp
1 tablespoon Old Bay seafood seasoning

Pour the beer into a large saucepan, insert a steamer basket, and add the shrimp. Sprinkle with the seafood seasoning. Bring the beer to a boil, cover, and steam for about 5 minutes, or until the shrimp curl and turn pink (do not overcook, or they will be tough and dry). Place in a large bowl and cool for about 5 minutes. Peel and devein the shrimp one by one, dipping them in cocktail sauce and eating as you go. Serve with cold beer, corn on the cob, and thick slices of the finest summer tomato you can find.

Yield: 2 servings

Nutritional data per serving: Calories, 225; protein, 47 g; carbohydrate, 0 g; dietary fiber, 0 g; total fat, 2 g; saturated fat, <1 g; cholesterol, 442 mg; sodium, 828 mg; vitamin A, 15% of Daily Value; vitamin C, 8%; vitamin D, 81%; vitamin E, 6%; calcium, 9%; iron, 39%; vitamin B_3 (niacin), 29%; magnesium, 19%; potassium, 12%; zinc, 24%; omega-3 fatty acids, 74%.

Don't Flounder Around

So many people tell me they'd love to eat more fish, but it seems so tricky to fix. Nothing could be further from the truth! Just start with a great seafood store and pick fresh, clean-smelling fish. The rest is easy. Just watch.

2 flounder filets (6 ounces each)
1/8 teaspoon salt
1 teaspoon walnut oil
1 tablespoon sliced almonds
2 wedges lemon

Line a baking sheet with foil and coat lightly with nonstick spray. Place the oven rack in the highest position.

Wash the fish, pat dry, and place on the baking sheet. Sprinkle with the salt, brush with the oil, and top with the almonds. Place the baking sheet on a broiler pan and broil at 375°F for about 5 minutes, or until the fish flakes easily with a fork. Place each filet on a dinner plate and garnish with a lemon wedge. Serve with Garlic Mashed Potatoes with Olive Oil (page 51) and a crisp green salad.

Yield: 2 servings

Nutritional data per serving: Calories, 193; protein, 33 g; carbohydrate, <1 g; dietary fiber, 0 g; total fat, 6 g; saturated fat, <1 g; cholesterol, 82 mg; sodium, 283 mg; vitamin A, 2% of Daily Value; vitamin C, 5%; calcium, 4%; iron, 3%; vitamin B_3 (niacin), 25%; vitamin B_6, 18%; vitamin D, 26%; vitamin E, 19%; magnesium, 15%; potassium, 18%; omega-3 fatty acids, 59%.

DOUBLE DUTY

The walnut oil isn't there just for the flavor—it's the best land-based source of omega-3 fatty acids!

Grilled Tuna with Capers and Olives

At our house, I make the sauce and my husband, Ted, does the grilling. Teamwork rocks!

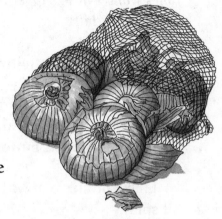

1 large red onion, thinly sliced
2 tablespoons walnut oil
1/2 cup dry red wine
1 tablespoon capers
2 tablespoons sliced black olives
1/2 teaspoon salt
Freshly ground black pepper to taste
2 tuna steaks (6 ounces each)
1 tablespoon chopped fresh oregano

In a medium saucepan over medium heat, sauté the onion in 1 tablespoon of the oil for about 5 minutes, or until soft but not brown. Stir in the wine, capers, olives, salt, and pepper. Reduce the heat to low and cook, stirring occasionally, until the sauce thickens and liquids evaporate. Meanwhile, brush the tuna with the remaining 1 tablespoon oil. Grill over a low fire just until cooked through. Place each steak on a dinner plate and top with half the sauce. Sprinkle with the oregano. This is exquisite served over angel hair pasta. *Mamma mia!*

Yield: 2 servings

Nutritional data per serving: Calories, 474; protein, 44 g; carbohydrate, 11 g; dietary fiber, 2 g; total fat, 24 g; saturated fat, 4 g; cholesterol, 69 mg; sodium, 858 mg; vitamin A, 108% of Daily Value; vitamin C, 10%; vitamin D, 71%; vitamin E, 13%; calcium, 6%; iron, 15%; vitamin B$_1$ (thiamin), 29%; vitamin B$_2$ (riboflavin), 28%; vitamin B$_3$ (niacin), 76%; vitamin B$_6$, 44%; magnesium, 28%; potassium, 19%; omega-3 fatty acids, 357%.

Grilled Grouper on Sourdough

After all my high-fiber, color-coded, nutrient-dense eating, I some-times want a little supper that's just kind of gentle and soft. Here's one that fills the bill.

6 ounces fresh grouper filet
$1/8$ teaspoon salt
2 slices sourdough bread
2 teaspoons creamy dill mustard
$1/2$ cup chopped butterhead lettuce

Line a broiler pan with foil and coat with olive oil spray.

Wash the fish, pat dry, and sprinkle with the salt. Place on the broiler pan and coat lightly with olive oil spray. Broil at medium heat for 5 to 10 minutes, or until the fish is translucent and flakes easily with a fork. Spread one slice of the bread with the mustard, top with the fish, then add the lettuce and the second slice of bread.

Yield: 1 serving

Nutritional data per serving: Calories, 338; protein, 40 g; carbohydrate, 27 g; dietary fiber, 2 g; total fat, 6 g; saturated fat, 1 g; cholesterol, 66 mg; sodium, 650 mg; vitamin A, 10% of Daily Value; vitamin C, 4%; calcium, 8%; iron, 17%; vitamin B_1 (thiamin), 26%; vitamin B_6, 27%; folate, 21%; magnesium, 17%; potassium, 23%; omega-3 fatty acids, 43%.

QUICK TRICK: Make this sandwich with any cold, leftover broiled fish.

Orange Orange Roughy

I love the sweet, melt-in-your-mouth flavor of delicate white fish, especially since the less you do to it, the better it tastes. This is simplicity itself.

2 orange roughy filets (6 ounces each)
1 navel orange, cut into thin slices
1/8 teaspoon salt
2 teaspoons walnut oil
1 teaspoon grated orange peel

Wash the fish and pat dry. Place the orange slices on a broiler pan, then top with the fish. Sprinkle with the salt and drizzle with the oil. Broil at medium heat for about 5 minutes, until the fish is translucent and flakes easily with a fork. Place each filet on a dinner plate and garnish with the orange peel.

Yield: 2 servings

Nutritional data per serving: Calories, 158; protein, 25 g; carbohydrate, 0 g; dietary fiber, 0 g; total fat, 6 g; saturated fat, 0 g; cholesterol, 34 mg; sodium, 122 mg; vitamin A, 4% of Daily Value; vitamin C, 0%; calcium, 5%; iron, 2%; vitamin B$_3$ (niacin), 26%; vitamin B$_6$, 26%; vitamin E, 5%; potassium, 15%; omega-3 fatty acids, 48%.

Bayside Crunchy Fish

I just love my fish crispy, crunchy, and buttery tasting. Here's the simplest approach I've found to get the taste I crave and still keep my meal in the "healthy" range.

8 ounces very thin fish filets (such as flounder or perch)
1/2 teaspoon Old Bay seafood seasoning
1 tablespoon bread crumbs
2 teaspoons butter

Preheat the oven to 450°F. Lightly coat a nonstick baking sheet with nonstick spray.

Wash the fish, pat dry, and place on the baking sheet. Dust with the seafood seasoning and sprinkle with the bread crumbs. In a small microwave-safe dish, microwave the butter on high until melted. Drizzle over the fish. Bake for about 10 minutes, or until crisp. Serve with Garlic Potato Crisps (page 54).

Yield: 2 servings

Nutritional data per serving: Calories, 150; protein, 22 g; carbohydrate, 2 g; dietary fiber, 0 g; total fat, 5 g; saturated fat, 3 g; cholesterol, 65 mg; sodium, 480 mg; vitamin A, 5% of Daily Value; vitamin C, 5%; calcium, 3%; iron, 3%; vitamin B$_3$ (niacin), 18%; vitamin D, 18%; vitamin E, 11%; potassium, 12%; omega-3 fatty acids, 29%

Lovely Leftovers

Sometimes, I double the recipe so I'll have cold fish for sandwiches the next day. It's great on a Kaiser roll with well-drained coleslaw.

Haddock Oscar

Okay, so it's not the classic veal dish. But it's a great way to skip the frying while still keeping the best parts of this tasty, deep-sea treasure.

2 haddock filets (4 ounces each)
4 ounces blue crab
10 spears asparagus, washed and tough stems removed
2 teaspoons butter
1/4 teaspoon salt
Freshly ground multicolored pepper to taste

Line a broiler pan with foil and coat lightly with olive oil spray. Wash the fish and pat dry. Place the filets on the broiler pan and top each with 2 ounces of the crabmeat. Lay the asparagus beside the fish. In a small microwave-safe dish, microwave the butter on high until melted. Drizzle over the fish and asparagus. Sprinkle with the salt and pepper. Broil at medium heat for about 10 minutes, or until the fish flakes easily with a fork and the asparagus is fork-tender. Serve with baked potatoes.

Yield: 2 servings

Nutritional data per serving: Calories, 207; protein, 35 g; carbohydrate, 3 g; dietary fiber, 1 g; total fat, 6 g; saturated fat, 3 g; cholesterol, 125 mg; sodium, 604 mg; vitamin A, 10% of Daily Value; vitamin C, 16%; calcium, 11%; iron, 12%; vitamin B_3 (niacin), 30%; vitamin B_6, 26%; vitamin D, 12%; vitamin E, 7%; folate, 37%; potassium, 20%; zinc, 20%; omega-3 fatty acids, 48%.

Oahu Mahi Mahi

Ready for a trip to the islands? Kick off your shoes, slip on your sarong, and let the tropical breeze blow through your hair.

8 ounces mahi mahi filet
1 very ripe Hawaiian plantain, thinly sliced
½ cup juice-packed crushed pineapple
1 ounce salted dry-roasted macadamia nuts, chopped

Coat a grill basket with nonstick spray.

Wash the fish and pat dry. Place the fish and plantain in the basket and grill over a medium fire until the fish flakes easily with a fork and the plantain is tender. Divide between two plates. Garnish each with ¼ cup of the pineapple and half of the macadamias.

Yield: 2 servings

Nutritional data per serving: Calories, 322; protein, 23 g; carbohydrate, 34 g; dietary fiber, 3 g; total fat, 12 g; saturated fat, 2 g; cholesterol, 82 mg; sodium, 146 mg; vitamin A, 13% of Daily Value; vitamin C, 24%; calcium, 3%; iron, 13%; vitamin B$_3$ (niacin), 39%; vitamin B$_6$, 34%; vitamin E, 3%; folate, 7%; potassium, 25%; omega-3 fatty acids, 14%.

**The
P·E·R·F·E·C·T
Companion**

For extra antioxidants, fill a tall, ice-packed glass with Juicy Juice tropical punch. Garnish with a banana slice. Aloha!

Langostino Pesto Pizza

This is not your kids' kind of pizza. Very adult. Very elegant. Very easy. Trust me.

2 individual fresh pizza crusts
2 tablespoons Classico pesto sauce
4 ounces frozen langostinos, thawed

Preheat the toaster oven to 475°F.

Spread each crust with 1 tablespoon of the sauce and arrange half of the langostinos on each. Place the pizzas directly on the rack in the toaster oven. Bake for about 10 minutes, or until the crust is crisp, the sauce is liquid, and the langostinos curl and turn pink. Serve with crisp salad and champagne.

Yield: 2 servings

Nutritional data per serving: Calories, 286; protein, 18 g; carbohydrate, 36 g; dietary fiber, 1.5 g; total fat, 6 g; saturated fat, 1 g; cholesterol, 112 mg; sodium, 670 mg; vitamin A, 4% of Daily Value; vitamin C, 2%; calcium, 13%; iron, 21%; vitamin B$_3$ (niacin), 7%; zinc, 6%; omega-3 fatty acids, 19%.

DOUBLE DUTY

This pesto sauce is loaded with calcium-rich cheese, so you don't have to add extra. It's great for helping to lower your blood pressure—one of the biggest risk factors for stroke.

Bay Scallops Provençal

Looking for a light, fresh entrée that takes just minutes to prepare?
Look no further. This delicate dish is just right for a breezy summer night.

2 teaspoons walnut oil
1 medium shallot, minced
1 pound fresh bay scallops
$1/2$ cup dry white wine
$1/4$ teaspoon salt
Freshly ground black pepper to taste
1 medium tomato, diced
1 teaspoon minced fresh dill
1 teaspoon chopped fresh thyme
1 teaspoon chopped fresh parsley

Warm the oil in a medium saucepan over medium-high heat. Add the shallot and sauté for about 3 minutes, or until tender. Stir in the scallops and sauté for 3 minutes, or until they begin to give up their liquid. Deglaze the pan with the wine. Sprinkle the scallops with the salt and pepper, then top with the tomato, dill, thyme, and parsley. Cook, stirring, until the tomatoes soften and the liquid thickens. Serve immediately over Butter Pecan Rice (page 396).

Yield: 4 servings

Nutritional data per serving: Calories, 133; protein, 20 g; carbohydrate, 5 g; dietary fiber, <1 g; total fat, 3 g; saturated fat, 0 g; cholesterol, 37 mg; sodium, 333 mg; vitamin A, 4% of Daily Value; vitamin C, 16%; calcium, 4%; iron, 4%; vitamin B_6, 10%; vitamin E, 7%; folate, 6%; magnesium, 17%; potassium, 13%; omega-3 fatty acids, 46%.

Baked Salmon Encrusted with Potato

At the Sea Bear salmon fishery, I learned that the best way to cook salmon is not the way you'd think—fast, over high heat. Nope. They taught me to cook it slowly with lower heat to save all the juices. Here's a prime, mouthwatering example.

2 salmon filets (4 ounces each)
1/4 teaspoon salt
Freshly ground black pepper to taste
1 cup Horseradish Mashed Potatoes
   (page 343)
1 teaspoon butter

Preheat the broiler to 400°F. Line a broiler pan with foil.

Wash the fish and pat dry. Coat the skin with nonstick spray and place skin side down on the broiler pan. Sprinkle with the salt and pepper. Place on the middle oven rack and broil for about 10 minutes, or just until barely done. Remove from the broiler and spread 1/2 cup of the potatoes on each filet. Dot each with 1/2 teaspoon of the butter. Increase the heat to high and broil for 3 to 5 minutes, or until the potatoes begin to brown.

Yield: 2 servings

Nutritional data per serving: Calories, 357; protein, 31 g; carbohydrate, 34 g; total fat, 10 g; saturated fat, 2.5 g; cholesterol, 77 mg; sodium, 739 mg; vitamin A, 8% of Daily Value; vitamin C, 23%; calcium, 16%; iron, 9%; vitamin B_1 (thiamin), 18%; vitamin B_2 (riboflavin), 28%; vitamin B_3 (niacin), 50%; vitamin B_6, 47%; vitamin D, 70%; potassium, 18%; omega-3 fatty acids, 223%.

Wokin' Salmon with Orzo

1 tablespoon olive oil
1/2 red onion, quartered and thinly sliced
1 clove garlic, minced or pressed
1 small yellow squash, cut into rounds
1 small zucchini, cut into rounds
1 teaspoon dried basil
Salt and freshly ground black pepper to taste
1 teaspoon capers
1 cup cooked orzo
4 ounces cooked salmon, flaked
1 ounce reduced-fat mozzarella cheese
2 Roma (plum) tomatoes, cut into rounds

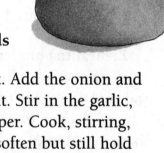

Heat the oil in a large wok over high heat. Add the onion and cook for 4 minutes, or until beginning to wilt. Stir in the garlic, yellow and green squash, basil, salt, and pepper. Cook, stirring, for about 5 minutes, or until the vegetables soften but still hold their shape. Stir in the capers and orzo and cook for 1 to 2 minutes, or just until warm. Gently stir in the fish and cook for 1 minute. Divide between two dinner plates. Top each serving with 1/2 ounce of the cheese and garnish with half the tomatoes. Serve with Italian bread and red wine. Wok on!

Yield: 2 servings

Nutritional data per serving: Calories, 333; protein, 23 g; carbohydrate, 28 g; dietary fiber, 4 g; total fat, 15 g; saturated fat, 3 g; cholesterol, 48 mg; sodium, 159 mg; vitamin A, 9% of Daily Value; vitamin C, 46%; calcium, 16%; iron, 14%; vitamin B$_1$ (thiamin), 26%; vitamin B$_2$ (riboflavin), 27%; vitamin B$_3$ (niacin), 38%; vitamin B$_6$, 39%; vitamin D, 40%; folate, 24%; potassium, 22%; omega-3 fatty acids, 139%.

Chocolate-Walnut Pudding

When I was a little kid, my favorite Easter treat was a chocolate fudge egg surrounded by walnuts. Only one store made it, and it is long since gone. But I still love that chocolate-walnut taste. Here's a quick little dessert that brings back those flavor memories.

1 package (3.4 ounces) instant
    chocolate pudding mix
2 cups fat-free milk
1 tablespoon walnut oil
¼ cup chopped walnuts
4 walnut halves

In a small bowl, combine the pudding mix, milk, oil, and chopped walnuts. With an electric mixer on low speed, beat for 2 minutes. Spoon into four small custard cups and top each with a walnut half. Refrigerate until ready to serve.

Yield: 4 servings

Nutritional data per serving: Calories, 210; protein, 6 g; carbohydrate, 29 g; dietary fiber, 1 g; total fat, 9 g; saturated fat, 1 g; cholesterol, 2 mg; sodium, 417 mg; vitamin A, 8% of Daily Value; vitamin C, 2%; calcium, 16%; iron, 4%; vitamin B$_2$ (riboflavin), 12%; vitamin D, 12%; folate 4%; omega-3 fatty acids, 104%.

SUPER SUB

Replacing whole milk with fat-free milk plus walnut oil banishes saturated fat and delivers a full day's supply of fishy fat.

CHAPTER
4

LOWER YOUR
TRIGLYCERIDES

HAVE AN OIL CHANGE

ALL RIGHT. F.A.T. = B.A.D. WE'VE ALL LEARNED THAT equation. But here comes some great news about fat: You can eat some—guilt-free! Not only that, but eating the right kind of fat can actually lower your triglycerides, those nasty little particles floating through your arteries that seriously increase your risk of heart attack and stroke.

A man I worked with, whom I'll call Tom, asked for help because he was afloat in a rising tide of triglycerides. The less fat and more carbohydrates he ate, the higher they went. "Relax, Tom," I told him, "and start enjoying your food. Would you like a peanut butter sandwich for lunch? Avocado on your salad? Olive oil with your pasta? Nuts in your cereal? Indulge!"

Tom thought I was crazy, but he followed my advice. And guess what? With the switch to more delicious eating, his triglycerides took a dive!

Tom was amazed. So are doctors all over the country. And yes, even the American Heart Association and the American Diabetes Association admit this diet works. As researchers tease out the taste-tempting truth about fat, healthy food is starting to taste great again!

Fat, it turns out, is similar to the fuel you put in your car. Use the right kind, and you'll zoom, top down, along the highway of life. Use the wrong kind, and watch out!

As we've learned in our struggle to cut down on burgers, fries, and premium ice cream, eating the wrong kind of fat—namely saturated fat and trans fat—is a lot like that. It raises cholesterol and triglycerides that clog our arteries' nooks and crannies and set us up for heart attacks and strokes.

Triglycerides are another type of blood fat, like cholesterol, that hangs out in your arteries and causes trouble when the level rises, although its workings are much less clear. What *is* clear is that the higher your triglyceride level, the higher your risk of heart attack and stroke. So keeping it down around 100 mg/dl is a good goal.

Here's how you do it.

♥ Minimize alcohol consumption.

♥ Replace highly processed sugars and starches with whole grains (see chapter 5).

♥ Ditch most saturated fats (chapter 1).

♥ Cut trans fats by eating foods without hydrogenated oils.

♥ Dump most polyunsaturated fats, such as vegetable and corn oils.

♥ Get heart-healthy fats by eating fish regularly (chapter 3).

♥ Cook with monounsaturated oils, such as olive, canola, and peanut oils; make sandwiches and sauces with peanut butter and other nut butters; and use nuts, avocado, and olives as garnishes.

On the last point, though, don't get carried away. No one is saying that you can curl up nightly with a big can of nuts and just munch away. Those babies do pack a ton of high-calorie fat that mounts up fast! Overeating anything, even good-for-you fat, can make you gain weight, and that will crank up your triglycerides again.

These suggestions sure sound different from those we usually hear. But you'll get used to it in a heartbeat—it's as easy as changing the oil you cook with or making a peanut butter and jelly sandwich. Come take a look!

Olive Array Appetizer

The world of olives has gone wild, with all the hot countries pitching in wonderful shapes, sizes, stuffings, and cures. Check out the gourmet section of your biggest supermarket for a mind-boggling experience, then pass it on to all your friends.

  8 ounces almond-stuffed green olives
  8 ounces ripe Cerignola olives
  8 ounces green Nicoise olives
  8 ounces sun-dried tomato–stuffed olives
  8 ounces Kalamata olives
  8 ounces oil-cured olives

Arrange the olives in a sectioned serving dish. Offer tiny plates so guests can discreetly dispose of pits.

Yield: 20 servings

Nutritional data per serving: Calories, 97; protein, 0 g; carbohydrate, 6 g; total fat, 9 g; saturated fat, <1 g; cholesterol, 0 mg; sodium, 1,115 mg; vitamin A, 2% of Daily Value; vitamin C, 1%; calcium, 4%; iron, 8% vitamin E, 6%.

Sicilian Tapenade

I stumbled across this appetizer in a natural foods store. I copied the ingredient list, then ran home and created my own version. It's tasty, and my guests love it!

¹/₂ cup whole almonds
1¹/₂ cups pimiento-stuffed Spanish olives
1 clove garlic, minced or pressed
1 tablespoon olive oil
3 sprigs parsley
1 tablespoon coarsely chopped chives
1 sprig thyme

In a food processor running on high, drop the almonds through the feeder tube. Process until finely chopped but not powdered. Add the olives, garlic, oil, parsley, chives, and thyme. Pulse until coarsely chopped. Scoop into a serving bowl. Serve chilled or at room temperature as a spread for toasted Italian bread.

Yield: 24 servings

Nutritional data per serving: Calories, 33; protein, <1 g; carbohydrate, 1 g; dietary fiber, <1 g; total fat, 3 g; saturated fat, 0 g; cholesterol, 0 mg; sodium, 73 mg; vitamin A, 0% of Daily Value; vitamin C, 1%; calcium, 1%; iron, 2%; vitamin E, 5%.

Lovely Leftovers

Mix the tapenade with water-packed white albacore tuna for a change from the same old mayonnaise and celery.

Fantastico Olive Oil Dip

Mangia…pane e olio d'oliva…'e fantistico!— *"Eat bread with olive oil…it's fantastic"*—*say the little dipping dishes I picked up at the Culinary Institute in California. My brother-in-law Joe likes his oil straight up, but my kids prefer this extra-savory version.*

- **1 cup extra virgin olive oil**
- **1 teaspoon dried basil**
- **1/2 teaspoon crushed red pepper**
- **1/4 teaspoon dried oregano**
- **1/2 teaspoon salt**
- **1 clove garlic, pressed**

In a cruet with a stopper or other container with a tight-fitting lid, combine the oil, basil, pepper, oregano, salt, and garlic. Refrigerate overnight or longer. At mealtime, pour a small amount of the flavored oil into a dipping dish. Return the cruet to the refrigerator. (Discard any leftover room-temperature oil.) Serve with crusty Italian bread.

Yield: 48 servings

Nutritional data per serving: Calories, 40; protein, 0 g; carbohydrate, 0 g; dietary fiber, 0 g; total fat, 4.5 g; saturated fat, <1 g; cholesterol, 0 mg; sodium, 24 mg; vitamin A, 0% of Daily Value; vitamin C, 0%; calcium, 0%; iron, 0%; vitamin E, 3%; omega-3 fatty acids, 3%.

SUPER SUB

When you dip into olive oil instead of slathering your bread with butter, you get 1/4 of the saturated fat and 8 times the vitamin E. Be still, my heart!

Asparagus Mousse Soup

Springtime asparagus invites yummy innovations. This creamy dream of a dish packs all the right fat.

1 pound asparagus
1 can (14½ ounces) fat-free chicken broth
⅓ cup nonfat dry milk
½ avocado, cut into chunks
⅛ teaspoon ground white pepper

Wash the asparagus and break off the tough stems. Cut off the tips and save for a salad or stir-fry. Cut the spears into 1-inch pieces, place in a small saucepan, and add just enough of the broth to cover. Bring to a boil, reduce the heat, and simmer for 5 to 10 minutes, or until tender. Remove from the heat and stir in the remaining broth.

In a food processor, combine the broth, asparagus, dry milk, avocado, and pepper. Process until creamy and cloud-like. Serve immediately with dinner rolls and salad.

Yield: 2 servings

Nutritional data per serving: Calories, 188; protein, 15 g; carbohydrate, 17 g; dietary fiber, 6 g; total fat, 8 g; saturated fat, 1 g; cholesterol, 2 mg; sodium, 624 mg; vitamin A, 18% of Daily Value; vitamin C, 106%; calcium, 21%; iron, 19%; vitamin B_2 (riboflavin), 25%; vitamin B_3 (niacin), 30%; vitamin E, 7%; folate, 70%; potassium, 23%.

Pumpkin-Seed Salad

In any other book, you'd find a spinach salad packed with bacon and eggs. But not in this one! We're going for more veggies and fruits— and pumpkin seeds for a totally awesome taste!

4 cups baby spinach, washed and spun dry
2 cups red bell pepper chunks
2 teaspoons olive oil
2 teaspoons red wine vinegar
Salt and freshly ground black pepper to taste
1/2 cup fresh pineapple chunks
2 tablespoons hulled pumpkin seeds

In a large salad bowl, combine the spinach and peppers. Add the oil, vinegar, salt, and pepper and toss until well blended. Garnish with the pineapple and sprinkle with the pumpkin seeds.

Yield: 4 servings

Nutritional data per serving: Calories, 99; protein, 3 g; carbohydrate, 13 g; dietary fiber, 3 g; total fat, 4 g; saturated fat, 1 g; cholesterol, 0 mg; sodium, 27 mg; vitamin A, 63% of Daily Value; vitamin C, 255%; calcium, 4%; iron, 9%; vitamin B_6, 13%; vitamin E, 7%; folate, 19%; magnesium, 15%; potassium, 12%.

SUPER SUB

1 CUP

When you add crunch to your salad with pumpkin seeds instead of croutons, you boost the trace minerals magnesium, potassium, copper, and zinc.

Zucchini-Basil Salad

Get out to your garden as fast as you can, and pick those baby zucchini before they turn into Baby Hueys!

4 baby zucchini (about 2 cups sliced)
1/4 cup slivered fresh basil
2 teaspoons extra virgin olive oil
3 teaspoons fresh lemon juice
1/4 teaspoon salt
Freshly ground black pepper to taste

Wash the zucchini and pat dry. Slice thinly into small rounds. In a medium bowl, combine the zucchini, basil, oil, lemon juice, salt, and pepper. Toss until well coated. Serve immediately or refrigerate. It's oh, so fresh with grilled fish or chicken. Easy, too!

Yield: 4 servings

Nutritional data per serving: Calories, 31; protein, 1 g; carbohydrate, 2 g; dietary fiber, 1 g; total fat, 2 g; saturated fat, 0 g; cholesterol, 0 mg; sodium, 147 mg; vitamin A, 3% of Daily Value; vitamin C, 13%; calcium, 1%; iron, 2%; vitamin E, 2%; folate, 4%; potassium, 5%.

Ginger-Sesame Dressing

When I want a light salad dressing with an Asian flair, I can zap this one together in less than a minute! So can you. Watch how easy it is.

3 tablespoons water
3 tablespoons white rice vinegar
2 tablespoons light soy sauce
4 teaspoons sesame oil
$\frac{1}{2}$ teaspoon sugar
$\frac{1}{8}$ teaspoon ground ginger
1 teaspoon minced garlic (from a jar)

In a small container with a tight-fitting lid, combine the water, vinegar, soy sauce, oil, sugar, ginger, and garlic. Cover and shake vigorously until well blended.

Yield: 4 servings

Nutritional data per serving: Calories, 44; protein, 0 g; carbohydrate, <1 g; dietary fiber, 0 g; total fat, 5 g; saturated fat, <1 g; cholesterol, 0 mg; sodium, 450 mg; vitamin A, 0% of Daily Value; vitamin C, 0%; calcium, 0%; iron, 0%; vitamin E, 1%; omega-3 fatty acids, 1%.

Lovely Leftovers Use extra dressing to marinate chicken or shrimp before grilling.

Lemon-Hazelnut Mayonnaise

Some dishes absolutely require mayonnaise. This one is so easy to make and so heart smart, you'll wonder how you survived this long without it!

1 medium egg
1 teaspoon salt
1 teaspoon honey
1 teaspoon Dijon mustard
2 tablespoons fresh lemon juice
1 1/4–1 1/2 cups hazelnut oil

In a blender, combine the egg, salt, honey, mustard, and lemon juice. Begin to blend, then remove the feeder cap and gradually drizzle in the oil until very thick. You may need to stop periodically to scrape down the sides of the jar and/or pulse occasionally as the mixture thickens. This is wonderful for fresh summer chicken and vegetable salads or, with a bit of dill added, as a sauce for grilled fish.

SUPER SUB

Replacing vegetable oil with nut oil slashes heart-stopping fat to 1/4 and triples heart-loving fat. Talk about a good deal!

Yield: 32 servings

Nutritional data per serving: Calories, 93; protein, 0 g; carbohydrate, 0 g; dietary fiber, 0 g; total fat, 10 g; saturated fat, <1 g; cholesterol, 6 mg; sodium, 78 mg; vitamin A, 0% of Daily Value; vitamin C, 0%; calcium, 0%; iron, 0%; vitamin E, 24%.

Buckwheat Breakfast Pancakes

When we were growing up, my dad loved to make Sunday morning breakfast. One of my favorites was a gigantic buckwheat pancake "sandwich" filled with butter, syrup, and bacon. Yikes! Here's how I do it now.

1 cup buckwheat pancake mix
1 egg
1 cup water
1 tablespoon almond oil
2 tablespoons almond butter
2 cups sliced fresh strawberries
2 tablespoons confectioners' sugar

DOUBLE DUTY

Almond butter serves as the flavorful fat for pancakes without the saturated fat of butter—with a bonus! It provides more than 1/3 of a day's quota of heart-lovin' vitamin E.

Preheat a nonstick griddle over medium-high heat. Place two plates in the oven on low to warm.

In a medium bowl, combine the pancake mix, egg, water, and oil. Stir with a fork just until smooth. Reduce the heat to medium and lightly coat the griddle with nonstick spray. Pour the batter by 1/4-cup measures onto the griddle and cook until bubbles form and the edges start to dry. Turn and cook just until the bottoms are brown. Place on the warmed plates and cover to keep warm until all batter is used. Spread each serving with 1 tablespoon of the almond butter and top with 1 cup of the strawberries. Dust with the sugar. They're still yummy after all these years!

Yield: 2 servings

Nutritional data per serving: Calories, 479; protein, 13 g; carbohydrate, 70 g; dietary fiber, 11 g; total fat, 21 g; saturated fat, 2 g; cholesterol, 93 mg; sodium, 1,224 mg; vitamin A, 6% of Daily Value; vitamin C, 157%; calcium, 16%; iron, 29%; vitamin E, 36%; folate, 24%; magnesium, 41%; potassium, 19%; omega-3 fatty acids, 46%.

Walnut Buckwheat Muffins

Would you believe that buckwheat's family is rhubarb, not wheat?

2 cups buckwheat pancake mix
$^1/_2$ teaspoon salt
$^1/_3$ cup nonfat dry milk
$^1/_4$ cup coarsely chopped walnuts
$^1/_4$ cup orange-flavored dried cranberries
2 tablespoons walnut oil
1 teaspoon vanilla extract
$^1/_3$ cup clover honey
1$^1/_2$ cups water

Preheat the oven to 375°F. Line a 12-cup muffin pan with paper liners.

In a medium bowl, combine the pancake mix, salt, dry milk, walnuts, and cranberries. Stir, then form a well in the center. Set aside.

In a small bowl, combine the oil, vanilla, honey, and water. Stir until the honey is dissolved. Pour into the well in the dry ingredients and stir with a fork just until wet. Spoon into the pan and bake for 18 to 20 minutes, or until a toothpick inserted in the center of a muffin comes out clean.

Yield: 12 servings

Nutritional data per serving: Calories, 168; protein, 7 g; carbohydrate, 26 g; dietary fiber, 3 g; total fat, 5 g; saturated fat, 0 g; cholesterol, 1 mg; sodium, 341 mg; vitamin A, 4% of Daily Value; vitamin C, 1%; calcium, 13%; iron, 4%; vitamin B$_1$ (thiamin), 10%; vitamin B$_2$ (riboflavin), 10%; potassium, 6%; omega-3 fatty acids, 46%.

Cashew Butter and Jam Sandwich

In a hurry? Don't fret. You can eat this simple breakfast sandwich on the go; it will make your heart and tummy happy, plus keep your body humming until lunchtime!

2 slices multigrain bread
2 tablespoons cashew butter
1 tablespoon apricot jam
¹/₄ teaspoon ground cinnamon

Toast the bread. In a microwave-safe dish, microwave the cashew butter on high for 30 to 60 seconds, or until melted. Stir in the jam and cinnamon. Spread on one slice of the toast and top with the remaining slice. Wrap it and go.

Yield: 1 serving

Nutritional data per serving: Calories, 356; protein, 10 g; carbohydrate, 50 g; dietary fiber, 11 g; total fat, 17 g; saturated fat, 3 g; cholesterol, 0 mg; sodium, 364 mg; vitamin A, 0% of Daily Value; vitamin C, 3%; calcium, 22%; iron, 19%; vitamin B_6, 44%; folate, 27%; copper, 36%; magnesium, 41%; potassium, 5%; zinc, 41%; omega-3 fatty acids, 65%.

Peanut Butter Oatmeal

This may be the ultimate breakfast for lowering your cholesterol, keeping your blood sugar under control, and keeping hunger at bay until lunchtime. Think of it as a hot peanut butter and jelly sandwich!

¹/₂ cup old-fashioned oats
1 cup fat-free milk
2 dried apricots, cut into sixths
1 teaspoon honey
1 tablespoon chunky peanut butter
¹/₄ teaspoon ground cinnamon

In a microwave-safe cereal bowl, combine the oats, milk, and apricots. Microwave on high for 3 minutes. Stir in the honey, peanut butter, and cinnamon.

Yield: 1 serving

Nutritional data per serving: Calories, 385; protein, 18 g; carbohydrate, 57 g; dietary fiber, 6 g; total fat, 12 g; saturated fat, 2 g; cholesterol, 4 mg; sodium, 207 mg; vitamin A, 25% of Daily Value; vitamin C, 5%; calcium, 34%; iron, 17%; vitamin D, 25%; potassium, 25%.

 The P·E·R·F·E·C·T Companion

In a heavy mug, pour boiling water over an English Breakfast tea bag. Steep for 3 to 5 minutes, then remove the tea bag. Drop in a Gilway golden sugar cube and stir to dissolve.

Olive Orange

My tall, skinny Italian friend, John Senatore, tells me that he and his brother grew up starting the day with this simple, nutritious treat. Orange you glad he shared it with us?

1 medium navel orange
1 teaspoon olive oil

Peel the orange and cut into chunks. Place in a small bowl and drizzle with the oil. Spoon it up!

Yield: 1 serving

Nutritional data per serving: Calories, 101; protein, 1 g; carbohydrate, 15 g; dietary fiber, 3 g; total fat, 5 g; saturated fat, <1 g; cholesterol, 0 mg; sodium, 0 mg; vitamin A, 3% of Daily Value; vitamin C, 116%; calcium, 5%; iron, 1%; vitamin E, 4%; folate, 10%; potassium, 7%; omega-3 fatty acids, 4%.

Garden Pizza

What could be better—or easier—than a luscious, full-flavored summer tomato baked on a pizza shell? Nothing—so give it a try!

1 individual fresh pizza crust
1 tablespoon extra virgin olive oil
1 thick slice large tomato
1 leaf fresh basil
1 paper-thin slice red onion
1/8 teaspoon salt
Freshly ground black pepper to taste
1 tablespoon freshly grated Parmesan cheese

Preheat the oven or toaster oven to 450°F.

Brush the pizza shell with the oil. On the crust, stack the tomato, basil, and onion. Bake for 6 to 8 minutes, or until the crust is crisp and the tomato begins to wilt. Sprinkle with the salt, pepper, and cheese. Grab a big napkin, then kick back and enjoy!

Yield: 1 serving

Nutritional data per serving: Calories, 322; protein, 7 g; carbohydrate, 40 g; dietary fiber, 2 g; total fat, 14 g; saturated fat, 2 g; cholesterol, 3 mg; sodium, 421 mg; vitamin A, 2% of Daily Value; vitamin C, 21%; calcium, 12%; iron, 12%; vitamin E, 9%; omega-3 fatty acids, 8%.

DOUBLE DUTY

Not only does olive oil make your heart sing, it also helps your body absorb the cancer-fighting lycopene from the tomato.

Tuna Garden Cups

This garden delight is pretty as a picture for a ladies' luncheon!

1 can (12 ounces) water-packed white albacore
    tuna, drained
¼ cup light canola oil mayonnaise*
Freshly ground black pepper to taste
8 canned artichoke bottoms
4 leaves red leaf lettuce
8 thick slices summer tomato
Dash of paprika
8 black olives

In a medium bowl, combine the tuna, mayonnaise, and pepper. Pile into the artichokes. Place a lettuce leaf on each of four plates. Top each with two slices of the tomato, then a filled artichoke. Dust each with the paprika and garnish with an olive. Serve with hot rolls and cold white wine.

Yield: 4 servings

Nutritional data per serving: Calories, 187; protein, 22 g; carbohydrate, 8 g; dietary fiber, 2 g; total fat, 7 g; saturated fat, <1 g; cholesterol, 36 mg; sodium, 668 mg; vitamin A, 8% of Daily Value; vitamin C, 38%; calcium, 4%; iron, 10%; vitamin E, 11%; potassium, 12%.

*Available in natural foods stores and some large supermarkets.

> **The
> P·E·R·F·E·C·T
> Companion**
>
> Fill 4 of your prettiest glasses with ice. Fill each with guava nectar and garnish with a lime wedge.

Devilishly Hot Grilled Chicken

Talk about opening up your sinuses! This one is not for the faint of heart.

4 boneless, skinless chicken breasts (about 4 ounces each)
1/2 teaspoon salt
2 tablespoons fresh lemon juice
1 tablespoon canola oil
2 tablespoons spicy Thai chili sauce*

Wash the chicken and pat dry. Trim off any fat. Sprinkle with the salt and brush with the lemon juice and oil. Grill over medium heat for about 10 minutes, turning every 2 to 3 minutes to prevent burning. Brush the tops with the sauce, close the grill, and cook for 2 to 3 minutes, or just until the sauce is set and the chicken is done. This is especially good with Coconut-Ginger Rice (page 117).

Yield: 4 servings

Nutritional data per serving: Calories, 167; protein, 26 g; carbohydrate, 3 g; dietary fiber, 0 g; total fat, 5 g; saturated fat, <1 g; cholesterol, 66 mg; sodium, 514 mg; vitamin A, 1% of Daily Value; vitamin C, 8%; calcium, 1%; iron, 5%; vitamin B$_3$ (niacin), 64%; vitamin B$_6$, 31%; vitamin E, 4%; potassium, 9%; omega-3 fatty acids, 35%.

*Available in many large supermarkets.

Thai Fish and Snow Peas

A little creativity turns the mundane—in this case, leftover rice—into a pretty elegant dish…with a little help from the freezer!

3 teaspoons peanut oil
4 ounces grouper filet
1 tablespoon water
1 teaspoon Thai green chile paste*
2 cups frozen snow peas
1 cup reheated jasmine rice
1 teaspoon light soy sauce
1 tablespoon chopped peanuts

Warm 2 teaspoons of the oil in a medium skillet over medium-high heat. Add the fish and cook for 2 minutes on each side. Reduce the heat to medium. Flake the fish into bite-size pieces, then move to one side of the skillet. Deglaze the pan with the water. Add the remaining 1 teaspoon oil and the chile paste. Stir, then mix with the fish. Add the snow peas, cover, and steam for 1 to 2 minutes, or just until the peas are heated through.

Divide the rice between two plates and spoon on the fish mixture. Sprinkle each serving with ½ teaspoon of the soy sauce and 1½ teaspoons of the peanuts. Dine in style!

Yield: 2 servings

Nutritional data per serving: Calories, 360; protein, 23 g; carbohydrate, 43 g; dietary fiber, 6 g; total fat, 10 g; saturated fat, 1.7 g; cholesterol, 27 mg; sodium, 323 mg; vitamin A, 6% of Daily Value; vitamin C, 59%; calcium, 11%; iron, 33%; vitamin B$_6$, 27%; vitamin E, 10%; folate, 30%; potassium, 19%; omega-3 fatty acids, 20%.

*Available in Asian markets and many large supermarkets.

Walnut-Oil Marinade

This tart and tangy marinade will tenderize your toughest meats and flavor them without a trace of salt. It's great as a salad dressing, too!

1/4 cup red wine vinegar
1/4 cup water
1 tablespoon walnut oil
1 small shallot, thinly sliced
1 teaspoon chopped garlic
1/2 teaspoon dried thyme
Freshly ground black pepper to taste

In a small bowl, combine the vinegar, water, oil, shallot, garlic, thyme, and pepper. With a wire whisk, stir until well blended. Pour over meat and let stand 1 hour or overnight.

Yield: As salad dressing, 4 servings

Nutritional data per serving: Calories, 40; protein, 0 g; carbohydrate, 3 g; dietary fiber, 0 g; total fat, 3 g; saturated fat, <1 g; cholesterol, 0 mg; sodium, 2 mg; vitamin A, 1% of Daily Value; vitamin C, 1%; calcium, 1%; iron, 1%; vitamin B_1 (thiamin), 5%; vitamin B_2 (riboflavin), 5%; omega-3 fatty acids, 35%.

Caribbean Peanut Plantains

Plantains are tricky little devils. They really look like bananas, and even taste like them, too...except that they're not sweet, and you can't eat them raw. So here's your big chance to make a quick island dish that looks like you worked all day in the sun. (Grab a cool drink and try to keep that sly smile to yourself.)

1 tablespoon peanut oil
2 large plantains, cut into ¹/₂-inch-thick slices
1 tablespoon water
1 tablespoon creamy peanut butter
1 teaspoon prepared jerk seasoning

Warm the oil in a medium nonstick skillet over medium-high heat. Add the plantains. Reduce the heat to medium, cover, and cook for about 3 minutes, or until brown. Turn to brown the other side.

Meanwhile, in a small microwave-safe dish, combine the water, peanut butter, and seasoning. Microwave on high for 20 to 30 seconds. With a fork, quickly stir until smooth. Place the plantains on a serving platter and drizzle with the sauce. Serve with chicken, fish, or shrimp.

Yield: 4 servings

Nutritional data per serving: Calories, 134; protein, 2 g; carbohydrate, 29 g; dietary fiber, 2 g; total fat, 2 g; saturated fat, <1 g; cholesterol, 0 mg; sodium, 59 mg; vitamin A, 10% of Daily Value; vitamin C, 27%; calcium, 0%; iron, 3%; vitamin B$_6$, 14%; vitamin E, 3%; folate, 6%; potassium, 14%.

St. Patty's Mashed Potatoes

On St. Patrick's Day, everyone is Irish. And along with the green beer, someone always dyes the potatoes green. This year, create these silky smooth spuds with a hint of natural color.

2 pounds potatoes, peeled and cubed
1 avocado, cubed
2/3 cup nonfat dry milk
1/2 teaspoon dried dillweed
1/2 teaspoon salt
1/8 teaspoon ground white pepper

Bring the potatoes to a boil in a large saucepan with just enough water to cover. Reduce the heat and cook for 10 minutes, or until tender. Drain, reserving 1 cup of the cooking water. Add the avocado and dry milk and, with an electric mixer, beat until smooth. Continue beating and add the reserved water, 1/3 cup at a time, until the potatoes are light, creamy, and fluffy. (You may not need all the water.) Add the dill, salt, and pepper and beat just until blended. Serve piping hot.

SUPER SUB

Replacing the traditional whole milk and butter with avocado cuts saturated fat to the bone and replaces it with the monounsaturated fat your heart craves.

Yield: 9 servings

Nutritional data per serving: Calories, 140; protein, 4 g; carbohydrate, 25 g; dietary fiber, 3 g; total fat, 3.5 g; saturated fat, <1 g; cholesterol, 0 mg; sodium, 164 mg; vitamin A, 4% of Daily Value; vitamin C, 45%; calcium, 8%; iron, 3%; vitamin B6, 18%; copper, 11%; potassium, 15%.

Coconut-Ginger Rice

Some good things are just too easy. This exotic rice will transport you to strange and romantic places…and best of all, someone else has done all the work!

1¹/₂ cups water
1 tablespoon peanut oil
1 package (7 ounces) A Taste of Thai coconut-ginger rice*

Bring the water to a boil in a medium saucepan over high heat. Add the oil and rice. Reduce the heat and simmer for 20 minutes, or until the water is absorbed. Serve with sautéed vegetables and grilled chicken.

Yield: 6 servings

Nutritional data per serving: Calories, 147; protein, 3 g; carbohydrate, 28 g; dietary fiber, 1 g; total fat, 2 g; saturated fat, <1 g; cholesterol, 0 mg; sodium, 287 mg; vitamin A, 0% of Daily Value; vitamin C, 0%; calcium, 0%, iron, 0%.

*Available in many large supermarkets.

SUPER SUB

When you substitute peanut oil for the butter called for on the package, you replace heart-stopping saturated fat with heart-lubricating monounsaturated fat.

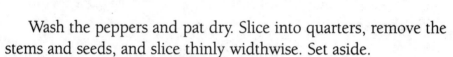

Pepperonata

Here's a gorgeous vegetable dish that will garner compliments all around. Oh, what a little slicing can do!

1 large red bell pepper
1 large green bell pepper
1 large yellow bell pepper
1 large onion, quartered lengthwise and
 thinly sliced
2 tablespoons extra virgin olive oil
2 cloves garlic, minced or pressed
1 can (14½ ounces) diced tomatoes
1 teaspoon dried basil

Wash the peppers and pat dry. Slice into quarters, remove the stems and seeds, and slice thinly widthwise. Set aside.

In a large, deep nonstick skillet over medium heat, sauté the onion in the oil for about 5 minutes, or just until beginning to soften. Stir in the garlic and peppers and cook, stirring occasionally, for 5 minutes. Add the tomatoes (with juice) and basil. Cook for about 20 minutes, or until the liquid evaporates but the peppers still hold their shape. Serve hot or cold with any meat or poultry. It's even good hot as a pasta sauce.

Yield: 8 servings

Nutritional data per serving: Calories, 74; protein, 2 g; carbohydrate, 10 g; dietary fiber, 3 g; total fat, 4 g; saturated fat, <1 g; cholesterol, 0 mg; sodium, 68 mg; vitamin A, 16% of Daily Value; vitamin C, 177%; calcium, 3%; iron, 3%; vitamin B$_6$, 10%; vitamin E, 5%; potassium, 5%.

Stuffin' Muffin

Kids' after-school appetites raging out of control? Here's a quick-as-a-wink snack that will satisfy even the pickiest eater. It's a healthier twist on an old favorite.

1 multigrain English muffin
2 tablespoons chunky peanut butter
6 seedless red grapes

Split and toast the English muffin. Spread each half with 1 tablespoon of the peanut butter. Pile the grapes on one half and add the top of the muffin. Stuff in your kid's mouth and watch him enjoy.

Yield: 1 serving

Nutritional data per serving: Calories, 451; protein, 22 g; carbohydrate, 55 g; dietary fiber, 4 g; total fat, 18 g; saturated fat, 4 g; cholesterol, 4 mg; sodium, 559 mg; vitamin A, 15% of Daily Value; vitamin C, 9%; vitamin E, 17%; calcium, 45%; iron, 16%; folate, 21%; potassium, 23%; omega-3 fatty acids, 6%.

 The P·E·R·F·E·C·T Companion

Every good pb&j deserves a tall, frosty glass of chocolate milk. Just stir a tablespoon of chocolate syrup into 1 cup fat-free milk.

Cheese 'n Garlic Popcorn

Well, it's true. Popcorn, because it uses the entire corn kernel, is a whole grain. Whoopee! But how do you get from a heart stopper loaded with salt and butter to a lip-smackin', finger-lickin', heart-lovin' treat? It's easy. Just do this...

½ cup popping corn
1 tablespoon olive oil
1 teaspoon garlic powder
2 tablespoons grated Parmesan cheese

Preheat an air popper by plugging it in and letting it run for about 3 minutes. Add the popcorn and pop into a large bowl. Place the oil in a mister and mist the popcorn, tossing constantly to coat. Sprinkle with the garlic powder and cheese and toss again. Then dig in!

Yield: 4 servings

Nutritional data per serving: Calories, 136; protein, 4 g; carbohydrate, 19 g; dietary fiber, 3 g; total fat, 6 g; saturated fat, 1 g; cholesterol, 2 mg; sodium, 58 mg; vitamin A, 1% of Daily Value; vitamin C, 0%; calcium, 4%; iron, 3%; vitamin B$_1$ (thiamin), 8%; vitamin E, 2%; potassium, 2%.

The Inside Skinny: Misto and other brands of oil sprayers are available at kitchenware stores. You fill them with the kind of oil you like, then get a little exercise pumping up the pressure to create a nonaerosol spray.

California Guacamole

Those Californians—they always seem to get it right before the rest of us. And whether it's a Super Bowl party or dinner on the deck, their guacamole with chips really hits the spot. This healthier version, sans mayo, is compliments of the California Avocado Commission. It packs the kind of fat your heart adores. So love it, and don't leave it!

2 ripe California avocados
3 tablespoons fresh lemon juice
¹/₂ cup diced onions
3 tablespoons chopped tomatoes
¹/₂ teaspoon salt
2 tablespoons minced fresh cilantro

Cut the avocados in half, remove the seeds, and scoop out the pulp. In a medium bowl, drizzle the avocados with the lemon juice, then mash. Add the onions, tomatoes, salt, and cilantro and stir until blended. Serve with baked tortilla chips.

Yield: 12 servings

Nutritional data per serving: Calories, 55; protein, <1 g; carbohydrate, 3 g; dietary fiber, 2 g; total fat, 5 g; saturated fat, <1 g; cholesterol, 0 mg; sodium, 101 mg; vitamin A, 2% of Daily Value; vitamin C, 8%; calcium, 1%; iron, 2%; vitamin B_6, 5%; vitamin E, 2%; folate, 5%; potassium, 6%.

Lovely Leftovers Cover extra guacamole with plastic wrap to keep it visible in the fridge. Store fresh-cut veggies nearby to tempt your snack sneakers.

Munch a Bunch of Chips

There are times when I must relent and serve some crispy, salty, chippy kinds of things along with all the veggies and healthy dips. You know, for the Super Bowl or for basketball fans, to celebrate March Madness. Here are a few good chips packed with only the best fat. But be careful…they're still high in calories.

1 package (3 ounces) garden-veggie flavor Skinny Sticks
1 package (7 ounces) Guiltless Gourmet baked chili
   lime tortilla chips
1 package (5 ounces) rosemary-flavored olive oil
   potato chips

Arrange the chips in small baskets, surrounded by lots of fresh fruits and veggies.

Yield: 15 servings

Nutritional data per serving: Calories, 128; protein, 2 g; carbohydrate, 19 g; dietary fiber, 1 g; total fat, 3.6 g; saturated fat, <1 g; cholesterol, 0 mg; sodium, 192 mg; vitamin A, 0% of Daily Value; vitamin C, 4%; calcium, 4%; iron, 4%.

Top-Shelf Smoothie

Just when I think there's nothing good left in the house to eat, I remember my top shelf, where I stash a few nutritional nuggets for safekeeping. Here's what I usually find.

1 box (8 ounces) orange juice
¹/₃ cup nonfat dry milk
1 tablespoon chocolate-hazelnut spread
1 tablespoon unsweetened cocoa powder

In a blender, combine the orange juice, dry milk, chocolate spread, and cocoa. Blend until smooth and creamy. Pour over ice for a tasty afternoon pick-me-up.

Yield: 2 servings

Nutritional data per serving: Calories, 287; protein, 13 g; carbohydrate, 46 g; dietary fiber, 3 g; total fat, 8 g; saturated fat, 2 g; cholesterol, 5 mg; sodium, 136 mg; vitamin A, 14% of Daily Value; vitamin C, 270%; calcium, 37%; iron, 8%; folate, 12%; potassium, 22%.

SUPER SUB

1 CUP

Using nonfat dry milk instead of liquid milk gets you a thick, creamy drink that packs the nutritional punch of a full glass of both milk and orange juice.

Macadamia Madness

Think everything you love is bad for you? Think again. This decadent dessert will make your heart and your taste buds jump for joy!

½ cup fresh pineapple chunks
½ cup fresh sweet cherries, halved and pitted
2 tablespoons Hershey's chocolate syrup
1 ripe papaya, halved lengthwise and seeded
1 ounce macadamia nuts, chopped

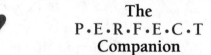

In a small bowl, combine the pineapple, cherries, and 1 tablespoon of the chocolate syrup. Toss until coated. Place each papaya half on a plate and top with the fruit. Drizzle with the remaining 1 tablespoon chocolate syrup and garnish with the macadamias.

Yield: 2 servings

Nutritional data per serving: Calories, 257; protein, 3 g; carbohydrate, 39 g; dietary fiber, 6 g; total fat, 12 g; saturated fat, 2 g; cholesterol, 0 mg; sodium, 52 mg; vitamin A, 5% of Daily Value; vitamin C, 171%; calcium, 6%; iron, 6%; vitamin E, 9%; folate, 16%; potassium, 16%.

♥ **The P·E·R·F·E·C·T Companion** ♥

In a teapot, pour 2 cups boiling water over a French Vanilla tea bag. Steep for 3 to 5 minutes. Sweeten with honey and pour into 2 very pretty cups. Sip and enjoy.

Peanut Butterscotch Pudding

This treat is to die for. Eat it instead of lunch. Think of it as a peanut butter sandwich for your heart and soul.

2 cups fat-free milk
1/4 cup creamy peanut butter
1 package (3.4 ounces) butterscotch instant pudding and
    pie filling mix

Pour the milk into a small bowl. Add the peanut butter and, with an electric mixer on low speed, beat for 1 minute. Add the pudding mix and beat on low speed for 2 minutes. Immediately pour into four small serving dishes. Dig in, and feel your cares melt away.

Yield: 4 servings

Nutritional data per serving: Calories, 228; protein, 8 g; carbohydrate, 32 g; dietary fiber, <1 g; total fat, 8 g; saturated fat, 2 g; cholesterol, 2 mg; sodium, 338 mg; vitamin A, 7% of Daily Value; vitamin C, 2%; calcium, 16%; iron, 2%; vitamin D, 12%; vitamin E, 8%; folate, 5%; magnesium, 10%; potassium, 9%.

CHAPTER 5

BEAT
DIABETES

LIGHTEN UP
AND GO FOR THE GRAINS

My MATERNAL GRANDFATHER WAS A DOCTOR WHO died of diabetes before I was born. This smart, determined man worked his way through pharmacy school, bought a pharmacy, then used the store's income to put himself through medical school. He was a lean, mean, medical machine, according to my mom. His Achilles heel? My mom said insulin turned him off, so he refused to use it. How sad.

His diabetes has hung over his descendants' heads like Damocles' sword, and—believe it or not—that has turned out to be a good thing. The American Heart Association reports that 20 percent of middle-aged adults and 35 percent of those over age 65 have type 2 diabetes—whether they know it or not. However, our focus on prevention has kept our family diabetes-free for three generations!

And we're willing to let you in on a few family secrets, along with up-to-the-minute scientific news you can use to fend off, or better manage, the big D. Here's what you need to do.

♥ **Keep your weight under control.** That's first and foremost. (Check that out in "A Word about Weight Control" on page 378.) Sure, it's a struggle, but it's worth it. Here's why. Weight gain in susceptible folks turns on the symptoms of diabetes. Weight loss turns them off. Yes, losing as few as 10 pounds for some people, or shedding 10 percent of body weight, is often enough. And even if you can't lose weight, at least stop gaining, so your risk doesn't get worse.

♥ **Get some exercise every day.** Not only will you look and feel better, but the exercise itself will help prevent or manage diabetes. Yes, it's true—in studies of identical twins with a family history of diabetes, those who exercise don't get the darned disease, while their couch potato sibs do. WOW! So put on your walking shoes and get your fanny out the door!

♥ **Eat whole grains every day.** This advice stems from the most recent scientific breakthrough. Studies of 42,000 men and 65,000 women showed a reduced risk of diabetes with just two daily servings of yummy stuff like oatmeal, wild rice, ground corn tortillas, woven wheat crackers, and whole wheat bread or pita pockets.

If your family is fighting off diabetes, you can protect your heart by lowering your cholesterol (chapter 1), blood pressure (chapter 2), stroke risk (chapter 3), and triglycerides (chapter 4). And eating more fruits and vegetables will deliver tons of antioxidants and phytochemicals to protect your eyes and arteries, as well as your sweet little feet. So dash on over to chapters 7 through 12 before you're done. Remember, an ounce of prevention is worth a pound of cure!

And now it's time for a taste bud tune-up. I realize that whole grain foods have taken a back seat to puffy white "balloon" bread, sugary cereals, doughnuts, and highly processed snack foods. I think of this stuff as *kid* food! And look where that's gotten us. Let's move on up to adult eating. Rich, earthy grains, the true staff of life, await you.

Quick-as-a-Wink Bean Dip

Got a house full of kids and nothing to feed them? Are unexpected guests knocking at your door? Quick, check your pantry. A few simple ingredients can save the day.

1 jar (16 ounces) mild or medium salsa
1 can (15½ ounces) black beans, rinsed and drained
1 teaspoon garlic powder
1 teaspoon dried cilantro

In a blender or food processor, combine the salsa, beans, garlic powder, and cilantro. Process until coarsely chopped to a chunky consistency. Place in a serving bowl and surround with baked tortilla chips.

Yield: 48 servings

Nutritional data per serving: Calories, 10; protein, <1 g; carbohydrate, 2 g; dietary fiber, 1 g; total fat, 0 g; saturated fat, 0 g; cholesterol, 0 mg; sodium, 68 mg; vitamin A, 1% of Daily Value; vitamin C, 2%; calcium, 1%; iron, 2%.

QUICK TRICK: Need chips? Stack 10 corn tortillas. Using a sharp chef's knife, cut them into sixths. Spread in a single layer on cookie sheets and mist lightly with olive oil spray. Bake at 450°F for 5 minutes, or until crisp and beginning to brown.

Mushroom Barley Soup

When I was a kid, I loved Campbell's vegetable beef soup, not because of the beef but because of the barley. Now I'm all grown up, but the kid in me still wants barley, so I've created lots of savory soups that deliver the goods. Here's one of my simple favorites.

1 cup chopped onions
1 tablespoon olive oil
2 cups sliced mushrooms, including
  stems
1/4 cup thinly sliced carrots
4 cups fat-free chicken broth
1/4 cup pearled barley, rinsed
4 sprigs fresh thyme or 1/4 teaspoon
  dried thyme
2 bay leaves
Freshly ground black pepper to taste

> **DOUBLE DUTY**
>
> That little bit of carrot adds color to the soup and is the sole source of vitamin A from beta-carotene.

In a deep saucepan over medium-high heat, sauté the onions in the oil for about 5 minutes, or until soft. Stir in the mushrooms and carrots and sauté for 2 minutes, or until the mushrooms begin to give up their liquid. Add the broth, barley, thyme, bay leaves, and pepper. Cover and bring to a boil. Reduce the heat and simmer for 1 hour. Before serving, remove the thyme sprigs and bay leaves.

Yield: 4 servings

Nutritional data per serving: Calories, 115; protein, 5 g; carbohydrate, 15 g; dietary fiber, 4 g; total fat, 4 g; saturated fat, <1 g; cholesterol, 0 mg; sodium, 466 mg; vitamin A, 12% of Daily Value; vitamin C, 6%; calcium, 2%; iron, 5%; vitamin E, 3%; magnesium, 4%.

Asiago Caesar Salad with Garlic Croutons

Start with a head of romaine lettuce and some shredded cheese, and you're on your way to a Caesar salad. But what about those croutons? Most are made with white bread and slathered with all the wrong kinds of fat, but here's a salad with healthy croutons. Hail, Caesar!

2 slices whole wheat bread, cubed
1 teaspoon olive oil
1 teaspoon garlic powder
Freshly ground black pepper to taste
1 head romaine lettuce, quartered lengthwise and
    cut into 1-inch strips
½ cup thinly sliced green bell peppers
1 ounce (about ¼ cup) shredded Asiago cheese
2 tablespoons Ken's light Caesar dressing

In a small bowl, drizzle the bread cubes with the oil. Toss until well coated. Sprinkle with the garlic powder and black pepper and toss again. Place on a tray in the toaster oven and toast until brown and crisp.

Meanwhile, in a large salad bowl, combine the lettuce, green peppers, cheese, and dressing. Toss well. Add the croutons and toss again. Divide between two plates and garnish with an extra pinch of cheese.

> **DOUBLE DUTY**
>
> The romaine lettuce in this salad feeds you half of your necessary folate and all of your vitamin C for the day.

Yield: 2 servings

Nutritional data per serving: Calories, 189; protein, 9 g; carbohydrate, 22 g; dietary fiber, 5 g; total fat, 8 g; saturated fat, 3 g; cholesterol, 13 mg; sodium, 356 mg; vitamin A, 35% of Daily Value; vitamin C, 101%; calcium, 20%; iron, 13%; folate, 44%; potassium, 15%.

Black-Eyed Tabbouleh Salad

When I need an easy but impressive summer party dish, I'll crank out this exotic salad the night before so it's nice and cold at blastoff time—and I have no last-minute hassles.

1 package (5¼ ounces) Near East tabbouleh
   wheat salad mix
1 cup boiling water
1 large tomato, diced
1 tablespoon fresh lemon juice
1 tablespoon olive oil
½ cup sliced black olives
¾ cup fresh blueberries

In a large serving bowl, combine the wheat and seasonings from the package. Add the water, stir, and cover. Refrigerate for 30 minutes. Add the tomato, lemon juice, oil, olives, and blueberries. Cover and refrigerate for 1 hour or overnight.

Yield: 7 servings

Nutritional data per serving: Calories, 109; protein, 3 g; carbohydrate, 21 g; dietary fiber, 5 g; total fat, 3 g; saturated fat, <1 g; cholesterol, 0 mg; sodium, 289 mg; vitamin A, 4% of Daily Value; vitamin C, 20%; calcium, 2%; iron, 6%; vitamin E, 4%.

Lovely Leftovers Toss tabbouleh with diced cold pork or chicken and toasted pine nuts for an enticing entrée.

Breakfast Burrito

Can't get enough Tex-Mex? My son Mike offered this idea, which gives a whole new meaning to the term hot meal.

1 teaspoon chopped green chile peppers
1/4 cup chopped red bell peppers
1 tablespoon sliced black olives
1 teaspoon peanut oil
1 medium egg, beaten
1 small corn tortilla
**Salt and freshly ground black pepper
     to taste**

In a medium nonstick skillet over medium-high heat, sauté the chile peppers, red peppers, and olives in the oil for about 3 minutes, or until the peppers are soft. Stir in the egg. Reduce the heat to medium and cook, stirring, until the egg reaches the preferred dryness.

Meanwhile, microwave the tortilla on high for 15 seconds, or until warm. Season the egg mixture with salt and pepper. Pile on the tortilla, roll it up, and get your day off to a very warm beginning.

Yield: 1 serving

Nutritional data per serving: Calories, 186; protein, 7 g; carbohydrate, 16 g; dietary fiber, 2 g; total fat, 11 g; saturated fat, 2 g; cholesterol, 187 mg; sodium, 165 mg; vitamin A, 29% of Daily Value; vitamin C, 121%; calcium, 8%; iron, 8%; folate, 14%; vitamin K, 37%.

> ### The
> ### P·E·R·F·E·C·T
> ### Companion
> Stir a tablespoon of unsweetened cocoa into your morning coffee. Dust it with some cinnamon for a perfect South-of-the-Border treat.

Hot Kasha Breakfast Blend

Brrr! A frosty morning makes you want to start the day with a hearty bowl of steaming cereal. Maybe this is the right day to climb out of your rut and try a new treat.

¹/₄ cup kasha
¹/₈ teaspoon salt
¹/₂ cup fat-free evaporated milk
1 teaspoon brown sugar
1 tablespoon toasted sliced almonds
2 dried figs, thinly sliced
¹/₂ teaspoon ground cinnamon

Bring 1¹/₄ cups water to a boil in a medium saucepan. Stir in the kasha and salt. Reduce the heat to medium and simmer for 11 minutes, or until all the water is absorbed. Add the milk, brown sugar, almonds, figs, and cinnamon. Stir well and heat through. Serve piping hot.

Yield: 1 serving

Nutritional data per serving: Calories, 389; protein, 17 g; carbohydrate, 75 g; dietary fiber, 10 g; total fat, 5 g; saturated fat, <1 g; cholesterol, 5 mg; sodium, 186 mg; vitamin A, 16% of Daily Value; vitamin C, 3%; calcium, 46%; iron, 13%; vitamin D, 26%; vitamin E, 8%; magnesium, 42%.

The Inside Skinny:
Kasha is another name for buckwheat. Don't confuse buckwheat with regular wheat; it's an entirely different grain with a three-cornered tan seed and a nutty flavor.

Vanilla-Almond Oatmeal

When I was a child, butter and brown sugar flavored my oatmeal. It sure did taste great, but there are healthier ways to eat oatmeal. You can, for example, trade the unhealthy fat in butter for the healthy fat in nuts. Then switch the refined sugar for some intriguing spice.

$1/2$ cup instant oats
2 tablespoons golden seedless raisins
1 cup fat-free milk
1 teaspoon honey
$1/2$ teaspoon vanilla extract
1 tablespoon toasted slivered almonds
$1/8$ teaspoon ground nutmeg

In a microwave-safe cereal bowl, combine the oats, raisins, and milk. Microwave on high for 3 to 4 minutes, or until the oats are cooked. Stir in the honey, vanilla, and almonds. (If the oatmeal is too thick, thin with warm water.) Dust with the nutmeg.

Yield: 1 serving

Nutritional data per serving: Calories, 375; protein, 17 g; carbohydrate, 60 g; dietary fiber, 5 g; total fat, 8 g; saturated fat, 1 g; cholesterol, 4 mg; sodium, 131 mg; vitamin A, 15% of Daily Value; vitamin C, 5%; calcium, 36%; iron, 13%; vitamin D, 25%; potassium, 22%.

Hearty Breakfast Teff

Once you learn to pass on kiddy cereals and dig into the whole grain, grownup stuff, your taste buds will start to nag you for more and more flavor. That's the time for teff. It's the world's smallest grain, and it hails from Ethiopia. You'll find it in natural foods stores or the health food section of many large supermarkets. It's packed with enough dark, hearty oomph to stand up to powerful garnishes. And one thing's for sure—you'll know you've had breakfast!

2 cups water
1/8 teaspoon salt
1/2 cup teff
1/3 cup orange-flavored dried cranberries
2 tablespoons orange marmalade
1/2 cup fat-free milk
2 tablespoons toasted slivered almonds

In a medium saucepan, bring the water and salt to a boil. Stir in the teff and cranberries. Reduce the heat, cover, and simmer for 15 to 20 minutes, or until the water is absorbed. Stir in the marmalade and milk. Divide between two cereal bowls and garnish each with 1 tablespoon almonds.

Yield: 2 servings

Nutritional data per serving: Calories, 340; protein, 8 g; carbohydrate, 68 g; dietary fiber, 3 g; total fat, 6 g; saturated fat, 0 g; cholesterol, 1 mg; sodium, 58 mg; vitamin A, 4% of Daily Value; vitamin C, 3%; calcium, 17%; iron, 141%; vitamin E, 9%; magnesium, 5%; potassium, 5%.

> ### The P·E·R·F·E·C·T Companion
>
> While you're waiting for your teff, have a cup of black tea sweetened with a lemon honey straw and a splash of fat-free milk. Ahhh, soothing…

Super Cereal Bowl

A hearty, carry-you-till-lunchtime breakfast is at your fingertips…no cooking needed! It's as easy as 1-2-3-4. Here are the ground rules.

1. Measure one serving of whole grain cereal into your bowl. The fiber and phytochemicals in whole grains fend off diabetes. Look at the label. "Whole grain" (of some kind) should be the first ingredient.

2. Add some fresh, dried, or canned fruit. Their fiber and antioxidants protect your heart, memory, and eyesight. Begin with a banana, then get creative with blueberries, strawberries, mangoes, dried apricots, raisins, mandarin oranges, or tropical fruit.

3. Top with 1 to 2 tablespoons of nuts or seeds. Healthy fats in these foods keep you fortified until lunchtime and add major minerals that work minor miracles in your body. Consider adding walnuts, pecans, hazelnuts, almonds, peanuts, or even macadamias.

4. Pour on the milk. Along with bone-building, fat-fighting calcium, you'll get blood pressure protection, too. Fat-free or 1%, chocolate, evaporated, buttermilk, lactase-loaded Lactaid, or calcium-fortified soy milk all do the milk magic trick.

Ready to try a super cereal bowl? Here are some combinations.

Kick-start: Kix cereal, blueberries, toasted pecans, and 1% milk.

Total Control: Whole Grain Total, sliced banana, chopped walnuts, and fat-free milk.

Get Movin': Bran Chex, chopped prunes, sliced almonds, and Lactaid.

It's gonna be a great day!

Broccoli Quesadilla

Everyone loves a grilled cheese sandwich! In Mexican cooking, it's called a quesadilla. These crispy little finger sandwiches make a quick, crunchy lunch.

2 small corn tortillas
1 tablespoon salsa
¼ cup reduced-fat four-cheese Mexican blend
¼ cup finely chopped broccoli florets

Warm a large skillet over high heat. Lightly coat one side of one tortilla with olive oil spray. Place with the oiled side down in the skillet and reduce the heat to medium. As the tortilla heats, spread with the salsa. Top with the cheese, broccoli, and the remaining tortilla. Lightly coat the top tortilla with olive oil spray. Cover and cook for 3 to 5 minutes, or until the bottom tortilla begins to brown and become crisp. Carefully flip the quesadilla. Cook for 3 to 5 minutes, or until light brown and crisp. On a cutting board, use a large knife to cut into six wedges. Let cool slightly before eating. Serve with vegetarian refried beans.

> ### The
> ### P·E·R·F·E·C·T
> ### Companion
>
> In a tall glass, combine the juice of 1 lime, 2 tablespoons super-fine sugar, and 1 cup cold green tea. Stir until the sugar dissolves. Fill with ice and garnish with a mint sprig.

Yield: 1 serving

Nutritional data per serving: Calories, 206; protein, 12 g; carbohydrate, 28 g; dietary fiber, 4 g; total fat, 6 g; saturated fat, 3 g; cholesterol, 10 mg; sodium, 369 mg; vitamin A, 4% of Daily Value; vitamin C, 31%; calcium, 32%; iron, 6%; folate, 20%; vitamin K, 45%.

Classic (Sort of) Turkey Club

I just love the taste of bacon. Sadly, it's nothing but fat and salt and preservatives, so I don't eat very much of it any more. Instead, I've learned to use it like an exclamation point in a few special dishes. Here's one.

1 small whole wheat pita pocket
2 ounces cooked turkey breast, diced
2 slices crisp bacon, crumbled
1 tablespoon reduced-fat mayonnaise
Freshly ground black pepper to taste
1/2 medium tomato, diced
1 leaf dark green romaine lettuce

Toast the pita until puffed, then split.

In a small bowl, combine the turkey, bacon, mayonnaise, and pepper. Stir well. Gently fold in the tomato. Pile the mixture on the lettuce, roll, and stuff into the pita.
Serve with baby carrots.

Yield: 1 serving

Nutritional data per serving: Calories, 363; protein, 28 g; carbohydrate, 43 g; dietary fiber, 6 g; total fat, 9 g; saturated fat, 3 g; cholesterol, 58 mg; sodium, 721 mg; vitamin A, 7% of Daily Value; vitamin C, 26%; calcium, 3%; iron, 20%; vitamin B$_3$ (niacin), 37%; vitamin B$_6$, 29%; vitamin E, 5%; folate, 17%; magnesium, 18%; potassium, 16%; omega-3 fatty acids, 17%.

SUPER SUB

Replacing traditional iceberg lettuce with romaine gives you 5 times more vitamins A and C. Your immune system loves that!

Jalapeño Tuna Tortilla

Sure, canned tuna is convenient. But when you want fresh-from-the-sea flavor, go for the fresh fish, grilled! (Sorry, Charlie.) And heck, if you make "planned-overs," you'll have convenience galore.

4 ounces grilled fresh tuna
1 recipe Jalapeño Mayo (page 333)
½ cup chopped red bell peppers
2 large whole wheat tortillas
1 cup spring mix salad greens

In a small bowl, combine the tuna, mayo, and peppers. Microwave the tortillas on high for 15 seconds, or until warm. Top each with half of the tuna mixture and ½ cup of the greens. Fold the bottom of each tortilla over the top, then fold in the sides.

Yield: 2 servings

SUPER SUB

Switching from tortillas made with white flour to whole wheat tortillas gives you more fiber, vitamin E, magnesium, and potassium.

Nutritional data per serving: Calories, 354; protein, 24 g; carbohydrate, 49 g; dietary fiber, 6 g; total fat, 11 g; saturated fat, 1 g; cholesterol, 28 mg; sodium, 684 mg; vitamin A, 72% of Daily Value; vitamin C, 127%; calcium, 6%; iron, 17%; vitamin B_3 (niacin), 41%; vitamin B_6, 28%; vitamin D, 28%; folate 15%; vitamin E, 12%; magnesium, 26%; potassium, 15%; omega-3 fatty acids, 86%.

Tuna Pita with Avocado

Tired of tuna with mayo? Try mashed avocado instead. Its rich, creamy texture adds just the right touch to a sandwich that's just packed with the vitamins and minerals your body craves. And stuffing it in a whole grain pita pocket will help keep diabetes off your family tree.

1 can (6 ounces) water-packed white albacore tuna, drained
1 avocado
1 wedge lime
2 small whole wheat pita pockets
2 leaves red leaf lettuce

In a small bowl, mash the tuna and avocado. Squeeze the lime over the mixture and stir until blended. Toast the pitas until puffed. Split the pitas and spread half the tuna inside each pocket. Stuff with a lettuce leaf and enjoy!

Yield: 2 servings

Nutritional data per serving: Calories, 271; protein, 24 g; carbohydrate, 21 g; dietary fiber, 5 g; total fat, 11 g; saturated fat, 1 g; cholesterol, 36 mg; sodium, 488 mg; vitamin A, 10% of Daily Value; vitamin C, 11%; calcium, 4%; iron, 12%; vitamin B_3 (niacin), 34%; vitamin B_6, 20%; vitamin D, 34%; vitamin E, 11%; folate, 11%; magnesium, 17%; potassium, 18%; omega-3 fatty acids, 87%.

SUPER SUB

A whole wheat pita delivers 4 times the fiber, 3 times the magnesium, twice the zinc, and more heart-smart vitamin E and potassium than a white pita. A real nutritional bargain!

Unstuffed Peppers

Stuffed peppers are delicious, but sometimes there just isn't time to do all the steps to make the real thing. Here's a busy-night recipe that captures all the flavors of the longer-cooking version.

2 cups thinly sliced green bell peppers
1 cup sliced green onions
1/2 cup sliced celery
1 tablespoon olive oil
4 ounces lean ground beef
1/2 cup water
1/4 teaspoon dried thyme
1/4 teaspoon salt
2 cups cooked rice

In a large skillet over medium-high heat, sauté the peppers, onions, and celery in the oil for about 10 minutes, until the vegetables begin to soften and the onions begin to brown. Crumble the beef into the pan and cook, stirring, until brown. Add the water and deglaze the pan. Stir in the thyme and salt. Reduce the heat, cover, and simmer for about 5 minutes, or until the water evaporates. Add the rice and stir to blend. Serve immediately. Add some crusty bread and your favorite bagged salad for a complete meal.

Yield: 4 servings

Nutritional data per serving: Calories, 210; protein, 9 g; carbohydrate, 31 g; dietary fiber, 3 g; total fat, 6 g; saturated fat, 2 g; cholesterol, 20 mg; sodium, 179 mg; vitamin A, 3% of Daily Value; vitamin C, 75%; calcium, 4%; iron, 9%; vitamin B$_3$ (niacin), 16%; vitamin B$_6$, 12%; potassium, 10%.

Basmati Chickpeas

1/2 cup chopped yellow onions
2 cloves garlic, minced
1 tablespoon peanut oil
1 small zucchini, cut lengthwise and thinly sliced
1 baby eggplant, cut lengthwise and thinly sliced
1 cup brown basmati rice
1 1/2 cups V8 vegetable juice
1 1/2 cups water
1 tablespoon parsley flakes
1 tablespoon paprika
1 can (15 1/2 ounces) chickpeas, rinsed and drained
6 tablespoons sunflower seeds

In a large skillet over medium-high heat, sauté the onions and garlic in the oil for about 5 minutes, or until soft. Stir in the zucchini and eggplant and cook, stirring constantly, for 5 minutes. Stir in the rice, V8, water, parsley, and paprika. Cover and bring to a boil, then reduce the heat to medium and simmer for 20 minutes. Stir in the chickpeas and cook for 10 minutes, or until all the water is absorbed. Ladle into individual bowls and top each serving with 1 tablespoon of the sunflower seeds.

Yield: 6 servings

Nutritional data per serving: Calories, 297; protein, 10 g; carbohydrate, 47 g; dietary fiber, 8 g; total fat, 9 g; saturated fat, 1 g; cholesterol, 0 mg; sodium, 356 mg; vitamin A, 13% of Daily Value; vitamin C, 34%; calcium, 6%; iron, 18%; vitamin B_6, 11%; vitamin E, 23%; folate, 31%; copper, 19%; magnesium, 12%; potassium, 11%, zinc, 9%.

Javanese Lamb Curry

Curry fans will fall in love with this quick-to-fix, fragrant dish. A little sitar music, anyone?

6 ounces lamb chunks
2 teaspoons peanut oil
1½ cups chicken broth
½ cup whole wheat couscous
1 teaspoon curry powder
1 tablespoon minced garlic (from a jar)
¼ teaspoon salt
Freshly ground black pepper to taste
½ cup dark seedless raisins
1 tablespoon chopped peanuts
1 tablespoon toasted flaked coconut

DOUBLE DUTY

Gamble (or gambol!) on lamb to provide protein and ¼ of your day's iron quota in a form that's absorbed better than iron from plants. This nutrient is especially beneficial for girls.

In a deep saucepan over medium-high heat, brown the lamb in the oil. Stir in the broth, couscous, curry powder, garlic, salt, pepper, and raisins. Cover and bring to a boil, then reduce the heat and simmer for 20 minutes, until all the liquid is absorbed. Ladle onto two plates and garnish each with ½ tablespoon of the peanuts and ½ tablespoon of the coconut.

Yield: 2 servings

Nutritional data per serving: Calories, 494; protein, 32 g; carbohydrate, 62 g; dietary fiber, 9 g; total fat, 14 g; saturated fat, 4 g; cholesterol, 80 mg; sodium, 676 mg; vitamin A, 0% of Daily Value; vitamin C, 2%; calcium, 6%; iron, 24%; vitamin B_2 (riboflavin), 19%; vitamin B_3 (niacin), 32%; vitamin E, 6%; zinc, 18%.

Chicken Barley Bowl

When the week ahead is looking as wild as a hurricane and kitchen time just isn't on my calendar, I put this dish on to cook while I'm enjoying my Sunday dinner. It's done when I am, and it's waiting for me on my busiest night.

1 cup thinly sliced carrots
1 cup coarsely chopped onions
1 cup sliced celery
6 ounces unbreaded chicken tenders,
    cut into 1-inch pieces
1 tablespoon canola oil
4 cups fat-free chicken broth
3/4 cup pearled barley, rinsed
Freshly ground black pepper to taste

> **The Inside Skinny:**
> Pearled barley is packed with fiber, mostly the soluble kind that helps rid your body of cholesterol.

In a deep soup pot over medium-high heat, sauté the carrots, onions, celery, and chicken in the oil for about 5 minutes, or until the vegetables are tender and the chicken begins to brown. Add the broth and deglaze the pan. Stir in the barley and pepper. Cover and bring to a boil, then reduce the heat and simmer for 50 to 60 minutes, or until most of the water is absorbed. Serve immediately or refrigerate and reheat later.

Yield: 4 servings

Nutritional data per serving: Calories, 300; protein, 19 g; carbohydrate, 37 g; dietary fiber, 8 g; total fat, 9 g; saturated fat, <1 g; cholesterol, 33 mg; sodium, 518 mg; vitamin A, 87% of Daily Value; vitamin C, 12%; calcium, 4%; iron, 9%; vitamin B$_3$ (niacin), 29%; vitamin B$_6$, 18%; vitamin E, 9%; vitamin K, 57%; potassium, 12%; omega-3 fatty acids, 68%.

Basic Wheatberries

Of all the whole grain foods out there, my favorite is definitely wheatberries. No, they don't grow on thorny bushes. They're just wheat kernels (yes, you could plant them) simmered in water or broth until they become soft and chewy. They're great served hot or cold, for breakfast, lunch, or dinner. Their only drawback is that they take a while to make, so plan ahead and cook up a whole pot. You'll find so many ways to use them.

1 cup whole grain wheat
4 cups water

At bedtime, place the wheat and water in a deep saucepan. Let stand overnight. In the morning, cover and bring to a boil. Reduce the heat and simmer for about 50 minutes (while you eat breakfast, read the paper, and get dressed for the day). Drain and refrigerate to use later; you can stir them into cold salads or hot vegetables, for example, or toss with pasta and beans.

Yield: 6 servings

Nutritional data per serving: Calories, 105; protein, 5 g; carbohydrate, 22 g; dietary fiber, 4 g; total fat, <1 g; saturated fat, 0 g; cholesterol, 0 mg; sodium, 0 mg; vitamin A, 0% of Daily Value; vitamin C, 0%; calcium, 1%; iron, 6%; vitamin E, 2%; copper, 7%; magnesium, 10%; potassium, 3%; zinc, 6%.

SUPER SUB

Wheatberries contain twice as much fiber as brown rice, wild rice, or oatmeal.

Summer Veggies and Wheatberries

Overrun with summer squash? Grab a couple of little ones and create this savory dish. It's all the best of summer in a bowl!

1 cup coarsely chopped yellow onions
1 tablespoon canola oil
1 small zucchini, washed and thinly sliced
1 small yellow squash, washed and thinly sliced
1 cup diced red bell peppers
2 cloves garlic, minced
1/4 cup slivered fresh basil
1/4 teaspoon salt
Freshly ground black pepper to taste
1 cup Basic Wheatberries (page 146)

In a large skillet over medium-high heat, sauté the onions in the oil until they begin to brown. Add the zucchini and yellow squash. Cook, stirring, until beginning to soften and brown. Add the red peppers, garlic, basil, salt, and black pepper. Cook, stirring, until the squashes are cooked through and the peppers begin to soften. Stir in the wheatberries and cook for 1 minute, or until heated through. Serve hot with grilled chicken or pork.

Yield: 4 servings

Nutritional data per serving: Calories, 92; protein, 3 g; carbohydrate, 14 g; dietary fiber, 3 g; total fat, 4 g; saturated fat, 0 g; cholesterol, 0 mg; sodium, 150 mg; vitamin A, 24% of Daily Value; vitamin C, 133%; calcium, 3%; iron, 5%; vitamin B$_6$, 12%; vitamin E, 6%; folate, 9%; potassium, 9%; omega-3 fatty acids, 35%.

Wild Rice Gone Mad

About once a year, usually in winter and often for Christmas, I spring for a box of outrageously expensive wild rice to serve to the people I love most. Why? Because the flavor is as rich as the price, and it's so outrageously good no one ever thinks of it as health food!

1 tablespoon minced garlic
½ cup diced yellow onions
4 ounces cremini mushrooms, cleaned and sliced
1 teaspoon canola oil
4 cups fat-free reduced-sodium beef broth
1 package (6 ounces) wild rice
¼ cup coarsely broken walnuts
¼ cup finely chopped fresh parsley
¼ teaspoon salt
Freshly ground black pepper to taste
1 tablespoon butter
4 sprigs parsley

In a large saucepan over medium-high heat, sauté the garlic, onions, and mushrooms in the oil for about 5 minutes, or until soft. Stir in the broth, rice, walnuts, chopped parsley, salt, and pepper. Bring to a boil. Reduce the heat, cover, and simmer for 50 to 60 minutes, or until all the liquid is absorbed. Stir in the butter. Spoon into a serving bowl and garnish with the parsley.

Yield: 6 servings

Nutritional data per serving: Calories, 192; protein, 9 g; carbohydrate, 26 g; dietary fiber, 3 g; total fat, 6 g; saturated fat, 2 g; cholesterol, 5 mg; sodium, 234 mg; vitamin A, 3% of Daily Value; vitamin C, 13%; calcium, 2%; iron, 6%; vitamin B₃ (niacin), 14%; folate, 10%; magnesium, 15%.

Beachy-Keen Kasha and Pasta

Longing for the beach but can't get there? Cook up this lovely dish that's reminiscent of the shore. Add a few shrimp for a taste of the ocean.

1 cup fat-free chicken broth
1 egg white
½ cup kasha
1 tablespoon butter
1 cup cooked small seashell pasta

In a small saucepan, heat the broth.

Meanwhile, in a small bowl, beat the egg white with a fork. Add the kasha and stir until well coated. Pour into a medium nonstick saucepan and cook, stirring, over high heat until the egg has dried and the kasha kernels have separated and are toasty brown. Stir in the hot broth and bring to a boil. Reduce the heat to medium and cook for 10 minutes, or until all the liquid is absorbed. Stir in the butter until well blended. Add the pasta and toss. Serve piping hot.

Yield: 4 servings

Nutritional data per serving: Calories, 149; protein, 6 g; carbohydrate, 24 g; dietary fiber, 3 g; total fat, 4 g; saturated fat, 2 g; cholesterol, 8 mg; sodium, 88 mg; vitamin A, 3% of Daily Value; vitamin C, 0%; calcium, 1%; iron, 8%; vitamin B₃ (niacin), 11%; folate, 7%; magnesium, 13%.

The Inside Skinny: Coating the kernels with egg white helps to keep them separate so they form a nice, fluffy pilaf instead of a sticky mess.

Traditional Polenta

Everything old is new again. Today, earthy, traditional recipes like this old-fashioned cornmeal dish can form the base for many a healthy meal. It's great with Southwestern, Spanish, and Eastern European cuisine.

3 cups water
¹/₂ teaspoon salt
2 tablespoons butter
1¹/₂ cups enriched
    stone-ground
    yellow cornmeal

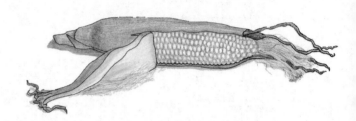

In a large saucepan, bring the water and salt to a boil. Stir in the butter. Pour in the cornmeal all at once, stirring rapidly with a wooden spoon to keep lumps from forming. When the mixture begins to bubble, reduce the heat to medium. Cook, stirring, for 10 to 15 minutes, or until all the water is absorbed and the polenta pulls away from the pan. Pour into a serving bowl and offer it hot, or pour into an oblong cake pan and refrigerate. When cold, cut into squares or diamonds to serve with hot bean dishes or grilled meat.

Yield: 6 servings

Nutritional data per serving: Calories, 145; protein, 3 g; carbohydrate, 25 g; dietary fiber, 2 g; total fat, 4 g; saturated fat, 2.5 g; cholesterol. 10 mg; sodium, 658 mg; vitamin A, 5% of Daily Value; vitamin C, 0%; calcium, 10%; iron, 12%; vitamin B₁ (thiamin), 22%; folate, 32%.

> **QUICK TRICK:** In a rush? Buy polenta in a roll (it looks like a fat yellow sausage). Just slice, heat, and serve.

Couscous and Pine Nut Pilaf

Warm up a winter's night with this savory, whole grain side dish that's quick to fix. Pine nuts make it elegant enough for company and tasty enough to seduce even the most reluctant whole wheat eaters.

1½ cups fat-free beef broth
1 tablespoon parsley flakes
½ teaspoon dried basil
¼ teaspoon dried cilantro
⅛ teaspoon garlic (from a jar)
1 cup whole wheat couscous
2 tablespoons pine nuts

In a medium saucepan, combine the broth, parsley, basil, cilantro, and garlic. Bring to a boil, then stir in the couscous. Reduce the heat to medium, cover, and simmer for 2 minutes, or until all the liquid is absorbed. Stir in the pine nuts.

Yield: 6 servings

Nutritional data per serving: Calories, 165; protein, 7 g; carbohydrate, 31 g; dietary fiber, 5 g; total fat, 2 g; saturated fat, 0 g; cholesterol, 0 mg; sodium, 41 mg; vitamin A, 1% of Daily Value; vitamin C, 3%; calcium, 2%; iron, 10%; copper, 2%; magnesium, 2%; potassium, 2%.

SUPER SUB

Whole wheat couscous serves up twice as much calcium and 4 times as much iron as regular couscous.

Seven-Grain Pilaf

Sure, this whole grain dish takes longer to prepare, but you can make it "instant." Cook it tonight while you're eating dinner, then reheat it instantly tomorrow night!

1 teaspoon walnut oil
1 package (5.6 ounces) Seeds of Change
    seven-grain pilaf blend
1 can (14½ ounces) reduced-sodium chicken broth
¾ cup water
1 tablespoon dehydrated onions
1 tablespoon parsley flakes
½ teaspoon dried tarragon
⅓ cup golden seedless raisins
¼ cup coarsely chopped walnuts
¼ teaspoon salt
Freshly ground black pepper to taste

Warm the oil in a 4-quart saucepan over medium-high heat. Add the pilaf blend, reserving the seasoning packet for another use. Sauté until the grain is coated and begins to brown. Add the broth, water, onions, parsley, tarragon, raisins, walnuts, salt, and pepper. Bring to a boil, then reduce the heat, cover, and simmer for about 1 hour, or until all the liquid is absorbed.

Yield: 4 servings

Nutritional data per serving: Calories, 244; protein, 6 g; carbohydrate, 40 g; dietary fiber, 5 g; total fat, 8 g; saturated fat, 1 g; cholesterol, 2 mg; sodium, 615 mg; vitamin A, 4% of Daily Value; vitamin C, 1%; calcium, 1%; iron, 5%; vitamin B$_1$ (thiamin), 12%; vitamin B$_3$ (niacin), 11%; folate, 4%; omega-3 fatty acids, 80%.

Pumpkin Muffins

When pumpkin is on special at holiday time, grab an extra can and stow it away. Then, when the mood strikes you, stir up these spicy muffins. You'll get a whiff of the holidays with a fraction of the work!

1½ cups white whole wheat flour*
2 teaspoons pumpkin pie spice
1 teaspoon baking soda
½ teaspoon baking powder
1 egg
1 cup canned pumpkin
½ cup honey
3 tablespoons canola oil
½ cup dark seedless raisins

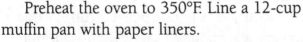

Preheat the oven to 350°F. Line a 12-cup muffin pan with paper liners.

In a large bowl, stir together the flour, spice, baking soda, and baking powder. In a small bowl, combine the egg, pumpkin, honey, and oil. Stir until well blended. Pour into the dry ingredients and stir just until mixed. Fold in the raisins and ladle into the pan. Bake for 25 minutes, or until a toothpick inserted in the center of a muffin comes out clean. Remove from the pan and cool on a rack. Wonderful with vegetable soup!

Yield: 12 servings

Nutritional data per serving: Calories, 159; protein, 3 g; carbohydrate, 30 g; dietary fiber, 3 g; total fat, 4 g; saturated fat, 0 g; cholesterol, 16 mg; sodium, 181 mg; vitamin A, 46% of Daily Value; vitamin C, 2%; calcium, 2%; iron, 7%; vitamin E, 5%; omega-3 fatty acids, 32%.

*Available in natural foods stores and some large supermarkets.

Brown Rice Custard

When I was a young homemaker, I was surprised to learn that the yummy dessert I wanted to make was not rice pudding, but rice custard. Here's the quick and easy way I make it now.

1 cup cold cooked instant brown rice
2 cups 2% milk
1 package (2.9 ounces) Jell-O Americana
    custard dessert mix
1/8 teaspoon ground nutmeg

Spoon 1/4 cup of the rice into each of four custard cups. In a medium saucepan over medium heat, combine the milk and custard mix. Cook, stirring constantly with a wire whisk, until the custard comes to a full rolling boil. Remove from the heat and ladle one-fourth of the custard over the rice in each cup. With a fork, gently stir each serving just enough to let the custard infiltrate the rice. Dust with the nutmeg and refrigerate for about 1 hour, or until firmly set.

Yield: 4 servings

Nutritional data per serving: Calories, 191; protein, 7 g; carbohydrate, 32 g; dietary fiber, <1 g; total fat, 4 g; saturated fat, 2 g; cholesterol, 128 mg; sodium, 202 mg; vitamin A, 7% of Daily Value; vitamin C, 2%; calcium, 20%; iron, 2%; vitamin B_2 (riboflavin), 17%; vitamin B_6, 4%; folate, 3%; potassium, 8%.

> **QUICK TRICK:** In place of the rice, use any leftover whole grain, such as quinoa, 7-grain blend, or even whole wheat pasta.

CHAPTER 6

BUILD BETTER BONES

THE MILKY WAY

WHEN I WAS JUST A LITTLE TYKE, I CHUCKED MY bottle out of my crib and pretty much threw in the diaper on drinking milk. Fortunately for me and my bones, both my parents were pretty tricky. My mom slipped milk into my baby cereal and later put nonfat dry milk in meat loaf. She served macaroni and cheese as an entrée and paired cheese toast with tomato soup.

My dad was no slouch, either. Always up for a game, he invented "skookie" by stirring vanilla extract and a little sugar into a glass of moo juice. He swore it wasn't milk, and I fell for it! Now, according to my most recent scan, I have bones that most 30-year-olds would kill for. Thanks for being so clever, Mom and Dad!

Bones are living tissue with a life cycle all their own. Calcium moves in and out of them every day, so their balance sheet changes all the time. Up until we're about 25, more calcium goes in than out, giving us a chance to build up a hefty bone bank account—enough for now and later. From age 25 to 35, the ins and outs are about even. But after age 50, things start going downhill—gradually for men, but sharply for women during menopause and then gradually in later years. (That's when our youthful bone bank comes in handy!)

Add Some Extra Sun

Over 50? Your body probably doesn't turn sunshine into vitamin D the way it used to. So the Institute of Medicine (that's the place that develops the Recommended Dietary Allowances) says you should take a 400 IU supplement of vitamin D daily.

Calcium researcher Dorothy Teegarden, Ph.D., of Purdue University, tells me that of all the possible calcium sources, milk is the most reliable. It's also one of the few food sources of vitamin D, which is also needed for bone health. "By age 16, your hip bone is as strong as it's ever going to be," she says, "and that's the one most likely to fracture if you develop osteoporosis in later life."

Of course, it's never too late to protect your bones. Getting enough calcium all through your life helps to keep bones strong. Here are modern science's top tips for building that bone bank and keeping a hefty balance.

♥ **Help your kids or grandkids drink 3 cups of milk every day.** The difference between drinking 1 cup and 3 means a 40 percent lower risk of osteoporosis later in life.

♥ **Drink milk at every meal yourself.** Children who drink the most milk are those whose mothers drink the most milk. And remember, while you're helping them, you're also helping yourself!

♥ **Exercise with your youngsters.** It helps pack calcium into their bones and keep it in yours. Hint: Women with the strongest muscles are those with the strongest bones!

♥ **Fill in with yogurt and cheese.** Although they lack milk's vitamin D, they do deliver the same protein, B vitamins, calcium, and other minerals as milk.

Of course, bones require more than calcium for peak performance (nothing is ever simple). They feast on lean protein (see chapter 1 for some great ways to get it). They bask in vitamin D, which you get from the sun and from some of the fish in chapter 3. They suck up trace minerals like magnesium and copper from whole grains (chapter 5) and nuts and seeds (chapter 4). And they crunch vitamin K from the dark green, leafy vegetables you'll find in chapters 7 and 12. Beyond dairy foods, you'll also find extra calcium in enriched soy products and fruit juice (check out chapter 14).

For most of your life, you'll need between 1,000 and 1,300 milligrams of calcium daily. One cup of milk (whether it's fat-free, 1%, 2%, whole, or chocolate), 1 cup of yogurt, or 1 ounce of cheese delivers about 300 milligrams. That's far more than, say, a cup of kale (179 milligrams), bok choy (158 milligrams), or turnip greens (197 milligrams), although that green cuisine can sure help out!

So grab your three-legged stool, head for the barn, and give old Bossy a pat on her rump. Then I'll show you a few of my family secrets for turning her milk into yummy treats that'll boost your bones.

Fresh Strawberry Cream Dip

Summer parties need light, fresh appetizers that tickle the tongue and dazzle the eye. Try this pretty-in-pink centerpiece.

2 cups sliced fresh strawberries
8 ounces fat-free cream cheese
1/2 teaspoon grated lemon peel
2 tablespoons strawberry preserves
Freshly grated nutmeg to taste

In a blender, combine the strawberries, cream cheese, lemon peel, and preserves. Pulse several times to blend. Spoon into a lotus bowl and sprinkle with the nutmeg. Surround with fresh fruit chunks for dipping.

Yield: 16 servings

Nutritional data per serving: Calories, 26; protein, 2 g; carbohydrate, 4 g; dietary fiber, <1 g; total fat, 0 g; saturated fat, 0 g; cholesterol, 1 mg; sodium, 79 mg; vitamin A, 4% of Daily Value; vitamin C, 20%; calcium, 3%; iron, 1%; folate, 2%.

SUPER SUB

1 cup

Fat-free cream cheese gives you double the calcium of the regular high-fat kind.

Clip 'n Snip Summer Vegetable Dip

I have pots of herbs on my deck, growing to beat the band. When I'm ready to make dip, I just clip and snip. Try it. It's easy, fresh, and delish.

1 cup fat-free plain yogurt
1/2 cup reduced-fat sour cream
1/4 cup snipped fresh chives
1/4 cup slivered fresh basil
Leaves from 4 sprigs thyme
2 tablespoons snipped parsley
2 cloves garlic, minced or pressed
1/4 teaspoon salt
1/8 teaspoon freshly ground pepper mélange

In a small bowl, combine the yogurt and sour cream and mix well. Add the chives, basil, thyme, parsley, garlic, salt, and pepper. Stir until well mixed. Serve surrounded by fresh vegetables.

Yield: 16 servings

Nutritional data per serving: Calories, 23; protein, 1 g; carbohydrate, 2 g; dietary fiber, 0 g; total fat, 1 g; saturated fat, <1 g; cholesterol, 6 mg; sodium, 52 mg; vitamin A, 3% of Daily Value; vitamin C, 3%; calcium, 4%; iron, 1%; vitamin K, 2%.

Lovely Leftovers

Drizzle over tossed salad—it's better than ranch dressing!

Creamy Broccoli Soup

1/2 cup chopped onions
1 teaspoon canola oil
2 cups fat-free milk
2 cups fat-free evaporated milk
4 cups small broccoli florets
1 tablespoon chicken bouillon granules
1/2 teaspoon dried dillweed
1 cup instant mashed potato granules
4 teaspoons butter
Dash of paprika

In a large saucepan over medium-high heat, sauté the onions in the oil until soft. Stir in the fat-free milk and evaporated milk, broccoli, bouillon, and dill. Reduce the heat to medium. Cook, stirring constantly, until the soup just begins to bubble around the edges. Reduce the heat and simmer for 10 minutes, or until the broccoli is tender. Stir in the potato granules and cook for 2 minutes, or until the soup begins to thicken. Ladle into four soup cups. Top each with 1 teaspoon of the butter and dust with paprika. Serve with a crisp salad for a complete meal.

Yield: 4 servings

Nutrition data per serving: Calories, 397; protein, 21 g; carbohydrate, 66 g; dietary fiber, 7 g; total fat, 6 g; saturated fat, 3 g; cholesterol, 17 mg; sodium, 503 mg; vitamin A, 37% of Daily Value; vitamin C, 117%; calcium, 57%; iron, 7%; vitamin D, 39%; vitamin K, 197%; potassium, 26%.

QUICK TRICK: Use a 10-ounce package of frozen broccoli instead of fresh broccoli florets.

Beans 'n Greens Tomato Soup

I just love tomato soup, and I've found lots of ways to gussy it up. Or I just go slumming and toss in all the little bits of leftovers in my fridge. Sometimes, such as when I scraped this one together, the soup turns out to be power-packed as well as delicious!

1 can (10³/₄ ounces) condensed tomato soup
1 soup can fat-free milk
1 cup cooked or rinsed and drained canned red
   kidney beans
¹/₂ cup cooked kale
1 tablespoon olive oil
2 tablespoons freshly grated Parmesan cheese

In a medium saucepan over medium-high heat, use a wire whisk to blend the milk into the soup. Stir in the beans, kale, and oil. Cook, stirring often, until almost boiling. Ladle into two large soup bowls. Top each serving with 1 tablespoon of the cheese.

Yield: 2 servings

Nutritional data per serving: Calories, 432; protein, 23 g; carbohydrate, 61 g; dietary fiber, 13 g; total fat, 12 g; saturated fat, 3 g; cholesterol, 9 mg; sodium, 1,087 mg; vitamin A, 48% of Daily Value; vitamin C, 161%; calcium, 41%; iron, 14%; vitamin B₂ (riboflavin), 34%; vitamin B₆, 16%; vitamin E, 22%; folate, 31%; magnesium, 23%; potassium, 22%; omega-3 fatty acids, 50%.

DOUBLE DUTY

Kale is one of those green leafy vegetables that add to your calcium quotient. Even more important, it serves up a huge dose of vitamin K, a nutrient also needed for bone health.

Figs, Feta, and Field Greens

Each summer, during that small window of opportunity when ripe figs appear in my supermarket, I have to splurge and buy a few. I fondly remember my grandmother and the fig tree that grew in her backyard. It seemed such an oddity, with those great big leaves and tiny fruits that were so sweet and wondrous.

4 cups mixed salad greens
4 large ripe figs
1 tablespoon olive oil
1 tablespoon balsamic vinegar
Salt and freshly ground black
    pepper to taste
2 ounces crumbled feta cheese
1 tablespoon toasted pine nuts

In a large salad bowl, combine the greens and figs. Drizzle with the oil and vinegar and toss until well coated. Season with the salt and pepper and toss again. Divide between two individual salad bowls. Top each with 1 ounce of the cheese and ½ tablespoon of the pine nuts.

Yield: 2 servings

Nutritional data per serving: Calories, 276; protein, 8 g; carbohydrate, 31 g; dietary fiber, 7 g; total fat, 16 g; saturated fat, 6 g; cholesterol, 25 mg; sodium, 347 mg; vitamin A, 35% of Daily Value; vitamin C, 34%; calcium, 25%; iron, 14%; vitamin E, 15%; folate, 37%; potassium, 20%; omega-3 fatty acids, 14%.

DOUBLE DUTY

Figs fork over 20% of the calcium and 60% of the fiber in this salad. How sweet!

Waffles with Ricotta and Fresh Apricots

Oops! We bought too many apricots this week. (They were so pretty and plentiful, we couldn't resist!). Now they're dead ripe and on the verge of going bad. Perfect for this delicious breakfast treat.

4 whole grain toaster waffles
1/2 cup low-fat ricotta cheese
1/2 cup diced fresh apricots, with peel
1 tablespoon orange marmalade
Freshly ground nutmeg to taste

Toast the waffles according to package directions, then divide between two large plates. Spread each with 2 tablespoons of the ricotta. In a small bowl, combine the apricots and marmalade and stir well. Spread 2 tablespoons on each waffle and dust with the nutmeg.

Yield: 2 servings

Nutritional data per serving: Calories, 275; protein, 13 g; carbohydrate, 45 g; dietary fiber, 4 g; total fat, 6 g; saturated fat, 2 g; cholesterol, 20 mg; sodium, 727 mg; vitamin A, 20% of Daily Value; vitamin C, 10%; calcium, 43%; iron, 34%; vitamin B_1 (thiamin), 25%; vitamin B_2 (riboflavin), 30%; vitamin B_3 (niacin), 24%; vitamin B_6, 39%; potassium, 10%.

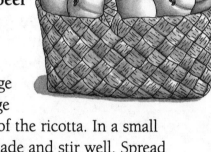

SUPER SUB

Ever wonder what a "highly processed diet" is? It's foods like white-flour waffles, margarine, and syrup. Whole grain waffles, ricotta, and fresh apricots are a close-to-natural combo that packs a nutritional wallop!

Bella Bella Pocket Salad

Although baby spinach has taken over in many produce departments, put your money on the grownup kind for this salad. Sturdy spinach leaves can handle onions, cheese, and an intense dressing.

10 ounces spinach, heavy stems removed
4 ounces baby bella mushrooms, cleaned
1 thin slice red onion, separated into rings
4 tablespoons light Catalina dressing
4 pieces Mini Babybel semisoft cheese (3/4 ounce each)
Freshly ground black pepper to taste
4 whole wheat pita pockets

Wash the spinach in running water, then spin dry. Tear into bite-size pieces and place in a large salad bowl. Thinly slice the mushrooms and add to the spinach. Add the onion. Drizzle with the dressing and toss until well coated. Unwrap the cheese and slice into thin rounds. Add to the salad, toss well, and season with the pepper. Toast the pitas until puffed, then split and fill each with one-fourth of the salad.

Yield: 4 servings

Nutritional data per serving: Calories, 265; protein, 15 g; carbohydrate, 41 g; dietary fiber, 6 g; total fat, 6 g; saturated fat, 2 g; cholesterol, 15 mg; sodium, 667 mg; vitamin A, 31% of Daily Value; vitamin C, 15%; calcium, 24%; iron, 17%; vitamin E, 8%; folate, 21%; vitamin K, 150%.

DOUBLE DUTY

Substituting spinach for the usual salad greens boosts vision with vitamin C to counter cataracts and lutein to fend off macular degeneration. The cheese provides calcium for your bones.

International Pizza

Pizza…tomato pie…I like to keep rearranging the ingredients to make new combinations. This pizza is awfully easy, especially considering the delicious mix of flavors.

1 French sourdough baguette (6 inches)
1/4 cup Italian pizza sauce
1/8 teaspoon dried Mexican oregano
1 teaspoon garlic (from a jar)
1 ounce imported Danish ham
2 tablespoons Italian-style Parmesan cheese
2 ounces Swiss cheese

Slice the bread in half lengthwise. In a small bowl, combine the sauce, oregano, and garlic. Spread equal portions on the cut sides of the bread. Cut the ham into strips and place evenly on top of the sauce. Sprinkle each pizza with 1 tablespoon of the Parmesan and top with 1 ounce of the Swiss. Place on a baking sheet and bake at 400°F for 5 to 10 minutes, or just until the cheese is melted. Serve with crisp green salad.

Yield: 2 servings

Nutritional data per serving: Calories, 328; protein, 19 g; carbohydrate, 34 g; dietary fiber, 2 g; total fat, 12 g; saturated fat, 7 g; cholesterol, 39 mg; sodium, 796 mg; vitamin A, 10% of Daily Value; vitamin C, 7%; calcium, 42%; iron, 11%; vitamin B$_1$ (thiamin), 31%; vitamin B$_2$ (riboflavin), 21%; vitamin E, 6%; folate, 15%.

SUPER SUB

Danish ham is nearly fat-free, while pepperoni packs 6 grams of fat per ounce.

Grilled Provolone and Tomato Sandwich

When I was a kid, I loved grilled cheese sandwiches that were ooz-ing thick, yellow cheese and dripping with butter. But neither my heart nor my hips can stand that treatment any more! Here's a grownup ver-sion for more sophisticated tastes (and tickers that need a little help!).

2 slices whole grain bread
2 slices provolone cheese (about 1 ounce)
1 thick slice very ripe large tomato
¼ teaspoon dried basil
Freshly ground black pepper to taste

Lightly coat one side of one slice of the bread with olive oil spray. Place oiled side down in a heavy skillet over medium heat and top with one slice of the cheese, then the tomato. Sprinkle the tomato with the basil and pepper. Top with the remaining cheese and bread. Coat lightly with olive oil spray. Cover and cook until the bottom begins to brown. With a spatula, carefully turn the sandwich. Cook for 1 to 2 minutes, or until the bottom is crisp and golden. Enjoy with a bowl of split pea soup.

Yield: 1 serving

Nutritional data per serving: Calories, 269; protein, 12 g; carbohydrate, 31 g; dietary fiber, 11 g; total fat, 13 g; saturated fat, 5 g; cholesterol, 20 mg; sodium, 412 mg; vitamin A, 10% of Daily Value; vitamin C, 17%; calcium, 42%; iron, 13%; vitamin B$_6$; 43%; folate, 22%; magnesium, 23%; zinc, 36%; omega-3 fatty acids, 71%.

QUICK TRICK: Cook your sandwich in a George Foreman grill and skip the flip!

Orzo with Vegetables and Fontina Cheese

My husband, Ted, came sniffing into the kitchen. "Mmmmm, mushrooms!" he said. "Oh, that looks good!" And it is!

4 ounces orzo
1 tablespoon olive oil
2 cups sliced brown mushrooms
6 ounces baby spinach
2 ounces shredded Fontina cheese

Cook the orzo according to package directions. Drain and set aside.

Meanwhile, warm the oil in a large, deep skillet over medium heat. Add the mushrooms in an even layer, then top with the spinach. Cover and steam for about 5 minutes, or until the mushrooms are cooked through and beginning to brown and the spinach is wilted. Fold in the orzo and mix well. Remove from the heat. Spread the cheese evenly over the mixture. Cover and let stand for 1 to 2 minutes, or until the cheese is melted.

Yield: 2 servings

Nutritional data per serving: Calories, 368; protein, 19 g; carbohydrate, 45 g; dietary fiber, 8 g; total fat, 10 g; saturated fat, 6 g; cholesterol, 33 mg; sodium, 317 mg; vitamin A, 65% of Daily Value; vitamin C, 40%; calcium, 25%; iron, 27%; vitamin E, 9%; folate, 66%; vitamin K, 425%; magnesium, 24%; potassium, 15%; omega-3 fatty acids, 36%.

SUPER SUB

1 CUP

Baby spinach stems are tender enough to eat, so you get twice as much fiber as you would from large spinach leaves with the heavy stems removed.

Ring Tum Ditty

My mother used to make this dish in a double boiler (does anyone even own one anymore?), but with a super nonstick saucepan, I can make it in half the time. This meal is simple but lip-smacking good.

1 can (10³/₄ ounces) condensed tomato soup
8 ounces shredded reduced-fat cheddar cheese
1 teaspoon Worcestershire sauce

In a nonstick saucepan over medium heat, combine the soup and cheese. Cook, stirring constantly with a whisk, until the cheese is melted and the sauce just begins to bubble (do not boil). Stir in the Worcestershire. Serve over crumbled crackers, or better still, mix quick-cooking brown rice with steamed broccoli and add the sauce for a perfect dinner in a bowl.

Yield: 4 servings

Nutritional data per serving: Calories, 215; protein, 19 g; carbohydrate, 10 g; dietary fiber, <1 g; total fat, 11 g; saturated fat, 7 g; cholesterol, 40 mg; sodium, 882 mg; vitamin A, 22% of Daily Value; vitamin C, 68%; calcium, 52%; iron, 6%; vitamin B$_2$ (riboflavin), 18%; vitamin E, 8%.

DOUBLE DUTY

Tomato soup is a super source of vitamin C, and it's loaded with cancer-fighting lycopene.

"Goddess" Wild Mushroom Pasta

I was having dinner the other night with Kathy Gottsacker, who hosts a TV food show in San Antonio, Texas. I got to wondering out loud what such a "foodie" cooks when she goes home at night, and she laughingly shared this recipe with me. "When I serve this," she said, "my husband thinks I'm a goddess!"

1½ teaspoons olive oil
1½ teaspoons butter
1 pound mushrooms (preferably 3 kinds,
    such as cremini, shiitake, and white buttons)
½ cup thinly sliced shallots
Salt and freshly ground black pepper to taste
¼ cup half-and-half
2 cups cooked bow-tie pasta
½ ounce shaved Parmesan cheese

In a large skillet over medium-high heat, warm the oil and butter until the butter is melted. Add the mushrooms, shallots, salt, and pepper. Cook, stirring, until the mushrooms soften and give up their liquid. Stir in the half-and-half and simmer until the sauce thickens and is reduced. Divide the pasta between two plates and pour half of the sauce over each serving. Garnish with the cheese. Watch your partner's eyes light up!

Yield: 2 servings

Nutritional data per serving: Calories, 428; protein, 19 g; carbohydrate, 59 g; dietary fiber, 5 g; total fat, 13 g; saturated fat, 6 g; cholesterol, 25 mg; sodium, 231 mg; vitamin A, 12% of Daily Value; vitamin C, 10%; calcium, 16%; iron, 23%; vitamin B_1 (thiamin), 39%; vitamin B_2 (riboflavin), 44%; folate, 34%; potassium, 17%.

Taco Pasta Shells

Here's a quick dinner that will make you the talk of the town. And really, when you can sit down to dine after only 15 minutes of prep, why would you bother with fast food?

8 ounces small pasta shells
8 ounces shredded low-fat
     cheddar cheese
½ cup sliced black olives
1 jar (15 ounces) mild salsa
½ teaspoon dried cilantro

Bring 4 quarts water to a rolling boil in a large saucepan. Stir in the pasta. Reduce the heat to medium and cook for 9 minutes, or according to package directions. Drain and return to the warm pan. Add the cheese, olives, and salsa and stir until the cheese is melted. Divide among four serving dishes and garnish with the cilantro. Serve with your favorite bagged salad.

Yield: 4 servings

Nutritional data per serving: Calories, 379; protein, 24 g; carbohydrate, 41 g; dietary fiber, 4 g; total fat, 13 g; saturated fat, 7 g; cholesterol, 42 mg; sodium, 1,029 mg; vitamin A, 25% of Daily Value; vitamin C, 25%; calcium, 58%; iron, 18%; vitamin B$_1$ (thiamin), 19%; vitamin B$_2$ (riboflavin), 25%; vitamin B$_3$ (niacin), 14%; folate, 24%, copper, 25%.

DOUBLE DUTY

Each serving of this dish delivers a double portion of low-fat cheese, so you get half your protein and calcium for the day but just ⅓ of your saturated fat. It's a bone-building bargain!

Salmon Radiatore with Asiago Cheese Sauce

Salmon is so darned good for your heart that I'm always looking for tasty ways to entice my friends into eating it.

1 cup fat-free evaporated milk
1 tablespoon cornstarch
1/4 teaspoon dry mustard
1/2 teaspoon chicken bouillon granules
1 ounce shredded Asiago cheese
Freshly ground black pepper to taste
4 cups cooked radiatore pasta
8 ounces grilled salmon, flaked

DOUBLE DUTY

Catch salmon and you reel in a day's worth of omega-3 fatty acids, along with 1/3 of your day's quota of vitamin D.

In a medium saucepan over medium heat, combine the milk, cornstarch, mustard, and bouillon. With a wire whisk, stir until well blended. Cook, whisking constantly, until thickened and almost boiling. Add the cheese and whisk until smooth and creamy. Add the pepper and whisk again. Add the pasta and toss until well coated. Divide among four individual pasta bowls and top each with one-fourth of the salmon. Serve with a crisp salad and cold white wine.

Yield: 4 servings

Nutritional data per serving: Calories, 312; protein, 22 g; carbohydrate, 39 g; dietary fiber, 1.5 g; total fat, 7 g; saturated fat, 2 g; cholesterol, 40 mg; sodium, 232 mg; vitamin A, 8% of Daily Value; vitamin C, 1%; calcium, 21%; iron, 12%; vitamin B$_1$ (thiamin), 25%; vitamin B$_2$ (riboflavin), 30%; vitamin B$_3$ (niacin), 33%; vitamin B$_6$, 25%; vitamin D, 42%; folate, 24%; omega-3 fatty acids, 106%.

Stovetop Eggplant Parmesan

The classic version of this dish requires a ton of breading, frying, baking, and time! But you can do a delicious imitation right in your skillet—and in just a few minutes. Give it a try; you'll look like a genius!

1 medium onion, chopped
1 medium eggplant, cut lengthwise into eighths
   and thinly sliced
1 tablespoon olive oil
2 medium tomatoes, cut into chunks
1/4 teaspoon dried oregano
1/4 teaspoon salt
Freshly ground black pepper to taste
2 cups cooked spiral pasta
1 ounce freshly grated Parmesan cheese

In a large skillet over medium-high heat, sauté the onion and eggplant in the oil for about 5 minutes, or until softened. Stir in the tomatoes, oregano, salt, and pepper. Reduce the heat to medium, cover, and simmer for 5 to 10 minutes, or until the eggplant is cooked through. Divide the pasta between two bowls. Top each with half of the eggplant mixture and garnish with 1/2 ounce of the cheese. Serve with salad and crusty rolls.

Yield: 2 servings

Nutritional data per serving: Calories, 422; protein, 17 g; carbohydrate, 64 g; dietary fiber, 11 g; total fat, 13 g; saturated fat, 3 g; cholesterol, 10 mg; sodium, 568 mg; vitamin A, 10% of Daily Value; vitamin C, 51%; calcium, 25%; iron, 19%; vitamin B_1 (thiamin), 34%; vitamin B_3 (niacin), 24%; vitamin B_6, 21%; folate, 43%; potassium, 28%.

Gouda Mac

My mother used to bone me up on calcium by feeding me mac and cheese. What could be more soothing, more comforting, or more loving than a creamy bowlful? Try this easy, tempting, gourmet version.

8 ounces elbow macaroni
1 tablespoon flour
1 cup fat-free evaporated milk
4 ounces freshly shredded smoked Gouda cheese

Bring a medium saucepan of water to a boil. Add the macaroni and cook according to package directions. Drain and return to the warm pan. Cover and set aside.

Meanwhile, in a small dish, combine the flour and 1 to 2 teaspoons of the milk. Stir until dissolved. Add another tablespoon or two of the milk and stir. Pour the remaining milk into a nonstick saucepan and use a wire whisk to stir in the flour mixture. Cook, stirring, over medium heat until very warm. Add the cheese a little at a time, stirring until melted. Cook, stirring, until the sauce is thick and very hot, but not boiling. Carefully add the macaroni and stir until well blended. Serve piping hot with a crisp green salad for a complete meal.

Yield: 4 servings

Nutritional data per serving: Calories, 368; protein, 19 g; carbohydrate, 52 g; dietary fiber, 1 g; total fat, 9 g; saturated fat, 5 g; cholesterol, 35 mg; sodium, 310 mg; vitamin A, 12% of Daily Value; vitamin C, 1%; calcium, 39%; iron, 14%; vitamin B_1 (thiamin), 42%; vitamin B_2 (riboflavin), 33%; vitamin D, 13%; folate, 36%; potassium, 10%.

Twice-Baked Sweet Potatoes

Instead of burying your sweet potato in butter, says registered dietitian Ann Dubner, try this creamy treat and get a calcium boost instead. Her daughters love it!

2 medium sweet potatoes
**¹/₂ cup reduced-fat ricotta
    cheese**
Ground cinnamon to taste

Scrub the potatoes well. On a microwave-safe plate, microwave on high, turning once, for 12 to 15 minutes (depending on the size of the potatoes and the power of your oven). Carefully split lengthwise and scoop out the insides, being careful not to tear the skins. Reserve the skins. In a food processor, combine the potatoes and ricotta. Process until smooth and fluffy. Pile the filling into the skins, dust with the cinnamon, and microwave for 5 minutes, or until heated through.

Yield: 2 servings

SUPER SUB

You could use cottage cheese in this recipe, but reduced-fat ricotta delivers 3 times the calcium.

Nutritional data per serving: Calories, 181; protein, 9 g; carbohydrate, 26 g; dietary fiber, 3 g; total fat, 5 g; saturated fat, 3 g; cholesterol, 19 mg; sodium, 86 mg; vitamin A, 138% of Daily Value; vitamin C, 28%; calcium, 19%; iron, 10%; copper, 14%; potassium, 11%.

Mashed Potatoes with Sour Cream and Chives

Long before anyone worried about osteoporosis, my mother taught me this trick for creating high-calcium mashed potatoes that are vitamin-packed. They're so creamy, who cares if they're good for you!

2 pounds red-skin potatoes, scrubbed
    and cubed
2/3 cup nonfat dry milk
1/2 teaspoon salt
Dash of ground white pepper
1 tablespoon butter
1/4 cup reduced-fat sour cream
2 tablespoons minced fresh chives

> **The Inside Skinny:**
> You recapture the vitamins that escaped into the cooking water by using the water with nonfat dry milk to mash the potatoes.

In a medium saucepan with just enough water to cover, bring the potatoes to a boil. Reduce the heat to medium and cook for 10 to 15 minutes, or until the potatoes are easily pierced with a fork. Drain, reserving 1 cup of the cooking water. In a large bowl, sprinkle the potatoes with the dry milk, salt, and pepper. Use an electric mixer to beat until lump-free. Add the butter, sour cream, and 1/2 cup of the reserved cooking water. Beat until creamy. Continue adding water and beating until the potatoes reach the desired consistency. Fold in the chives and serve piping hot.

Yield: 6 servings

Nutritional data per serving: Calories, 179; protein, 6 g; carbohydrate, 32 g; dietary fiber, 2 g; total fat, 3 g; saturated fat, 2 g; cholesterol, 11 mg; sodium, 270 mg; vitamin A, 9% of Daily Value; vitamin C, 95%; calcium, 13%; iron, 7%; vitamin B$_6$, 21%; copper, 20%; potassium, 26%.

Zucchini with Three Cheeses

Cheese brings out the best in so many vegetables. Combining the flavors turns ho-hum zucchini into a dinnertime star!

1 cup coarsely chopped yellow onions
2 cups thinly sliced baby zucchini
2 teaspoons olive oil
1 clove garlic, minced
$1/4$ cup slivered fresh basil
$1/4$ teaspoon salt
Freshly ground pepper mélange to taste
1 tablespoon grated Romano cheese
1 tablespoon grated Parmesan cheese
$1/2$ cup shredded reduced-fat mozzarella cheese

In a large skillet over medium-high heat, sauté the onions and zucchini in the oil until beginning to brown. Add the garlic, basil, salt, and pepper. Reduce the heat and cook, stirring, for about 5 minutes, or until the zucchini are cooked through. Sprinkle the Romano, Parmesan, and mozzarella evenly over the vegetables, ending with the mozzarella. Cover and remove from the heat. Let stand for 2 minutes, or until the mozzarella is melted. Serve hot with Boca Italian sausage or grilled chicken.

Yield: 4 servings

Nutritional data per serving: Calories, 95; protein, 6 g; carbohydrate, 6 g; dietary fiber, 2 g; total fat, 6 g; saturated fat, 2 g; cholesterol, 11 mg; sodium, 263 mg; vitamin A, 6% of Daily Value; vitamin C, 15%; calcium, 15%; iron, 3%; folate, 6%; potassium, 7%.

Cheddar Cheese Sauce

Lots of the healthiest veggies, such as broccoli, brussels sprouts, and spinach, taste kind of bitter to me. But, to borrow an idea from Mary Poppins, a spoonful of cheese sauce makes the vegetables go down—in the most delightful way! This sauce provides calcium (a quarter of your day's supply) without clogging your arteries.

1 cup fat-free evaporated milk
1 tablespoon cornstarch
1/4 teaspoon dry mustard
1/2 teaspoon chicken bouillon granules
1 ounce shredded cheddar cheese
Freshly ground black pepper to taste

In a medium saucepan over medium heat, combine the milk, cornstarch, mustard, and bouillon. Use a wire whisk to stir until well blended. Cook, whisking constantly, until the sauce is thickened and almost boiling. Add the cheese and whisk until smooth and creamy. Add the pepper and whisk again. Serve over your favorite vegetables.

Yield: 4 servings

Nutritional data per serving: Calories, 89; protein, 7 g; carbohydrate, 9 g; dietary fiber, 0 g; total fat, 3 g; saturated fat, 2 g; cholesterol, 10 mg; sodium, 257 mg; vitamin A, 10% of Daily Value; vitamin C, 1%; calcium, 24%; iron, 1%; vitamin B$_2$ (riboflavin), 13%; vitamin D, 13%; potassium, 6%.

"Skookie"

Nothing is better than cookies and milk, unless you're not a big fan of milk. Here's my dad's secret recipe for the drink that fooled me into drinking milk and helped make my bones what they are today.

 1 cup 2% milk
 1 teaspoon vanilla extract
 1 teaspoon sugar

Pour the milk into a small glass. Add the vanilla and sugar and stir until the sugar is dissolved. Serve with Fig Newtons for a special taste treat.

Yield: 1 serving

Nutritional data per serving: Calories, 270; protein, 10 g; carbohydrate, 36 g; dietary fiber, 2 g; total fat, 8 g; saturated fat, 4 g; cholesterol, 18 mg; sodium, 242 mg; vitamin A, 14% of Daily Value; vitamin C, 4%; calcium, 30%; iron, 5%; vitamin B$_2$ (riboflavin), 24%; vitamin D, 24%; potassium, 13%.

1 CUP

SUPER SUB

Still too "plain vanilla" for you? Stir in chocolate syrup instead of vanilla and sugar. No one can resist that!

Banana-Coconut Shake

I'm the envy of all my friends because I own a hammock. Once in a while, I even have time to lie in it! When I do, I whirl up this special drink to celebrate the occasion. It's a slightly exotic treat.

2/3 cup light coconut milk
1 very ripe banana
1 cup Edy's fat-free vanilla frozen
    yogurt
1 large strawberry

In a blender, combine the coconut milk and banana. Blend on high until smooth. Add the frozen yogurt and blend until thick and creamy. Pour into a tall glass and garnish with the strawberry. Drink until you get a coconut-milk mustache.

Yield: 1 serving

Nutritional data per serving: Calories, 379; protein, 9 g; carbohydrate, 72 g; dietary fiber, 3 g; total fat, 8 g; saturated fat, 5 g; cholesterol, 0 mg; sodium, 91 mg; vitamin A, 1% of Daily Value; vitamin C, 18%; calcium, 61%; iron, 6%; vitamin B_6, 34%; folate, 6%; potassium, 13%.

SUPER SUB

Coconut is one of the few plant foods that contain saturated fat. Using light coconut milk cuts total fat and saturated fat by 23 grams!

Apricot Sunset

If the sun has gone over the yardarm and you'd rather drink your dinner than eat it, get out your blender and create this nutrition-packed smoothie.

1 cup Stonyfield fat-free apricot-mango yogurt
4 apricots, washed, halved, and pitted
6 large pecan halves, toasted
1/2 teaspoon vanilla extract
Dash of ground cinnamon

In a blender, combine the yogurt, apricots, pecans, vanilla, and cinnamon. Blend on high until thick and creamy. Pour into a coconut shell (or a tall glass) and sip your cares away.

Yield: 1 serving

Nutritional data per serving: Calories, 313; protein, 11 g; carbohydrate, 48 g; dietary fiber, 4 g; total fat, 9 g; saturated fat, <1 g; cholesterol, 0 mg; sodium, 127 mg; vitamin A, 37% of Daily Value; vitamin C, 30%; calcium, 47%; iron, 8%; vitamin E, 8%; potassium, 13%.

> **QUICK TRICK:** Apricots out of season? Use dried apricots instead. Add 1 to 2 tablespoons water if the mixture is too thick.

Strawberry-Thyme Smoothie

Summer is definitely the time to wallow in fresh strawberries. When you've had your fill of plain, luscious berries, whirl a few into this cold and creamy treat.

1 cup Stonyfield fat-free strawberry yogurt
1 cup sliced fresh strawberries
1/4 teaspoon dried thyme
1 whole strawberry

In a blender, combine the yogurt, sliced strawberries, and thyme. Blend on high until smooth and creamy. Pour into a tall glass and garnish with the whole strawberry. Have a sip of strawberry heaven.

Yield: 1 serving

Nutritional data per serving: Calories, 211; protein, 9 g; carbohydrate, 43 g; dietary fiber, 4 g; total fat, <1 g; saturated fat, 0 g; cholesterol, 0 mg; sodium, 127 mg; vitamin A, 1% of Daily Value; vitamin C, 164%; calcium, 48%; iron, 7%; vitamin K, 29%; potassium, 8%.

> **QUICK TRICK:** Put the yogurt in a bowl and pile the strawberries on top for a refreshing snack or light lunch.

Cherry-Chocolate Hazelnut Cup

A friend recently introduced me to Nutella, the European equivalent of chocolate peanut butter. Since Europeans are big on hazelnuts, not peanuts, here's this jar full of chocolatey, nutty stuff that will drive you insane no matter what you spread it on. Here's something to put it in.

1 tablespoon chocolate-hazelnut spread
1/2 cup fat-free vanilla yogurt
2 tablespoons frozen dark sweet cherries, thawed

In a small microwave-safe dish, microwave the spread on high for 15 to 30 seconds, or until melted. Place the yogurt in a medium dessert dish. Stir in the melted spread until well blended. Top with the cherries. Find a quiet corner so you can savor every spoonful.

Yield: 1 serving

Nutritional data per serving: Calories, 213; protein, 8 g; carbohydrate, 32 g; dietary fiber, <1 g; total fat, 7 g; saturated fat, 2 g; cholesterol, 4 mg; sodium, 85 mg; vitamin A, 1% of Daily Value; vitamin C, 2%; calcium, 25%; iron, 3%; vitamin B$_2$ (riboflavin), 14%.

SUPER SUB

Hazelnuts treat you to twice as much heart-healthy monounsaturated fat, vitamin E, calcium, copper, and iron as peanuts.

1 CUP

Honey-Stuffed Figs

I no longer end a meal with a thick slab of cheesecake or a big bowl of ice cream, the way I once did. But I still like a little something sweet to let my tummy know I'm finished eating. This luscious treat fills the bill.

3 tablespoons reduced-fat ricotta cheese
1½ teaspoons clover honey
8 large black mission figs
4 leaves butterhead lettuce
Freshly ground nutmeg to taste

In a small bowl, combine the ricotta and honey and stir well. Wash the figs and pat dry. With a sharp knife, slice each fig nearly in half from stem to blossom end, revealing the interior but leaving the halves attached. Top each fig with a heaping teaspoon of the cheese mixture. Place a lettuce leaf on each of four small plates and top each with two filled figs. Dust with the nutmeg.

Yield: 4 servings

Nutritional data per serving: Calories, 120; protein, 2 g; carbohydrate, 28 g; dietary fiber, 4 g; total fat, 1 g; saturated fat, <1 g; cholesterol, 4 mg; vitamin A, 4% of Daily Value; vitamin C, 5%; calcium, 8%; iron, 3%; vitamin B6, 8%; vitamin E, 6%; potassium, 9%.

Lovely Leftovers The honey-cheese mixture is outrageously good on whole wheat toast for breakfast.

Fresh Strawberries and Frozen Yogurt

I remember picking fresh strawberries with my kids when they were little. We sort of got going and couldn't stop, so we ended up with more fresh berries than we knew what to do with! But those berries were so sweet, we mostly just ate them plain or with a little frozen yogurt.

2 cups mashed fresh strawberries
2 cups Edy's Grand Light vanilla
    frozen yogurt*
2 cups sliced fresh strawberries
2 tablespoons chopped walnuts

Divide the mashed strawberries evenly among four small dessert dishes. Top each with 1/2 cup of the yogurt, then 1/2 cup of the sliced strawberries. Sprinkle with the walnuts.

Yield: 4 servings

Nutritional data per serving: Calories, 180; protein, 7 g; carbohydrate, 33 g; dietary fiber, 5 g; total fat, 3 g; saturated fat, 0 g; cholesterol, 2 mg; sodium, 66 mg; vitamin A, 1% of Daily Value; vitamin C, 189%; calcium, 33%; iron, 5%; vitamin B$_2$ (riboflavin), 20%; folate, 12%; magnesium, 10%; potassium, 16%; omega-3 fatty acids, 50%.

*Edy's packs more calcium than any other brand.

> **QUICK TRICK:** In winter, use 4 cups individually frozen whole strawberries. Whirl in the blender for instant strawberry sauce.

CHAPTER 7

OUTWIT CANCER

BECOME A CABBAGE PATCH KID

My friend Phyllis McShane is the only person I've ever met who knows what kohlrabi are, and she had an absolute *crush* on them. One summer, she even grew them in her tiny Baltimore backyard garden. She was cool with kohlrabi because those mild-tasting little bulbs with all the funny stems look so amusing—she said they looked like something drinking at that bar in *Star Wars!*

But for Phyllis, kohlrabi's real draw was their membership in the cabbage, a.k.a. cruciferous, family of vegetables. At the time, Phyllis was the top dietitian at the cancer unit at Johns Hopkins University Hospital, so she—of all people—knew that an ounce of prevention was worth a pound of cure. It's long been known, you

185

see, that folks who eat the most cabbage (and its relatives) have the lowest rates of many kinds of cancer.

The cruciferous family is large, offering lots of choices besides the comical kohlrabi. There's everybody's favorite, broccoli (okay, everybody except George Bush, the elder), as well as broccoli sprouts (great in sandwiches and salads), Chinese bok choy (super for stir-fries), the much-maligned brussels sprout (better than you think), cabbage itself (what's a picnic without coleslaw?), creamy white cauliflower (my husband, Ted's, favorite vegetable), kale (my personal top pick), collard and mustard greens (real down-home flavor), rutabaga and turnips (the secret to great stews), and lovely little watercress.

Hmmm…the list of crucifers is long, but let's face it, they're not at the top of Americans' hit parade. But that's okay. Past is past. We're grownups now, and we're discovering the joys of expanding our palates. With clever cooking, saucing, and tossing, we're learning to savor the flavors that grow healthy bodies as well as make our taste buds happy.

So, with a few tricks of the trade, you can learn to love a few more cabbages and cash in on their secret cancer-fighting ingredients. They're packed with flavonoids, organosulfides, coumarins, and terpenes that protect your cells against cancer-causing agents. And there's a

Think Fresh Is Always Best?

Think again. You'll get more lycopene from tomatoes when you eat them cooked—as in pizza sauce, pasta sauce, stewed tomatoes, or even ketchup! When you put fresh tomatoes on your sandwich or salad, skip the fat-free dressing and go for a little olive oil or other healthy fat for better lycopene absorption.

bonus: They also defend against heart disease. Now that's a double bang for your buck!

But, ladies, if you're committed to food for cancer protection and can't get your man to go for the green, help him see red. Offer him a piece of pizza, a bowlful of pasta with marinara sauce, or a slice of juicy red watermelon. Both tomatoes and watermelon are packed with lycopene, the food component most likely to fend off prostate cancer.

Then, when you both need a little coddling, indulge in a pot of tea. Whether you choose green or black, iced or hot, you'll get a hefty dose of cancer-fighting flavonols. Ahhhhh…life is good!

Cancer, of course, is pretty tricky, and outsmarting it gets easier if you follow the advice of the American Institute for Cancer Research. Here's what they recommend.

♥ **Section your dinner plate into thirds.** Pile two-thirds with vegetables and fruit (see chapters 2, 8, 9, 10, 12, and 14 for loads of lovely ideas), whole grains (stride to chapter 5), and beans (run to chapter 1). Save just one-third of your plate for fish (hook up with chapter 3), poultry, or lean meat (have fun with chapter 1).

♥ **Stay trim.** Maintain a healthy weight.

♥ **Get physical.** Take a brisk 30-minute walk every day.

♥ **Skip happy hour.** Drink alcohol only in moderation, if at all.

♥ **Eat less salt and fat.** Preparing foods low in salt and fat is easy to do with this book full of recipes!

So let's get started. I just poured myself a cup of tea. Want to join me? While we're sipping our cares away, we'll find the perfect veggie for tonight's dinner.

Elegant Pickled Veggie Tray

Tired of run-of-the-mill veggie trays? For your next party, try these spicy sweet pickles that add a bit of style to healthy eating.

1 jar (12 ounces) Hogue Farms pickled asparagus, drained
1 jar (12 ounces) Hogue Farms pickled crunchy
    carrot sticks, drained
1 jar (12 ounces) Hogue Farms pickled bell
    peppers, drained
1/4 cup low-fat mayonnaise
1 clove garlic, minced
1/2 teaspoon dried dillweed
Freshly ground black pepper to taste

Arrange the asparagus, carrots, and bell peppers on a serving platter, leaving a space in the center. In a small serving bowl, stir together the mayonnaise, garlic, dill, and black pepper. Place in the center of the tray for dipping.

Yield: 18 servings

Nutritional data per serving: Calories, 28; protein, 0 g; carbohydrate, 5 g; dietary fiber, 0 g; total fat, 0 g; saturated fat, 0 g; cholesterol, 0 mg; sodium, 27 mg; vitamin A, 21% of Daily Value; vitamin C, 10%; calcium, 0%; iron, 1%.

Lovely Leftovers

These low-sodium pickled veggies add a spicy crunch to lunch. Keep them handy!

Gotta-Love-It Salsa

My friend Judy Renie served up this fruity salsa for post-tennis refreshment, and our whole team called it a smash! It's oh, so summery and refreshing. Healthy, too, when scooped up with baked tortilla chips.

1 cup cilantro-flavored salsa
1 cup diced fresh peaches
2/3 cup diced fresh pineapple
Juice of 1 lime

In a medium bowl, combine the salsa, peaches, pineapple, and lime juice. Mix well. Refrigerate before serving.

Yield: 16 servings

Nutritional data per serving: Calories, 13; protein, 0 g; carbohydrate, 3 g; dietary fiber, <1 g; total fat, 0 g; saturated fat, 0 g; cholesterol, 0 mg; sodium, 48 mg; vitamin A, 1% of Daily Value; vitamin C, 5%; calcium, 0%; iron, 1%.

QUICK TRICK: Combine the salsa with canned, juice-packed peaches and pineapple.

Bev's Hot Summer Salsa

Bev has been my manicurist practically forever. (Yes, someone who cooks and types all day needs a manicure!) We've dished a lot of dirt and traded some great recipes. Bev likes her salsa hot, but you can turn down the heat, she says, by cutting back on the jalapeños.

4 cups diced tomatoes
1 small jalapeño chile pepper, diced
1 medium onion, diced
$^1/_2$ cup chopped fresh cilantro
$^1/_4$ teaspoon salt
Freshly ground black pepper to taste

In a large bowl, combine the tomatoes, jalapeño pepper, onion, cilantro, salt, and black pepper. This salsa is best, Bev says, if you refrigerate it overnight to blend the flavors, but you can eat it right away if you're in a hurry. Serve with baked tortilla chips or as a sauce over chicken or fish.

Yield: 32 servings

Nutritional data per serving: Calories, 6; protein, 0 g; carbohydrate, 1 g; dietary fiber, <1 g; total fat, 0 g; saturated fat, 0 g; cholesterol, 0 mg; sodium, 20 mg; vitamin A, 1% of Daily Value; vitamin C, 9%; calcium, 0%; iron, 1%.

QUICK TRICK: When winter comes and the fresh summer tomatoes go, substitute a 28-ounce can diced tomatoes and 2 tablespoons diced canned jalapeño chile peppers for fresh.

Tomato Bread Soup

Reportedly, Tuscan peasants make this soup to use up stale bread. It's my method for cleaning out the refrigerator. (No pink mold included!) I toss in onion bits left over from cooking other dishes, the outer celery ribs that I don't usually fill with peanut butter because their taste is too strong, and an assortment of stale bread ends—the grainier, the better. The ingredients are a bit haphazard, but the soup is amazingly delicious!

1 medium onion, diced
2 ribs celery, thinly sliced
2 tablespoons olive oil
2 cloves garlic, minced or pressed
1 can (28 ounces) crushed tomatoes
3 cups water
2 cups cubed stale bread
1 teaspoon dried basil
Freshly ground black pepper to taste

DOUBLE DUTY

While the olive oil is busy helping you absorb the lycopene from the tomatoes, it also creates a lovely, rich flavor.

In a large, heavy saucepan over medium-high heat, sauté the onion and celery in the oil for about 5 minutes, or just until wilted. Add the garlic and cook for 1 minute. Add the tomatoes and water and simmer for about 20 minutes, or until the vegetables are soft. Stir in the bread, basil, and pepper and cook for 5 minutes, until the bread is soft. Serve piping hot or at room temperature.

Yield: 6 servings

Nutritional data per serving: Calories, 130; protein, 4 g; carbohydrate, 21 g; dietary fiber, 6 g; total fat, 5 g; saturated fat, <1 g; cholesterol, 0 mg; sodium, 232 mg; vitamin A, 10% of Daily Value; vitamin C, 26%; calcium, 12%; iron, 14%; vitamin B$_6$, 22%; vitamin E, 7%; folate, 11%; magnesium, 13%; potassium, 14%; zinc, 11%.

Village Salad

Sometimes, the tomatoes are so ripe and flavorful that you want to keep the focus on them. In this recipe, a few simple ingredients make plum tomatoes the stars of the show.

6 very ripe Roma (plum) tomatoes, cut into rounds
1 pickling cucumber, cut into thin rounds
1 small red onion, thinly sliced
2 tablespoons light Caesar dressing
1 ounce feta cheese

In a medium bowl, combine the tomatoes, cucumber, onion, and dressing. Toss until well coated. Divide between two small salad bowls and crumble ½ ounce of feta over each.

Yield: 2 servings

Nutritional data per serving: Calories, 135; protein, 5 g; carbohydrate, 16 g; dietary fiber, 3 g; total fat, 7 g; saturated fat, 2 g; cholesterol, 13 mg; sodium, 476 mg; vitamin A, 15% of Daily Value; vitamin C, 69%; calcium, 10%; iron, 7%; potassium, 17%.

DOUBLE DUTY

The fat in the salad dressing helps your heart and arteries work better to fend off heart disease. It also helps you absorb more of the cancer-fighting lycopene from the tomatoes.

Guiseppi's Favorite Salad

On a hot August evening, I served this salad to my brother-in-law Joe Bucci, and he paid me his highest compliment. "It looks so Italian!" he said. Then he asked for just a little olive oil to drizzle over the top. Mamma mia!

8 thick slices large tomatoes
8 large leaves fresh basil
2 ounces freshly shaved
    Parmesan cheese
2 tablespoons toasted pine nuts

Place two slices of tomato on each of four small salad plates and top each slice with a basil leaf. Garnish with the cheese and pine nuts. Serve with cruets of olive oil and balsamic vinegar.

Yield: 4 servings

Nutritional data per serving: Calories, 78; protein, 4 g; carbohydrate, 5 g; dietary fiber, 1 g; total fat, 5 g; saturated fat, 2 g; cholesterol, 13 mg; sodium, 166 mg; vitamin A, 7% of Daily Value; vitamin C, 35%; calcium, 8%; iron, 5%; vitamin B_2 (riboflavin), 10%; folate, 5%; magnesium, 6%; potassium, 6%.

 The P·E·R·F·E·C·T Companion

For a cooling summer treat and a big jolt of vitamin C, mix your iced tea half and half with passionfruit juice.

Apple and Orange Kohl Slaw

You can turn almost any cabbagey vegetable into "cole" slaw. This time, let's do it with kohlrabi!

2 cups shredded peeled kohlrabi
2 cups shredded peeled Fuji apples
¼ cup orange juice
1 tablespoon walnut oil
¼ cup orange-flavored dried cranberries
2 tablespoons coarsely broken walnuts
¼ teaspoon salt
Freshly ground black pepper to taste

In a medium bowl, combine the kohlrabi, apples, and orange juice. Stir well to blend and keep the apples from turning brown. Add the oil, cranberries, walnuts, salt, and pepper. Refrigerate until ready to serve.

Yield: 6 servings

Nutritional data per serving: Calories, 95; protein, 1 g; carbohydrate, 15 g; dietary fiber, 4 g; total fat, 4 g; saturated fat, 0 g; cholesterol, 0 mg; sodium, 106 mg; vitamin A, 1% of Daily Value; vitamin C, 55%; calcium, 1%; iron, 2%; copper, 5%; potassium, 7%; omega-3 fatty acids, 48%.

Lovely Leftovers Pile extra slaw on shredded romaine lettuce for an instant fruity salad!

Orzo and Chunky Vegetable Salad

My daughter Bobbi made this salad for a bunch of guys who were having a meeting at her house. They seemed to think that salad is a more macho dish without lettuce. Whatever it takes…

2 medium cucumbers, peeled and cut into chunks
1 large green bell pepper, cut into chunks
1 cup grape tomatoes
1 medium yellow squash, cut into chunks
1 cup cooked orzo
4 ounces crumbled feta cheese
1/2 teaspoon dried oregano
1/2 cup Ken's light Caesar dressing

In a large bowl, combine the cucumbers, pepper, tomatoes, squash, orzo, feta, and oregano. Drizzle with the dressing and toss gently until coated.

Yield: 8 servings

Nutritional data per serving: Calories, 120; protein, 4 g; carbohydrate, 12 g; dietary fiber, 2 g; total fat, 6 g; saturated fat, 2 g; cholesterol, 13 mg; sodium, 462 mg; vitamin A, 5% of Daily Value; vitamin C, 46%; calcium, 9%; iron, 4%; vitamin B_2 (riboflavin), 10%; folate, 9%; potassium, 7%; omega-3 fatty acids, 6%.

Lovely Leftovers

Actually, make "planned-overs," and pack the extra for lunch the next day.

Turnip-Potato Salad

You can sneak turnips into potato dishes in lots of great ways. Here, they fairly vanish in this colorful veggie jumble.

1 pound turnips, peeled and diced
1 pound red-skin potatoes, scrubbed and diced
1 cup chopped red bell peppers
1 cup chopped green bell peppers
1 cup chopped yellow squash
2 tablespoons sunflower seeds
1/4 cup light Catalina dressing

In a 4-quart saucepan with enough water to cover, bring the turnips and potatoes to a boil. Cook for 5 to 10 minutes, or until tender. Drain and cool. In a large bowl, combine the potatoes, turnips, red and green peppers, squash, and sunflower seeds. Add the dressing and toss until well blended.

Yield: 12 servings

Nutritional data per serving: Calories, 70; protein, 2 g; carbohydrate, 13 g; dietary fiber, 2 g; total fat, 1 g; saturated fat, 0 g; cholesterol, 0 mg; sodium, 177 g; vitamin A, 10% of Daily Value; vitamin C, 72%; vitamin E, 4%; calcium, 2%; iron, 2%; folate, 4%; potassium, 7%.

QUICK TRICK: Let kids use a celery "shovel" to eat their salad. It will disappear in no time at all!

Italian Broccoli Slaw

Tired of slaws laden with mayonnaisey calories? Pump up the volume of this broccoli-based slaw by piling on the fresh basil and oregano.

1 package (12 ounces) Mann's broccoli coleslaw
1/2 cup slivered fresh basil
1/4 cup chopped fresh oregano
1/2 cup chopped onions
1/4 cup chopped celery
1/4 cup Ken's light Caesar
**   dressing**

In a large bowl, combine the coleslaw, basil, oregano, onions, celery, and dressing. Toss until well coated.

Yield: 4 servings

Nutritional data per serving: Calories, 44; protein, 2 g; carbohydrate, 8 g; dietary fiber, 4 g; total fat, <1 g; saturated fat, 0 g; cholesterol, 0 mg; sodium, 113 mg; vitamin A, 3% of Daily Value; vitamin C, 118%; calcium, 7%; iron, 5%; folate, 15%; potassium, 10%.

Lovely Leftovers

Pile extra slaw on sandwiches for a tasty change from lettuce and tomato.

Sloppy Chicken

Many people I counsel tell me they don't cook—and they mean it! They just want to come home and eat. This meal is about as simple as it gets, especially if you use the new packaged chopped cooked white-meat chicken. It's easy for kids to make, too.

4 hamburger buns
8 ounces chopped cooked chicken breast
1 can (14¹⁄₂ ounces) sloppy Joe sauce
4 leaves romaine lettuce

Place each bun on a paper plate. Top each with 2 ounces of the chicken, then one-fourth of the sauce. Microwave each sandwich on high for 1 to 2 minutes, or until warm. Top each with a lettuce leaf. Close cover before munching. Pour a glass of milk for each person. Finish with an apple—it keeps the doctor away!

Yield: 4 servings

SUPER SUB

When you replace iceberg lettuce with romaine, you'll get 8 times the vitamin A, 6 times the vitamin C, and double the folate and potassium!

Nutritional data per serving: Calories, 509; protein, 35 g; carbohydrate, 83 g; dietary fiber, 11 g; total fat, 5 g; saturated fat, 1 g; cholesterol, 53 mg; sodium, 1,460 mg; vitamin A, 57% of Daily Value; vitamin C, 15%; calcium, 37%; iron, 24%; vitamin B₃ (niacin), 49%; vitamin B₆, 23%; folate, 15%; potassium, 23%; zinc, 12%.

Tomato-Ricotta Potato

Nothing makes me happier than a piping hot baked potato stuffed with good things. Here's what I had for lunch today.

1 medium russet potato, scrubbed
¼ cup Hunt's diced tomatoes with
  green peppers and onions
¼ cup low-fat ricotta cheese
Salt and freshly ground black
  pepper to taste

Pierce the potato and microwave on high for 10 minutes. Turn and cook for 5 minutes, or until soft.

Meanwhile, in a small bowl, combine the tomatoes and ricotta. Stir until well blended. Set aside.

Place the potato on a plate. Cut a cross in the top, then squeeze the sides to open. Spread with the tomato-ricotta mixture and season with the salt and pepper.

Yield: 1 serving

Nutritional data per serving: Calories, 223; protein, 9 g; carbohydrate, 38 g; dietary fiber, 4 g; total fat, 3 g; saturated fat, 1.5 g; cholesterol, 15 mg; sodium, 295 mg; vitamin A, 9% of Daily Value; vitamin C, 34%; calcium, 22%; iron, 10%; vitamin B$_6$, 21%; copper, 19%; potassium, 15%.

SUPER SUB

Replacing sour cream with ricotta cheese triples the calcium and cuts fat dramatically.

Grilled Samburger on a Bun

1 cup instant or old-fashioned oats
12 ounces flaked cooked salmon
1 large egg
$\frac{1}{2}$ cup chopped fresh chives
$\frac{1}{2}$ cup chopped fresh basil
$\frac{1}{2}$ teaspoon salt
Freshly ground black pepper to taste
4 hamburger buns
4 leaves romaine lettuce
4 thick slices tomato
4 slices red onion

> **The Inside Skinny:**
> Choose the darkest lettuce and the meatiest tomato for maximum cancer-fighting power.

Place the oats in a blender and blend on high to make oat flour. Measure $\frac{1}{2}$ cup into a large bowl, reserving the rest for another use. Add the salmon, egg, chives, basil, salt, and pepper. Stir with a fork until blended. Form into four patties and mist both sides with olive oil spray. Refrigerate to cook later, or head straight for the grill. Grill over medium-high heat for about 5 minutes on each side, or until cooked through and brown. Nestle each burger on a roll, then top with a lettuce leaf, a tomato slice, and an onion slice. Add condiments of your choice.

Yield: 4 servings

Nutritional data per serving: Calories, 367; protein, 31 g; carbohydrate, 35 g; dietary fiber, 3 g; total fat, 12 g; saturated fat, 3 g; cholesterol, 114 mg; sodium, 590 mg; vitamin A, 12% of Daily Value; vitamin C, 27%; calcium, 8%; iron, 19%; vitamin B_1 (thiamin), 38%; vitamin B_2 (riboflavin), 39%; vitamin B_3 (niacin), 53%; vitamin B_6, 46%; folate, 27%; potassium, 22%; omega-3 fatty acids, 191%.

Lemon-Tuna Tomatoes

Kick off your shoes, slip into your baggy shorts, and take advantage of this refreshing, best-of-summer treat.

1 tuna steak (5 ounces)
1/8 teaspoon garlic powder
1/8 teaspoon Old Bay seafood seasoning
2 tablespoons light canola oil mayonnaise
1/2 teaspoon grated lemon peel
2 leaves fresh basil, finely slivered
1/8 teaspoon salt
Freshly ground black pepper to taste
2 large leaves red lettuce
4 large thick slices tomato

Mist one side of the tuna with olive oil spray, then sprinkle with half of the garlic powder and seafood seasoning. Grill, seasoned side up, over medium-high heat for 5 minutes, or until cooked halfway through. Turn, top with the remaining garlic powder and seafood seasoning, and cook for 5 minutes. Place in a medium bowl and flake with a fork. Stir in the mayonnaise, lemon peel, basil, salt, and pepper. Refrigerate until chilled. On each of two plates, arrange a lettuce leaf, then two tomato slices side by side. Spread one-fourth of the tuna on each. Serve with corn on the cob.

Yield: 2 servings

Nutritional data per serving: Calories: 136; protein, 18 g; carbohydrate, 6 g; dietary fiber, 1.5 g; total fat, 4 g; saturated fat, 0 g; cholesterol, 33 mg; sodium, 122 mg; vitamin A, 13% of Daily Value; vitamin C, 39%; calcium, 3%; iron, 5%; vitamin B$_3$ (niacin), 36%; vitamin B$_6$, 33%; potassium, 17%; omega-3 fatty acids, 17%.

The Sandwich Board

Have you ever thought of a sandwich as a health food? Many people don't! That's not surprising, really, if they're thinking about greasy fried chicken patties or double-stacked burgers on cottony buns. But with the right fixings, you can have healthy meals in minutes—without cooking! Just follow these easy guidelines.

1. Start with whole grain breads to get fiber, folate, and phytochemicals that fend off cancer, heart disease, and diabetes. Read the label on the wrapper to make sure the first ingredient is something "whole." Check out whole wheat, multigrain, rye, and pumpernickel. And don't forget pita pockets, corn or whole wheat tortillas, and multigrain English muffins.

2. Fill your sandwich with 2 to 3 ounces of low-fat protein to build muscle, bone, and your immune system. Lean roast beef, ham, turkey, chicken, tuna or other fish, shrimp, beans, tofu, or veggie patties all do nicely.

3. Add a slice of cheese to build bones, cut body fat, and control blood pressure. Reduced-fat is good, but even regular, full-fat cheese is okay as long as you have just one slice and the rest of your diet is low in saturated fat. Swiss, mozzarella, American, cheddar, Jack, you name it—they all count.

4. Pile on the veggies for antioxidant vitamins and fiber that protect everything from your memory and your eyesight to the way your bowels work. Try dark green lettuce, tomatoes, peppers, zucchini, yellow squash, onions, and eggplant. If you can slice it, you can stack it on a sandwich.

5. Kiss it with some healthy fat to help your heart and absorb more carotenes from the veggies. Try canola oil mayo, avocado, sliced olives, nuts or sunflower seeds, Garlic Aioli (page 320), olive oil, peanut butter or other nut butters, or flavored oils.

6. Zap it with herbs or spice to intensify flavors. Try hot and sweet mustard, horseradish, ketchup, chopped chile peppers, garlic from a jar, oregano, dill, or basil.

Sound good? Let's apply those six rules to achieve super sandwiches. Here's our sandwich board.

The Turkey Trot: Pumpernickel bread, turkey breast, Muenster cheese, romaine lettuce, sliced tomato, canola oil mayo, and a pinch of dill and freshly ground black pepper.

California Dreamin': Whole wheat bread, white albacore tuna, mozzarella cheese, green leaf lettuce, yellow tomato and red onion slices, mashed avocado, hot and sweet mustard.

Veggie Wedge: Multigrain English muffin, sliced spiced tofu, soy cheese, romaine lettuce, yellow and green squash, chopped black olives, and fresh basil leaves.

Ham on Rye: Rye bread, lean ham, Swiss cheese, lettuce and tomato, canola oil mayo, and horseradish mustard.

Where's the Beef?: 12-grain bread, lean roast beef, jalapeño Jack cheese, red leaf lettuce, red and green bell pepper rings, chile oil, and ketchup.

By George, I think you've got it!

Shrimp Mediterranean

1/4 cup diced onions
1 large clove garlic, minced
1 tablespoon olive oil
1 can (15 ounces) diced tomatoes with basil,
    garlic, and oregano
1/2 teaspoon aniseeds
Dash of ground red pepper
1/2 pound shrimp, peeled,
    deveined, and tails removed
2 cups cooked linguine
1 ounce crumbled feta cheese

In a large skillet over medium heat, sauté the onions and garlic in the oil for about 5 minutes, or until soft but not brown. Add the tomatoes (with juice), aniseeds, and pepper. Stir until well mixed. Add the shrimp and simmer for 7 to 10 minutes, or until they curl and turn pink. Divide the linguine between two bowls. Top each with half of the shrimp mixture and garnish with 1/2 ounce of the cheese. Serve with salad and garlic bread.

Yield: 2 servings

Nutritional data per serving: Calories, 391; protein, 12 g; carbohydrate, 61 g; dietary fiber, 5 g; total fat, 11 g; saturated fat, 3 g; cholesterol, 13 mg; sodium, 1,257 mg; vitamin A, 15% of Daily Value; vitamin C, 28%; calcium, 22%; iron, 30%; folate, 27%; omega-3 fatty acids, 11%.

QUICK TRICK: Use vermicelli (very thin spaghetti) instead of linguine. It cooks in 5 minutes instead of 10.

Upside-Down Pasta

My friend and colleague Edee Hogan sympathizes with the American struggle to eat more veggies. Her solution? Pump up your pasta sauce with plenty of fresh vegetables, serve twice as much sauce as noodles, and you're on your way to Five a Day!

6 ounces campanelle pasta
1/2 teaspoon salt
1 jar (26 ounces) chunky tomato-basil pasta sauce
2 cups kale, washed and finely chopped
1 1/2 cups green beans, cut into bite-size pieces
1 small zucchini, washed, halved lengthwise,
    and thinly sliced
1/2 teaspoon dried oregano
6 tablespoons freshly grated Parmesan cheese

Bring 4 quarts water to a boil in a large saucepan. Stir in the pasta and salt. Reduce the heat to medium and cook for 6 to 7 minutes, or according to package directions.

Meanwhile, in a medium saucepan, bring the sauce to a boil. Stir in the kale, beans, zucchini, and oregano. Reduce the heat, cover, and simmer until the pasta is done.

Drain the pasta. Ladle 1 cup of sauce into each of six pasta bowls. Top each with 1/2 cup pasta and sprinkle with 1 tablespoon of the cheese.

Yield: 6 servings

Nutritional data per serving: Calories, 194; protein, 8 g; carbohydrate, 35 g; dietary fiber, 4 g; total fat, 2 g; saturated fat, 1 g; cholesterol, 5 mg; sodium, 412 mg; vitamin A, 20% of Daily Value; vitamin C, 28%; calcium, 14%; iron, 11%; folate, 12%; vitamin K, 115%; potassium, 17%.

Chicken and Broccoli

Here's an easy, one-dish meal that will have you taking bows like a top-notch chef from a fine Chinese restaurant.

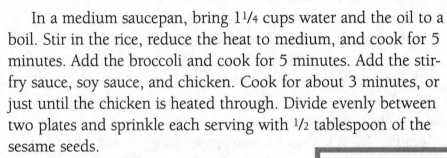

1 teaspoon peanut oil
1 cup instant brown rice
4 cups broccoli florets
1 tablespoon Szechuan spicy stir-fry sauce
1 tablespoon light soy sauce
6 ounces grilled chicken breast, thinly
 sliced
1 tablespoon toasted sesame seeds

In a medium saucepan, bring 1¼ cups water and the oil to a boil. Stir in the rice, reduce the heat to medium, and cook for 5 minutes. Add the broccoli and cook for 5 minutes. Add the stir-fry sauce, soy sauce, and chicken. Cook for about 3 minutes, or just until the chicken is heated through. Divide evenly between two plates and sprinkle each serving with ½ tablespoon of the sesame seeds.

Yield: 2 servings

Nutritional data per serving: Calories, 390; protein, 35 g; carbohydrate, 45 g; dietary fiber, 6 g; total fat, 8 g; saturated fat, 1 g; cholesterol, 72 mg; sodium, 641 mg; vitamin A, 22% of Daily Value; vitamin C, 221%; calcium, 8%; iron, 15%; vitamin B$_3$ (niacin), 72%; vitamin B$_6$, 38%; folate, 26%; vitamin K, 364%; potassium, 27%; omega-3 fatty acids, 23%.

DOUBLE DUTY

While the broccoli is busy delivering cancer-fighting sulphorafane, it's also serving up a 3-day supply of bone-building vitamin K!

Broccoli Rabe with Pasta

½ pound broccoli rabe
½ cup sliced onions
1 tablespoon coarsely chopped
　　almonds
1 clove garlic, minced
1 tablespoon olive oil
½ cup slivered red bell peppers
2 cups cooked spiral pasta
¼ cup freshly grated Parmesan
　　cheese

DOUBLE DUTY

Broccoli rabe—all by itself—gives you a full day's supply of both vitamin A (from beta-carotene) and vitamin C. Potent!

Bring a deep saucepan three-quarters full of water to a boil.
On a cutting board, use a sharp knife to trim about 2 inches off the tough broccoli rabe stems. Cut the remaining broccoli rabe into 2-inch pieces. Wash, then drop into the boiling water. Reduce the heat to medium, simmer for 5 minutes, and drain.

In a deep skillet over medium heat, sauté the onions, almonds, and garlic in the oil for about 5 minutes, or until the vegetables are soft. Stir in the broccoli rabe and peppers. Increase the heat to medium-high and cook for about 5 minutes, or until the peppers just begin to soften. Divide the pasta between two individual pasta bowls and top each with half of the broccoli rabe mixture. Sprinkle each with 2 tablespoons of the cheese.

Yield: 2 servings

Nutritional data per serving: Calories, 380; protein, 16 g; carbohydrate, 50 g; dietary fiber, 4 g; total fat, 14 g; saturated fat, 4 g; cholesterol, 10 mg; sodium, 257 mg; vitamin A, 150% of Daily Value; vitamin C, 243%; calcium, 22%; iron, 15%; vitamin E, 11%; folate, 28%.

Quickie Chickie Cacciatore

When I was a young, stay-at-home wife, I made a wonderful dish that took hours. Now I make cacciatore for two in about 15 minutes!

4 ounces whole wheat pasta
1 boneless, skinless chicken breast (6 ounces), halved
1 teaspoon olive oil
1/4 cup dry white wine
2 cups canned chopped tomatoes
1/2 cup diced onions
1 clove garlic, minced or pressed
1/8 teaspoon dried oregano
1/2 teaspoon dried basil
Dash of ground red pepper
1 ounce deli-sliced provolone cheese

Bring 3 quarts water to a boil in a 4-quart saucepan. Add the pasta and cook for 11 minutes. Meanwhile, wash the chicken and pat dry. In a small nonstick skillet over medium-high heat, brown the chicken in the oil. Deglaze the pan with the wine. Stir in the tomatoes (with juice), onions, garlic, oregano, basil, and pepper. Reduce the heat to medium and simmer until the sauce thickens and the pasta is done. Drain the pasta and divide between two large soup bowls. Top each serving with half of the chicken, sauce, and cheese. Serve with tossed salad.

Yield: 2 servings

Nutritional data per serving: Calories, 445; protein, 35 g; carbohydrate, 63 g; dietary fiber, 13 g; total fat, 8 g; saturated fat, 3 g; cholesterol, 59 mg; sodium, 484 mg; vitamin A, 14% of Daily Value; vitamin C, 41%; calcium, 20%; iron, 21%; vitamin B$_3$ (niacin), 63%; vitamin B$_6$, 35%; folate, 13%; potassium, 14%.

Bok Choy and Chicken

Ted and I love stir-fries because we get to eat a great big plateful of food that's very low in calories. Here's one of our favorites.

1 tablespoon low-sodium soy sauce
1 tablespoon fish sauce*
1 tablespoon sugar
1 tablespoon sesame seeds
1 tablespoon peanut oil
2 large cloves garlic, minced or pressed
2 cups thinly sliced bok choy
1/2 cup thinly sliced green onion tops
1 large yellow bell pepper, cut into strips
1/2 cup snow peas, washed and trimmed
6 ounces cooked chicken breast, cut into strips

In a small bowl, combine the soy sauce, fish sauce, and sugar. Stir until the sugar dissolves. Set aside. In a small nonstick skillet over high heat, toast the sesame seeds until golden. Place in a bowl and set aside to cool. Heat the oil in a wok over high heat. Add the garlic and bok choy and cook, stirring constantly, for 3 minutes. Add the onions, peppers, snow peas, chicken, and sauce. Cook, stirring constantly, for 3 minutes. Divide between two dinner plates and top with the sesame seeds. Serve with cooked brown rice.

Yield: 2 servings

Nutritional data per serving: Calories, 285; protein, 27 g; carbohydrate, 24 g; dietary fiber, 6 g; total fat, 10 g; saturated fat, 2 g; cholesterol, 49 mg; sodium, 1,170 mg; vitamin A, 53% of Daily Value; vitamin C, 439%; calcium, 25%; iron, 24%; folate, 41%; magnesium, 29%; potassium, 30%.

*Available in Asian markets and many large supermarkets.

Spaghetti Squash with Vermicelli

My friend Kathy Pontone loves a big pile of pasta, but she's always counting calories as well as trying to eat more veggies. One of her eye-fooling tricks is to mix her pasta and veggies together. Here's a sample.

1 cup cooked spaghetti squash, separated into strands
1 cup cooked vermicelli
1 cup Healthy Choice chunky mushroom and sweet pepper pasta sauce
2 tablespoons freshly grated Parmesan cheese

In a medium bowl, combine the squash and vermicelli and toss until well blended. Top with the sauce and sprinkle with the cheese. Eat until your tummy is full.

Yield: 1 serving

SUPER SUB

By replacing 1 cup pasta with 1 cup spaghetti squash, you'll get ⅕ the calories and 5 times the potassium.

Nutritional data per serving: Calories, 386; protein, 17 g; carbohydrate, 68 g; dietary fiber, 9 g; total fat, 5 g; saturated fat, 3 g; cholesterol, 10 mg; sodium, 1,042 mg; vitamin A, 8% of Daily Value; vitamin C, 29%; calcium, 29%; iron, 26%; vitamin B$_1$ (thiamin), 23%; folate, 28%; potassium, 7%; zinc, 10%; omega-3 fatty acids, 20%.

Sun-Dried Tomato Pizza

I can make these little pizzas faster than Domino's can get to my door. Plus, the flavor is richer, there's more tomato, and the portion is controlled. Perfect!

2 individual fresh pizza crusts
¹/₄ cup Classico sun-dried tomato pasta sauce
1 ounce freshly grated Parmesan cheese

Preheat the toaster oven to 475°F. Top each crust with half of the sauce, then half of the cheese. Place on the rack and bake for 8 minutes, or until the crust is crisp and the cheese begins to brown. Serve with salad and have fruit for dessert.

Yield: 2 servings

Nutritional data per serving: Calories, 282; protein, 12 g; carbohydrate, 39 g; dietary fiber, 2 g; total fat, 8 g; saturated fat, 3.5 g; cholesterol, 16 mg; sodium, 956 mg; vitamin A, 4% of Daily Value; vitamin C, 1%; calcium, 28%; iron, 11%; zinc, 6%.

SUPER SUB

When you replace traditional mozzarella with grated Parmesan, you get a double dose of calcium, which may help fend off colon cancer.

Brussels Sprouts with Oregano

I know, I know. More than half the people reading this book probably hate brussels sprouts. If you're dead set against giving them one more try, then move on to another cruciferous recipe. The rest of you, whether you're brussels spouts lovers (and there are plenty of you) or are just willing to give it a shot, should try this savory approach to enjoying these yummy little mini-cabbages.

2 cups fresh brussels sprouts (all about equal size)
1 small red onion
¹/₂ teaspoon dried oregano
2 teaspoons walnut oil
Salt and freshly ground black pepper to taste

Trim the bottoms off the sprouts and remove the tough outer leaves. Cut a little "x" in the bottom of each sprout to help even the cooking time. Peel and slice the onion, then separate into rings. Put about 1 inch of water in the bottom of a pot large enough to allow the lid to fit snugly when a steamer basket is inserted. Arrange the sprouts in the basket, top with the onion rings, and sprinkle with the oregano. Cover and bring to a boil over high heat. Reduce the heat to medium and cook for 5 minutes. In a large bowl, combine the vegetables with the oil, salt, and pepper and toss well.

Yield: 4 servings

Nutritional data per serving: Calories, 59; protein, 2 g; carbohydrate, 8 g; dietary fiber, 2 g; total fat, 3 g; saturated fat, 0 g; cholesterol, 0 mg; sodium, 201 mg; vitamin A, 6% of Daily Value; vitamin C, 82%; calcium, 3%; iron, 6%; folate, 12%; potassium, 8%; omega-3 fatty acids, 37%.

Coins of the Realm

I used to be a broccoli snob. You know, I was the kind of person who ate only the florets. But throwing away the stems bugged me because it seemed so wasteful. So, I finally gave in and started looking for ways to use them. Here's a pretty little side dish that will brighten up any meal. The broccoli and carrot slices remind me of coins.

1 cup thinly sliced peeled broccoli stems
1 cup thinly sliced carrots
1 cup low-fat chicken broth, or to cover
Freshly ground black pepper to taste

In a small saucepan, bring the broccoli, carrots, and broth to a boil over high heat. Reduce the heat to medium-low, cover, and cook for about 5 minutes, or until tender. Drain off the broth. Divide the coins between two plates and season with the pepper. Buy yourself good health!

Yield: 4 servings

Nutritional data per serving: Calories, 26; protein, 2 g; carbohydrate, 5 g; dietary fiber, 2 g; total fat, 0 g; saturated fat, 0 g; cholesterol, 0 mg; sodium, 236 mg; vitamin A, 97% of Daily Value; vitamin C, 36%; calcium, 2%; iron, 2%; vitamin E, 3%; folate, 5%; potassium, 5%.

SUPER SUB

Low-fat chicken broth is also lower in sodium, so you get lots more flavor with a lot less salt.

BroCauliflower with Lemon Butter

When I'm zooming around my kitchen on an everyday basis, my food goes straight from the pot to the plate. Who has time for serving bowls and platters? But when company comes (even if it's just my kids or sibs), I like a little display—just to show I care. Sample this example.

2 cups broccoli florets
2 cups cauliflower florets
1 tablespoon butter
2 tablespoons fresh lemon juice

Pour about 1 inch of water into a deep saucepan and insert a steamer basket. Add the broccoli and cauliflower, cover, and bring to a boil. Reduce the heat to medium and steam for 5 minutes, or just until the broccoli is bright green and the florets are crisp-tender.

Meanwhile, in a microwave-safe dish, microwave the butter and lemon juice on medium until the butter is melted and the juice is hot. Stir until well blended and set aside.

With tongs, place a floret flower side down in a deep, 4-cup bowl. Press into the bowl, then continue with the remaining vegetables, alternating green and white. Press again to pack tightly. Cover with a large serving dish, then flip and gently remove the packing bowl. You'll have a beautiful mound of brightly colored veggies. Pour on the lemon butter and serve immediately.

Yield: 8 servings

Nutritional data per serving: Calories, 25; protein, 1 g; carbohydrate, 3 g; dietary fiber, 1 g; total fat, 2 g; saturated fat, 1 g; cholesterol, 4 mg; sodium, 27 mg; vitamin A, 7% of Daily Value; vitamin C, 50%; calcium, 1%; iron, 2%; vitamin B$_6$, 4%; vitamin E, 2%; folate, 7%; potassium, 4%; omega-3 fatty acids, 6%.

Crumby Cauliflower

Cauliflower is the vegetable my family eats most often. It's mild-flavored for such a power-packed vegetable, it's available year-round, and it's oh, so easy to prepare. Here's the tasty way we like to eat it. Grab a fork and pull up a chair.

1 head cauliflower
1/4 teaspoon salt
1 tablespoon butter
1/4 cup Italian-style bread crumbs

Wash and trim the cauliflower and cut into florets. Pour about 1 inch of water into a deep saucepan and insert a steamer basket. Add the cauliflower and sprinkle with the salt. Cover and bring to a boil. Reduce the heat to medium and steam for 5 minutes, or until crisp-tender. Remove the basket and cauliflower and pour out the water. Return the saucepan to high heat. Melt the butter, then stir in the bread crumbs. Cook, stirring, until toasted. Reduce the heat to medium and add the cauliflower. Cook, stirring, until well coated with crumbs.

Yield: 4 servings

Nutritional data per serving: Calories, 87; protein, 4 g; carbohydrate, 12 g; dietary fiber, 3 g; total fat, 3 g; saturated fat, 2 g; cholesterol, 8 mg; vitamin A, 3% of Daily Value; vitamin C, 147%; calcium, 5%; iron, 4%; potassium, 11%.

Lovely Leftovers

Mix cold cauliflower with diced lean ham and stuff into a pita pocket for lunch.

Spiced Tomato Casserole

1 tablespoon butter
1 tablespoon canola oil
1/4 cup finely chopped onions
3 cups fresh multigrain bread cubes
3 tablespoons brown sugar
1/4 teaspoon ground cloves
1/4 teaspoon ground cinnamon
1 can (28 ounces) diced tomatoes

Melt the butter in a large skillet over medium heat. Add the oil and onions. Cook, stirring, for about 5 minutes, or until the onions are soft but not brown. Stir in the bread cubes. Increase the heat to medium-high and cook, stirring, for 5 to 10 minutes, or until the bread cubes are toasted but not burned. Remove from the heat and stir in the brown sugar, cloves, and cinnamon. Continue stirring until the sugar is melted and the bread cubes are well coated with spices. Measure out 1/3 cup of the bread cubes and set aside. Place half of the remaining bread cubes in a 6-cup baking dish and top with half of the tomatoes (with juice). Add the remaining bread cubes and tomatoes. Sprinkle the reserved bread cubes on top. Bake at 350°F for 25 minutes. Let cool slightly before serving.

Yield: 12 servings

Nutritional data per serving: Calories, 146; protein, 4 g; carbohydrate, 23 g; dietary fiber, 4 g; total fat, 5 g; saturated fat, 1 g; cholesterol, 5 mg; sodium, 308 mg; vitamin A, 7% of Daily Value; vitamin C, 16%; calcium, 4%; iron; 6%; vitamin E, 3%; omega-3 fatty acids, 24%.

Baby Broccolini with Hot Lemon-Garlic Sauce

8 ounces baby broccolini
1 tablespoon canola oil
1 clove garlic, minced
1/4 teaspoon crushed red pepper
1 tablespoon butter
1 tablespoon fresh lemon juice

Pour about 1 inch of water into a deep saucepan and insert a steamer basket. Use a large knife to trim about 1/2 inch off the broccolini stalks. Wash the remaining broccolini under running water and add to the steamer basket. Cover and bring to a boil. Reduce the heat to medium and steam for 8 minutes, or until the broccolini is bright green and the stems are crisp-tender. Drain and place in a serving bowl. In a small saucepan, combine the oil, garlic, and pepper. Bring to a boil, then reduce the heat and simmer for 5 minutes. Remove from the heat and stir in the butter and lemon juice. Drizzle over the broccolini. Serve piping hot.

Yield: 4 servings

Nutritional data per serving: Calories, 80; protein, 2 g; carbohydrate, 4 g; dietary fiber, 1 g; total fat, 6 g; saturated fat, 2 g; cholesterol, 8 mg; sodium, 46 mg; vitamin A, 13% of Daily Value; vitamin C, 87%; calcium, 4%; iron, 3%; vitamin E, 4%; omega-3 fatty acids, 36%.

Lovely Leftovers Dip cold steamed broccolini in ranch dressing for a powerful afternoon snack.

Watermelon Refresher

Watermelon, despite its size, is a pretty fragile fruit. You can't dehydrate it or can it or cook it into anything. You just have to grab it while it's ripe and sweet and eat as much as you can!

½ cup fat-free plain yogurt
¼ teaspoon ground cinnamon
3 cups seedless watermelon cubes

In a blender, combine the yogurt, cinnamon, and 1 cup of the watermelon. Blend on high to make a smooth sauce. Pile the remaining 2 cups watermelon into a tall pilsner or parfait glass and pour on the sauce. Eat with an iced-tea spoon.

Yield: 1 serving

Nutritional data per serving: Calories, 198; protein, 8 g; carbohydrate, 45 g; dietary fiber, 3 g; total fat, 2 g; saturated fat, 0; cholesterol, 2 mg; sodium, 77 mg; vitamin A, 17% of Daily Value; vitamin C, 73%; calcium, 19%; iron, 5%; vitamin B_1 (thiamin), 24%; potassium, 15%.

SUPER SUB

Good news! Seedless watermelon contains more lycopene than the seedy kind!

CHAPTER 8

CRANK UP YOUR
IMMUNE SYSTEM

YOU CAN "BETA" YOUR LIFE ON IT

I DON'T KNOW ABOUT YOU, BUT I JUST DON'T HAVE TIME to get sick. I don't care whether the problem is something as "small" as a cold or the flu or as big as cancer, I'd rather be out playing and having fun than draggin' around feeling crummy. So I rely on some of my favorite foods to keep up my defenses against invading germs.

The best immune-system boosters brim with beta-carotene. They are:

♥ **Carrots.** Those little babies are my constant companions.

♥ **Apricots, peaches, and nectarines.** If I want a juicy treat, I'll indulge in one of these potent fruits.

♥ **Mango and papaya.** Like a vacation in the tropics, these foods make wintertime germs irrelevant.

219

♥ **Sweet potatoes and butternut squash.** Despite their warm, fuzzy names, they are fierce fighters.

♥ **Pumpkins.** When you long for a sweet treat, try some pumpkin custard.

♥ **Cantaloupe.** For a refreshing summer lift, I put ice-cold chunks of it on my menu.

Notice a trend here? Every one of these foods is orange. That's your clue that they're loaded with beta-carotene, one of Mother Nature's best immune-system boosters. It gobbles up free radicals so they can't attack your cells, smashes cancer-causing carcinogens before they can get a foothold, and helps your cells communicate better for a lock-step defense. Best of all, it creates a physical barrier (think Great Wall of China) against invading viruses and germs by beefing up the mucous membranes lining your eyes, nose, mouth, lungs, and intestinal tract. Great job!

Eating orange food is more than just fun. It's the fruit-and-vegetable way to safely create all the vitamin A your body can use. Sure, you can get ready-made vitamin A from liver, fish-liver oil, margarine, butter, milk products, and eggs. And a little of that is okay, but high doses can be toxic. Fortunately, you can only overdose on vitamin A if you take super supplements (more than 10,000 IU daily), eat too many fortified foods, or dine on polar bear liver! To protect yourself, check the labels on vitamins and fortified cereals and limit the retinol form of vitamin A.

Another big benefit of these orange foods is

> ### Battered Bones
> Postmenopausal women who take supplements of preformed vitamin A (retinol) are 40% more likely to suffer hip fractures than women who don't take these supplements. So skip the pills, and eat your carrots and cantaloupe. Their beta-carotene safely converts to all the vitamin A you need.

that they serve as a sort of boot camp for a huge family of beta-carotene cousins called carotenoids. This family has more than 500 members, which work in many ways, singly and together, to provide possibly countless health benefits.

Pills Aren't Peachy

Foods high in beta-carotene reduce lung cancer risk. For a while, hefty beta-carotene supplements were all the rage. Then, two big studies showed that supplements actually *increased* lung cancer risk in smokers. So, have a peach instead, sweetie!

Virtually every tasty bite of these foods fills your body with a battalion of protective nutrients. Powerful! Two relatives, beta-cryptoxanthin and alpha-carotene, can become vitamin A, while cousins lutein and zeaxanthin protect vision (more about that in chapter 12), and lycopene fends off prostate cancer (check out chapter 7).

But for the best defense against marauding invaders, of course, you'll need an entire army of nutrients, not just beta-carotene. Count on the B vitamins, iron, and zinc to run your bone marrow factory, which churns out white blood cells for guard duty (see chapter 1 for recipes loaded with all three). Vitamin E, which you get from healthy fats (chapter 4) and whole grains (chapter 5), helps muster the troops that kill viruses.

The mineral copper acts like a growth hormone, helping fighter cells mature into full-fledged warriors; you can get it from shellfish (chapter 3) and green vegetables (chapter 7). For quercetin, a flavonoid that helps keep pathogens from sabotaging us, pile on the garlic and onions (chapter 11), sip lots of tea (chapter 7), and stock up on fruits and vegetables (chapters 2, 10, and 12).

But for now, you'd beta get movin' toward the "orange grove," my little Pumpkin. Good things are in store!

Butternut Squash Dippers

I was looking for a new veggie appetizer and happened upon this tasty treat. It's bright, pretty, crisp, and attention-getting. No one will notice that it's nutrition-packed, too.

1 small butternut squash
¼ cup light Thousand Island dressing
¼ cup light ranch dressing

Wash the squash and pat dry. On a cutting board, use a large, heavy knife to halve the squash lengthwise. Remove the seeds. Place each half cut side down on the cutting board and cut off the neck pieces, leaving the "cups" intact. Cut the neck into 1-inch pieces. Peel the rind off each piece, then cut into ⅛-inch-thick slices. Set aside.

Arrange the squash cups on one side of a serving platter with the cut sides together to form a butterfly. Fill one cup with the Thousand Island dressing and the other with the ranch dressing. Arrange the reserved slices to fill the plate. Invite guests to dip the slices in their favorite dressing.

Yield: 4 servings

Nutritional data per serving: Calories, 67; protein, 1 g; carbohydrate, 11 g; dietary fiber, 2 g; total fat, 3 g; saturated fat, 0 g; cholesterol, 3 mg; sodium, 159 mg; vitamin A, 54% of Daily Value; vitamin C, 19%; calcium, 3%; iron, 3%; folate, 4%; potassium, 7%.

Lovely Leftovers Cut leftovers into strips and stir into soup.

Ginger ApriCottas

Here's a little something different for your appetizer tray. Be sure the apricots are ripe but firm, so they hold up as finger food. Zingy!

8 small ripe apricots, halved and pitted
1/4 cup reduced-fat ricotta cheese
1 tablespoon ginger preserves
Dash of ground cinnamon

Arrange the apricots on a serving tray. In a small bowl, combine the ricotta and preserves. Stir until well blended. Fill each apricot half with 1 teaspoon of the ricotta mixture and dust with the cinnamon.

Yield: 8 servings

Nutritional data per serving: Calories, 32; protein, 1 g; carbohydrate, 6 g; dietary fiber, 1 g; total fat, <1 g; saturated fat, 0 g; cholesterol, 2 mg; sodium, 6 mg; vitamin A, 10% of Daily Value; vitamin C, 6%; calcium, 3%; iron, 1%; vitamin E, 2%; potassium, 3%.

The Inside Skinny: Ginger preserves add both the sweetness and the zing to the ricotta filling—with very little work on your part.

Chilled Honey-Nectarine Soup

Mmmm...this soup is beautiful. It feeds the eye as well as the tummy. And it's sweet enough to begin, or even end, a meal.

3 cups sliced nectarines, with peel
2 tablespoons fresh lime juice
1 tablespoon honey
1 tablespoon frozen cranberry juice concentrate, thawed
1 teaspoon pumpkin pie spice
1 cup apple juice
4 tablespoons reduced-fat sour cream

In a food processor, combine the nectarines, lime juice, honey, cranberry juice, and spice. Process on high until smooth but flecked with bits of red nectarine peel. Pour into a bowl. Stir in the apple juice and blend well. Cover and refrigerate for 1 to 2 hours. To serve, ladle into four lotus bowls and garnish each with 1 tablespoon of the sour cream.

Yield: 4 servings

Nutritional data per serving: Calories, 131; protein, 2 g; carbohydrate, 28 g; dietary fiber, 2 g; total fat, 2 g; saturated fat, 1 g; cholesterol, 8 mg; sodium, 11 mg; vitamin A, 12% of Daily Value; vitamin C, 60%; calcium, 4%; iron, 2%; vitamin E, 5%; potassium, 10%.

Lovely Leftovers Blend leftover soup with frozen yogurt for a delicious frozen treat.

Curried Carrot and Chickpea Soup

Just give me a bowl of this with a piece of warm bread and a glass of milk, and I'm happy as can be.

1/2 cup coarsely chopped onions
1 tablespoon peanut oil
3 cups fat-free chicken broth
2 cups sliced carrots
1 can (15 1/2 ounces) chickpeas, rinsed and drained
1/4 teaspoon curry powder, or to taste
Freshly ground black pepper to taste
4 tablespoons reduced-fat sour cream

In a medium saucepan over medium heat, sauté the onions in the oil for 5 minutes, or until soft but not brown. Stir in the broth and carrots. Cover and bring to a boil. Reduce the heat and simmer for 10 to 12 minutes, or until the carrots are fork-tender. Drain, reserving the liquid. In a food processor, combine half of the carrots and one-third of the reserved liquid. Process until smooth, then return to the pan. Repeat with the remaining carrots and half of the remaining liquid. In the food processor, combine the last of the liquid and the chickpeas. Process until smooth, then stir into the carrots. Add the curry powder and pepper. Warm over medium heat just until boiling. Ladle into four bowls and top each with 1 tablespoon of the sour cream.

Yield: 4 servings

Nutritional data per serving: Calories, 444; protein, 16 g; carbohydrate, 67 g; dietary fiber, 15 g; total fat, 13 g; saturated fat, 4 g; cholesterol, 16 mg; sodium, 1,194 mg; vitamin A, 391% of Daily Value; vitamin C, 23%; calcium, 17%; iron, 21%; vitamin B$_6$, 69%; folate, 41%; copper, 29%; potassium, 24%; zinc, 18%.

Pumpkin Bisque

Making this exotic-tasting soup is as simple as opening a couple of cans, but it tastes like you slaved all day over a hot stove. Now that's the kind of cooking I like!

2 cans (12 ounces each) fat-free evaporated milk
1 can (15 ounces) prepared pumpkin
1 medium shallot, diced (about 1/3 cup)
1 small clove garlic, minced
1 tablespoon hazelnut oil
1 teaspoon honey
1/4 teaspoon ground cinnamon
1/8 teaspoon ground nutmeg
1/8 teaspoon ground turmeric
1/8 teaspoon curry powder
1/2 teaspoon salt

In a 4-quart saucepan over medium heat, use a wire whisk to gradually stir the milk into the pumpkin until silky.

Meanwhile, in a small nonstick skillet over medium heat, sauté the shallot and garlic in the oil until soft. Add to the pumpkin mixture. Add the honey, cinnamon, nutmeg, turmeric, curry powder, and salt. Whisk until smooth. Cook, whisking occasionally, until hot but not boiling. Serve immediately or refrigerate to serve later. (Reheat over medium heat; do not boil.)

Yield: 8 servings

Nutritional data per serving: Calories, 119; protein, 8 g; carbohydrate, 18 g; dietary fiber, 2 g; total fat, 2 g; saturated fat, 0 g; cholesterol, 3 mg; sodium, 260 mg; vitamin A, 147% of Daily Value; vitamin C, 7%; calcium, 30%; iron, 7%; vitamin D, 19%; potassium, 13%.

Golden Accent Carrot Salad

When my kids were little, I used to make them this salad to help brighten a rainy day. It seems to add a touch of sunshine!

1 cup grated carrots
$^1/_2$ cup well-drained juice-packed pineapple
$^1/_4$ cup golden seedless raisins
Freshly ground black pepper to taste
2 tablespoons light French dressing
2 leaves romaine lettuce
2 tablespoons coarsely chopped walnuts,
   toasted

In a small bowl, combine the carrots, pineapple, raisins, pepper, and dressing. Stir until well blended. Place a lettuce leaf on each of two salad plates. Spoon half of the carrot mixture onto each leaf and garnish with 1 tablespoon of the walnuts.

Yield: 2 servings

Nutritional data per serving: Calories, 189; protein, 2 g; carbohydrate, 33 g; dietary fiber, 4 g; total fat, 7 g; saturated fat, <1 g; cholesterol, 0 mg; sodium, 157 mg; vitamin A, 162% of Daily Value; vitamin C, 24%; calcium, 4%; iron, 6%; vitamin B$_6$, 9%; vitamin E, 5%; vitamin K, 100%; copper, 11%; potassium, 11%; omega-3 fatty acids, 70%.

Lovely Leftovers   Mix with canned chicken and pile on a sandwich.

Wormy Salad

Having a hard time getting your kids to eat their veggies? This spiral pasta that I found in the health food section of a large local supermarket looks a bit like worms. (And kids are sure to believe you if you say so!) They make a youngster's salad definitely squirmy—and therefore worth eating.

2 ounces Eddie's organic corkscrew pasta
2 cups torn butterhead lettuce
1 small pickling cucumber, thinly sliced
1/4 cup grated carrots
2 tablespoons light ranch dressing
8 grape tomatoes

Bring 4 quarts water to a rolling boil in a large saucepan. Gradually add the pasta and stir gently to prevent sticking. Reduce the heat to medium-high and cook for 7 minutes, or until al dente. Drain and rinse quickly with cold water to stop the cooking process. Set aside.

In a medium bowl, toss the lettuce, cucumber, carrots, and dressing until well blended. Divide equally among four small salad bowls. Garnish each with 2 grape tomatoes and one-fourth of the "worms." Say "Eeeew!" when you serve it.

Yield: 4 servings

Nutritional data per serving: Calories, 83; protein, 3 g; carbohydrate, 14 g; dietary fiber, 1 g; total fat, 2 g; saturated fat, 0 g; cholesterol, 2 mg; sodium, 87 mg; vitamin A, 59% of Daily Value; vitamin C, 26%; calcium, 3%; iron, 8%; folate, 29%; vitamin K, 20%; potassium, 13%.

Nectarine and Honeydew Salad

Juicy summer fruits just blow me away! I like them mixed with a few veggies for fun.

1 ripe nectarine, pitted and cut
   into wedges
1 cup honeydew melon balls
1/2 cup seedless red grapes
1/2 cup thinly sliced pickling
   cucumbers
4 baby carrots, thinly sliced
4 tablespoons light French dressing
2 cups torn butterhead lettuce
2 cups shredded romaine lettuce
2 tablespoons chopped walnuts

DOUBLE DUTY

Walnuts deliver heart-smart omega-3 fatty acids and enough monounsaturated fat to help you absorb the beta-carotene from the nectarines and lettuce.

In a medium bowl, combine the nectarine, melon, grapes, cucumbers, and carrots. Add 2 tablespoons of the dressing and toss. Set aside.

In another medium bowl, combine the butterhead and romaine lettuce and the remaining 2 tablespoons dressing. Toss until well coated. Divide the lettuce among four luncheon plates. Top each with one-fourth of the fruit mixture and garnish with 1/2 tablespoon of the walnuts.

Yield: 4 servings

Nutritional data per serving: Calories, 159; protein, 3 g; carbohydrate, 23 g; dietary fiber, 3 g; total fat, 8 g; saturated fat, <1 g; cholesterol, 0 mg; sodium, 140 mg; vitamin A, 33% of Daily Value; vitamin C, 46%; calcium, 4%; iron, 6%; vitamin E, 8%; folate, 20%; potassium, 16%; omega-3 fatty acids, 99%.

Sweet Cantaloupe Salad Dressing

If you're looking for a light, summery dressing to brighten up hearty greens, you've gotta give this sweetie a try. Its unusual flavor is surprisingly good—and it's refreshing!

2 cups cantaloupe cubes
1 teaspoon canola oil
2 teaspoons balsamic vinegar
⅛ teaspoon salt
Freshly ground black pepper to taste

In a blender, combine the cantaloupe, oil, vinegar, salt, and pepper. Blend on high until smooth. Refrigerate before serving.

Yield: 8 servings

Nutritional data per serving: Calories, 19; protein, 0 g; carbohydrate, 4 g; dietary fiber, 0 g; total fat, <1 g; saturated fat, 0 g; cholesterol, 0 mg; sodium, 8 mg; vitamin A, 13% of Daily Value; vitamin C, 28%; calcium, 0%; iron, 1%; omega-3 fatty acids, 8%.

Lovely Leftovers — Surprise! This dressing is great over vanilla ice cream, too. Top with fresh berries for a taste treat.

Breakfast Fruit Bowl

Let the heady perfume of ripening fruit draw you, barefoot, into the kitchen. Grab a knife and a spoon. You're about to get this lazy day started off on the right foot.

1 large peach, pitted and sliced
2 medium apricots, pitted and
   sliced
1 mango, pitted and sliced
2 cups low-fat plain yogurt
2 tablespoons strawberry jam
2 tablespoons toasted sliced
   almonds

In a medium bowl, combine the peach, apricots, and mango. In a small bowl, blend the yogurt and jam. Stir the yogurt into the fruit. Divide between two cereal bowls and garnish each serving with 1 tablespoon of the almonds.

Yield: 2 servings

Nutritional data per serving: Calories, 363; protein, 16 g; carbohydrates, 63 g; dietary fiber, 5 g; total fat, 8 g; saturated fat, 3 g; cholesterol, 27 mg; sodium, 172 mg; vitamin A, 57% of Daily Value; vitamin C, 69%; calcium, 44%; iron, 3%; vitamin E, 16%; potassium, 28%.

SUPER SUB

Of all nuts, almonds are highest in vitamin E.

Cashew-Peach Waffles

Once July hits, the farm near me offers a new kind of peach almost every week. Here's what I do with the Hale Haven variety on a hot summer morning. Share it with your sweetie.

2 Nutri-Grain multigrain waffles
2 tablespoons cashew butter
Freshly ground nutmeg to taste
1 large peach, pitted and sliced

Toast the waffles. In a small microwave-safe dish, microwave the cashew butter on high for 30 to 60 seconds, or until melted. Stir in the nutmeg. Spread 1 tablespoon on each waffle and top with peach slices. Enjoy with a frosty glass of milk.

Yield: 1 serving

Nutritional data per serving: Calories, 415; protein, 12 g; carbohydrate, 55 g; dietary fiber, 9 g; total fat, 21 g; saturated fat, 4 g; cholesterol, 0 mg; sodium, 586 mg; vitamin A, 8% of Daily Value; vitamin C, 17%; calcium, 12%; iron, 30%; vitamin B$_2$ (riboflavin), 27%; vitamin B$_6$, 25%; vitamin E, 8%; folate, 13% copper, 40%; magnesium, 23%; potassium, 14%.

SUPER SUB

Replacing butter or margarine with cashew butter cuts harmful fat. Instead, you slather on heart-smart monounsaturated fat and minerals, such as copper, iron, magnesium, potassium, and zinc.

1 CUP

Blackberry and Cantaloupe Bowl

One of the best things about those nice, round little western cantaloupes is that they make super bowls for other fruit, ice cream, yogurt, and even cold soup! Try this quick treat for melt-in-your-mouth summer fun.

**1 cup fresh blackberries, gently washed and
  patted dry
1 cup fat-free vanilla yogurt
1 small cantaloupe, halved and seeded
1/4 teaspoon ground cinnamon**

In a small bowl, combine the blackberries and yogurt. Stir until well mixed. Pile half in each cantaloupe bowl and dust with the cinnamon.

Yield: 2 servings

Nutritional data per serving: Calories, 245; protein, 9 g; carbohydrate, 54 g; dietary fiber, 6 g; total fat, 1 g; saturated fat, 0 g; cholesterol, 2 mg; sodium, 109 mg; vitamin A, 90% of Daily Value; vitamin C, 221%; calcium, 27%; iron, 6%; vitamin E, 5%; folate, 21%; potassium, 36%.

> **QUICK TRICK:** Use frozen blackberries and mix with blackberry pie–flavored yogurt.

Pork with French Apricot Sauce

Grilling is cool, just when fresh apricots are hot. Try this unusual sauce to make the most of very ripe apricots.

1 tablespoon butter
1/2 cup thinly sliced shallots
1 thin slice garlic
1 sprig fresh thyme or 1/8 teaspoon dried thyme
1 cup apricots, pitted and cut into slivers
1 teaspoon sugar
Freshly ground black pepper to taste
1/2 cup dry white wine
12 ounces cooked pork tenderloin

Melt the butter in a small saucepan over medium heat. Stir in the shallots, garlic, and thyme. Sauté for 3 to 5 minutes, or until the shallots soften but still hold their shape. Stir in the apricots, sugar, and pepper. Cook for 2 minutes. Add the wine and simmer for 10 minutes, or until the sauce thickens. Remove the garlic and thyme sprig (if using). Place 2 tablespoons of sauce in a large pool on each of four dinner plates. Arrange 3 ounces of pork on top of each apricot pool and drizzle the remaining sauce over the meat.

Yield: 4 servings

Nutritional data per serving: Calories, 255; protein, 27 g; carbohydrate, 9 g; dietary fiber, 1 g; total fat, 10 g; saturated fat, 4 g; cholesterol, 88 mg; sodium, 88 mg; vitamin A, 16% of Daily Value; vitamin C, 12%; calcium, 2%; iron, 10%; vitamin B_1 (thiamin), 57%; vitamin B_2 (riboflavin), 20%; vitamin B_3 (niacin), 23%; vitamin B_6, 27%; potassium, 17%; zinc, 18%.

Stir-Fried Sweet Potatoes

Stir-frying doesn't always require a vast array of veggies. Sometimes, it's just a nice way to get a simple, crisp-tender side dish.

2 teaspoons peanut oil
1 slice fresh ginger
Dash of crushed red pepper
1 large sweet potato
1/2 cup diagonally sliced celery
Salt and freshly ground black pepper to taste

In a small wok over high heat, warm the oil, ginger, and pepper. Quarter the sweet potato lengthwise, then cut crosswise into 1/2-inch pieces. Add the sweet potato and celery to the wok. Cook, stirring, over high heat until the vegetables are crisp-tender. Season with the salt and pepper and remove the ginger. Great as a side dish with ham or pork tenderloin.

Yield: 2 servings

Nutritional data per serving: Calories, 108; protein, 1 g; carbohydrate, 16 g; dietary fiber, 2 g; total fat, 5 g; saturated fat, <1 g; cholesterol, 0 mg; sodium, 39 mg; vitamin A, 131% of Daily Value; vitamin C, 28%; calcium, 3%; iron, 2%; folate, 6%; potassium, 9%.

Lovely Leftovers — Stir any extra sweet potatoes into black beans for intense color and super-power nutrition.

Silky Dinner Squash

Okay, squash is never an easy sell, but it offers such dynamite nutrition that it's always worth one more try. This version is as thick and creamy as mashed potatoes. It adds color to the plate and is really rich and flavorful.

½ cup finely chopped onions
2 teaspoons olive oil
1 cup fat-free beef broth
1 package (14 ounces) frozen cooked squash, thawed
2 teaspoons butter
Freshly ground black pepper to taste

In a small saucepan over medium heat, sauté the onions in the oil for about 5 minutes, or until soft but not brown. Stir in the broth, cover, and simmer for 5 minutes, or until the onions are very soft. Add the squash, butter, and pepper. Cook, stirring, until heated through.

Yield: 4 servings

Nutritional data per serving: Calories, 87; protein, 3 g; carbohydrate, 11 g; dietary fiber, 3 g; total fat, 4 g; saturated fat, 1.5 g; cholesterol, 5 mg; sodium, 62 mg; vitamin A, 32% of Daily Value; vitamin C, 9%; calcium, 2%; iron, 3%; folate, 5%; potassium, 6%.

Lovely Leftovers Thin with additional beef broth and use as "gravy" for roast beef or pork.

Garlic-Roasted Carrot Sticks

Want a replacement for french fries that will spruce up your next sandwich? Give these colorful "fries" a try.

4 large carrots
1 teaspoon olive oil
¼ teaspoon salt
1 teaspoon garlic powder
Freshly ground black pepper to taste

Place a baking sheet in the oven and preheat to 425°F. Meanwhile, halve the carrots, then cut lengthwise into fourths or sixths to make carrot sticks. In a small bowl, combine the carrots and oil. Toss until well coated. Sprinkle with the salt, garlic powder, and pepper. Toss until the carrots are evenly coated with spices. Carefully arrange in a single layer on the baking sheet. Bake for 8 minutes, or until tender and beginning to brown. Remove with a spatula and divide among four plates.

Yield: 4 servings

Nutritional data per serving: Calories, 43; protein, 1 g; carbohydrate, 8 g; dietary fiber, 2 g; total fat, 1 g; saturated fat, 0 g; cholesterol, 0 mg; sodium, 171 mg; vitamin A, 203% of Daily Value; vitamin C, 11%; calcium, 2%; iron, 2%; vitamin K, 131%; potassium, 7%.

> **QUICK TRICK:** Buy precut carrot sticks from the produce department of your supermarket. Just toss with the oil and spices, then bake.

Oven-Crisp Sweet Potatoes

I'm constantly amazed at how many people tell me they love sweet potatoes but eat them only at Thanksgiving. Here's a delicious way to get them into your food life all year 'round!

2 medium sweet potatoes, peeled and thinly sliced
1/4 teaspoon salt
1/8 teaspoon freshly ground black pepper
1/4 teaspoon garlic powder

Lightly coat a baking sheet with olive oil spray.

Arrange the potatoes in a single layer on the baking sheet, then coat lightly with olive oil spray. Sprinkle on the salt, pepper, and garlic powder. Bake at 400°F for 10 to 15 minutes, or until crisp. Use a stiff spatula to remove from the baking sheet and serve immediately.

Yield: 2 servings

Nutritional data per serving: Calories; 158; protein, 2 g; carbohydrate, 28 g; dietary fiber, 3 g; total fat, 5 g; saturated fat, <1 g; cholesterol, 0 mg; sodium, 571 mg; vitamin A, 249% of Daily Value; vitamin C, 47%; calcium, 3%; iron, 3%; potassium, 11%.

SUPER SUB

When you mist your yams with olive oil, you help lower cholesterol and triglycerides. On the other hand, frying them in hydrogenated margarine packed with trans fats raises your risk of heart disease.

Red Yams with Fiery Peanut Sauce

My friend Phyllis once spent hours cooking up an African peanut stew that drove us all wild. Here are the best elements of that dish served up in 10 minutes flat.

1 large red yam, peeled
1 tablespoon creamy peanut butter
1 tablespoon fat-free milk
1/8 teaspoon ground red pepper

Split the yam lengthwise and place on a microwave-safe plate. Microwave on high for 5 to 7 minutes, or until cooked through. In a small microwave-safe dish, combine the peanut butter and milk. Microwave for 20 seconds, or until warm. Add the pepper and stir vigorously until well blended. Cube the yam, then drizzle with the sauce. It's wonderful with lean pork or chicken. Just keep a fire extinguisher handy.

Yield: 2 servings

Nutritional data per serving: Calories, 167; protein, 4 g; carbohydrate, 30 g; dietary fiber, 4 g; total fat, 4 g; saturated fat, <1 g; cholesterol, 0 mg; sodium, 53 mg; vitamin A, 248% of Daily Value; vitamin C, 47%; calcium, 4%; iron, 4%; vitamin E, 6%; folate, 8%; magnesium, 9%; potassium, 13%.

The P·E·R·F·E·C·T Companion

Make your own fire extinguisher. Empty a 12-ounce can of guava nectar (find it in the international foods section of your supermarket) into a tall glass filled with ice. Add a squeeze of lime juice.

Fresh Peach and Apricot Freeze

An endless heat wave broke today, so I whipped some fresh fruit into a cold and creamy lunch and enjoyed the noontime sunshine and cool breezes. Heaven!

¼ cup peach or apricot nectar
1 large peach, pitted and sliced
2 large apricots, pitted and halved
1 tablespoon apricot preserves
1 cup vanilla frozen yogurt

Place the nectar in a blender, cover, and begin to blend on high. Remove the feeder cap, drop in the peach and apricots, and blend until smooth. Add the preserves and blend for 10 seconds. Remove the lid and add the frozen yogurt. Cover and blend for 10 to 20 seconds. Pour into two tall glasses and serve with straws and iced-tea spoons.

Yield: 2 servings

Nutritional data per serving: Calories, 365; protein, 8 g; carbohydrate, 85 g; dietary fiber, 5 g; total fat, <1 g; saturated fat, 0 g; cholesterol, 0 mg; sodium, 100 mg; vitamin A, 35% of Daily Value; vitamin C, 89%; calcium, 63%; iron, 5%; vitamin E, 9%; potassium, 17%.

SUPER SUB

Some frozen yogurts pile on the calcium, with 30 to 40% of your daily requirement, while others offer only a measly 8%. Be sure to check the label so you get the most of this important mineral.

Peach Pie Smoothie

Fresh peaches are so absolutely luscious that I just can't think of enough ways to eat them. This way, with soy, they help cool my hot flashes, too!

6 ounces Silk cultured soy yogurt
1 large peach, with peel, pitted and sliced
1 tablespoon peach preserves
1 teaspoon pumpkin pie spice

In a blender, combine the yogurt, peach (reserving one slice), preserves, and spice. Blend on high for about 1 minute, or until smooth, creamy, and thick. Pour into a large glass and garnish with the reserved peach slice.

Yield: 1 serving

Nutritional data per serving: Calories, 284; protein, 5 g; carbohydrate, 64 g; dietary fiber, 4 g; total fat, 2 g; saturated fat, 0 g; cholesterol, 0 mg; sodium, 31 mg; vitamin A, 9% of Daily Value; vitamin C, 20%; calcium, 52%; iron, 3%; vitamin E, 6%; potassium, 10%.

QUICK TRICK: Winter got you down? Whip up this summer smoothie—just use frozen peaches.

Cantaloupe and Tonic

I like to be sure my guests have tempting nonalcoholic choices when cocktails are being served. This golden goodie comes naturally packed with vitamins and minerals.

2 cups cold cantaloupe cubes
1 cup cold tonic water
3 cups ice cubes
2 large wedges lime

In a blender, combine the cantaloupe and tonic. Blend on high until smooth. Fill two tall glasses with ice, then with the cantaloupe mixture. Garnish each with a lime wedge and a straw.

Yield: 2 servings

Nutritional data per serving: Calories, 99; protein, 1 g; carbohydrate, 25 g; dietary fiber, 1 g; total fat, 0 g; saturated fat, 0 g; cholesterol, 0 mg; sodium, 10 mg; vitamin A, 52% of Daily Value; vitamin C, 115%; calcium, 2%; iron, 2%; vitamin B$_6$, 9%; folate, 7%; potassium, 14%.

SUPER SUB

So you're the designated driver? Cool! Substitute this drink for a gin and tonic and get half your vitamin A and all your vitamin C for the day!

Neon Carrot Cocktail

I'm not a big fan of "juicing" because you end up throwing away the fibrous pulp—and let's face it, most of us need all the help we can get in that department! On the other hand, when you blend your own juice, you get all the goodies. Be fore-warned, though, the color is shocking!

1 cup ruby red grapefruit blend with calcium
¹/₈ teaspoon ground ginger
1 cup baby carrots
1 cup ice cubes

In a blender, combine the grapefruit juice and ginger. Begin to blend on high, remove the feeder cap, and drop in the carrots one by one until all the carrots are pureed. Drop in the ice cubes one at a time and blend until finely crushed. Divide between two glasses.

Yield: 2 servings

Nutritional data per serving: Calories, 93; protein, 1 g; carbohydrate, 22 g; dietary fiber, 1 g; total fat, 0 g; saturated fat, 0 g; cholesterol, 0 mg; sodium, 42 mg; vitamin A, 106% of Daily Value; vitamin C, 75%; calcium, 7%; iron, 3%; folate, 7%.

DOUBLE DUTY

This one little cock-tail meets your entire day's needs for vitamin A. It delivers most of your vitamin C, too.

Cantaloupe Smoothie

Feeling too hot and lazy to lift a fork? Collapse in your beach chair and sip a whole day's worth of vitamins A and C right through a straw!

½ cup cold fat-free evaporated milk
3 cups cold cantaloupe cubes
¼ teaspoon vanilla extract
Dash of ground cinnamon

In a blender, combine the milk, cantaloupe, vanilla, and cinnamon. Blend until smooth. Pour into a tall glass and sip through a fat straw.

Yield: 1 serving

Nutritional data per serving: Calories, 271; protein, 13 g; carbohydrate, 55 g; dietary fiber, 4 g; total fat, 1.6 g; saturated fat, 0 g, cholesterol, 5 mg; sodium,190 mg; vitamin A, 170% of Daily Value; vitamin C, 340%; calcium, 42%; iron, 8%; vitamin B_6, 31%; vitamin D, 26%; folate, 23%; potassium, 55%; omega-3 fatty acids, 30%.

DOUBLE DUTY

Cantaloupe and evaporated milk team up to deliver half your potassium and almost as much calcium—a double whammy for fighting high blood pressure.

Peaches and Apricots
with Wheatberries

This is to die for...or maybe live with!

1 cup diced peaches, with peel
1 cup diced apricots, with peel
1 cup Basic Wheatberries (page 146)
¹/₂ teaspoon sugar
¹/₈ teaspoon grated lime peel
¹/₄ cup reduced-fat sour cream
2 tablespoons coarsely broken toasted pecans

In a medium bowl, combine the peaches, apricots, wheatberries, sugar, lime peel, and sour cream. Gently fold together until well mixed. Spoon into six individual serving dishes and garnish with the pecans.

Yield: 6 servings

Nutritional data per serving: Calories, 109; protein, 3 g; carbohydrate, 15 g; dietary fiber, 3 g; total fat, 5 g; saturated fat, 1 g; cholesterol, 5 mg; sodium, 7 mg; vitamin A, 11% of Daily Value; vitamin C, 8%; calcium, 3%; iron, 4%; vitamin E, 4%; potassium, 6%.

> **The Inside Skinny:** It's easier to absorb beta-carotene from fruits than from vegetables, so your body may be getting a lot more than the numbers suggest.

Mango Cream Cake

Under the gun, I whipped up this sensuous dessert in just minutes. My guests were impressed!

1 large ripe mango, peeled, pitted, and diced
¼ cup sour cream
4 slices angel food cake
¼ cup large fresh blueberries

In a blender, combine the mango and sour cream. Blend to make a thick, luxurious sauce. Place a slice of cake on each of four dessert plates. Top each with one-fourth of the sauce and garnish with a few blueberries.

Yield: 4 servings

Nutritional data per serving: Calories, 138; protein, 2 g; carbohydrate, 26 g; dietary fiber, 1 g; total fat, 3 g; saturated fat, 2 g; cholesterol, 6 mg; sodium, 221 mg; vitamin A, 23% of Daily Value; vitamin C, 24%; calcium, 6%; iron, 1%; vitamin B$_2$ (riboflavin), 11%; folate, 5%; potassium, 4%.

Lovely Leftovers

Spread mango cream sauce on waffles or pancakes for breakfast.

Peach Cobbler

4 peaches, with peel, pitted and thinly sliced
3 tablespoons sugar
2 teaspoons cornstarch
1/2 teaspoon ground cinnamon
1/2 cup cold water
1/2 cup Arrowhead Mills multigrain
   pancake and waffle mix
1 tablespoon peanut oil
1 tablespoon honey

Preheat the oven to 400°F. Arrange the peach slices in the bottom of an 8-inch by 8-inch baking pan. Set aside.

In a small saucepan, combine the sugar, cornstarch, and cinnamon. Stir until blended. Stir in the cold water until the cornstarch is dissolved. Bring to a boil over medium heat and cook, stirring constantly, for about 2 minutes, or until thick. Pour over the peaches.

In a small bowl, combine the waffle mix, oil, honey, and 2 tablespoons water. Stir just until blended. Spoon over the peaches to form four "biscuits." Bake for 15 to 20 minutes, or until crisp and brown. Serve warm or at room temperature.

> ### The
> ### P·E·R·F·E·C·T
> ### Companion
>
> Fill a tea ball with loose Queen Mary tea. Drop it into a teapot and fill with boiling water. Steep for 5 minutes, then remove the tea ball. Serve with milk and sugar.

Yield: 4 servings

Nutritional data per serving: Calories, 215; protein, 3 g; carbohydrate, 45 g; dietary fiber, 5 g; total fat, 4 g; saturated fat, <1 g; cholesterol, 0 mg; sodium, 140 mg; vitamin A, 9% of Daily Value; vitamin C, 17%; calcium, 6%; iron, 3%; vitamin E, 8%; potassium, 9%.

Berries with Mango Sorbet

Last night, we ended dinner with this cool, luscious treat. It just doesn't get any better than this.

1 cup sliced fresh strawberries
1 tablespoon confectioners'
   sugar
6 ounces fresh raspberries
1 cup mango sorbet

In a small bowl, combine the strawberries and sugar and mix well. Rinse the raspberries and pat dry. Gently fold into the strawberries. Divide between two dessert dishes. By spoonfuls, top each with ½ cup of the sorbet. Let stand for 3 to 5 minutes before serving so the sorbet softens.

Yield: 2 servings

SUPER SUB

Replacing high-fat ice cream with mango sorbet wipes out saturated fat and fills in with lots of beta-carotene and plenty of natural flavor.

Nutritional data per serving: Calories, 201; protein, 1 g; carbohydrate, 50 g; dietary fiber, 2 g; total fat, <1 g; saturated fat, 0 g; cholesterol, 0 mg; sodium, 0 mg; vitamin A, 21% of Daily Value; vitamin C, 134%; calcium, 3%; iron, 4%; folate, 9%; vitamin K, 15%; potassium, 8%.

Peach Melba

Now here's an old-fashioned dessert that's usually made with lots of sugary syrups. But not this one. This baby is as pure as the juiciest summer fruits.

1 small very ripe summer peach
½ cup low-fat vanilla ice cream
½ cup fresh raspberries, crushed
1 leaf mint

Peel and pit the peach and slice into a stemmed dessert dish. Top with the ice cream and pour on the raspberries. Garnish with the mint. Eat it in a sunny outdoor spot that's warm enough to melt the ice cream. Mmmmmm…

Yield: 1 serving

Nutritional data per serving: Calories, 174; protein, 4 g; carbohydrate, 35 g; dietary fiber, 7 g; total fat, 2 g; saturated fat, 1 g; cholesterol, 5 mg; sodium, 45 mg; vitamin A, 11% of Daily Value; vitamin C, 34%; calcium, 12%; iron, 2%; vitamin E, 4%; folate, 5%; potassium, 7%.

DOUBLE DUTY

While you're focused on the melt-in-your-mouth flavors, the ice cream sneaks in some calcium, while the raspberries slip in a big dose of fiber. And both protect against colon cancer.

CHAPTER 9

RELIEVE
INTESTINAL
DISTRESS

SELECT SPECIAL FOODS
TO EASE THE WAY

RECENTLY, WHEN I SUGGESTED TO A GROUP OF HIGH school athletes, their parents, and coaches that high-fiber foods (fruits, vegetables, and whole grains) were healthier choices than all those processed foods they were eating, one of the dads spluttered at me in frustration. "High-fiber food takes longer to chew," he said. "I'm so busy driving my kids around that I don't have time to chew!"

Well, doesn't that sum up the state of American nutrition!

The casual dismissal of healthful high-fiber foods is a real problem on several levels. Of course, crisp apples and crunchy

carrots deliver a pile of nutrients that build and protect all
your body parts. On another
level, they also help take out
the garbage, and life doesn't get
much more basic than that.

Keep It Moving

For best bowel function, complement your high-fiber diet
by exercising regularly and
drinking plenty of water.

So let's have a show of
intestinal fortitude here and do a quick tour of the more mundane
ways that insoluble fiber (what your grandma called "roughage")
works for you. It can:

♥ **Prevent constipation** by rhythmically rocking your intestines to keep food rolling along toward its final destination.

♥ **Fend off diverticulosis and hemorrhoids** by absorbing
water, swelling in size, and creating soft, bulky stools that you can
pass easily without straining.

♥ **Help you eat more slowly** (yes, this is a benefit!) so your
body has time to recognize when you've eaten enough.

♥ **Scrub your pearly whites** and protect them from decay.
Sticky, starchy foods cling to your teeth and create the perfect
growth medium for decay-causing bacteria. Munching fresh pears
or celery cleans your teeth, sweeping away nasty germs and
plaque.

♥ **Fill your tummy** with indigestible fiber that helps you feel
full. Think about finishing a big bowl of salad greens versus eating a slice of white bread. Same calories,
different feeling.

Okay, I know what you're thinking: Will fiber prevent colon cancer?
Well, the jury is still out on that one,
but research is clear about a mountain
of other benefits.

♥ Piling on the fruits and vegetables can

Relieve Intestinal Distress   251

lower blood pressure.

♥ Two or three whole grains daily help fend off diabetes.

♥ Cabbage and tomatoes are known cancer fighters.

♥ Nectarines, carrots, and other orange fruits and veggies boost your immune system.

♥ Blueberries and beets help keep your memory sharp.

♥ Garlic and onions battle the common cold.

♥ Melons, berries, and peppers protect vision.

♥ Asparagus and citrus fruit fight birth defects.

Chew on this: What have you got to lose besides a few pounds, your current cold, and that chronic constipation that makes you feel so sluggish? You could trade them all for some chocolate-dipped strawberries, Persian sweets, or smoky eggplant spread. Come on—your table is waiting.

Don't Step On the Gas

Increase high-fiber foods gradually and drink lots of water. Easing into a high-fiber diet allows your intestines to adjust, thus minimizing gas production and pain.

Artichoke Tapenade

Have you been looking for a different sort of appetizer? One with rich, tender flavors? Search no more. You can create this sensational dish in no time using ingredients you already have on hand.

12 almonds
1 package (8 ounces) frozen
    artichoke hearts, thawed
1 tablespoon canola oil
1/4 teaspoon salt
1/2 teaspoon red wine vinegar
1/2 teaspoon dried thyme

In a food processor running on high, drop the almonds through the feeder tube one by one. Process until finely chopped. Turn off the processor and add the artichokes, oil, salt, vinegar, and thyme. Pulse to make a coarse spread. Serve with thin, toasted baguette slices or water crackers.

Yield: 32 servings

Nutritional data per serving: Calories, 10; protein, <1 g; carbohydrate, 1 g; dietary fiber, 0.5 g; total fat, <1 g; saturated fat, 0 g; cholesterol, 0 mg; sodium, 5 mg; vitamin A, 0% of Daily Value; vitamin C, 1%; calcium, 0%; iron, 0%; folate, 2%.

Lovely Leftovers Use this spread on a grilled chicken sandwich to increase fiber and add flavor.

Smoky Eggplant Spread

*My husband, Ted, and I took this yummy spread to our friends'
annual Preakness party. True, we had to coax folks into trying it
because it looked a little funny. Once they tasted it, though, they kept
coming back for more. In fact, some of them were so busy eating they
almost missed post time!*

3 medium eggplants, washed and dried
1 medium sweet onion, very finely chopped
2 tablespoons white vinegar
¼ cup olive oil
Salt and freshly ground black pepper to taste

Place the eggplants on a grill over high heat and close the lid.
Turn every 10 minutes, or until the eggplants are soft and the skin
blisters and turns black in places. Remove from the grill and place
in a brown paper bag. Close the bag and let stand for 10 minutes
to loosen the skin. Scrape the flesh away from the skin into a
large bowl. Stir in the onion, vinegar, oil, salt, and pepper. Cover
and refrigerate. Serve with party rye bread.

Yield: 48 servings

*Nutritional data per serving: Calories, 22; protein, 0 g; carbohydrate, 3 g;
dietary fiber, 1 g; total fat, 1 g; saturated fat, 0 g; cholesterol, 0 mg; sodium,
26 mg; vitamin A, 0% of Daily Value; vitamin C, 1%; calcium, 0%; iron, 1%;
vitamin B$_6$, 2%; folate, 1%; vitamin E, 1%; potassium, 2%.*

Lovely Leftovers Wow your friends with this fabulous spread
by using it to make vegetarian sandwiches.

Tuscan Bean Spread

Desperate for an off-the-cuff appetizer for guests who are just pulling into your driveway? Here's a taste of the lovely Italian countryside that's very easy to concoct. You'll come off looking like a celebrity chef.

1 can (15½ ounces) cannellini beans,
   rinsed and drained
1 teaspoon chopped garlic (from a jar)
1 tablespoon olive oil
2 tablespoons balsamic vinegar
2 tablespoons chopped onions
¼ teaspoon dried sage
Dash of ground red pepper

In a food processor, combine the beans, garlic, oil, vinegar, onions, sage, and pepper. Process to make a semi-smooth paste. Serve with raw vegetables or toasted baguette slices.

Yield: 22 servings

Nutritional data per serving: Calories, 18; protein, 1 g; carbohydrate, 3 g; dietary fiber, 1 g; total fat, <1 g; saturated fat, 0 g; cholesterol, 0 mg; sodium, 60 mg; vitamin A, 0% of Daily Value; vitamin C, 0%; calcium, 1%; iron, 1%; potassium, 1%.

Lovely Leftovers   Create a Tuscan wrap. Fill a dark green romaine lettuce leaf with bean spread, then roll it up and stuff it into a pita pocket.

Three-Bean Slaw

My mother created a wonderful, sweet slaw dressing that I've used for years to entice reluctant vegetable eaters. Try it on your hang-back friends.

2 cups shredded red cabbage
2 cups shredded green cabbage
1 cup shredded carrots
1 cup rinsed and drained canned black beans
1 cup rinsed and drained canned pinto beans
1 cup rinsed and drained canned chickpeas
1 cup well-drained juice-packed crushed
   pineapple
1/3 cup apple cider vinegar
1/3 cup sugar
2/3 cup low-fat mayonnaise
Salt and freshly ground black pepper to taste

In a large bowl, combine the red and green cabbage, carrots, black beans, pinto beans, chickpeas, and pineapple. Set aside.

In a small bowl, combine the vinegar, sugar, mayonnaise, salt, and pepper. Use a wire whisk to blend into a smooth sauce. Pour the dressing over the vegetables. Refrigerate for 4 hours or overnight to let the flavors blend.

Yield: 16 servings

Nutritional data per serving: Calories, 91; protein, 3 g; carbohydrate, 18 g; dietary fiber, 3 g; total fat, 1 g; saturated fat, 0 g; cholesterol, 0 mg; sodium, 321 mg; vitamin A, 20% of Daily Value; vitamin C, 21%; calcium, 3%; iron, 5%; folate, 7%; potassium, 5%.

Triple Wedge Salad

I remember when a serving of "hearts of lettuce" was no more than a chunk of iceberg with Thousand Island dressing. No more! Now lettuce really has heart, and it will do a better job of protecting yours.

1 small head romaine lettuce
1 head butterhead lettuce
1 head radicchio
4 thin slices red onion
1 tablespoon chopped fresh basil
1 tablespoon chopped fresh parsley
4 teaspoons olive oil
2 tablespoons red wine vinegar
1/4 teaspoon kosher salt
Freshly ground black pepper to taste

The Inside Skinny:
In a New England medical study, dieters who ate moderate amounts of healthy fat ate more vegetables than dieters on a low-fat regimen. They probably did so because veggies taste better when they're dressed with a touch of fat, says researcher Kathy McManus, R.D.

Quarter each lettuce head lengthwise. On each of four salad plates, arrange three lettuce hearts, one from each head. Separate the onion slices into rings and scatter them over the lettuce. In a small bowl, combine the basil, parsley, oil, vinegar, salt, and pepper. Use a wire whisk to blend well. Drizzle equal portions of the dressing over the salads.

Yield: 4 servings

Nutritional data per serving: Calories, 68; protein, 2 g; carbohydrate, 6 g; dietary fiber, 2 g; total fat, 5 g; saturated fat, <1 g; cholesterol, 0 mg; sodium, 130 mg; vitamin A, 19% of Daily Value; vitamin C, 35%; calcium, 4%; iron, 6%; vitamin E, 7%; folate, 31%; potassium, 11%.

Variegated Tomato Salad

Tomatoes come in so many shapes and sizes. Tossed together, they make a tempting array. This salad is absolutely beautiful, and it tastes even better than it looks.

1 large red tomato, coarsely chopped
1 large yellow tomato, coarsely chopped
1 medium green tomato, coarsely chopped
10 cocktail tomatoes, halved
10 pear-shaped yellow tomatoes
10 grape tomatoes
4 tablespoons Ken's light Caesar dressing
2 cups chopped spinach
2 cups torn butterhead lettuce
4 tablespoons crumbled feta cheese

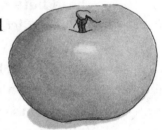

In a medium bowl, combine the tomatoes. Add the dressing and toss. Arrange a mixture of spinach and lettuce leaves on each of four salad plates. Top each with one-fourth of the tomato mixture and garnish with 1 tablespoon of the cheese.

Yield: 4 servings

Nutritional data per serving: Calories, 117; protein, 5 g; carbohydrate, 14 g; dietary fiber, 3 g; total fat, 6 g; saturated fat, 2 g; cholesterol, 8 mg; sodium, 458 mg; vitamin A, 24% of Daily Value; vitamin C, 85%; calcium, 9%; iron, 10%; folate, 27%; vitamin K, 85%; potassium, 22%.

> **The**
> **P·E·R·F·E·C·T**
> **Companion**
>
> Fill a tall glass with ice. Pour in some Westsoy Chai and garnish with a lime wedge. (This product is sweetened, spiced tea that comes ready-made in quart containers.)

Fort Myers Color-Burst Salad

While I was visiting my sister, Linda, lots of things in her garden ripened lusciously all at once. So we washed, peeled, chopped, and tossed until we created this stunning salad that tumbles all over the plate in a riot of color. A feast for the eyes as well as the palate!

4 medium tomatoes
¼ teaspoon salt
1 pink papaya, peeled and chopped, seeds reserved
Juice of ½ lime
1 mango, peeled, seeded, and chopped
1 avocado, peeled, seeded, and chopped
¼ cup toasted hulled pumpkin seeds

Place the tomatoes on their stem ends. With a sharp knife, form "flowers" by slicing each into six wedges without cutting all the way through. Place each on a luncheon plate and sprinkle with the salt.

In a medium bowl, sprinkle the papaya with the lime juice. Add the mango and avocado and stir gently to combine. Pile an equal portion of fruit into each tomato. Sprinkle with the pumpkin seeds and garnish each plate with the reserved papaya seeds (yes, you can eat them!). Serve with crab, tuna, or chicken salad and a dinner roll.

Yield: 4 servings

Nutritional data per serving: Calories, 174; protein, 3 g; carbohydrate, 24 g; dietary fiber, 6 g; total fat, 9 g; saturated fat, 1 g; cholesterol, 0 mg; sodium, 164 mg; vitamin A, 32% of Daily Value; vitamin C, 125%; calcium, 3%; iron, 7%; vitamin E, 11%; folate, 18%; vitamin K, 22%; potassium, 23%.

Move-Along Muffins

Let's say you're feelin' a little sluggish. You've probably lost your appetite and don't want to eat all those foods that are good for what ails you, like fruits and vegetables. Maybe a warm muffin will do. You can whip these up in no time and be on your way.

1 package (7 ounces) wheat bran muffin mix
1 egg
1/2 cup water
1/2 cup chopped pitted prunes

Preheat the oven to 400°F. Lightly coat a six-cup muffin pan with nonstick spray.

In a small bowl, combine the muffin mix, egg, water, and prunes. Stir with a fork just until blended. Spoon into the pan and bake for 20 minutes, or until a toothpick inserted in the center of a muffin comes out clean. Remove from the pan and cool on a rack.

Yield: 6 servings

Nutritional data per serving: Calories, 175; protein, 4 g; carbohydrate, 33 g; dietary fiber, 3 g; total fat, 5 g; saturated fat, 1 g; cholesterol, 31 mg; sodium, 241 mg; vitamin A, 4% of Daily Value; vitamin C, 1%; calcium, 2%; iron, 9%; vitamin B$_3$ (niacin), 10%; vitamin E, 5%; folate, 8%; potassium, 5%.

Instant Comfort: Really stuck? Wash down your muffin with a 4-ounce glass of prune juice.

Bran Buds with Cherries

Okay, you can probably guess that choosing a bran cereal like this one will keep your busy life moving in high gear. But the big surprise is that it also delivers a healthy dose of potassium. Think bran cereal tastes like sticks and twigs? Try it in this yummy, sundae-style breakfast.

1 cup fat-free chocolate-cheesecake yogurt
1/2 cup Bran Buds cereal
1/2 cup canned juice-packed sweet cherries
Dash of ground cinnamon

Put 1/2 cup of the yogurt in a cereal bowl. Add the cereal and cherries (with juice). Top with the remaining 1/2 cup yogurt. Stir gently until blended and dust with the cinnamon.

Yield: 1 serving

Nutritional data per serving: Calories, 413; protein, 13 g; carbohydrate, 100 g; dietary fiber, 20 g; total fat, 2 g; saturated fat, <1 g; cholesterol, 5 mg; sodium, 466 mg; vitamin A, 36% of Daily Value; vitamin C, 43%; calcium, 30%; iron, 46%; magnesium, 35%; potassium, 27%; zinc, 66%.

 The P·E·R·F·E·C·T Companion

This coffee recipe brews such a wonderful potion, you will spring from your bed each morning for that first fabulous sip. For each cup, grind 1/2 tablespoon doughnut-shop coffee beans with 1/2 tablespoon flavored coffee beans. (Cinnamon-hazelnut is my favorite.) Brew as usual, and inhale deeply. It's gonna be a great day!

Wheatberries with Pecans and Raspberries

I'm such a lucky girl. Because my dad's job was installing air-conditioning units, I grew up with heat relief when everyone else was still wondering if air conditioning was healthy. (Can you remember when?) All these years later, I still marvel at the simple pleasure I get from a good night's sleep and a hearty, hot breakfast, even in the heat of a Maryland summer. Try cooking up this no-sweat recipe for a steaming bowl of cereal just when the raspberries are at their peak!

½ cup Basic Wheatberries (page 146)
1 cup fat-free milk
1 teaspoon sugar
½ teaspoon vanilla extract
2 tablespoons chopped toasted pecans
1 cup fresh raspberries

In a microwave-safe bowl, combine the wheatberries, milk, sugar, and vanilla. Microwave on high for 2 to 5 minutes, or until piping hot. Stir in the pecans and raspberries.

Yield: 1 serving

Nutritional data per serving: Calories, 363; protein, 15 g; carbohydrate, 54 g; dietary fiber, 13 g; total fat, 12 g; saturated fat, 1 g; cholesterol, 4 mg; sodium, 127 mg; vitamin A, 17% of Daily Value; vitamin C, 56%; calcium 35%; iron, 12%; vitamin E, 8%; folate, 15%; potassium, 22%; omega-3 fatty acids, 29%.

> **QUICK TRICK:** To prepare this hearty breakfast in winter, just stir in frozen raspberries, then return the bowl to the microwave for 1 minute.

Oat 'n Fruit Smoothie

Looking for a high-fiber breakfast-on-the-run? Whip up this fruity drink that will keep you going like the Energizer bunny until lunchtime!

1/2 cup fat-free evaporated milk
1/2 cup high-calcium cottage cheese
1 cup Cheerios cereal
1/4 cup juice-packed crushed pineapple
1/2 banana
1/2 cup unsweetened applesauce
1 tablespoon orange marmalade

In a blender, combine the milk, cottage cheese, cereal, pineapple, banana, applesauce, and marmalade. Blend on high until smooth. Pour into a tall glass and sip through a fat straw.

Yield: 1 serving

Nutritional data per serving: Calories, 453; protein, 25 g; carbohydrate, 86 g; dietary fiber, 5 g; total fat, 3 g; saturated fat, 1.5 g; cholesterol, 15 mg; sodium, 761 mg; vitamin A, 44% of Daily Value; vitamin C, 85%; calcium, 63%; iron, 39%; vitamin B$_2$ (riboflavin), 48%; vitamin B$_6$, 41%; vitamin D, 34%; folate, 26%; potassium, 24%.

SUPER SUB

Despite its milky nature, natural cottage cheese is not high in calcium. It's discarded in producing the curds. High-calcium cottage cheese restores the missing mineral.

Corn and Refried Bean Burrito

I love melted cheese oozing out of my burrito. And I'll have a little crunch on the side please, so make it baby carrots.

½ cup grilled or canned yellow corn
½ cup vegetarian refried beans
1 ounce shredded reduced-fat cheddar cheese
2 red chile tortillas
2 tablespoons medium cilantro-flavored salsa

Warm a nonstick skillet over medium heat.

In a small bowl, combine the corn, beans, and cheese. Stir until well mixed. Spread half of the mixture in the center of each tortilla. Fold the ends over and place fold side down in the skillet. Cover and cook for 1 to 2 minutes, then turn and cook for 1 to 2 minutes, or until the centers are hot and the cheese begins to melt. Place each on a plate and top with a tablespoon of salsa.

Yield: 2 servings

Nutritional data per serving: Calories, 348; protein, 15 g; carbohydrate, 56 g; dietary fiber, 7 g; total fat, 9 g; saturated fat, 1 g; cholesterol, 3 mg; sodium, 841 mg; vitamin A, 20% of Daily Value; vitamin C, 8%; calcium, 10%; iron, 13%; folate, 6%; potassium, 4%.

> **QUICK TRICK:** Place each burrito on a paper plate. Microwave each on high for 30 to 60 seconds, or until the center is hot.

Bowl o' BLT

One of my fondest childhood memories is the unparalleled taste of the BLTs my dad made me. He grew the tomatoes, of course, and he cooked the bacon really crisp, then slathered on the mayo and added just a smidge of iceberg lettuce. Oh, well, we all know better now. Here's an updated BLT that puts all those remarkable flavors in healthier proportions.

2 slices whole wheat bread, cubed
2 cups chopped romaine lettuce
1 large ripe tomato, cubed
1 teaspoon olive oil
1 teaspoon balsamic vinegar
1/8 teaspoon salt
Freshly ground black pepper to taste
2 slices very crisp bacon, crumbled

> **The P·E·R·F·E·C·T Companion**
>
> Add a glass of fat-free milk for a complete lunch. For just 400 calories, you'll get 40% or more of your protein, vitamins B1 and B2, folate, vitamin C, calcium, and potassium for the day—a power-packed lunch!

Spread the bread cubes on a toaster-oven tray and mist lightly with olive oil spray. Toast until crisp and brown.

Meanwhile, in a large bowl, combine the lettuce, tomato, oil, vinegar, salt, and pepper. Toss well. Add the bread cubes and toss again. Pile into a salad bowl and garnish with the bacon.

Yield: 1 serving

Nutritional data per serving: Calories, 321; protein, 20 g; carbohydrate, 38 g; dietary fiber, 8 g; total fat, 12 g; saturated fat, 3 g; cholesterol, 27 mg; sodium, 1,070 mg; vitamin A, 40% of Daily Value; vitamin C, 103%; calcium, 10%; iron, 24%; vitamin B$_1$ (thiamin), 53%; vitamin B$_3$ (niacin), 24%; vitamin B$_6$, 25%; vitamin E, 12%; folate, 52%; potassium, 30%.

Martin's Hummus Chicken Salad Sandwich

My stepson, Martin, called me one day with a funny question: Could he use hummus instead of mayonnaise as the "glue" in chicken salad? Turns out, this combo makes a delicious, low-fat sandwich filler. Great idea, Martin!

2 ounces diced grilled chicken
¼ cup grated carrots
¼ cup diced red peppers
¼ cup diced cucumbers
¼ cup roasted-garlic–flavored hummus
1 small whole wheat pita pocket

In a small bowl, combine the chicken, carrots, peppers, cucumbers, and hummus. Use a fork to mix well. Toast the pita until puffed and let cool slightly. Split halfway and stuff with the chicken salad.

Yield: 1 serving

Nutritional data per serving: Calories, 393; protein, 30 g; carbohydrate, 50 g; dietary fiber, 10 g; total fat, 10 g; saturated fat, <1 g; cholesterol, 48 mg; sodium, 630 mg; vitamin A, 100% of Daily Value; vitamin C, 125%; calcium, 6%; iron, 25%; vitamin B$_3$ (niacin), 52%; vitamin B$_6$, 39%; vitamin E, 6%; folate, 23%; vitamin K, 58%; copper, 29%; magnesium, 29%; potassium, 17%; zinc, 19%.

Lovely Leftovers Too much chicken salad? Pile it on crackers for a light lunch or quick snack.

Orange and Black Bean Salad

Here's a salad hearty enough to serve as dinner. It would be espe-cially welcome on a hot summer night. Plus, it has enough color to make a rainbow jealous!

1 can (15½ ounces) black beans, rinsed and drained
1 can (11 ounces) mandarin oranges in light
    syrup, drained
1 cup diced red bell peppers
1 pickling cucumber, halved lengthwise and sliced
6 green onions, including some of the green tops,
    thinly sliced
1 tablespoon peanut oil
2 tablespoons fresh lime juice
2 teaspoons dried cilantro
½ teaspoon ground cumin

In a medium bowl, combine the beans, oranges, peppers, cucumber, and onions. In a small bowl, use a wire whisk to combine the oil, lime juice, cilantro, and cumin. Pour over the bean mixture and stir. Refrigerate for about 1 hour to let the flavors blend.

DOUBLE DUTY

Beans provide both the protein and the fiber in this salad, which is something that meat, chicken, and fish can't do.

Yield: 4 servings

Nutritional data per serving: Calories, 183; protein, 7 g; carbohydrate, 31 g; dietary fiber, 8 g; total fat, 4 g; saturated fat, <1 g; cholesterol, 0 mg; sodium, 389 mg; vitamin A, 22% of Daily Value; vitamin C, 134%; calcium, 4%; iron, 14%; folate, 18%; potassium, 12%.

Maple-Grilled Turkey Salad

I love to make a one-bowl meal. Here's one of the ways I pile it on.

½ cup Vermont sweet 'n sour marinade and
    grilling sauce
2 turkey cutlets (about 4 ounces each)
4 cups mixed salad greens
¼ cup shredded carrots
½ cup grilled yellow corn
½ avocado, cubed
2 tablespoons sunflower seeds
2 slices whole wheat bread, cubed
    and toasted

> ### The
> ### P·E·R·F·E·C·T
> ### Companion
>
> Drop 2 cold-brew tea bags into a 2-quart pitcher and fill ⅔ full with water. Steep for 3 minutes, then remove the tea bags. Stir in ½ cup cranberry juice concentrate. Fill with ice.

In a glass dish, brush the marinade on the turkey, reserving 2 tablespoons. Cover and refrigerate for 30 minutes. Grill for 4 to 5 minutes on each side, or until cooked through and juices are clear. Remove from the heat and slice into long, thin strips. Set aside.

In a large bowl, combine the greens, carrots, corn, avocado, sunflower seeds, and bread cubes. Add the reserved marinade and toss until well coated. Divide between two salad bowls and top each with half of the turkey strips.

Yield: 2 servings

Nutritional data per serving: Calories, 465; protein, 34 g; carbohydrate, 41 g; dietary fiber, 9 g; total fat, 20 g; saturated fat, 3 g; cholesterol, 60 mg; sodium, 613 mg; vitamin A, 74% of Daily Value; vitamin C, 44%; calcium, 12%; iron, 25%; vitamin E, 29%; folate, 52%; potassium, 27%.

Grilled Salmon and Corn with Limas

We always grill a very large slab of salmon. After dinner, I cut the leftover fish into 4-ounce chunks, wrap each in plastic, and pop them into the freezer. By planning ahead, I always have wonderful grilled salmon at my fingertips.

1 cup yellow corn, cut from the cob
1 cup cooked lima beans
1/2 cup diced red bell peppers
1 tablespoon balsamic vinegar
6 leaves fresh basil, slivered
Salt and freshly ground black pepper to taste
2 leaves red lettuce
2 grilled salmon filets (4 ounces each)

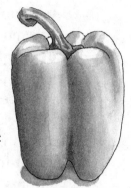

In a medium bowl, combine the corn, lima beans, bell peppers, vinegar, basil, salt, and black pepper. Mix well. Place a lettuce leaf on each of two plates and top with the corn mixture. Nestle a salmon fillet into each.

Yield: 2 servings

Nutritional data per serving: Calories, 406; protein, 38 g; carbohydrate, 42 g; dietary fiber, 9 g; total fat, 11 g; saturated fat, 2 g; cholesterol, 81 mg; sodium, 301 mg; vitamin A, 29% of Daily Value; vitamin C, 138%; calcium, 5%; iron, 21%; vitamin B$_1$ (thiamin), 39%; vitamin B$_2$ (riboflavin), 40%; vitamin B$_3$ (niacin), 68%; vitamin B$_6$, 66%; vitamin D, 79%; vitamin E, 12%; folate, 24%; potassium, 40%; omega-3 fatty acids, 258%.

SUPER SUB

Corn and limas outrank all other vegetables when it comes to forking over fiber.

Jiffy Jambalaya

6 ounces deveined peeled shrimp
2 unbreaded chicken tenders, cut into $1/2$-inch rounds
4 ounces low-fat smoked sausage or kielbasa, cut into
    $1/2$-inch pieces
$1/2$ teaspoon crushed red pepper
1 tablespoon peanut oil
1 cup chopped red onions
1 cup chopped green bell peppers
1 cup sliced celery
3 cloves garlic, minced
1 cup V8 vegetable juice
1 cup fat-free chicken broth
$1/2$ cup instant brown rice
$1/4$ teaspoon dried thyme
Dash of ground cloves

> **DOUBLE DUTY**
>
> V8 delivers plenty of veggie flavor, which means you can skip chopping and cooking some vegetables. It has lots of salt, too, so you don't have to add more.

In a large saucepan over high heat, sauté the shrimp, chicken, sausage, and red pepper in the oil until the meat begins to brown. Stir in the onions, green peppers, celery, and garlic. Cook, stirring, for 1 to 2 minutes, or until the vegetables begin to soften. Add the V8, broth, rice, thyme, and cloves. Bring to a boil. Reduce the heat, cover, and simmer for 10 minutes, or until the rice is cooked. Serve with whole grain bread and cold beer.

Yield: 4 servings

Nutritional data per serving: Calories, 255; protein, 24 g; carbohydrate, 25 g; dietary fiber, 3 g; total fat, 6 g; saturated fat, 1 g; cholesterol, 115 mg; sodium, 652 mg; vitamin A, 11% of Daily Value; vitamin C, 93%; calcium, 7%; iron, 15%; vitamin B_3 (niacin), 23%; vitamin B_6, 17%; potassium, 11%.

Beef and Broccoli Rabe Stir-Fry

4 ounces lean beef round, thinly sliced
4 teaspoons peanut oil
$^1/_2$ cup sliced onions
$^1/_2$ cup sliced shiitake mushrooms
$^1/_2$ cup slivered red bell peppers
$^1/_2$ pound broccoli rabe, cooked*
1 can (15 ounces) baby corn, drained
$^1/_2$ cup beef broth
1 tablespoon cornstarch
1 tablespoon teriyaki stir-fry sauce

The P·E·R·F·E·C·T Companion

Of course, you'll want green tea, but this time try the lemon-flavored variety. Put 2 tea bags in a teapot and pour in 4 cups boiling water. Cover and steep for 5 minutes. Remove the tea bags and serve.

In a wok over high heat, cook the beef in 3 teaspoons of the oil, just until cooked through. Remove with a slotted spoon and set aside. Add the onions, mushrooms, peppers, and the remaining 1 teaspoon oil. Cook for 3 to 5 minutes, just until beginning to wilt. Stir in the broccoli rabe, corn, and reserved beef. Reduce the heat to low.

In a small bowl, combine the broth, cornstarch, and sauce. Stir until the cornstarch dissolves. Add to the vegetable mixture and cook for 5 minutes, or until the sauce thickens and the vegetables are heated through. Serve over cooked brown rice.

Yield: 4 servings

Nutritional data per serving: Calories, 147; protein, 12 g; carbohydrate, 12 g; dietary fiber, 2 g; total fat, 6 g; saturated fat, 1 g; cholesterol, 20 mg; sodium, 396 mg; vitamin A, 77% of Daily Value; vitamin C, 123%; calcium, 2%; iron, 9%; zinc, 10%.

*See Broccoli Rabe with Pasta on page 207.

Nutty Chicken Nuggets

1 cup instant or old-fashioned oats
1/4 cup toasted pecans, finely chopped
1/2 cup fat-free evaporated milk
4 unbreaded chicken tenders, cut into
    1-inch pieces

Preheat the oven to 450°F. Lightly coat a baking sheet with nonstick spray.

In a blender running on high, remove the feeder cap and pour in the oats. Blend for a few seconds to make oat flour. Pour into a cereal bowl, add the pecans, and stir until well mixed. Pour the milk into another cereal bowl.

Use a fork or toothpick to spear the chicken chunks one by one, dipping them first into the milk and then into the flour mixture. As they're coated, place on the baking sheet. Lightly coat with nonstick spray. Bake for 10 to 15 minutes, or until cooked through and beginning to brown. Let cool slightly. Serve with light ranch dressing or apricot jam thinned with water for dipping.

Yield: 4 servings

Nutritional data per serving: Calories, 168; protein, 16 g; carbohydrate, 10 g; dietary fiber, 2 g; total fat, 7 g; saturated fat, 1 g; cholesterol, 33 mg; sodium, 56 mg; vitamin A, 2% of Daily Value; vitamin C, 2%; calcium, 6%; iron, 6%, vitamin B$_3$ (niacin), 33%; vitamin B$_6$, 17%; magnesium, 14%.

SUPER SUB

These nutty nuggets slash total fat and saturated fat by 1/3 and provide 8 times more fiber than average chicken nuggets.

Samba Fruit Salsa

Salsa isn't always spicy hot or even made of vegetables. It's really just a sauce made of chopped ingredients. This one is naturally sweet and heady with cinnamon. It's wonderful with grilled chicken or shrimp.

1 cup diced fresh pineapple
1 mango, peeled, pitted, and diced
1 red banana, cut lengthwise
   and sliced
1/4 teaspoon ground cinnamon
1/2 teaspoon dried cilantro
1/2 teaspoon grated lime peel

In a medium bowl, combine the pineapple, mango, and banana. Stir until well blended. Sprinkle with the cinnamon, cilantro, and lime peel and gently fold together. Refrigerate until ready to use.

Yield: 4 servings

Nutritional data per serving: Calories, 76; protein, 1 g; carbohydrate, 20 g; dietary fiber, 2 g; total fat, 0 g; saturated fat, 0 g; cholesterol, 0 mg; sodium, 2 mg; vitamin A, 20% of Daily Value; vitamin C, 38%; calcium, 1%; iron, 2%; vitamin B_6, 12%; potassium, 7%.

Lovely Leftovers Combine leftover salsa with plain yogurt for a luscious pre-workout treat.

Farmers' Market Casserole

At the end of summer, when roadside stands and farmers' markets are packed with just-picked vegetables, I'm a happy girl. I run right home and cook up a mix of everything too good to resist that day. Here's a sample.

1 medium eggplant, cubed
1 medium onion, thinly sliced
1 small zucchini, thinly sliced
1 small yellow squash, thinly sliced
1 medium red bell pepper, cut into 2-inch strips
2 tomatoes, quartered and sliced
2 cups rinsed and drained canned soybeans
1/2 teaspoon salt
Freshly ground black pepper to taste
1/2 cup fresh basil, chopped
1 tablespoon garlic (from a jar)
1 cup shredded reduced-fat mozzarella cheese

In a 2-quart microwave-safe baking dish, combine the eggplant, onion, zucchini, squash, red pepper, tomatoes, soybeans, salt, pepper, basil, and garlic. Cover and microwave on high for 8 to 10 minutes, turning every 3 to 4 minutes, until soft. Sprinkle with the cheese. Cover and let stand for 2 minutes, or until the cheese is melted.

Yield: 6 servings

Nutritional data per serving: Calories, 217; protein, 18 g; carbohydrate, 20 g; dietary fiber, 8 g; total fat, 9 g; saturated fat, 3 g; cholesterol, 10 mg; sodium, 483 mg; vitamin A, 22% of Daily Value; vitamin C, 103%; calcium, 27%; iron, 22%; vitamin E, 7%; folate, 15%; potassium, 25%.

Black Japonica Rice with Hazelnuts

Black Japonica is a beautiful, rich, dark blend of whole grain black and mahogany rice. It's originally from Japan but is now grown in California by Lundberg Family Farms. You'll find it in natural foods stores or the natural foods section of most large supermarkets. Once you've eaten it, you'll go back for more.

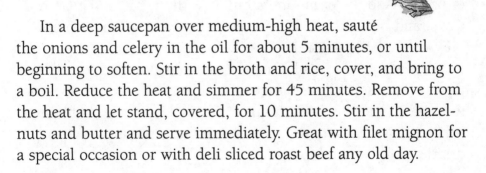

1 cup coarsely chopped yellow onions
1/2 cup finely chopped celery
1 teaspoon hazelnut oil
2 cups fat-free beef broth
1 cup Lundberg Black Japonica
   rice
1/4 cup chopped toasted hazelnuts
1 tablespoon butter

In a deep saucepan over medium-high heat, sauté the onions and celery in the oil for about 5 minutes, or until beginning to soften. Stir in the broth and rice, cover, and bring to a boil. Reduce the heat and simmer for 45 minutes. Remove from the heat and let stand, covered, for 10 minutes. Stir in the hazelnuts and butter and serve immediately. Great with filet mignon for a special occasion or with deli sliced roast beef any old day.

Yield: 6 servings

Nutritional data per serving: Calories, 189; protein, 6 g; carbohydrate, 29 g; dietary fiber, 3 g; total fat, 7 g; saturated fat, 1.5 g; cholesterol, 5 mg; vitamin A, 2% of Daily Value; vitamin C, 7%; calcium, 2%; iron, 6%; vitamin E, 7%; vitamin B_6, 11%; magnesium, 14%; potassium, 7%.

Green Beans with Lemony Sauce

Most sauces strangle your veggies (and your arteries) with fat. A dollop of this refreshing dressing will turn ho-hum green beans into a special treat.

1/2 **pound green beans, washed and trimmed**
1/8 **teaspoon salt**
1/4 **teaspoon dried cilantro**
2 **tablespoons light canola oil mayonnaise***
2 **tablespoons fat-free milk**
1/8 **teaspoon grated lemon peel**
Freshly ground pepper mélange to
   taste

Pour 1 inch of water into a deep saucepan and insert a steamer basket. Add the beans and sprinkle with the salt and cilantro. Cover and bring to a boil. Reduce the heat and steam for 5 minutes, or until crisp-tender.

Meanwhile, in a small saucepan over medium heat, combine the mayonnaise, milk, lemon peel, and pepper. Use a wire whisk to blend into a silky smooth sauce. Gently heat just to bubbling. When the beans are done, spoon them into a serving bowl and drizzle with the sauce.

Yield: 4 servings

Nutritional data per serving: Calories, 38 calories; protein, 1g; carbohydrate, 5 g; dietary fiber, 2 g; total fat, 2 g; saturated fat, 0 g; cholesterol, 0 mg; sodium, 45 mg; vitamin A, 4% of Daily Value; vitamin C, 16%; calcium, 3%; iron, 3%; vitamin K, 34%; potassium, 4%.

*Available in natural foods stores and some large supermarkets.

Chewy Fruit 'n Flax Cookies

These high-fiber cookies, just bursting with all-natural ingredients, are really good for what ails you!

2 tablespoons creamy peanut butter
1/2 cup unsweetened applesauce
6 tablespoons flaxseeds
1/2 cup brown sugar
1 egg
1 teaspoon vanilla extract
1/2 teaspoon salt
1/2 cup enriched all-purpose flour
3/4 cup old-fashioned oats
1/2 cup dark seedless raisins

DOUBLE DUTY

In addition to easing intestinal distress, these cookies provide the same healthful fat found in fish. The secret is the flaxseeds. Hook just one of these tasty little nuggets, and you'll reel in 3/4 of your day's supply of that special fat!

Preheat the oven to 400°F.

In a medium bowl, combine the peanut butter, applesauce, flaxseeds, brown sugar, egg, vanilla, and salt. With an electric mixer, beat until well blended. Add the flour and oats and beat until blended. Stir in the raisins. Drop by level measuring tablespoons onto an ungreased baking sheet. Bake for 10 minutes. With a spatula, immediately remove from the baking sheet and place on a rack to cool. Store in a covered container—if they last long enough.

Yield: 14 servings

Nutritional data per serving: Calories, 94; protein, 3 g; carbohydrate, 14 g; dietary fiber, 2 g; total fat, 3 g; saturated fat, <1 g; cholesterol, 15 mg; sodium, 105 mg; vitamin A, 1% of Daily Value; vitamin C, 3%; calcium, 2%; iron, 5%; vitamin E, 3%; folate, 6%; magnesium, 8%; omega-3 fatty acids, 76%.

Baked Apple Cocktail

Tired of the same old orange juice for breakfast? Dust off your blender and put it to work on this fruity treat. It will really perk up your morning!

1 cup cold ruby red grapefruit blend with calcium
¹/₄ teaspoon ground cinnamon
1 cold medium sweet apple, quartered and cored

In a blender, combine the grapefruit juice and cinnamon. Begin to blend on high, then remove the feeder cap. Drop in the apples one by one and blend until finely chopped. Pour into a highball glass, sip, and savor.

Yield: 1 serving

Nutritional data per serving: Calories, 212; protein, 1 g; carbohydrate, 54 g; dietary fiber, 5 g; total fat, 0 g; saturated fat, 0 g; cholesterol, 0 mg; sodium, 35 mg; vitamin A, 1% of Daily Value; vitamin C, 138%; calcium, 11%; iron, 2%; folate, 2%; potassium, 10%.

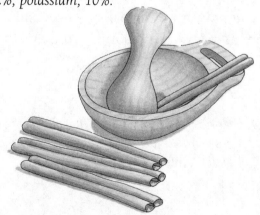

DOUBLE DUTY

An apple with its peel is a two-for-the-price-of-one treat, providing both soluble fiber to help lower cholesterol and insoluble fiber to keep your bowels working.

Peach Melba Swirl

Right now, my supermarket is overflowing with the sweetest fresh raspberries I've ever eaten. I've eaten them every way you can think of, but today, I decided to drink a few for lunch. So sweet, so easy, and oh, so refreshing.

1 cup peach-flavored kefir*
1 cup fresh raspberries
Ground cinnamon to taste

In a blender, combine the kefir and raspberries. Blend on high until smooth and creamy. Pour over ice in a tall glass and dust with the cinnamon. Grab a straw and a favorite book, then head for the patio.

Yield: 1 serving

Nutritional data per serving: Calories, 220; protein, 15 g; carbohydrate, 35 g; dietary fiber, 8 g; total fat, 3 g; saturated fat, 1.5 g; cholesterol, 10 mg; sodium, 125 mg; vitamin A, 12% of Daily Value; vitamin C, 55%; calcium, 33%; iron, 4%; vitamin D, 25%; folate, 8%.

*A cultured milk beverage available in the dairy department, near the milk and yogurt.

DOUBLE DUTY

Raspberries are not only high in vitamin C, they're also team leaders in the fiber department, delivering 1/3 of your day's requirement in just 1 cupful.

Persian Sweets

My mother-in-law used to make these tidy tidbits for Christmas every year. They're jam-packed with natural sugars guaranteed to satisfy the most jaded sweet tooth! It's fun to make them with the kids, too.

1 pound pitted dates
1/2 pound dried figs
1/2 cup walnuts
1/4 cup sugar

Feed the dates, figs, and walnuts into a food grinder, catching the mixture in a medium bowl. Use a teaspoon to scoop up enough to form small balls. In a small bowl or dish, roll each ball in the sugar.

Yield: 50 servings

Nutritional data per serving: Calories, 49; protein, <1 g; carbohydrate, 11 g; dietary fiber, 1 g; total fat, <1 g; saturated fat, 0 g; cholesterol, 0 mg; sodium, <1 mg; vitamin A, 0% of Daily Value; vitamin C, 0%; calcium, 1%; iron, 2%; folate, 1%; potassium, 2%.

DOUBLE DUTY

Dates and figs are not simply sweet treats. They help you sneak a little extra calcium into your diet.

Blackberries with Banana Cream Pudding

I admit it—fresh blackberries are not that easy to find. When they do appear in my market, I snag them and dash home to make this luscious treat.

4 cups blackberries, washed and patted dry
1 banana
2 cups 2% milk
**1 package (3.4 ounces) banana cream
   instant pudding mix**
Dash of ground nutmeg

Divide the blackberries among four dessert bowls. On a plate, use a fork to thoroughly mash the banana. Set aside.

In a medium bowl, combine the milk and pudding mix. Use a wire whisk to blend for 2 minutes, or until beginning to thicken. Whisk in the nutmeg and banana until well blended. (The pudding will remain soft and custardlike.) Spoon ¼ cup over each bowl of blackberries. Refrigerate leftover pudding for later use.

Yield: 4 servings

Nutritional data per serving: Calories, 164; protein, 3 g; carbohydrate, 36 g; dietary fiber, 8 g; total fat, 2 g; saturated fat, <1g; cholesterol, 5 mg; sodium, 216 mg; vitamin A, 6% of Daily Value; vitamin C, 54%; calcium, 12%; iron, 5%; vitamin E, 6%; folate, 14%; potassium, 12%.

Lovely Leftovers

The pudding is great all by itself or spooned over toasted pound cake.

CHAPTER 10

SHARPEN YOUR MIND

REMEMBER TO EAT THE RED AND THE BLUE

I'D LOVE TO TELL YOU A FUNNY STORY ABOUT HOW I GOT smarter by eating blueberries, but I can't just yet. That's because I'm not an old lab rat.

I do eat lots of blueberries, especially in June and July when they're fat and fresh and tumbling out of the market faster than I can tote them to my car. I stir them into my oatmeal, bake them into a sweet and savory blueberry crisp, toss them into salads, and, of course, make blueberry pancakes. I eat them in winter, too, frozen or canned, and whip them into smoothies or fold them into muffins. (Yes, all their brain-protective nutrients are intact!) But am I smarter because of it? I'm too young to know!

Now if I were an old lab rat, I'd be bragging about my

bodacious brain. At Tufts University in Boston, a group of medical researchers have been feeding blueberry concentrate to elderly rats, then checking how well the rats find their way through a maze. And, surprise—it turns out that eating blueberries actually improves their memory! So I'll keep eating my blueberries and drop you a note in 20 or 30 years to let you know how I'm doing.

Beyond blueberries, what else helps protect your gray matter? Research on the way food affects your brain is too new, so no one can say for sure, but some amazing trends are emerging.

♥ **Get to the heart of the matter.** The most surprising is that just about anything that's good for your heart is good for your brain. Take lowering your cholesterol. If your arteries are clogged with sludge, the blood carrying needed oxygen has trouble flowing to your brain, so you can't think as well, which sets you up for memory loss, says Jim Joseph, Ph.D., the Tufts blueberry doc.

♥ **Take your medicine.** Diabetes and high blood pressure take a toll, too. But in French and Finnish studies, folks with these conditions who shaped up their plates and took their medicine put the

The Best Brain Boosters

Folks over 50 need a multivitamin that serves up a full day's supply of three vital brain-boosting nutrients that are absorbed better from supplements than from food. They are vitamin B_{12} (2.4 micrograms), folic acid (400 micrograms), and vitamin D (400 IU), according to the National Academy of Sciences Institute of Medicine, which sets the Recommended Dietary Allowances.

brakes on mental decline. Fruits and veggies played a big part. Here's why.

Your brain sucks up a ton of oxygen while tending to its daily chores. Just resting, it takes about 20 percent of your body's total supply. And thinking can hog 40 to 50 percent of all the oxygen your heart and lungs can pump out.

Processing oxygen comes with a high price tag, however. It produces free radical garbage that can clutter up your brain or damage its delicate structures. Add that to chronic diseases that can pile up, magnifying one another's effects, and down you go into the swirling vortex of memory loss.

But sweet little blueberries are prepared to come to the rescue! They're loaded with antioxidants that fight free radicals. Fortunately, they may have help. In another lab at Tufts, researchers are testing fruits and veggies for their antioxidant power. Some of the top picks: blueberries, blackberries, kale, strawberries, spinach, brussels sprouts, plums, broccoli, beets, red grapes, red peppers, cherries, and kiwifruit.

Now, what do these foods have in common, you may ask? Don't tax your brain—I'll tell you: intense colors, such as blue, purple, red, and green.

In this chapter, we're going to have some fun with the blues, purples, and reds (you'll find plenty of information about greens in chapters 7 and 12). But first, I'll show you how to make that blueberry crisp. We'll eat it while it's nice and warm, then think about some cool things to do with strawberries, raspberries, raisins, plums, prunes, red radishes, and red peppers.

Roasted-Pepper and Green Olive Spread

Whip out your food processor and whirl up this knock-your-socks-off spread. Your family and friends will keep coming back for more!

1 jar (7 ounces) roasted red peppers
1/2 cup pimiento-stuffed Spanish olives
1 clove garlic, minced or pressed
1 teaspoon balsamic vinegar
1 1/2 teaspoons olive oil
1/2 teaspoon dried basil
Freshly ground black pepper to taste

In a food processor, combine the red peppers, olives, garlic, vinegar, oil, basil, and black pepper. Process until coarsely chopped but not pureed. Spoon onto toasted Italian bread rounds.

Yield: 16 servings

Nutritional data per serving: Calories, 13, protein, 0 g; carbohydrate, 1 g; dietary fiber, 0 g; total fat, 1 g; saturated fat, 0 g; cholesterol, 0 mg; sodium, 137 mg; vitamin A, 5% of Daily Value; vitamin C, 12%; calcium, 0%; iron, 1%.

Lovely Leftovers Use as a super sandwich spread. It beats the heck out of mayonnaise!

Chilled Blueberry Soup

This soup is a hot-weather favorite at my house. It's icy cold and refreshing. An added benefit is that you can whip up this cool beauty in no time.

2 pints fresh blueberries,
   washed and patted dry
½ cup lemonade
2 tablespoons honey
2 tablespoons chopped fresh mint
4 tablespoons sour cream

In a blender or food processor, combine the blueberries, lemonade, honey, and mint. Process on high until smooth and creamy. Ladle into four soup cups or stemmed glasses and garnish each with 1 tablespoon of the sour cream. Refrigerate until ready to serve.

Yield: 4 servings

Nutritional data per serving: Calories, 158; protein, 1 g; carbohydrate, 34 g; dietary fiber, 4 g; total fat, 4 g; saturated fat, 2 g; cholesterol, 6 mg; sodium, 20 mg; vitamin A, 4% of Daily Value; vitamin C, 32%; calcium, 3%; iron, 2%; vitamin E, 8%; omega-3 fatty acids, 14%.

Lovely Leftovers Create a high-calcium treat by stirring extra blueberry soup into plain yogurt.

Chipotle Ranch Salad

Sometimes, I want lots of dressing on my salad, but I just can't help hating all those calories! My solution? A blend of salsa and ranch dressing, which ups the veggies instead of the fat. I'm especially fond of the smoky, Southwestern flavor of chipotle chile pepper blend.

1/4 cup Pace chipotle salsa
1 tablespoon light ranch dressing
2 cups mesclun or field greens
2 baby carrots, thinly sliced
1/2 cup sliced red bell peppers
5 grape tomatoes
1/4 avocado, cut into chunks
1 ounce shredded reduced-fat four-cheese blend
1 tablespoon hulled pumpkin seeds

In a small bowl, combine the salsa and dressing. Set aside.

In a large salad bowl, combine the greens, carrots, peppers, tomatoes, and avocado. Add the dressing and toss until well coated. Place in a single-serving bowl and garnish with the cheese and pumpkin seeds.

Yield: 1 serving

Nutritional data per serving: Calories, 325; protein, 16 g; carbohydrate, 24 g; dietary fiber, 9 g; total fat, 21 g; saturated fat, 6 g; cholesterol, 24 mg; sodium, 704 mg; vitamin A, 135% of Daily Value; vitamin C, 312%; calcium, 36%; iron, 26%; vitamin B$_6$, 29%; vitamin E, 14%; folate, 52%; magnesium, 31%; potassium, 35%; zinc, 19%.

DOUBLE DUTY

Along with those cancer-fighting red pigments, the peppers deliver a 3-day supply of vitamin C. It's eye-deal for protecting your vision.

Sweet Beet Salad

The most important thing I ever learned from a salad bar is how much I love beets on my greens. Their sweet, earthy flavor helps smooth out the sharper, sometimes bitter flavor of other veggies. It's amazing how it all works together!

2 cups mixed salad greens
1/2 cup shredded red cabbage
1/2 cup drained canned
   sliced beets
4 wedges tomato
1/4 cup broccoli florets
1/8 cup sliced red
   radishes
1 tablespoon sunflower seeds
1 hard-boiled egg, sliced
1 tablespoon Ken's light Caesar dressing

At the salad bar, pile the greens, cabbage, beets, tomatoes, broccoli, radishes, sunflower seeds, and egg into a take-home container. At home, transfer the salad to one of your own pretty salad bowls, toss with the dressing, and enjoy!

Yield: 1 serving

Nutritional data per serving: Calories, 244; protein, 12 g; carbohydrate, 24 g; dietary fiber, 8 g; total fat, 13 g; saturated fat, 2 g; cholesterol, 186 mg; sodium, 664 mg; vitamin A, 48% of Daily Value; vitamin C, 132%; calcium, 12%; iron, 24%; vitamin E, 30%; folate, 51%.

Flaming Wasabi Salad

If you like your salad with a bit of a kick, this red beauty is just what you're looking for. Red radishes, jalapeño Jack cheese, and wasabi-coated toasted soy nuts fan the flames. Keep a tall, cool drink handy!

4 cups torn red leaf lettuce
1 cup torn radicchio
1 cup cherry tomatoes
4 red radishes, sliced
1/2 cup thinly sliced red bell
    peppers
1/4 cup light French dressing
1/2 cup wasabi-coated toasted soy nuts
2 ounces reduced-fat jalapeño Jack
    cheese, cubed

In a large bowl, combine the lettuce, radicchio, tomatoes, radishes, peppers, and dressing. Toss until well coated. Divide among four salad bowls and top each serving with 2 tablespoons of the soy nuts and 1/2 ounce of the cheese.

Yield: 4 servings

Nutritional data per serving: Calories, 150; protein, 9 g; carbohydrate, 15 g; dietary fiber, 5 g; total fat, 7 g; saturated fat, 1 g; cholesterol, 5 mg; sodium, 403 mg; vitamin A, 30% of Daily Value; vitamin C, 67%; calcium, 19%; iron, 5%; vitamin E, 4%; folate, 4%; potassium, 9%.

The P·E·R·F·E·C·T Companion

In a 2-cup heatproof measuring cup, pour 1 cup boiling water over a jasmine green tea bag. Steep for 3 minutes, then remove the tea bag. Stir in 1 teaspoon honey, then 1 cup crushed ice. Stir until the ice melts and pour into a tall, ice-filled glass.

"The Color Purple" Salad

My eyes lit up when I found this salad mix of red and green leaf lettuce, and, can you believe it, purple Savoy kale! I couldn't resist tossing it with some other pretty purple things.

1 package (6 ounces) Fresh Express royal salad blend
1 medium black or red bell pepper, thinly sliced
1/2 cup torn radicchio
12 oil-cured olives
1 cup purple grapes, halved and pitted
1 tablespoon olive oil
2 tablespoons balsamic vinegar
1/4 teaspoon salt
Freshly ground black pepper to taste

In a large salad bowl, combine the greens, bell pepper, radicchio, olives, and grapes. Drizzle with the oil and vinegar and sprinkle with the salt and black pepper. Toss until well coated.

Yield: 6 servings

Nutritional data per serving: Calories, 53; protein, 1 g; carbohydrate, 7 g; dietary fiber, 1 g; total fat, 3 g; saturated fat, 0 g; cholesterol, 0 mg; sodium, 165 mg; vitamin A, 2% of Daily Value; vitamin C, 43%; calcium, 3%; iron, 3%; vitamin E, 3%.

DOUBLE DUTY

While providing their protective pigments, the olives also help you absorb the fat-soluble vitamins A and E from the veggies.

Spicy Hot Fruit Compote

This warm and cozy fruit compote has become a family favorite for our Christmas morning brunch. It practically makes itself, and it gives the house a wonderful, welcoming fragrance.

8 ounces dried pitted apricots
8 ounces dried pitted plums (prunes)
1 cup fresh cranberries
2 cups water
1 cup dry white wine
1 teaspoon ground cinnamon
1/2 teaspoon ground mace
1/2 teaspoon ground cloves

In a slow cooker, combine the apricots, dried plums, cranberries, water, wine, cinnamon, mace, and cloves. Cook on low for about 2 hours, or until the fruit is plump. Stir as little as possible so the fruit stays whole.

Yield: 12 servings

Nutritional data per serving: Calories, 112; protein, 1 g; carbohydrate, 25 g; dietary fiber, 3 g; total fat, 0 g; saturated fat, 0 g; cholesterol, 0 mg; sodium, 3 mg; vitamin A, 5% of Daily Value; vitamin C, 8%; calcium, 2%; iron, 7%; potassium, 12%.

DOUBLE DUTY

In addition to fighting memory loss, just 1/4 cup dried cranberries contains enough condensed tannins to fend off urinary tract infections.

Chocolate-Raspberry Pancakes

³/₄ cup Arrowhead Mills multigrain pancake
    and waffle mix
³/₄ cup water
2 teaspoons walnut oil
2 tablespoons flaxseeds
2 tablespoons chocolate-hazelnut spread
1 cup fresh raspberries

Preheat a nonstick griddle over medium-high heat. Place two plates in the oven on low to warm.

In a medium bowl, combine the pancake mix, water, oil, and flaxseeds. Stir with a fork just until smooth. Reduce the heat to medium and lightly coat the griddle with nonstick spray. Use a gravy ladle to spoon the batter onto the griddle. Cook until bubbles form and the edges begin to dry. Turn and cook just until the bottoms brown. Place on the warmed plates and cover to keep warm until all batter is used. Dot each pancake with the chocolate spread and top each serving with ¹/₂ cup of the raspberries.

SUPER SUB

Walnut oil, flaxseeds, and hazelnuts combine to deliver 2 days' supply of omega-3s, the fats that work to protect you from stroke.

Yield: 2 servings

Nutritional data per serving: Calories, 383; protein, 11 g; carbohydrate, 52 g; dietary fiber, 12 g; total fat, 16 g; saturated fat, 2 g; cholesterol, 2 mg; sodium, 400 mg; vitamin A, 1% of Daily Value; vitamin C, 26%; calcium, 22%; iron, 16%; omega-3 fatty acids, 229%.

Whole Grain Waffles with Hot Raisin Syrup

I was raised on King syrup, but that's kid stuff. Now I like my sweets with a little more nutritional punch. How about you? Try this sweet, spicy sauce, and you'll be glad you're a grownup.

½ cup frozen cranberry juice concentrate,
    thawed
½ cup water
1 teaspoon cornstarch
½ cup dark seedless raisins
½ teaspoon ground cloves
½ teaspoon ground cinnamon
8 round whole grain waffles
1 cup low-fat ricotta cheese

In a small saucepan over medium heat, stir together the cranberry juice, water, and cornstarch until the cornstarch is dissolved. Stir in the raisins, cloves, and cinnamon. Bring to a boil. Reduce the heat, cover, and simmer for 10 minutes, or until the sauce is thickened and the raisins are plump. Toast the waffles and spread each with 2 tablespoons of the ricotta. Top with 2 tablespoons of the syrup.

Yield: 4 servings

Nutritional data per serving: Calories, 411; protein, 14 g; carbohydrate, 63 g; dietary fiber, 3 g; total fat, 12 g; saturated fat, 4 g; cholesterol, 89 mg; sodium, 313 mg; vitamin A, 12% of Daily Value; vitamin C, 29%; calcium, 42%; iron, 12%; vitamin D, 8%; vitamin E, 6%; potassium, 10%.

Grilled Tuna Cobb Salad

4 leaves dark green romaine lettuce
4 ounces grilled tuna, chilled and lightly flaked
8 cocktail or cherry tomatoes
1 cup frozen peas, cooked until crisp-tender and chilled
1 hard-boiled egg, quartered lengthwise
4 tablespoons sliced black olives
1/2 cup sliced red radishes
1 tablespoon olive oil
1 tablespoon balsamic vinegar
1 teaspoon chopped garlic (from a jar)
1/8 teaspoon salt
Freshly ground black pepper to
    taste
2 sprigs fresh basil

On each of two luncheon plates, arrange two of the lettuce leaves to cover the plate. On the lettuce, arrange 2 ounces of the tuna, four of the tomatoes, 1/2 cup of the peas, two pieces of the egg, 2 tablespoons of the olives, and 1/4 cup of the radishes.

In a small bowl, combine the oil, vinegar, garlic, salt, and pepper. Use a wire whisk to beat until well blended. Drizzle over the salads and garnish each with a basil sprig.

Yield: 2 servings

Nutritional data per serving: Calories, 283; protein, 26 g; carbohydrate, 20 g; dietary fiber, 6 g; total fat, 12 g; saturated fat, 2 g; cholesterol, 139 mg; sodium, 232 mg; vitamin A, 22% of Daily Value; vitamin C, 58%; calcium, 8%; iron, 18%; vitamin B$_1$ (thiamin), 40%; vitamin B$_2$ (riboflavin), 18%; vitamin B$_3$ (niacin), 43%; vitamin B$_6$, 43%; folate, 26%; vitamin E, 11%; potassium, 23%; omega-3 fatty acids, 28%.

Cuppa Red Pasta Sauce

1 tablespoon olive oil
1 cup sliced red onions
1/2 cup baby carrots, quartered lengthwise
4 ounces ground pork
1 cup sliced red bell peppers
1 cup sliced red radishes
2 cups coarsely chopped ripe tomatoes
2 cloves garlic, minced
8 oil-cured olives, chopped
1 teaspoon aniseeds
1 teaspoon salt
Freshly ground black pepper to taste

Warm the oil in a deep skillet over high heat. Add
the onions and carrots and sauté, stirring often, for
about 5 minutes, or until beginning to brown.
Push the vegetables to the sides. Place the pork in
the center of the pan and cook until brown. Add the red peppers,
radishes, tomatoes, garlic, olives, aniseeds, salt, and black pepper.
Stir until well mixed. Reduce the heat to medium-low, cover, and
simmer for 15 to 20 minutes, or until the vegetables are soft.
Serve over your favorite pasta, dusted with Parmesan cheese.

Yield: 4 servings

*Nutritional data per serving: Calories, 170; protein, 7 g; carbohydrate,
13 g; dietary fiber, 3 g; total fat, 11 g; saturated fat, 3 g; cholesterol, 20 mg;
sodium, 676 mg; vitamin A, 72% of Daily Value; vitamin C, 170%; calcium,
4%; iron, 9%; folate, 10%; potassium, 15%.*

Romanian Red Slaw

My husband, Ted, has been in the kitchen again, whipping up a taste of home. Along with his wonderful cooking, I get a little boy's tales about life in the Carpathian Mountains. Cabbages, he tells me, were shredded by the head into a tall wooden barrel. That barrel provided enough cabbage for a winter's worth of sauerkraut. Here's his recipe for enough fresh slaw to last a few days. If you don't have a Romanian cabbage slicer, you can slice the cabbage with a sharp knife or, easier still, chop it in a food processor.

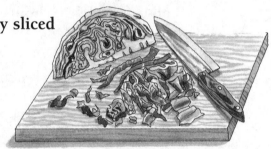

1 head red cabbage, very thinly sliced
1 medium onion, grated
1 tablespoon caraway seeds
1/4 cup olive oil
1 tablespoon white vinegar
1 teaspoon salt

In a large bowl, combine the cabbage, onion, caraway seeds, oil, vinegar, and salt. Cover and refrigerate for at least 24 hours for best flavor.

Yield: 16 servings

Nutritional data per serving: Calories, 55; protein, 1 g; carbohydrate, 6 g; dietary fiber, 1 g; total fat, 4 g; saturated fat, <1 g; cholesterol, 0 mg; sodium, 153 mg; vitamin A, 0% of Daily Value; vitamin C, 51%; calcium, 3%; iron, 2%; folate, 3%; potassium, 4%.

Lovely Leftovers

Toss a big spoonful of this slaw with a bowl full of chopped romaine lettuce. Sprinkle with grated Parmesan for a "red Caesar salad."

Beets with Risotto

1 can (15 ounces) sliced beets
1 tablespoon butter
1 tablespoon olive oil
½ medium onion, thinly sliced
1 cup Arborio rice
½ cup dry white wine
2 cans (15 ounces each) chicken broth
2 ounces freshly grated Parmesan cheese
Freshly ground black pepper to taste

Drain the beets, reserving the liquid. Dice the beets and set aside in a small bowl.

In a large, heavy saucepan over medium heat, melt the butter with the oil. Add the onion and sauté for about 5 minutes, or until soft but not brown. Add the rice and stir until evenly coated and warm. Add the wine and cook, stirring, until completely absorbed. Add the beets and reserved liquid and cook, stirring, until the liquid is absorbed. Add the broth ½ cup at a time, cooking and stirring after each addition, until absorbed. The rice should be creamy on the outside but firm on the inside when tasted. (This may not require all of the broth.) When the rice is done, add the cheese and pepper and stir to blend. Garnish with a thin curl of cheese and serve with chicken or pork.

Yield: 8 servings

Nutritional data per serving: Calories, 209; protein, 6 g; carbohydrate, 27 g; dietary fiber, 1 g; total fat, 7 g; saturated fat, 3 g; cholesterol, 11 mg; sodium, 738 mg; vitamin A, 7% of Daily Value; vitamin C, 4%; calcium, 11%; iron, 4%; vitamin E, 2%; folate, 4%; potassium, 3%.

Oven-Roasted Beets

Eons ago, I tried shredding fresh beets for a salad. What a mess. There was red juice everywhere! Now I neatly roast them. Want to learn my secret? Read on.

4 medium beets
Salt to taste
4 teaspoons prepared horseradish

Preheat the oven to 450°F. Line a baking sheet with foil and mist lightly with olive oil spray.

Trim the tops off the beets, leaving 1 inch of stem and the root attached to prevent "bleeding." (Save the leaves to make Cranberry Beet Greens, page 299.) Gently but thoroughly wash the beets to remove any sand or soil without breaking the skin. Slice in half from top to bottom. Place cut side down on the baking sheet and mist lightly with olive oil spray. Bake for 45 minutes, or until tender and becoming crisp. Place two halves cut side up on each of four dinner plates and sprinkle with the salt. Top each half with ½ teaspoon of the horseradish.

Yield: 4 servings

Nutritional data per serving: Calories, 43; protein, 1 g; carbohydrate, 8 g; dietary fiber, 2 g; total fat, <1 g; saturated fat, 0 g; cholesterol, 0 mg; sodium, 80 mg; vitamin A, 0% of Daily Value; vitamin C, 9%; calcium, 2%; iron, 4%; folate, 23%.

The Inside Skinny:

Beets' red color comes from betacyanin, a pigment some folks can't process very well, so it turns their urine or feces red or pink. Don't be alarmed if this happens to you; it's perfectly harmless.

Cranberry Beet Greens

Actually, beet leaves and stems (the "greens") are kind of red, so they make a colorful side dish that turns a pale meal downright pretty.

2 cups beet greens
1/2 cup cranberry juice cocktail
1 teaspoon cornstarch
1/2 cup cold water

Wash the beet greens thoroughly to remove any sand or soil. Cut into 2-inch pieces. In a small saucepan over high heat, combine the greens with the cranberry juice and bring to a boil. Reduce the heat, cover, and simmer for 10 minutes, or until the stems are tender.

Meanwhile, in a small bowl, stir the cornstarch into the water until dissolved. When the beet tops are done, stir in the cornstarch mixture and cook for 1 to 2 minutes, or until thick. Serve immediately with lean pork, turkey, or chicken.

Yield: 2 servings

Nutritional data per serving: Calories, 80; protein, 4 g; carbohydrate, 18 g; dietary fiber, 4 g; total fat, 0 g; saturated fat, 0 g; cholesterol, 0 mg; vitamin A, 73% of Daily Value; vitamin C, 97%; calcium, 17%; iron, 16%; vitamin B_2 (riboflavin), 25%; vitamin B_6, 10%; copper, 19%; magnesium, 25%; potassium, 38%.

DOUBLE DUTY

Beet greens are fabulous for fiber, and they're a gold mine of minerals such as calcium, copper, magnesium, and potassium, all important for lowering blood pressure.

Berry Memorable Spinach

Spinach has so much to offer, but I often find it a bit bitter. I balance the taste by stirring in a sweet, flavorful fruit. I might use strawberries, oranges, cranberries, or mangos. In June, it's usually blueberries.

1 bag (10 ounces) fresh spinach, washed
    and heavy stems removed
¹/₄ teaspoon salt
1 teaspoon butter
¹/₂ cup fresh blueberries,
    washed and patted dry
1 tablespoon toasted pine
    nuts

Place the spinach in a deep, heavy saucepan with just the water that clings to the leaves after washing. Sprinkle with the salt. Cover and bring to a boil. Reduce the heat and cook for 5 minutes, stirring occasionally, until wilted. Drain, place in a serving bowl, and toss with the butter. Stir in the blueberries and garnish with the pine nuts.

Yield: 4 servings

Nutritional data per serving: Calories, 43; protein, 2 g; carbohydrate, 5 g; dietary fiber, 2 g; total fat, 2 g; saturated fat, <1 g; cholesterol, 3 mg; sodium, 201 mg; vitamin A, 39% of Daily Value; vitamin C, 31%; calcium, 6%; iron, 10%; vitamin E, 7%; folate, 28%; vitamin K, 284%; potassium, 10%.

QUICK TRICK: Got the winter blues? Make this dish with frozen spinach and frozen blueberries.

Cranberry-Grape Relish

Here's a slight twist on an old favorite to perk up your next turkey.

1 can (16 ounces) jellied cranberry sauce
2 cups black seedless grapes

In a medium bowl, use a fork to mash the cranberry sauce. Set aside.

In a blender, quickly pulse the grapes once or twice for 1 or 2 seconds each time, just until roughly chopped. Stir into the cranberry sauce. Serve with turkey, pork, or chicken.

Yield: 12 servings

Nutritional data per serving: Calories, 73; protein, 0 g; carbohydrate, 19 g; dietary fiber, 1 g; total fat, 0 g; saturated fat, 0 g; cholesterol, 0 mg; sodium, 9 mg; vitamin A, 0% of Daily Value; vitamin C, 5%; calcium, 0%; iron, 0%; potassium, 1%.

Lovely Leftovers This sauce tastes great over vanilla ice cream or stirred into plain yogurt.

Lemon-Blueberry Muffins

Blueberry muffins have been a favorite of mine since I was a little kid, but now I like them to be really hearty and not quite so sweet. Would that suit you? Then try these.

2 cups Arrowhead Mills multigrain pancake and waffle mix
1/2 cup nonfat dry milk
1 teaspoon grated lemon peel
1 teaspoon baking powder
1/4 cup honey
1 egg
1/2 cup canola oil
3/4 cup water
2 cups fresh blueberries, washed and patted dry

Preheat the oven to 400°F. Lightly coat a 12-cup muffin pan with nonstick spray.

In a large bowl, combine the waffle mix, dry milk, lemon peel, and baking powder. Stir until well mixed. Add the honey, egg, oil, and water. Stir with a fork just until mixed. Fold in the blueberries. Spoon the batter into the pan and bake for 15 to 20 minutes, or until a toothpick inserted in the center of a muffin comes out clean. Loosen the muffins with a knife, remove from the pan, and cool on a rack. Serve with a kiss of butter and a drop of honey.

Yield: 12 servings

Nutritional data per serving: Calories, 211; protein, 4 g; carbohydrate, 28 g; dietary fiber, 3 g; total fat, 10 g; saturated fat, 1 g; cholesterol, 16 mg; sodium, 149 mg; vitamin A, 4% of Daily Value; vitamin C, 22%; calcium, 13%; iron, 4%; vitamin E, 11%; omega-3 fatty acids, 86%.

Peanut Butter and Jelly Sipper

Oh, this is so completely yummy. And it's sure to carry you through the day until lunchtime.

1 cup fat-free plain yogurt
2 tablespoons creamy peanut butter
2 tablespoons grape jelly

In a blender, combine the yogurt, peanut butter, and jelly. Blend until smooth. Pour into a 10-ounce glass or large travel mug. Sip yourself to heaven.

Yield: 1 serving

Nutritional data per serving: Calories, 390; protein, 18 g; carbohydrate, 53 g; dietary fiber, 2 g; total fat, 16 g; saturated fat, 3 g; cholesterol, 5 mg; sodium, 304 mg; vitamin A, 0% of Daily Value; vitamin C, 0%; calcium, 31%; iron, 3%; vitamin B_3 (niacin), 21%; vitamin E, 16%; magnesium, 13%.

DOUBLE DUTY

The purple grapes used in grape jelly contain natural ingredients shown to fend off heart disease as well as urinary tract infections. They may also boost your memory.

Blueberry-Basil Smoothie

In the heat of July, try to remember to whirl up this cold and creamy treat. The basil gives it just a hint of something different. See if your friends can identify your secret ingredient.

1 cup Stonyfield fat-free blueberry yogurt
1 cup fresh blueberries, washed and patted dry
¹/₂ teaspoon dried basil
1 sprig fresh basil

In a blender, combine the yogurt, blueberries, and dried basil. Blend on high until thick and smooth. Pour into a tall glass and garnish with the fresh basil.

Yield: 1 serving

Nutritional data per serving: Calories, 243; protein, 9 g; carbohydrate, 52 g; dietary fiber, 4 g; total fat, <1 g; saturated fat, 0 g; cholesterol, 0 mg; sodium, 134 mg; vitamin A, 2% of Daily Value; vitamin C, 37%; calcium, 47%; iron, 5%; vitamin E, 7%.

DOUBLE DUTY

Blueberries are packed with antioxidants that help to keep your memory in top form. And, like cranberries, they're loaded with tannins that fight urinary tract infections.

Double Grape Crush

I was browsing through the produce department of my favorite store this morning and found some gorgeous purple-black seedless grapes. Sure, they're wonderful to eat just as they are, but without seeds, it's easy to use them for this luscious drink.

1 cup black seedless grapes
1 cup fat-free plain yogurt
2 tablespoons grape jelly
2 cups ice cubes
2 small clusters grapes

In a blender, combine the grapes, yogurt, and jelly. Blend on high for about 1 minute. Add the ice cubes and blend until crushed. Pour into two 12-ounce glasses and garnish each with a grape cluster. Serve with an iced-tea spoon and a straw.

Yield: 2 servings

Nutritional data per serving: Calories, 157; protein, 6 g; carbohydrate, 38 g; dietary fiber, 1 g; total fat, 0 g; saturated fat, 0 g; cholesterol, 0 mg; sodium, 79 mg; vitamin A, 1% of Daily Value; vitamin C, 14%; calcium, 16%; iron, 1%; vitamin E, 3%; potassium, 4%.

The Inside Skinny: Research at Tufts University in Boston has shown that red grapes pack 90% more cancer-fighting antioxidants than green grapes.

Deep Purple Plums

I just thought about canned plums for the first time in eons, so I had to zip over to the store and get some. As a kid, I loved rolling them around in the dish, trying to cut them in half with a spoon (skill development, I guess). They're still as yummy as I remember, and now their color makes them extra-cool! I'm tired of chasing them, though, so into the blender they go.

**2 canned purple plums in 2 tablespoons
  heavy syrup**
1 cup fat-free plain yogurt
½ teaspoon ground cinnamon

Halve the plums and remove the pits. In a blender, combine the plums, plum syrup, yogurt, and cinnamon. Blend until smooth and creamy. Pour into a thick mug and eat with a spoon.

Yield: 1 serving

Nutritional data per serving: Calories, 219; protein, 14 g; carbohydrate, 40 g; dietary fiber, 1 g; total fat, <1 g; saturated fat, 0 g; cholesterol, 4 mg; sodium, 205 mg; vitamin A, 3% of Daily Value; vitamin C, 4%; calcium, 50%; iron, 6%; vitamin B$_2$ (riboflavin), 36%; vitamin E, 3%; folate, 8%; magnesium, 13%; potassium, 20%.

DOUBLE DUTY

This creamy dessert silently slips in half your calcium and 20% of your potassium for the day—great for controlling blood pressure.

Double Berry Decadence

My supermarket is having a two-for-one sale on strawberries and raspberries. Perfect for Father's Day!

1 quart ripe strawberries
1 pint ripe raspberries
2 tablespoons Cointreau (orange-flavored liqueur)
4 tablespoons whipped cream

Gently wash the strawberries under running water, drain, and pat dry. Remove and discard the caps. Place small berries in a medium bowl. Slice large berries from top to bottom (to keep that unique strawberry shape!) and place in the bowl. Set aside.

Gently wash, drain, and dry the raspberries. In a wire mesh strainer over a small bowl, use the back of a wooden spoon to mash until nothing is left in the strainer but seeds. Discard the seeds. Pour in the Cointreau and blend well. Spoon the strawberries into four stemmed serving dishes or champagne glasses. Ladle the raspberry puree on top and garnish each serving with 1 tablespoon of the whipped cream.

Yield: 4 servings

Nutritional data per serving: Calories, 116; protein, 2 g; carbohydrate, 20 g; dietary fiber, 8 g; total fat, 4 g; saturated fat, 2 g; cholesterol, 10 mg; sodium, 4 mg; vitamin A, 4% of Daily Value; vitamin C, 169%; calcium, 4%; iron, 5%; vitamin B_2 (riboflavin), 10%; folate, 11%; vitamin K, 27%; potassium, 10%.

DOUBLE DUTY

Along with hefty doses of vitamin C and the B vitamin folate, strawberries and raspberries also pile on ellagic acid, thought to be a potent cancer fighter.

Blue Moon Fruit Sauce
with Frozen Yogurt

I just love Bing cherries, and I usually eat them out of hand. But once in a blue moon, I split them and pit them and serve them to my family and friends over frozen yogurt. My guests are always grateful!

20 large Bing cherries
1 cup fresh blueberries, washed and patted dry
1 cup fat-free plain yogurt
2 tablespoons seedless black raspberry preserves
2 cups fat-free raspberry frozen yogurt

Halve the cherries and remove the pits. In a small bowl, combine the cherries and blueberries.

In another small bowl, combine the yogurt and preserves. Stir until well mixed and the color is even. Pour over the fruit and stir until well blended. Divide the frozen yogurt among four dessert dishes and spoon one-fourth of the sauce over each.

Yield: 4 servings

Nutritional data per serving: Calories, 183; protein, 7 g; carbohydrate, 38 g; dietary fiber, 2 g; total fat, <1 g; saturated fat, 0 g; cholesterol, 1 mg; sodium, 96 mg; vitamin A, 1% of Daily Value; vitamin C, 13%; calcium, 43%; iron, 2%; potassium, 8%.

> **QUICK TRICK:** Serving a crowd? Use a cherry pitter. You'll find them at most kitchenware stores—or ask your grandmother if she still has hers!

Baked Black Plums

I can't get over those huge black plums with the tiny seeds inside. They're so incredibly sweet. Right around the pit, though, they're still kind of sour. Here's how to outsmart that tart.

2 large ripe black plums
2 tablespoons coarsely broken toasted walnuts
2 tablespoons dark seedless raisins
1 tablespoon brown sugar
$1/2$ teaspoon ground cinnamon
2 tablespoons fat-free vanilla frozen yogurt

Remove the pit and some of the center of each plum. Place tablespoon of water in the bottom of two microwave-safe custard cups and set a plum in each.

In a small bowl, combine the walnuts, raisins, brown sugar, and cinnamon. Stir until well mixed. Stuff half into each plum. Microwave on high for 3 to 4 minutes, or until cooked through and bubbly. Let stand for 5 minutes. Top each serving with 1 tablespoon of the frozen yogurt. Eat with a spoon.

Yield: 2 servings

Nutritional data per serving: Calories, 170; protein, 3 g; carbohydrate, 31 g; dietary fiber, 3 g; total fat, 6 g; saturated fat, <1 g; cholesterol, 0 mg; sodium, 12 mg; vitamin A, 3% of Daily Value; vitamin C, 16%; calcium, 5%; iron, 4%; vitamin E, 4%; copper, 11%; potassium, 9%; omega-3 fatty acids, 68%.

> **QUICK TRICK:** Use an apple corer to easily remove the plum pits.

Pink Sunset Parfait

Here's a feast for your eyes as well as your palate—and a great ending for a light supper.

1 cup fat-free raspberry frozen yogurt
1 cup mango sorbet
6 ounces fresh raspberries, washed and dried
6 teaspoons Hershey's chocolate syrup
2 tablespoons whipped cream
2 teaspoons finely chopped walnuts

Let the yogurt and sorbet stand for about 5 minutes, or until slightly softened.

In each of two parfait glasses, place a spoonful of yogurt, then a spoonful of sorbet, a few raspberries, and 1 teaspoon of the chocolate syrup. Repeat twice, using all the yogurt, sorbet, raspberries, and syrup. Top each parfait with 1 tablespoon of the whipped cream and garnish with 1 teaspoon of the walnuts. Serve with an iced-tea spoon.

Yield: 2 servings

Nutritional data per serving: Calories, 334; protein, 7 g; carbohydrate, 73 g; dietary fiber, 7 g; total fat, 3 g; saturated fat, <1 g; cholesterol, 4 mg; sodium, 79 mg; vitamin A, 22% of Daily Value; vitamin C, 57%; calcium, 20%; iron, 5%; vitamin B_2 (riboflavin), 17%; folate, 9%; magnesium, 9%; potassium, 10%; omega-3 fatty acids, 33%.

"Be An Angel" Cherry-Frosted Cake

When all my kids are "eating light," we celebrate birthdays with this sweet treat. Everyone goes home happy.

**1 package (1 pound) frozen pitted unsweetened dark
     sweet cherries, thawed**
2 cups low-fat vanilla yogurt
1 angel food cake (12 inches)

In a blender, coarsely chop half of the cherries. Add the yogurt and pulse until blended. Pour half of the sauce over the cake and top with half of the remaining cherries. Combine the remaining cherries and sauce and spoon a little over each slice after cutting.

Yield: 12 servings

Nutritional data per serving: Calories, 143; protein, 4 g; carbohydrate, 31 g; dietary fiber, 1 g; total fat, <1 g; saturated fat, 0 g; cholesterol, 3 mg; sodium, 235 mg; vitamin A, 1% of Daily Value; vitamin C, 1%; calcium, 10%; iron, 2%; vitamin B_2 (riboflavin), 13%; folate, 3%; potassium, 2%.

The
P·E·R·F·E·C·T
Companion

While the group is gathered round, put 4 red raspberry herb tea bags in a large teapot. Fill with boiling water and steep for 3 to 5 minutes. Pour into pretty cups and serve with a little milk and honey.

Cherry Vanilla Pudding

This dessert is simplicity itself. And it's simply delicious.

1 package (3.4 ounces) vanilla instant pudding mix
2 cups 2% milk
1 cup canned unsweetened sweet cherries

In a medium bowl, combine the pudding mix and milk. With an electric mixer on low, beat until the pudding begins to thicken. Stir in the cherries. Ladle into four small dessert dishes and top each with a cherry. Serve immediately or refrigerate.

Yield: 4 servings

Nutritional data per serving: Calories, 187; protein, 5 g; carbohydrate, 37 g; dietary fiber, 1 g; total fat, 3 g; saturated fat, 1.5 g; cholesterol, 9 mg; sodium, 429 mg; vitamin A, 8% of Daily Value; vitamin C, 4%; calcium, 18%; iron, 2%; vitamin B_2 (riboflavin), 15%; vitamin D, 12%; potassium, 9%.

DOUBLE DUTY

Indulging in a creamy dessert made with milk gives you a burst of calcium. You get a few rays of sunshine vitamin D, too.

CHAPTER
11

CHILL THE
COMMON COLD

HEAT UP YOUR DIET

Would you be surprised to learn that on our recent trip to Transylvania, we found that not one person was wearing garlic to fend off vampires? The folks there cook with a lot of garlic, though, so they do know how to fend off colds and flu.

Here's some advice that has nothing to do with Dracula and everything to do with staying healthy when those nasty bugs are going around.

♥ **Become a friend of the family.** Evidence is mounting that garlic and other members of its plant family (such as onions, leeks, and chives) that contain a compound called allicin can help fend off colds and flu (and—not inconsequentially—cancer) as well as lower cholesterol and help control high blood pressure.

Bright bulbs!

Another good part of this breaking news is that you don't have to bury yourself in the stuff to get the benefit. Just drop some garlic into pasta sauce, put a slice of onion on your sandwich, or stir some fresh chives into cream cheese. Your body will take it from there!

♥ **Try going to seed.** Toss some chive seeds into the ground, then stand back. They'll start growing in no time, and you can cut and eat them right away. Anytime you want instant zest for soups or potatoes, just snip some fresh chives from your own crop. Nothing could be easier. The plants are so hardy that they just keep coming back year after year. And here's a bonus: Each spring, they'll sprout purple blooms that make stunning, edible garnishes for special dishes or everyday salads.

♥ **Shed a few tears.** Onions are worth crying for. In addition to allicin, they're loaded with quercetin, an antioxidant more powerful than vitamin E, so your immune system will get a boost. You can get quercetin from tea, apples, and wine, too.

♥ **Start your day right.** Folks who skip breakfast get the most colds, so remember

A Pill is Not a Clove

Cooking with garlic is not the same as taking a high-dose garlic supplement, which may increase the action of anticoagulant (blood-thinning) drugs such as warfarin (Coumadin) or decrease blood levels of the anti-HIV drug saquinavir. If you take prescription drugs, be sure to tell your doctor about everything else that you're taking, including garlic supplements.

what your mama said, and chow down when you wake up.

♥ **Eat wisely and well.** Researchers nationwide all tell me the same thing: What your immune system really needs is a healthy, well-balanced diet bursting with such a complete array of nutrients that it works like a well-oiled machine to keep you healthy and disease-free.

What if you slip up and get a cold anyway? Here are some tips.

♥ **Fire up your chile supply.** These hot little peppers are packed with capsaicin, which pours on the heat. Your body responds to it with a flood of endorphins, the natural painkillers that boost mood and help you forget your worries. Hot peppers also make your nose run, which clears your sinuses and sends germs packing. Think they're too hot for you? Relax and start with just a little, but eat up. Your body will learn to tolerate the heat, and you'll discover a world of flavors that also fight heart disease, cancer, and premature aging, along with fending off colds.

♥ **Giddyup with horseradish.** It's another sinus blaster that clears your head so you can function in spite of your misery.

♥ **Savor the flavor.** Garlic, onions, chile peppers, and horseradish are packed with potent flavors that break

Chill the Common Cold 315

through to your taste buds when nothing else will. That means you can eat and enjoy the healthy foods that will get you back on your feet again, fast.

Now, I know you're wondering—and you've patiently waited to ask—what about vitamin C supplements? Sorry, but despite all the hype, study after study reveals that there is no one magic nutrient for preventing or treating the common cold—not even vitamin C. Typically, without high doses of vitamin C, a cold lasts two weeks. With them, it lasts about 13½ days! But cheer up. While you're piling on the fruits and vegetables, you'll get all the C you need for a healthy immune system, along with plenty of other nutritional coworkers to get the job done right.

Now I've got something savory on the stove. Take a whiff. Can you smell it? If it starts with onions and garlic, it has to be good, so follow me out to the kitchen.

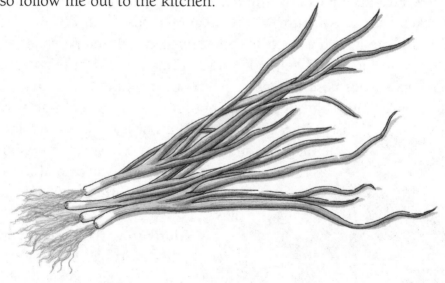

Hot Chicks and Cute Tomatoes

Remember when a tomato was, well, just a tomato? Now they've gone wild. And all the sizes and shapes are so much fun to play with!

1 can (15½ ounces) chickpeas, rinsed and drained
1 tablespoon peanut oil
3 tablespoons fat-free milk
1 clove garlic, minced
2 tablespoons hot prepared horseradish
¼ teaspoon ground red pepper
1/16 teaspoon ground white pepper
1 teaspoon Worcestershire sauce
2 teaspoons lemon juice
½ teaspoon sugar
½ teaspoon kosher salt
1 pint red grape tomatoes
1 pint tiny pear-shaped yellow tomatoes

In a food processor, combine the chickpeas, oil, milk, garlic, horseradish, red pepper, white pepper, Worcestershire, lemon juice, sugar, and salt. Process on high for 30 seconds. Scrape down the sides and blend until creamy and smooth. Place in a lotus bowl on a serving plate and surround with the tomatoes. Dip away.

Yield: 8 servings

Nutritional data per serving: Calories, 74; protein, 3 g; carbohydrate, 11 g; dietary fiber, 3 g; total fat, 2.5 g; saturated fat, 0 g; cholesterol, 0 mg; sodium, 283 mg; vitamin A, 3% of Daily Value; vitamin C, 24%; calcium, 3%; iron, 4%; folate, 5%; potassium, 6%.

Some Like It Hot Pepper Platter

When winter winds blow and all your friends are feeling stuffy, start your party with this decongestant appetizer tray. Just keep plenty of tissues handy!

1 jar (16 ounces) hot giardiniera vegetables, drained
1 jar (16 ounces) pepperoncini, drained
1 jar (16 ounces) hot cherry peppers, drained

Arrange the vegetables, pepperoncini, and peppers on a sturdy tray, then stand out of the way.

Yield: 12 servings

Nutritional data per serving: Calories, 32; protein, 1 g; carbohydrate, 6 g; dietary fiber, 2 g; total fat, 0 g; saturated fat, 0 g; cholesterol, 0 mg; sodium, 1,077 mg; vitamin A, 30% of Daily Value; vitamin C, 22%; calcium, 3%; iron, 4%; potassium, 2%.

DOUBLE DUTY

The carrots in the giardiniera are loaded with beta-carotene to boost your immune system as it gears up to battle offending germs, while the cherry peppers turn your nose into a garden hose.

Oven-Roasted Garlic

Want to be a kitchen wizard? Turn raw garlic's pungent bite into a gentle purr—by roasting. It's a magic trick you'll get the hang of in no time.

1 large bulb garlic
1 teaspoon olive oil

On a cutting board, turn the garlic on its side. Use a large, sharp knife to cut off a third of the top so the insides of the cloves are visible. Place the bulb upright on a square of foil and drizzle with the oil. Seal in the foil. Bake at 350°F in the oven or toaster oven for 1 hour, or until soft. Let cool. Separate the cloves and squeeze the garlic onto a cutting board. Use a fork to mash into a coarse paste. Place in a serving dish and surround with crackers, toasted baguette rounds, or fresh Italian bread.

Yield: 12 servings

Nutritional data per serving: Calories, 8; protein, 0 g; carbohydrate, 1 g; dietary fiber, 0 g; total fat, 0 g; saturated fat, 0 g; cholesterol, 0 mg; sodium, 0 mg; vitamin A, 0% of Daily Value; vitamin C, 1%; calcium, 1%; iron, 0%; vitamin B_6, 2%.

Lovely Leftovers
Stir into tuna, egg, or chicken salad for a real taste treat.

Garlic Aioli

Having a hard time getting your gang to eat their veggies? Whirl up this garlicky mayonnaise spread and enjoy the veggie vanishing act. Since I made my first batch, I've never been without it in my fridge.

6 cloves garlic, minced or pressed
2 egg yolks
1½ teaspoons boiling water
1 teaspoon salt
Freshly ground pepper mélange
    to taste
5 tablespoons hazelnut or peanut oil
5 tablespoons olive oil
1 tablespoon fresh lemon juice

> **The Inside Skinny:**
> Aioli is a natural way to get your vitamin E.

In a blender, combine the garlic and egg yolks. Begin to blend on high, then remove the feeder cap. Add the water, salt, and pepper. Add the nut and olive oils 1 teaspoon at a time, eventually adding larger amounts until incorporated. Add the lemon juice. (You may have to stop the blender from time to time to stir the ingredients.) Place the aioli in a serving bowl and surround with steamed vegetables such as artichokes, cauliflower, green beans, and broccoli.

Yield: 8 servings

Nutritional data per serving: Calories, 101; protein, 0 g; carbohydrate, 0 g; dietary fiber, 0 g; total fat, 11 g; saturated fat, 1 g; cholesterol, 24 mg; sodium, 130 mg; vitamin A, 1% of Daily Value; vitamin C, 1%; calcium, 0%; iron, 1%; vitamin E, 13%.

Cozy Comfort (Quick) Chicken Soup

Researchers tell me that a big pot of chicken soup cooked up from scratch really does help relieve the symptoms of a cold. But when I have a cold, the last thing I want to do is spend all day in the kitchen! So I whipped up this 10-minute version, then checked it out with Stephen Rennard, M.D., a researcher at the University of Nebraska Medical Center. He says this has all the right stuff to unstuff you. And it's oh, so soothing!

1 envelope Lipton Ring-O-Noodle soup mix
10 baby carrots, thinly sliced
1 rib celery, thinly sliced
½ yellow onion, chopped
1 tablespoon parsley flakes
1 tablespoon garlic (from a jar)
1 can (5 ounces) boned light-meat
  chicken

> **Instant Comfort:**
> Enjoy a cup of raspberry sorbet. It will soothe your aching throat.

Bring 4 cups water to a boil in a large heavy saucepan. Stir in the soup mix, carrots, celery, onion, parsley, and garlic. Reduce the heat, cover, and simmer for 10 minutes, or until the noodles are tender. Remove the lid and inhale deeply. Stir in the chicken and cook for 1 minute. Inhale again. Ladle into your favorite bowls and enjoy.

Yield: 5 servings

Nutritional data per serving: Calories, 116; protein, 8 g; carbohydrate, 12 g; dietary fiber, 1 g; total fat, 4 g; saturated fat, 1 g; cholesterol, 30 mg; sodium, 738 mg; vitamin A, 32% of Daily Value; vitamin C, 7%; calcium, 2%; iron, 8%; vitamin B_1 (thiamin), 14%; vitamin B_3 (niacin), 15%.

Creamy Leek Soup

It turns out that washing the sand out of leeks is a lot easier than I had been led to believe. Like a baby crawling on the beach, they probably don't like being all sandy, either.

6 leeks, roots and tough green tops removed
2 teaspoons canola oil
1½ cups water
1 teaspoon chicken bouillon granules
¾ cup fat-free evaporated milk
⅛ teaspoon salt
Freshly ground black pepper to taste
2 teaspoons butter

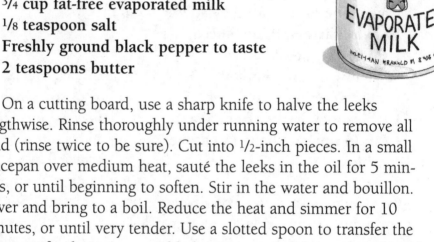

On a cutting board, use a sharp knife to halve the leeks lengthwise. Rinse thoroughly under running water to remove all sand (rinse twice to be sure). Cut into ½-inch pieces. In a small saucepan over medium heat, sauté the leeks in the oil for 5 minutes, or until beginning to soften. Stir in the water and bouillon. Cover and bring to a boil. Reduce the heat and simmer for 10 minutes, or until very tender. Use a slotted spoon to transfer the leeks to a food processor. Add about ½ cup of the cooking liquid and process until smooth. Return to the pan and stir in the milk, salt, and pepper. Cook over medium heat until warm. Spoon into two soup bowls and garnish each with 1 teaspoon of the butter.

Yield: 2 servings

Nutritional data per serving: Calories, 270; protein, 11 g; carbohydrate, 40 g; dietary fiber, 4 g; total fat, 10 g; saturated fat, 3 g; cholesterol, 14 mg; sodium, 619 mg; vitamin A, 17% of Daily Value; vitamin C, 28%; calcium, 39%; iron, 24%; folate, 25%; magnesium, 20%; potassium, 19%; omega-3 fatty acids, 73%.

Oniony Lentil Soup

I think lentils are the coolest of all the dried beans because they're so quick to fix. No overnight soaking, no long hours of cooking. In just 30 minutes, you've got yourself a pot of really fine soup, hearty enough to fill in for both meat and potatoes.

1 cup coarsely chopped yellow onions
1 cup thinly sliced celery
1 cup diced carrots
1 tablespoon olive oil
1 cup dried lentils, washed
4 cups fat-free chicken broth
Freshly ground black pepper to taste

In a large saucepan over medium-high heat, sauté the onions, celery, and carrots in the oil for 5 to 10 minutes, or until beginning to soften. Stir in the lentils, broth, and pepper. Cover and bring to a boil. Reduce the heat and simmer for 20 minutes, or until the lentils are tender. Serve piping hot with a crisp salad and some crusty bread.

Yield: 4 servings

Nutritional data per serving: Calories, 188; protein, 12 g; carbohydrate, 28 g; dietary fiber, 10 g; total fat, 4 g; saturated fat, <1 g; cholesterol, 0 mg; sodium, 490 mg; vitamin A, 91% of Daily Value; vitamin C, 15%; calcium, 5%; iron, 20%; folate, 50%; vitamin K, 59%; potassium, 18%.

Lovely Leftovers
Puree extra soup in a blender with some plain yogurt to boost calcium.

French Onion Soup

4 large yellow onions, quartered and thinly sliced
  (about 4 cups)
2 tablespoons butter
1 tablespoon olive oil
2 tablespoons flour
4 cups fat-free reduced-sodium beef broth
1 cup dry red wine
1 teaspoon Worcestershire sauce
1 bay leaf
Freshly ground black pepper to taste
4 very thin slices French bread
4 ounces freshly shredded Emmental cheese

In a deep pot, sauté the onions in the butter and oil for about 15 minutes, or until brown. Stir in the flour, coating the onions well. Stir in 2 cups of the broth and deglaze the pan. Add the wine, Worcestershire, bay leaf, pepper, and the remaining 2 cups broth. Bring to a boil, then reduce the heat and simmer for 20 minutes. When ready to serve, toast the bread until golden brown. Remove the bay leaf and ladle the soup into four small bowls or crocks. Top each with a toasted bread slice, then sprinkle with 1 ounce of the cheese. Serve with crisp green salad.

Yield: 4 servings

Nutritional data per serving: Calories, 403; protein, 17 g; carbohydrate, 29 g; dietary fiber, 3 g; total fat, 20 g; saturated fat, 7 g; cholesterol, 26 mg; sodium, 316 mg; vitamin A, 7% of Daily Value; vitamin C, 13%; calcium, 33%; iron, 11%; vitamin B$_3$ (niacin), 24%; folate, 15%; potassium, 15%.

Shallot Summer Salad

I don't like big hunks of onion in my green salad. No, indeed; what I really want is thin little rings. That's why I go for shallots. They never get all big and overgrown.

2 cups shredded romaine lettuce
1 small yellow squash, cut into rounds
2 Roma (plum) tomatoes, cut into rounds
1/2 cup rinsed and drained canned cannellini beans
1 large shallot, thinly sliced and separated into rings
2 teaspoons olive oil
1 tablespoon balsamic vinegar
Salt and freshly ground black pepper to taste
2 tablespoons sliced black olives

In a medium bowl, combine the lettuce, squash, tomatoes, beans, and shallot. Drizzle with the oil and vinegar and toss until well coated. Sprinkle with the salt and pepper and toss again. Divide between two salad plates and garnish each with 1 tablespoon of the olives.

Yield: 2 servings

Nutritional data per serving: Calories, 150; protein, 6 g; carbohydrate, 20 g; dietary fiber, 6 g; total fat, 6 g; saturated fat, <1 g; cholesterol, 0 mg; sodium, 227 mg; vitamin A, 22% of Daily Value; vitamin C, 57%; calcium, 7%; iron, 15%; vitamin E, 7%; folate, 27%; potassium, 16%.

DOUBLE DUTY

The beans in this salad provide the protein along with a hefty dose of the heart-protective B vitamin folate.

Vidalia Onion Salad with Wheatberries

For the longest time, I thought I didn't like raw onions, but then I tasted my first Vidalia. It's one of summer's sweetest treats and deserves a starring role in this best-of-summer salad.

1 cup coarsely chopped Vidalia onions
1 pickling cucumber, thinly sliced
1 medium tomato, coarsely chopped
1 cup Basic Wheatberries (page 146)
4 leaves fresh basil, slivered
1 teaspoon olive oil
1 tablespoon balsamic vinegar
Salt and freshly ground black pepper to taste

In a medium bowl, combine the onions, cucumber, tomato, and wheatberries. Stir in the basil, oil, vinegar, salt, and pepper. Mix well. Cover and refrigerate for 1 hour before serving.

Yield: 4 servings

Nutritional data per serving: Calories, 77; protein, 2 g; carbohydrate, 15 g; dietary fiber, 3 g; total fat, 1.5 g; saturated fat, 0 g; cholesterol, 0 mg; sodium, 217 mg; vitamin A, 3% of Daily Value; vitamin C, 17%; calcium, 2%; iron, 4%; vitamin E, 3%; potassium, 6%.

Lovely Leftovers

Toss whatever extras you have with some lean ham and cheese and pile it all on a bed of romaine lettuce for a super chef's salad.

Salmon and Tomato with Onion Sprouts

I was scouting for sprouts the other day and discovered these teensy-weensy onions. Their delicate but distinct flavor is exactly right when I want just a hint of onion. They're pretty, too.

**1/2 cup canned salmon with bones
1 tablespoon light ranch dressing
Freshly ground black pepper to taste
1 large tomato, cut into 4 thick slices
1/2 cup onion sprouts, thoroughly
    washed and drained**

In a small bowl, combine the salmon, dressing, and pepper. Arrange the tomato slices on a large plate. Top each with one-fourth of the salmon and garnish with one-fourth of the sprouts. Serve with a crusty roll and a chilled glass of white wine.

Yield: 1 serving

Nutritional data per serving: Calories, 183; protein, 18 g; carbohydrate, 11 g; dietary fiber, 2 g; total fat, 8 g; saturated fat, 2 g; cholesterol, 36 mg; sodium, 531 mg; vitamin A, 16% of Daily Value; vitamin C, 60%; calcium, 20%; iron, 10%; vitamin D, 42%; vitamin E, 9%; folate, 10%; potassium, 20%; omega-3 fatty acids, 97%.

DOUBLE DUTY

Canned salmon is rich in heart-smart omega-3 fatty acids. It also provides plenty of calcium when you eat the bones!

Garlic and Onion Pizza

Years ago, my friends Charlie and Colleen LoPresto made me an onion pizza. It was a shock to find no red sauce. Now I've added a few twists of my own. What a delicious way to fight off a cold!

> 1 jumbo English muffin
> 2 teaspoons chopped fresh or dried chives
> 2 tablespoons Oven-Roasted Garlic (page 319)
> 1 ounce shredded reduced-fat mozzarella cheese
> 2 thin slices sweet onion, separated into rings
> 4 thin slices shallot, separated into rings
> Salt and freshly ground black pepper to taste

Split the English muffin. In a small bowl, combine the chives and garlic. Spread evenly over each of the muffin halves and sprinkle each with 1/2 ounce of the cheese. Arrange the onion and shallot rings to cover both halves. Season with the salt and pepper and mist lightly with olive oil spray. Bake at 500°F in the toaster oven for 10 minutes, or until the cheese is melted and the onions begin to soften and brown.

Yield: 1 serving

Nutritional data per serving: Calories, 372; protein, 18 g; carbohydrate, 54 g; dietary fiber, 4 g; total fat, 11 g; saturated fat, 3 g; cholesterol, 14 mg; sodium, 200 mg; vitamin A, 8% of Daily Value; vitamin C, 22%; calcium, 38%; iron, 19%; vitamin B_6, 22%; zinc, 10%.

> **QUICK TRICK:** No oven-roasted garlic? Use chopped garlic from a jar.

Five-Alarm Chicken Finger Sandwich

*Want to sneeze? Sweat? Blast your taste buds to Kingdom Come?
Then you're in for a total treat with a sandwich you won't soon forget!*

4 ounces unbreaded chicken tenders
1 teaspoon Ragin' Cajun seasoning mix*
1 small whole wheat pita pocket,
   toasted and split
1/2 cup well-drained coleslaw

Line a toaster-oven tray with foil and
mist lightly with olive oil spray.

Mist the chicken with olive oil spray. On
a plate, coat with the seasoning. (This is where
you'll sneeze.) Place on the tray and bake at 400°F for 10
to 15 minutes, or until cooked through and slightly brown. Let
cool. Cut the chicken to fit, if necessary, and stuff into the pita.
Fill with the coleslaw. Grab a cold drink (now comes the sweat-
ing).

Yield: 1 serving

*Nutritional data per serving: Calories, 526;
protein, 34 g; carbohydrate, 61 g; dietary fiber, 8 g;
total fat, 17 g; saturated fat, 3 g; cholesterol, 74 g;
sodium, 698 mg; vitamin A, 10% of Daily Value;
vitamin C, 59%; calcium, 5%; iron, 17%; vitamin
B_3 (niacin), 73%; vitamin B_6, 40%; copper, 12%;
magnesium, 17%; potassium, 11%; zinc, 13%.*

*See Ragin' Cajun Roasted Potatoes on page 399.

**The
P·E·R·F·E·C·T
Companion**

Need to put out the
fire? Snag a nonalco-
holic beer and add a
squeeze of lime juice.

Albuquerque Taco Salad

1 cup slivered romaine lettuce
2 very ripe Roma (plum) tomatoes, diced
¼ cup thinly sliced jalapeño chile peppers
2 tablespoons light ranch dressing
1 ounce shredded reduced-fat cheddar cheese
2 ounces sliced cooked chicken breast
⅛ avocado, cut into chunks
1 teaspoon toasted pine nuts
1 ring green bell pepper
1 ounce baked tortilla chips

In a large bowl, combine the lettuce, tomatoes, jalapeño peppers, and 1 tablespoon of the dressing. Toss until well coated. Pile the salad in the center of a large plate. Top with the cheese, chicken, and avocado. Sprinkle with the pine nuts, garnish with the pepper ring, and surround with tortilla chips. Drizzle with the remaining 1 tablespoon dressing.

Yield: 1 serving

SUPER SUB

By surrounding your salad with baked tortilla chips instead of a fried flour-tortilla shell, you'll get more fiber, vitamins, and minerals and less artery-clogging fat.

Nutritional data per serving: Calories, 423; protein, 30 g; carbohydrate, 38 g; dietary fiber, 6 g; total fat, 18 g; saturated fat, 3 g; cholesterol, 63 mg; sodium, 859 mg; vitamin A, 27% of Daily Value; vitamin C, 79%; calcium, 20%; iron, 16%; vitamin E, 7%; folate, 29%; potassium, 26%; zinc, 10%.

Roast Beef Blastoff

Feel like you need a jackhammer to clear your stuffy head enough so that flavor comes through? Try this sure-fire sandwich that's guaranteed to reach even the most reluctant taste buds!

2 slices pumpernickel bread
1 tablespoon Inglehoffer sweet hot chili mustard
2 ounces lean roast beef
3 lengthwise slices baby zucchini
4 thin slices red onion
¹/₂ cup fresh arugula

Spread one slice of the bread with the mustard. Layer on the beef, zucchini, onions, and arugula. Top with the second slice of bread and grab a cold drink!

Yield: 1 serving

Nutritional data per serving: Calories, 371; protein, 26 g; carbohydrate, 44 g; dietary fiber, 5 g; total fat, 10 g; saturated fat, 3 g; cholesterol, 59 mg; sodium, 734 mg; vitamin A, 3% of Daily Value; vitamin C, 15%; calcium, 8%; iron, 29%; potassium, 11%; zinc, 22%.

Instant Comfort: When the fire gets too hot to handle, cool off your taste buds with a glass of cold milk or a cup of frozen yogurt. Dairy foods douse the flames.

Fire-Breathing Chicken Nuggets

Think chicken nuggets are just for kids? Think again. These babies will set the night—and your palate—on fire. You're gonna love them!

8 ounces unbreaded chicken tenders
1/4 cup Inglehoffer sweet hot chili mustard

Wash the chicken and pat dry. Cut into 1-inch-long pieces. Place the mustard in a plastic bag and add the chicken. Roll the pieces around until well coated. Broil for 5 to 10 minutes, or until cooked through. Stuff into a pita pocket or use as a salad topper along with some cubed avocado to help cool the fire.

Yield: 2 servings

SUPER SUB

Replacing deep-fried nuggets—full of grease and fatty skin—with your own nuggets made from skinless breast meat slashes total fat and saturated fat to 1/4.

Nutritional data per serving: Calories, 163; protein, 12 g; carbohydrate, 16 g; dietary fiber, <1 g; total fat, 6 g; saturated fat, 1 g; cholesterol, 35 mg; sodium, 436 mg; vitamin A, 0% of Daily Value; vitamin C, 3%; calcium, 2%; iron, 3%.

Jalapeño Mayo

Kiss your next sandwich with this distinctive spread. Next thing you know, you'll be whipping up a big batch to serve at your next party!

¹/₄ cup light canola oil mayonnaise*
2 tablespoons jalapeño mustard or other hot mustard
1 tablespoon well-drained juice-packed crushed pineapple

In a small bowl, combine the mayonnaise, mustard, and pineapple. Stir until well mixed. Refrigerate until ready to use. Great on cold turkey sandwiches or grilled burgers.

Yield: 4 servings

Nutritional data per serving: Calories, 42; protein, 0 g; carbohydrate, 2 g; dietary fiber, 0 g; total fat, 3 g; saturated fat, 0 g; cholesterol, 0 mg; sodium, 148 mg; vitamin A, 0% of Daily Value; vitamin C, 0%; calcium, 0%; iron, 0%.

*Available in natural foods stores and some large supermarkets.

The
 P·E·R·F·E·C·T
Companion

Take the easy way out. Drop a cold-brew tea bag into a tall glass with 16 ounces of cold water. Steep for 3 minutes, dunking the tea bag occasionally, then remove it. Perk up your tea with honey, lemon, and lots of ice. Olé!

Cajun Red Beans and Kale

My husband, Ted, is not so hot on foods that burn. On the other hand, I would slide down a fire pole any day to get to a zingy dish like this. So I make it for lunch when he's not around.

1/8 teaspoon crushed red pepper
1 tablespoon peanut oil
1 cup rinsed and drained canned red kidney beans
4 cups cooked kale
1/2 teaspoon liquid smoke
1/8 teaspoon salt

In a heavy nonstick skillet over medium-high heat, sauté the pepper in the oil for about 2 minutes, or until the oil is well flavored. Reduce the heat to medium and stir in the beans. Cook, stirring constantly, for about 2 minutes, or until warmed through. Pile the kale on top of the beans and sprinkle with the liquid smoke and salt. Cover and simmer for about 2 minutes, or until the kale is warm. Serve with lean ham or roasted chicken.

Yield: 2 servings

Nutritional data per serving: Calories, 247; protein, 12 g; carbohydrate, 35 g; dietary fiber, 14 g; total fat, 8 g; saturated fat, 1 g; cholesterol, 0 mg; sodium, 47 mg; vitamin A, 96% of Daily Value; vitamin C, 89%; calcium, 9%; iron, 7%; folate, 27%; copper, 23%; magnesium, 18%; potassium, 8%; omega-3 fatty acids, 34%.

Lovely Leftovers

Stuff extras—hot or cold—into a pita pocket for a quick and filling lunch.

Black Beans Caribbean

This dish is quick but stunningly exotic. Whenever I eat it, I feel as though I'm on a mini vacation. No-stress cooking, no-stress cleanup, and a little island music on the CD player…all great for the heart!

1/2 cup frozen chopped onions
1 tablespoon chopped garlic (from a jar)
1 teaspoon ground ginger
1/2 teaspoon dried thyme
1/8 teaspoon ground mace
2 teaspoons peanut oil
1 can (15 1/2 ounces) black beans, rinsed and drained
1/2 cup pineapple juice

In a medium saucepan over medium heat, sauté the onions, garlic, ginger, thyme, and mace in the oil until the onions are soft but not brown. Stir in the beans and pineapple juice. Reduce the heat to low and cook for about 15 minutes, or until thick. Serve over cooked rice.

Yield: 2 servings

Nutritional data per serving: Calories, 169; protein, 8 g; carbohydrate, 31 g; dietary fiber, 10 g; total fat, 5 g; saturated fat, <1 g; cholesterol, 0 mg; sodium, 798 mg; vitamin A, 0% of Daily Value; vitamin C, 4%; calcium, 12%; iron, 33%; folate, 21%; potassium, 26%.

> **The P·E·R·F·E·C·T Companion**
>
> Pour a can of mango nectar into a glass filled with crushed ice. Garnish with a strawberry.

Smoked Salmon Chili

On a trip to a salmon fishery in Washington State, I learned that their version of smoked salmon—thick cut and fully cooked over an open, smoky fire—is the one I like best. You can enjoy that same wonderful smoky flavor in this chili.

1 teaspoon olive oil
2 teaspoons minced garlic
1/2 cup diced celery
1/2 cup diced onions
1 cup sliced mushrooms
2 cups water
1 can (15 1/2 ounces) great Northern beans, rinsed and drained
1 can (14 1/2 ounces) Del Monte zesty tomatoes with mild chiles
4 ounces Northwestern smoked salmon, flaked
1 teaspoon liquid smoke

DOUBLE DUTY

The beans in this recipe provide carbohydrate for energy and soluble fiber to help lower your cholesterol. Really!

Warm the oil in a 4-quart saucepan over medium-high heat. Add the garlic, celery, onions, and mushrooms. Sauté about for 5 minutes, or until the vegetables begin to wilt. Stir in the water, beans, tomatoes, salmon, and liquid smoke. Bring to a boil, then reduce the heat and simmer for 15 minutes.

Yield: 5 servings

Nutritional data per serving: Calories, 136; protein, 11 g; carbohydrate, 24 g; dietary fiber, 6 g; total fat, 2 g; saturated fat, 0 g; cholesterol, 5 mg; sodium, 1,000 mg; vitamin A, 1% of Daily Value; vitamin C, 16%; calcium, 10%; iron, 15%; vitamin D, 21%; potassium, 13%; omega-3 fatty acids, 10%.

Hot 'n Cold Peanut Noodles

Imagine my delight when I can get two of my favorite foods—peanut butter and chile peppers—in the same dish!

4 ounces enriched very thin spaghetti
¼ cup crunchy peanut butter
½ teaspoon Thai green chile paste*
1 tablespoon reduced-sodium soy sauce
¼ cup fat-free evaporated milk
Dash of grated lime peel

Bring 3 quarts water to a boil in a saucepan. Add the spaghetti and cook for 5 minutes, or according to package directions (do not overcook). Drain and place in a serving bowl. Set aside.

Meanwhile, in a small bowl, combine the peanut butter, chile paste, and soy sauce. Use a wire whisk to stir until well blended. Gradually whisk in the milk and lime peel. Pour over the spaghetti and toss until well mixed. Cover and refrigerate for at least 1 hour. Serve with steamed chilled snow peas, baby corn, and water chestnuts.

Yield: 2 servings

Nutritional data per serving: Calories, 429; protein, 18 g; carbohydrate, 54 g; dietary fiber, 4 g; total fat, 17 g; saturated fat, 3 g; cholesterol, 1 mg; sodium, 496 mg; vitamin A, 4% of Daily Value; vitamin C, 1%; calcium, 12%; iron, 17%; vitamin B_1 (thiamin), 43%; vitamin B_2 (riboflavin), 23%; vitamin B_3 (niacin), 45%; vitamin B_6, 12%; vitamin E, 12%; folate, 41%; copper, 16%; magnesium, 22%; potassium, 13%; zinc, 13%.

*Available in Asian markets and many large supermarkets.

Chile-Tuna Grill

Here's yet another great thing about fish: It's so tender, you don't have to marinate it very long. And because it cooks so quickly, it becomes faster than a drive-thru meal!

1 pound tuna filets, about 1 inch thick
¹/₂ cup Tropical Grill 10-minute marinade
1 tablespoon minced fresh garlic
Freshly ground black pepper to taste
2 tablespoons hot jalapeño jelly
2 tablespoons chopped green chile peppers

Place the tuna in a glass dish. In a small bowl, combine the marinade and garlic. Pour over the tuna, turning once to coat both sides. Refrigerate for 10 minutes. Grill over medium-high heat, turning every 2 minutes, until cooked through.

Meanwhile, in a microwave-safe dish, microwave the jelly on high for 10 to 15 seconds, or just until melted. Stir in the peppers. When the tuna is done, divide among four plates and spread each filet with 1 tablespoon of the jelly mixture. Hot dog!

Yield: 4 servings

Nutritional data per serving: Calories, 164; protein, 25 g; carbohydrate, 11 g; dietary fiber, 0 g; total fat, 1 g; saturated fat, 0 g; cholesterol, 53 mg; sodium, 59 mg; vitamin A, 2% of Daily Value; vitamin C, 9%; calcium, 4%; iron, 8%; vitamin B₃ (niacin), 87%; vitamin B₆, 50%; potassium, 14%; omega-3 fatty acids, 29%.

Pan-Fried Leeks

My son, Mike, was the first in our family to give leeks a try. He offered me instructions over the phone while he was making dinner for a friend. Mmmm, I could almost smell their sweet fragrance through the wire.

2 medium leeks, roots and tough green tops removed
1 teaspoon canola oil
1 teaspoon butter
1/8 teaspoon salt

On a cutting board, use a sharp knife to halve the leeks lengthwise. Rinse thoroughly under running water to remove all sand (rinse twice to be sure).

In a medium nonstick saucepan over medium heat, warm the oil and butter until the butter is melted. Add the leeks cut side down. Cover and cook for about 4 minutes, or until well browned. Turn and cook for 3 to 4 minutes, or until beginning to brown. Sprinkle the cut sides with the salt. Place two halves on each of two dinner plates. They're great with lean pork chops or chicken.

Yield: 2 servings

Nutritional data per serving: Calories, 57; protein, 1 g; carbohydrate, 9 g; dietary fiber, 1 g; total fat, 2 g; saturated fat, <1 g; cholesterol, 3 mg; sodium, 329 mg; vitamin A, 2% of Daily Value; vitamin C, 9%; calcium, 4%; iron, 8%; folate, 8%; potassium, 3%.

QUICK TRICK: Sear the leeks on a George Foreman grill.

Sautéed Leeks and Fennel

Leeks are such gentle onions, and fennel offers up just a hint of licorice, so this delicate dish is great with fish. Unusual, yes, but easy to love.

1 tablespoon olive oil
1 tablespoon butter
1 clove garlic, minced
2 cups sliced leeks
2 cups sliced fennel
1/4 teaspoon salt
Freshly ground black pepper to taste
1/2 cup slivered red bell peppers
6 large leaves fresh basil, coarsely chopped
1 tablespoon balsamic vinegar

In a deep saucepan over medium heat, warm the oil and butter. Stir in the garlic, leeks, fennel, salt, and black pepper. Cook for about 15 minutes, stirring occasionally, until the leeks are soft. Stir in the red peppers and cook for 2 minutes. Remove from the heat and stir in the basil and vinegar. Serve immediately.

Yield: 4 servings

Nutritional data per serving: Calories, 100, protein, 1 g; carbohydrate, 10 g; dietary fiber, 2 g; total fat, 7 g; saturated fat, 2 g; cholesterol, 8 mg; sodium, 207 mg; vitamin A, 9% of Daily Value; vitamin C, 48%; calcium, 5%; iron, 7%; vitamin E, 5%; folate, 11%; potassium, 8%.

Lovely Leftovers

Toss with cold pasta, grated cheese, and olive oil for a unique pasta salad.

Chili-Lime Asparagus

Asparagus is my favorite vegetable, and I can be pretty happy eating it just plain. But every now and then, I like to spice it up, especially if the rest of the meal is on the sedate side.

10 spears asparagus, washed and tough stems removed
1/8 teaspoon salt
1/2 fresh lime
1/2 teaspoon chili powder, or to taste

Coat the asparagus lightly with olive oil spray and sprinkle with the salt. Grill or broil for about 5 minutes, or until slightly charred and crisp-tender. Divide between two dinner plates. Squeeze the lime over the spears, then sprinkle with the chili powder. Great with grilled chicken or pork.

Yield: 2 servings

Nutritional data per serving: Calories, 22; protein, 2 g; carbohydrate, 4 g; dietary fiber, 1 g; total fat, <1 g; saturated fat, 0 g; cholesterol, 0 mg; sodium, 29 mg; vitamin A, 6% of Daily Value; vitamin C, 18%; calcium, 2%; iron, 4%; folate, 28%; potassium, 4%.

Lovely Leftovers Cut extra spears into 1-inch pieces and toss them into your next bowl of soup.

Refried Greens

Sure, most of the time, we refry beans. But here's a way to create greens that you and your friends will remember!

2 teaspoons peanut oil
2 cups steamed kale or other leafy greens
1 small clove garlic, minced or pressed
4 slices jalapeño chile pepper, diced
1/8 teaspoon salt

Warm the oil in a nonstick skillet over medium-high heat. Stir in the kale, garlic, and jalapeño peppers. Cook, stirring, for about 5 minutes, or until the greens are hot and well coated with oil. Sprinkle with the salt and serve piping hot.

Yield: 4 servings

Nutritional data per serving: Calories, 39; protein, 1 g; carbohydrate, 4 g; dietary fiber, 1 g; total fat, 2.5 g; saturated fat, 0 g; cholesterol, 0 mg; sodium, 103 mg; vitamin A, 48% of Daily Value; vitamin C, 45%; calcium, 5%; iron, 3%; vitamin E, 4%; potassium, 4%; omega-3 fatty acids, 7%.

DOUBLE DUTY

This tiny serving of kale really packs a wallop, bolstering your immune system with half your daily requirement of vitamins A and C.

Horseradish Mashed Potatoes

Nothing's more soothing and heartwarming than mashed potatoes. And if they can boost your bones and clear your sinuses, so much the better!

1¹⁄₃ cups water
²⁄₃ cup fat-free evaporated milk
1 tablespoon horseradish
¹⁄₂ teaspoon garlic powder
¹⁄₄ teaspoon salt
²⁄₃ cup instant mashed potato granules

In a medium saucepan, combine the water, milk, horseradish, garlic powder, and salt. Bring to a boil. Remove from the heat and stir in the potato granules. Let stand for 1 minute, then fluff with a fork.

Yield: 4 servings

Nutritional data per serving: Calories, 159; protein, 6 g; carbohydrate, 34 g; dietary fiber, 3 g; total fat, 0 g; saturated fat, 0 g; cholesterol, 2 mg; sodium, 373 mg; vitamin A, 5% of Daily Value; vitamin C, 23%; calcium, 14%; iron, 3%; vitamin B$_6$, 16%; folate, 5%; magnesium, 11%; potassium, 11%.

Lovely Leftovers

Form cold mashed potatoes into patties, then brown them in a little olive oil.

Tom's Savory Onion Sauce

"I know it sounds strange to put prunes in a sauce with onions, but just taste it," my brother-in-law urged me. So I did—and it was great! He says he got the idea from a TV cooking show, but by now the ingredient list has taken on a life of its own.

3 large onions, thinly sliced
1 tablespoon canola oil
¹/₂ cup pitted prunes, cut into thirds
1 tablespoon balsamic vinegar
¹/₂ teaspoon salt
Freshly ground black pepper to taste

In a large skillet over medium-high heat, sauté the onions in the oil for 5 to 10 minutes, or until soft and brown. Stir in the prunes and cook for 5 minutes. Add the vinegar, salt, and pepper and heat through. An amazingly good companion for beef, pork, or lamb.

Yield: 4 servings

SUPER SUB

This sauce is a great gravy stand-in, created mostly from fruits and vegetables (can you ever get enough?) and just a kiss of the right heart-healthy fat.

Nutritional data per serving: Calories, 132; protein, 2 g; carbohydrate, 25 g; dietary fiber, 3 g; total fat, 4 g; saturated fat, 0 g; cholesterol, 0 mg; sodium, 295 mg; vitamin A, 4% of Daily Value; vitamin C, 12%; calcium, 4%; iron, 4%; vitamin B₆, 11%; potassium, 10%; omega-3 fatty acids, 32%.

CHAPTER
12

SAVE YOUR
EYESIGHT

KEEP A LOOKOUT FOR LUTEIN

Every chance I get, I try to sneak some dark green, leafy vegetables into my husband, Ted. It's more than just that age-old admonition to eat something green every day. It's also because Ted's eye doctor has hinted that he may have the beginnings of cataracts. In addition, his mother developed age-related macular degeneration (ARMD) late in life, and I'm worried that Ted may be at risk, too. So I've embarked on a vision mission, and I'm pretty excited about it. I slip in a little spinach, broccoli, kale, or collard or mustard greens—whatever is dark and green. When he's not looking, I:

♥ Mix them with salad greens

♥ Toss them into soups and stews

345

♥ Sliver them into pasta dishes

♥ Shred them into mashed potatoes

Although we've long been helpless in the face of fading eyesight, new research sheds light on some diet strategies that appear to keep us looking good and seeing straight.

Dark green vegetables are bursting with some beta-carotene relatives called lutein and zeaxanthin (we'll call them L and Z for short). These same two nutrients show up in megadoses in a spot in the center of your eye. Called the macula, that little spot is what lets you see straight ahead, such as when you're reading, driving, or just looking at the face of someone you love. If the macula degenerates, central vision fades.

Now here's a surprise: People who eat the most vegetables rich in L and Z tend to have the most of both nutrients in the macula of their eyes. Furthermore—and here's where it gets good—they also have a 40 percent lower risk of macular degeneration. Wow! I like that.

But what's the connection? Researchers suspect that L and Z filter out and protect against some harmful light that can damage the macula and lead to vision loss. That's why I sneakily try to make sure that Ted eats those powerful veggies.

Other foods that deliver modest amounts of L and Z include egg yolks, green peas, pumpkin, celery, yellow corn, cucumbers, and green beans. (Ted likes all of those, except celery.)

Look into "Vitamin Eye"

The National Institutes of Health recommends that everyone over 55 have an eye exam to check for macular degeneration. If it shows that you have a problem, talk to your doctor about taking supplements of vitamin C (500 milligrams), vitamin E (400 IU), beta-carotene (15 milligrams), zinc (80 milligrams), and copper (2 milligrams). These amounts have been shown to reduce the odds of disease progression by 25%.

♥ **Pick peeper-protecting antioxidants.** There's a second good reason to make dark, leafy greens absolutely irresistible. It looks like they also help slow cataracts, and not just because of L and Z. The green foods your mother harped on are also exploding with antioxidant vitamins C and E. Along with all the other ways these vitamins protect your body, they appear to help the lens of your eye fend off the cell damage that becomes a cataract. I'm telling you, that green cuisine is serious stuff!

When it comes to vitamin C, the greens don't have to go it alone. Citrus fruits such as oranges, grapefruit, and tangerines are stuffed with C, too. And don't forget berries (you'll see lots of them in chapter 11) and melons (look at chapters 7 and 8). You'll find more vitamin E in whole grains (glance through chapter 5) and nuts (take a peek at chapter 4). Oh, and one more thing. Eating less sunflower and corn oil—the fats that ooze out of junk food—and more of the healthy fats from fish, walnuts, and flaxseed also appears to lower the risk of ARMD (set your sights on chapter 3).

♥ **It's time to go green!.** Let's face it, dark green veggies aren't everyone's favorite (although I'll show you how to make them so luscious your family can't resist!), so we have to do the best we can. Load up on the greens when possible, and mix in the more modest L and Z foods for variety. Every little bit helps.

Okay, it's time to put on your apron and get cooking. And you're going to love it. We'll use a little healthy fat so your veggies will taste good, and you'll want to eat them. Plus, the fat will boost your lutein absorption by 88 percent! Cool. Come take a look.

Very Red Spread

When my kids arrive for a family celebration, they come home hungry—and they expect to find something healthy and delicious to hold them until dinner is served. I, on the other hand, expect a quick fix. This little appetizer spread meets all our needs.

1 jar (7 ounces) roasted red peppers, drained
1 cup reduced-fat ricotta cheese
1 tablespoon chopped garlic (from a jar)
1 tablespoon red wine vinegar
½ teaspoon ground red pepper
½ teaspoon paprika
½ teaspoon dried oregano

In a blender, combine the roasted peppers, ricotta, garlic, vinegar, red pepper, paprika, and oregano. Blend until smooth. Serve with toasted whole wheat pita triangles.

Yield: 12 servings

Nutritional data per serving: Calories, 35; protein, 3 g; carbohydrate, 2 g; dietary fiber, 0 g; total fat, 2 g; saturated fat, 1 g; cholesterol, 6 mg; sodium, 134 mg; vitamin A, 10% of Daily Value; vitamin C, 16%; calcium, 6%; iron, 1%.

Lovely Leftovers This spread is especially good on grilled chicken or turkey sandwiches.

Ham and Gold Bites

Looking for a quick-fix appetizer that's just bursting with sunny goodness? Try these yummy, salty-sweet treats made with yellow kiwi, which is sweeter than the green. The folks who grow New Zealand kiwifruit thought up this pretty dish.

2 Zespri gold kiwifruit
2 ounces very thinly sliced lean ham

Peel the kiwi and quarter lengthwise. Twist a piece of the ham on a fancy toothpick, then spear the kiwi. It's bright, and smart, too!

Yield: 8 servings

Nutritional data per serving: Calories, 19; protein, 2 g; carbohydrate, 3 g; dietary fiber, <1 g; total fat, <1 g; saturated fat, 0 g; cholesterol, 3 mg; sodium, 101 mg; vitamin A, 0% of Daily Value; vitamin C, 39%; calcium, 0%; iron, 0%; vitamin B$_1$ (thiamin), 4%; vitamin E, 2%; potassium, 1%.

SUPER SUB

1 CUP

Ounce for ounce, kiwifruits pack more vitamin C than oranges.

Fresh Yellow Corn and Clam Chowder

The next time you're grilling corn, throw on a couple of extra ears. Use them to make this summery soup.

¹/₃ cup diced sweet onions
1 teaspoon butter
1 teaspoon walnut oil
¹/₃ cup diced red bell peppers
2 large ears grilled yellow corn
1 medium red-skin potato, diced
1 bottle (16 ounces) clam juice
1 can (6¹/₂ ounces) chopped clams
¹/₂ teaspoon Old Bay seafood
    seasoning

> ### The Inside Skinny:
> When you're slicing corn off the cob, try to capture all of the little yellow "germs" in the kernels. That's where most of the vitamins and minerals are hiding!

In a deep saucepan over medium-high heat, sauté the onions in the butter and oil for 5 minutes, or until beginning to soften. Stir in the peppers and sauté for 2 minutes.

Meanwhile, use a sharp knife to cut the corn from the cobs. Stir into the onion mixture. Add the potato, clam juice, clams (with juice), and seafood seasoning. Cover and bring to a boil. Reduce the heat and simmer for 10 to 20 minutes, or until the potatoes are cooked through.

Yield: 2 servings

Nutritional data per serving: Calories, 265; protein, 15 g; carbohydrate, 46 g; dietary fiber, 6 g; total fat, 6 g; saturated fat, 2 g; cholesterol, 29 mg; sodium, 1,293 mg; vitamin A, 22% of Daily Value; vitamin C, 123%; calcium, 5%; iron, 19%; vitamin E, 14%; folate, 20%; copper, 50%; magnesium, 21%; potassium, 33%; omega-3 fatty acids, 30%.

Spinach-Tortelloni Soup

My childhood memories of spinach—from a can—are definitely not inviting! But nowadays, baby spinach, prewashed and ready to use, really turns me on with instant cooking fun!

2 cans (14½ ounces each) fat-free
    chicken broth
1 tablespoon minced garlic (from a jar)
1 cup Barilla ricotta and spinach tortelloni
2 cups baby spinach, washed and spun dry

In a 4-quart saucepan, bring the broth and garlic to a boil. Stir in the tortelloni and return to a boil. Reduce the heat to medium and cook for 10 minutes. Stir in the spinach and cook for 2 to 3 minutes, or just until wilted. Ladle into lotus bowls.

Yield: 4 servings

Nutritional data per serving: Calories, 70; protein, 4 g; carbohydrate, 8 g; dietary fiber, 1.5 g; total fat, 2 g; saturated fat, 1 g; cholesterol, 10 mg; sodium, 518 mg; vitamin A, 10% of Daily Value; vitamin C, 8%; calcium, 4%; iron, 4%; folate, 7%; potassium, 7%.

> **QUICK TRICK:** Use refrigerated tortelloni instead of these dehydrated ones and cut cooking time by 7 minutes.

Oyster Mushroom and Spinach Salad

Yellow, flower-shaped oyster mushrooms may look delicate, but they are rich and earthy enough to help this intensely colorful salad hold its own against spicy dishes like Three-Pound Goulash (page 23). A glass of Cabernet Sauvignon helps, too.

4 cups baby spinach, washed and spun dry
1/2 large red bell pepper, thinly sliced
4 ounces oyster mushrooms, cleaned and sliced
3 tablespoons Ken's light country French dressing
1 tablespoon sunflower seeds
2 small mushroom caps
2 large black olives
1 ounce feta cheese

In a large bowl, combine the spinach, pepper, and sliced mushrooms. Add 2 tablespoons of the dressing and toss until well coated. Divide the salad between two bowls. Sprinkle each serving with half of the sunflower seeds and garnish with a mushroom cap and a black olive. Crumble the feta and sprinkle on each salad, then drizzle with half of the remaining dressing.

Yield: 2 servings

Nutritional data per serving: Calories, 167; protein, 7 g; carbohydrate, 15 g; dietary fiber, 3.5 g; total fat, 9 g; saturated fat, 3 g; cholesterol, 13 mg; sodium, 600 mg; vitamin A, 67% of Daily Value; vitamin C, 123%; calcium, 14%; iron, 18%; vitamin E, 18%; folate, 34%; vitamin K, 306%; potassium, 14%.

DOUBLE DUTY

Certainly, spinach is in the vanguard of vision protection. It also builds bone and helps blood clot properly.

Arugula and Green Soybean Salad

Getting beyond iceberg lettuce has taken me a lifetime, but it was worth it because of the amazing flavors available from "rabbit food." Arugula, or rocket, is peppery. If it's too strong for you, mix it with greens you already love. Soon, your palate will crave more of the new taste.

1 head arugula
1 tablespoon hazelnut oil
2 tablespoons fresh lemon juice
1/8 teaspoon dried oregano
1 red pear, quartered, cored, and
    thinly sliced
1/4 cup cooked green soybeans*
2 tablespoons freshly grated Parmesan cheese

Wash the arugula, remove the stems, and spin dry. In a large salad bowl, combine the arugula, oil, lemon juice, and oregano. Toss until well coated. Add the pear and toss. Divide among four salad plates. Top each salad with 1 tablespoon of the soybeans and sprinkle with the cheese.

Yield: 4 servings

Nutritional data per serving: Calories, 92; protein, 3 g; carbohydrate, 9 g; dietary fiber, 2 g; total fat, 5 g; saturated fat, <1 g; cholesterol, 2 mg; sodium, 65 mg; vitamin A, 6% of Daily Value; vitamin C, 17%; calcium, 10%; iron, 4%; vitamin E, 10%; folate, 9%; potassium, 6%; omega-3 fatty acids, 9%.

* See Slurp-It-Up Edamame on page 412.

DOUBLE DUTY

Sure, the soybeans are busy providing the protein in this salad, but they'll also help lower your cholesterol.

Sesame Spinach Salad

The eyes have it when it comes to this ultra-simple but simply delicious salad.

10 ounces spinach
1 can (8 ounces) sliced water
    chestnuts, rinsed and drained
¹/₂ cup Ginger-Sesame
    Dressing (page 103)
1 tablespoon toasted
    sesame seeds

Wash the spinach and spin dry. Remove the heavy stems and tear the leaves into bite-size pieces. In a large salad bowl, combine the spinach, water chestnuts, and dressing. Toss until well coated and sprinkle with the sesame seeds.

Yield: 12 servings

Nutritional data per serving: Calories, 15; protein, 1 g; carbohydrate, 4 g; dietary fiber, 1 g; total fat, 2 g; saturated fat, 0 g; cholesterol, 0 mg; sodium, 175 mg; vitamin A, 20% of Daily Value; vitamin C, 14%; calcium, 0%; iron, 17%; vitamin E, 3%; folate, 15%; potassium, 5%; omega-3 fatty acids, 4%.

> **QUICK TRICK:** Toast sesame seeds by placing them in a heavy nonstick skillet over high heat. Shake the pan constantly. When the seeds start to "pop" and turn golden, they're done.

Shrimp and White Bean Tomato Toss

Grilling shrimp? Make extra and hide it in the fridge. Tomorrow, you can toss together this lovely salad when friends come to call.

12 ounces grilled shrimp
1 can (15½ ounces) cannellini beans, rinsed and drained
2 large ripe tomatoes, diced
1 large yellow bell pepper, cut into chunks
2 tablespoons olive oil
2 tablespoons fresh lime juice
Crushed red pepper to taste
4 leaves red lettuce
2 ounces feta cheese

In a large bowl, combine the shrimp, beans, tomatoes, and yellow pepper. Drizzle with the oil and lime juice and dust with the red pepper. Toss until well blended. Arrange a lettuce leaf on each of four luncheon plates. Top each with one-fourth of the shrimp mixture and sprinkle with ½ ounce of the cheese. Serve with hot rolls and cold white wine.

Yield: 4 servings

Nutritional data per serving: Calories, 342; protein, 29 g; carbohydrate, 33 g; dietary fiber, 8 g; total fat, 12 g; saturated fat, 3 g; cholesterol, 178 mg; sodium, 387 mg; vitamin A, 30% of Daily Value; vitamin C, 198%; calcium, 21%; iron, 35%; vitamin D, 31%; vitamin E, 11%; folate, 25%; omega-3 fatty acids, 42%.

> **QUICK TRICK:** No grill in sight? Thaw frozen cooked, peeled, and deveined shrimp under running water, then drain, dry, and toss with the other ingredients.

Syracuse Blue Portobello Salad

My friend Brenda Keith is a dietitian in charge of the nutrition department at a hospital in upstate New York. She taught me how to make this artistic salad that's a big hit there.

2 large portobello mushrooms, cleaned and stems removed
4 cups field greens
2 tablespoons spicy French dressing
2 tablespoons blue cheese

Mist the mushrooms with olive oil spray. Grill over medium-high heat for about 3 minutes on each side, just until beginning to soften. On a cutting board, cut into ½-inch-wide strips. Set aside.

In a medium bowl, combine the greens and dressing, Toss until well coated. Divide between two individual salad bowls. Top each with half of the mushroom slices and garnish with 1 tablespoon of the cheese.

Yield: 2 servings

Nutritional data per serving: Calories, 142; protein, 6 g; carbohydrate, 11 g; dietary fiber, 4 g; total fat, 10 g; saturated fat, 3 g; cholesterol, 6 mg; sodium, 365 mg; vitamin A, 34% of Daily Value; vitamin C, 31%; calcium, 11%; iron, 11%; vitamin B_2 (riboflavin), 32%; folate, 37%; potassium, 23%.

The Inside Skinny: Ten grams of fat are a must to help you absorb all the carotenes in this salad, which become vitamin A in your body.

Strawberry Sea Breeze

Sometimes, I'm just too busy to make a real breakfast. But that's no problem; I just push a button!

1 cup fat-free orange-mango yogurt
1 cup fat-free milk
1 cup frozen strawberries

In a blender, combine the yogurt, milk, and all but two of the strawberries. Push the "high" button and blend until thick and smooth. Top each serving with a reserved strawberry.

Yield: 2 servings

Nutritional data per serving: Calories, 131; protein, 9 g; carbohydrate, 24 g; dietary fiber, 2 g; total fat, 0 g; saturated fat, 0 g; cholesterol, 5 mg; sodium, 130 mg; vitamin A, 8% of Daily Value; vitamin C, 59%; calcium, 34%; iron, 4%; folate, 5%; potassium, 14%.

DOUBLE DUTY

Strawberries not only serve up anti-cataract vitamin C, they also dole out cancer-fighting ellagic acid. Two good!

MicroEgg

Here's an eye-deal way to zap an egg in a hurry.

1 teaspoon olive oil
1 large egg
¹/₈ teaspoon salt
Freshly ground black pepper to taste

Place the oil in a custard cup or other small microwave-safe dish. Break the egg into the dish and pierce the yolk. Cover with plastic wrap and pierce to vent. Microwave on low for 1 to 1¹/₂ minutes, or until the egg is cooked through. Sprinkle with the salt and pepper.

Yield: 1 serving

Nutritional data per serving: Calories, 130; protein, 7 g; carbohydrate, <1 g; dietary fiber, 0 g; total fat, 11 g; saturated fat, 2.5 g; cholesterol, 246 mg; sodium, 363 mg; vitamin A, 10% of Daily Value; vitamin C, 0%; vitamin D, 8%; calcium, 3%; iron, 4%; vitamin B₂ (riboflavin), 18%; vitamin E, 6%; folate, 6%; omega-3 fatty acids, 7%.

SUPER SUB

Replace egg-white omelets with the real thing. It's the egg yolks that are bursting with vitamins, minerals, and healthy fats as well as visionary lutein.

Grilled Chicken and Spinach Pita

I love pita pockets because they can capture runaway ingredients, like loose spinach leaves. So feel free to pack in a ton of salad instead of just a smidgen.

1 small whole wheat pita pocket
3 ounces grilled chicken breast
2 tablespoons Roasted-Pepper and Green Olive Spread
  (page 285)
1 cup baby spinach, washed and spun dry

Toast the pita until puffed. When cool to the touch, split one edge to form a pocket. Slather the chicken with the pepper spread. Stuff into the pita and fill with the spinach.

Yield: 1 serving

Nutritional data per serving: Calories, 343; protein, 34 g; carbohydrate, 38 g; dietary fiber, 6 g; total fat, 7 g; saturated fat, 1 g; cholesterol, 72 mg; sodium, 701 mg; vitamin A, 31% of Daily Value; vitamin C, 38%; calcium, 5%; iron, 21%; vitamin B$_1$ (thiamin), 20%; vitamin B$_2$ (riboflavin), 12%; vitamin B$_3$ (niacin), 68%; vitamin B$_6$, 37%; folate, 21%; potassium, 14%.

DOUBLE DUTY

True, chicken is a great low-fat protein source. It's also bursting with B vitamins that help your body use that protein, produce energy, and protect nerves.

Grilled Swiss with Spinach and Mushrooms

Grilled cheese goes gourmet! Who says great cooking has to be hard?

2 slices rye bread
1 tablespoon creamy dill mustard
2 thin slices reduced-fat Swiss cheese
  (1 ounce)
1/2 cup sliced mushrooms
1/2 cup baby spinach, washed and spun dry

Heat a nonstick skillet over medium-high heat.

Lightly coat one side of each slice of bread with nonstick spray. Spread the opposite sides with the mustard. On one slice of bread, layer the mustard side with one slice of the cheese, 1/4 cup of the mushrooms, the spinach, the remaining 1/4 cup mushrooms, and the remaining slice of cheese. Top with the second slice of bread. Place in the skillet, cover, and reduce the heat to medium. Cook for about 3 minutes, or until the bottom is brown. Turn the sandwich, cover, and cook for 2 to 3 minutes, or until brown. Place on a plate and let cool for 1 to 2 minutes. Cut in half diagonally.

Yield: 1 serving

Nutritional data per serving: Calories, 260; protein, 14 g; carbohydrate, 37 g; dietary fiber, 4 g; total fat, 6 g; saturated fat, 1.5 g; cholesterol, 10 mg; sodium, 498 mg; vitamin A, 12% of Daily Value; vitamin C, 9%; calcium, 33%; iron, 14%; vitamin B_1 (thiamin), 20%; vitamin B_2 (riboflavin), 28%; vitamin D, 10%; vitamin E, 6%; folate, 21%; potassium, 10%.

Beans 'n Greens 'n Pasta

My hairdresser, Michael, is a talented guy who is also a master of the quick Mediterranean meal. Here's one of his simplest and healthiest creations, using leftovers from a too-large restaurant meal.

1 cup cooked pasta
½ cup cooked greens (such as collards, spinach, and kale)
1 cup cooked or rinsed and drained canned cannellini beans
2 tablespoons olive oil
2 tablespoons freshly shredded Parmesan cheese
Salt and freshly ground black pepper to taste

Place the pasta in a medium bowl. In a nonstick skillet, sauté the greens and beans in the oil until heated through. Ladle over the pasta. Sprinkle with the cheese, salt, and pepper.

Yield: 1 serving

Nutritional data per serving: Calories, 496; protein, 15 g; carbohydrate, 40 g; dietary fiber, 5 g; total fat, 32 g; saturated fat, 6 g; cholesterol, 9 mg; sodium, 312 mg; vitamin A, 124% of Daily Value; vitamin C, 59%; calcium, 35%; iron, 31%; folate, 55%.

> **QUICK TRICK:** You don't *need* restaurant leftovers to make this dish. Just use frozen mixed greens and canned beans instead.

Flounder Florentine

When I'm home alone and fishin' for something fancy, but I don't want to mess with all the cleaning up that follows a gourmet project, I turn to this lovely flounder dish.

1 very thin flounder filet (4 ounces)
1 tablespoon hazelnut oil
1 small red-skin potato, scrubbed and
    thinly sliced
Freshly ground black pepper to taste
4 cups baby spinach, washed and
    spun dry
1/8 teaspoon salt
1 wedge lemon

> **DOUBLE DUTY**
>
> Spinach shines with both vitamin C and vitamin A—a double bonus for eye health.

Wash the fish and pat dry. Warm the oil in a medium nonstick skillet over medium-high heat. Arrange the potato slices in a single layer in the skillet and sprinkle with the pepper. Pile on the spinach and sprinkle with the salt. Lay the fish on the spinach and squeeze on the lemon. Reduce the heat to medium, cover, and cook for 10 minutes, or until the fish is cooked through, the spinach is wilted, and the potatoes are brown. Carefully slide onto a dinner plate so the layers remain intact. Put the skillet in the dishwasher, pour a glass of white wine, and chill out.

Yield: 1 serving

Nutritional data per serving: Calories, 323; protein, 27 g; carbohydrate, 21 g; dietary fiber, 5 g; total fat, 16 g; saturated fat, 1 g; cholesterol, 54 mg; sodium, 221 mg; vitamin A, 82% of Daily Value; vitamin C, 92%; calcium, 15%; iron, 24%; vitamin B_3 (niacin), 28%; vitamin B_6, 36%; vitamin D, 17%; vitamin E, 54%; folate, 64%; potassium, 45%; omega-3 fatty acids, 38%.

My Best Friend's Wedding Pasta

My friend Brenda is getting married in a couple of months, and she's all in a whirl. But in the middle of a phone call about hairdressers, wedding shoes, and her mom's crazy adventures, she took a minute to pass on this especially summery pasta salad recipe.

2 cups cooked bow-tie pasta
1 cup cooked yellow corn, cut from the cob
$\frac{1}{2}$ cup sliced green onions, including tops
$\frac{1}{2}$ cup Ken's light Caesar dressing
1 large ripe tomato, diced
8 ounces grilled salmon, flaked
4 sprigs parsley
4 wedges lemon

In a large bowl, combine the pasta, corn, onions, and dressing. Toss until well coated. Gently fold in the tomato and salmon until well mixed. Refrigerate until ready to serve. Garnish with the parsley and lemons.

Yield: 8 servings

Nutritional data per serving: Calories, 169; protein, 10 g; carbohydrate, 19 g; dietary fiber, 2 g; total fat, 6 g; saturated fat, <1 g; cholesterol, 20 mg; sodium, 324 mg; vitamin A, 3% of Daily Value; vitamin C, 15%; calcium, 1%; iron, 6%; vitamin B_3 (niacin), 21%; vitamin B_6, 16%; folate; 14%; potassium, 10%; omega-3 fatty acids, 63%.

QUICK TRICK: Use well-drained canned salmon if you haven't used the grill lately. Canned or frozen corn works, too.

Tex-Mex Grilled Corn

I try to buy my corn as close as possible to where it's grown, so I get really sweet ears that haven't turned starchy yet. A touch of spice sets them off perfectly.

6 ears yellow corn, with husks
1 tablespoon ground red pepper
3 tablespoons ground cumin
1/2 cup medium salsa

> ### The Inside Skinny:
> Brushing corn with butter or other fat helps your body absorb more of the lutein and zeaxanthin that's so good for your eyes!

Remove the heavy outer husks from the corn. Peel back the inner husks and remove the silk.

In a small dish, combine the pepper and cumin. Sprinkle about 1 teaspoon on each ear of corn. Pull the husks back into place, then twist and fold over the tops. Hold in place with rubber bands. Soak the corn in ice water for 30 minutes, drain, and remove the rubber bands. Place on a grill over medium heat, close the lid, and cook for 15 to 20 minutes, turning every 5 minutes. Serve with the salsa and a small amount of melted butter.

Yield: 6 servings

Nutritional data per serving: Calories, 95; protein, 4 g; carbohydrate, 20 g; dietary fiber, 4 g; total fat, 2 g; saturated fat, 0 g; cholesterol, 0 mg; sodium, 111 mg; vitamin A, 8% of Daily Value; vitamin C, 16%; calcium, 3%; iron, 8%; vitamin B$_1$ (thiamin), 13%; folate, 11%; potassium, 9%.

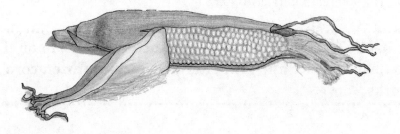

Spinach Asiago

Quick as a wink, you can serve up this colorful side dish that's pretty to look at and powerful protection for your eyes.

1 bag (10 ounces) baby spinach, washed but not dried
1/8 teaspoon salt
Freshly ground black pepper to taste
1/2 yellow bell pepper, thinly sliced into 1-inch strips
2 tablespoons shredded Asiago cheese

In a large, deep skillet over high heat, sprinkle the wet spinach with the salt and black pepper. Top with the yellow pepper. Cover and bring to a boil. Reduce the heat to medium and steam for about 5 minutes, stirring occasionally, until the spinach is wilted and the peppers are crisp-tender. Spoon into a serving bowl and garnish with the cheese.

Yield: 4 servings

DOUBLE DUTY

Sure, spinach is hard at work doling out the vitamin C and lutein that protect your eyes. But it also serves up hefty doses of folate and vitamin E to safeguard your heart.

Nutritional data per serving: Calories, 40; protein, 4 g; carbohydrate, 5 g; dietary fiber, 3 g; total fat, 1 g; saturated fat, <1 g; cholesterol, 3 mg; sodium, 92 mg; vitamin A, 62% of Daily Value; vitamin C, 98%; calcium, 12%; iron, 14%; folate, 32%; vitamin E, 10%; magnesium, 20%; potassium, 16%; omega-3 fatty acids, 12%.

Arugula with Olives and Figs

Arugula is a very peppery, bitter green. I like the bite of it, but I also like to tame it with buttery, oil-cured olives and dried figs. This combination will drive your taste buds wild.

1/4 cup thinly sliced onions
1 tablespoon walnut oil
1 clove garlic, minced or pressed
2 dried figs, thinly sliced
4 oil-cured olives, pitted and sliced
1 cup coarsely chopped fresh basil
1 bunch arugula (about 4 cups), washed and
     stems removed
1 teaspoon balsamic vinegar
Dash of ground red pepper
1 tablespoon coarsely chopped toasted walnuts

In a large, deep nonstick skillet over medium heat, sauté the onions in the oil just until soft. Stir in the garlic and cook for 1 minute. Add the figs and olives and cook just until warm. Add the basil and arugula and cook, stirring constantly, until wilted and tender. Stir in the vinegar and pepper and mix well. Divide between two plates and top each with half of the walnuts.

Yield: 4 servings

Nutritional data per serving: Calories, 85; protein, 1 g; carbohydrate, 9 g; dietary fiber, 2 g; total fat, 5 g; saturated fat, <1 g; cholesterol, 0 mg; sodium, 35 mg; vitamin A, 7% of Daily Value; vitamin C, 8%; calcium, 6%; iron, 5%; folate, 7%; magnesium, 6%; potassium, 5%; omega-3 fatty acids, 58%.

Bella Spinach Sauté

1 package (10 ounces) spinach, washed and
   heavy stems removed
2 teaspoons butter
1 package (10 ounces) baby bella
   mushrooms, cleaned and sliced
1 clove garlic, minced or pressed
1 ounce feta cheese, crumbled

Place the spinach in a heavy saucepan with just the water that clings to the leaves after washing. Cover and bring to a boil. Reduce the heat to medium and cook, stirring occasionally, for about 5 minutes, until wilted but still firm.

Meanwhile, in a large sauté pan over medium heat, melt the butter. Stir in the mushrooms and garlic, cover, and cook until the spinach is done. Drain the spinach and add to the mushrooms. Cook, stirring, for 1 minute, or until blended. Divide among four plates and garnish each serving with the cheese.

Yield: 4 servings

Nutritional data per serving: Calories, 69; protein, 3 g; carbohydrate, 5 g; dietary fiber, 2 g; total fat, 4 g; saturated fat, 2 g; cholesterol, 11 mg; sodium, 147 mg; vitamin A, 41% of Daily Value; vitamin C, 27%; calcium, 9%; iron, 9%; vitamin B_2 (riboflavin), 20%; vitamin E, 6%; folate, 31%; magnesium, 12%; potassium, 15%; omega-3 fatty acids, 11%.

> **QUICK TRICK:** Use frozen spinach and canned mushrooms if you're in a rush.

Salsa Turnip Greens

"Greens" tend to be a Southern favorite in the United States. But they take on local charm with any change of seasonings. This Tex-Mex version is a cool adventure for those who like it hot!

1 teaspoon peanut oil
2 cups lightly steamed turnip or other greens
¼ teaspoon ground cumin
½ cup hot cilantro-flavored salsa

Warm the oil in a large skillet over medium heat. Add the greens and sauté for about 4 minutes, or until hot. Add the cumin and stir until well blended. Stir in the salsa and cook for 2 to 3 minutes, or until hot.

Yield: 4 servings

Nutritional data per serving: Calories, 35; protein, 1 g; carbohydrate, 5 g; dietary fiber, 3 g; total fat, 1 g; saturated fat, 0 g; cholesterol, 0 mg; sodium, 421 mg; vitamin A, 41% of Daily Value; vitamin C, 33%; calcium, 10%; iron, 3%; vitamin E, 7%; folate, 21%; potassium, 4%.

SUPER SUB

Cooking in peanut oil instead of butter replaces saturated fat with heart-happy monounsaturated fat—and adds a whole different flavor.

Kung Pao Collards

Peanuts and collard greens are a natural Southern combination. Add a few Asian spices, and you'll think you're in the south of China!

2 cups cooked collard greens
2 tablespoons chunky peanut butter
1 tablespoon reduced-sodium soy sauce
¼ teaspoon Chinese five-spice powder*

Place the greens in a medium microwave-safe dish, cover, and microwave on high for about 2 minutes, or until steaming. Set aside, covered, to keep warm.

In a smaller microwave-safe dish, microwave the peanut butter for 1 minute, or until warm. Stir in the soy sauce and five-spice powder. Drizzle over the greens and toss until well coated. Microwave 1 minute to reheat, if necessary.

Yield: 4 servings

Nutritional data per serving: Calories, 75; protein, 4 g; carbohydrate, 7 g; dietary fiber, 3 g; total fat, 4 g; saturated fat, 1 g; cholesterol, 0 mg; sodium, 197 mg; vitamin A, 30% of Daily Value; vitamin C, 29%; calcium, 12%; iron, 4%; vitamin E, 7%; folate, 24%; potassium, 9%; omega-3 fatty acids, 9%.

*Available in Asian markets and many large supermarkets.

Thai Turnip Greens

Tired of eating turnip greens with cornbread? Okay, let's cross a few borders and time zones to see how you might eat the same greens in Thailand.

2 pounds turnip greens, washed and stems removed
1 teaspoon sesame oil
1 teaspoon spicy red Thai chili sauce,* or to taste
¹/₈ teaspoon salt

In a large covered saucepan, bring the greens and ¹/₂ cup water to a boil. Reduce the heat and simmer for 10 to 15 minutes, or just until tender. Drain. Warm the oil in a nonstick skillet over medium-high heat. Stir in the sauce. Add the greens and sauté until heated through and well coated. Sprinkle with the salt. Serve hot with chicken or catfish.

Yield: 2 servings

Nutritional data per serving: Calories, 34; protein, 1 g; carbohydrate, 3 g; dietary fiber, 3 g; total fat, 2 g; saturated fat, 0 g; cholesterol, 0 mg; sodium, 191 mg; vitamin A, 40% of Daily Value; vitamin C, 33%; calcium, 10%; iron, 3%; vitamin E, 7%; folate, 21%; potassium, 4%; omega-3 fatty acids, 5%.

*Available in Asian markets and many large supermarkets.

Lovely Leftovers Mix the greens with cold chicken and stuff into a pita pocket for lunch.

Kale with Walnuts and Raisins

Trying to break into a little green cuisine? Then go a little nutty.

1 tablespoon coarsely chopped walnuts
2 teaspoons walnut oil
1 small clove garlic, minced or pressed
2 cups cooked kale
$1/8$ teaspoon salt
Freshly ground black pepper to taste
1 tablespoon dark seedless raisins

In a large, heavy skillet over medium-high heat, sauté the walnuts in the oil for about 2 minutes, or until toasted. Stir in the garlic and cook for 1 minute. Pile on the kale, sprinkle with the salt and pepper, and top with the raisins. Reduce the heat to low, cover, and simmer for 1 to 2 minutes, or until the kale is heated through. Stir until well blended and divide between two plates. It's great with fish or pork tenderloin.

Yield: 2 servings

Nutritional data per serving: Calories, 117; protein, 3 g; carbohydrate; 12 g; dietary fiber, 3 g; total fat, 8 g; saturated fat, <1 g; cholesterol, 0 mg; sodium, 45 mg; vitamin A, 96% of Daily Value; vitamin C, 90%; calcium, 10%; iron, 8%; vitamin B_6, 11%; vitamin E, 7%; folate, 5%; potassium, 10%; omega-3 fatty acids, 95%.

DOUBLE DUTY

Kale builds bone with calcium and vitamin K. See, there's more here than meets the eye!

Pink Lemonade Crush

Tired of artificial colors and flavors? You'll get a pink you can rely on when you swirl fresh strawberries into your lemonade. Pull up a sand chair and chill out!

1 cup Minute Maid natural lemonade
1 cup sliced fresh strawberries
2 cups ice cubes
1 sprig mint

In a blender, combine the lemonade, strawberries, and ice cubes. Blend on high until the ice is crushed and the berries are well blended. Pour into a tall glass and garnish with the mint.

Yield: 1 serving

Nutritional data per serving: Calories, 160; protein, 1 g; carbohydrate, 43 g; dietary fiber, 4 g; total fat, <1 g; saturated fat, 0 g; cholesterol, 0 mg; sodium, 27 mg; vitamin A, 0% of Daily Value; vitamin C, 157%; calcium, 2%; iron, 4%; folate, 7%; vitamin K, 29%; potassium, 8%.

DOUBLE DUTY

One cup of fresh strawberries delivers more than a day's worth of vitamin C, along with a hefty dose of fiber.

Guava Colada in the Shade

What makes Hawaiian Punch such a pretty pink? Guava! Make your own pink and frosty grownup drink in the blender. (It's okay for kids to indulge, too.)

12 ounces Goya guava nectar*
1/2 cup light coconut milk*
2 cups ice cubes
1/2 banana
2 slices banana

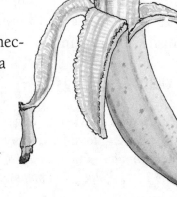

In a blender, combine the guava nectar, coconut milk, ice, and the banana half. Blend on high until the ice is crushed and the ingredients are well blended. Pour into two tall glasses and garnish each with a banana slice.

Yield: 2 servings

Nutritional data per serving: Calories, 159; protein, 1 g; carbohydrate, 34 g; dietary fiber, 2 g; total fat, 3 g; saturated fat, 2 g; cholesterol, 0 mg; sodium, 20 mg; vitamin A, 2%; vitamin C, 57%; calcium, 1%; iron, 3%; vitamin B_6, 9%; potassium, 5%.

*Available in the imported foods section of many supermarkets.

Island Papaya Cup

When you're in a lazy, tropical kind of mood, the last thing you want to do is spend hours making dessert. Here's the best of everything natural.

1 very ripe papaya
1 tablespoon shredded toasted coconut
2 wedges lime

Halve the papaya and remove the seeds. Scoop out the pulp and cut into chunks. Divide between two small, stemmed dessert dishes (wine glasses work, too). Sprinkle with the coconut and garnish with the limes.

Yield: 2 servings

Nutritional data per serving: Calories, 45; protein, 1 g; carbohydrate, 9 g; dietary fiber, 2 g; total fat, 1 g; saturated fat, 1 g; cholesterol, 0 mg; sodium, 10 mg; vitamin A, 2% of Daily Value; vitamin C, 80%; calcium, 2%; iron, 1%; vitamin E, 4%; folate, 7%; potassium, 6%.

Lovely Leftovers
Fruit getting overripe? Peel and slice it, then combine it with a little yogurt and cinnamon.

CHAPTER 13

FIGHT FATIGUE

EAT, SLEEP, AND BE MERRY

W HEN HERB RAYMOND CAME TO SEE ME, HE WAS REALLY draggin' his wagon. He couldn't haul himself out of bed to go running in the morning. He couldn't control his snacking at night, and so he couldn't control his weight. He couldn't do his briefcase full of legal work when he got home. He was too tired to enjoy activities with his daughter. "What can I eat," he asked me, "to get more energy?"

"Nothing," I said, "and everything."

There is no magic food—no energy bar or vitamin-fortified water—that will fix this problem. And that's the good news.

If you feel tired most of the time—just able to get through the day, with no oomph left over for fun and games—maybe you need to rebalance your life. You have to work less, obsess less, play more, sleep more, maintain a healthy weight, and exercise every day.

Then, choosing the right foods and changing the way you eat will boost your energy levels all day long—big time! For example, one young man I met recently complained that his afternoons were awful. He was stressed, irritable, and headachy, and he couldn't get anything done. It turned out that he thought eating lunch was a time-wasting luxury he couldn't afford. I talked him into taking a 20-minute lunch break to enjoy a peanut butter and jelly sandwich, some raw veggies, and a piece of fruit.

"Your body needs fuel all day long," I told him. "Eat lunch." When he started eating at midday, his afternoon "stress" all but vanished, and his productivity soared. He had just been plain old hungry.

Here's how to keep your energy sizzling throughout the day.

♥ **Eat something every 3 to 5 hours.** I meet others who run on empty all day long, then load up at dinnertime. I tell them to imagine getting into a car with an empty gas tank, driving to New York, and filling up after they get there. It can't be done. If you want more energy, you need to provide your body with fuel all day long. Keep the foods healthy and the portions small.

♥ **Watch your weight.** Lugging around excess pounds really wears you out. Think not? Try toting a 25-

pound turkey (or even a 10-pound bag of sugar) all day and see how you feel. (See "A Word about Weight Control" on page 378 for some helpful information.)

♥ **Eat the right stuff.** If you're like me and you feel fatigued when you eat too many sweets or processed foods, you'll want to:

1. Check out the whole grains in chapter 5.

2. Combine them with the healthy fats in chapter 4 to avoid energy drops between meals.

3. Monitor your protein, because eating too much can dehydrate you and sap your energy. Stick to 2- to 3-ounce portions of meat, for example.

4. Keep things moving. Constipation is another energy robber, so drink plenty of water and eat lots of fruits and vegetables. They're in chapters 2 and 7 through 12.

Let this little poem become your mantra.

Get some sleep.
Move your feet.
Try to balance what you eat.

Now, how about taking a nap? When you wake up, come on out to the kitchen. I'll be cooking up some high-energy dishes that are to die for. And you won't believe how easy they are to prepare.

A Word about Weight Control

Are you tired of feeling guilty about your weight? Weary of losing the same pounds over and over and gaining back more each time? Maybe you need to shift gears. Do yourself a favor and take the easy way out. Forget about losing weight; just stop gaining it.

All you have to do is these two things.

1. Have more fun. Research makes it clear that being fatter but fitter is much better for you than being a skinny couch potato. And getting fit—if you take your time and do it gradually—is really a kick! In fact, if you're like most people, you'll feel more energetic just a few days after starting a simple daily walking program. Then, the better you feel, the more you'll want to do. Before you know it, your weekends and vacations will be filled with bicycling, walking on the beach, going to museums, hiking in the mountains, and enjoying loads of fun and games with the kids. Oh, you're going to love this!

2. Eat better food, but less of it. What could be better than eating deliciously, day after day? This book is packed with fabulous food that tastes *really good*! No sacrifice required. All you have to do is manage your portion sizes, and I've made that part pretty easy by sharing recipes that you can cook in small batches.

Want a few more fat-prevention tips? Here's what I tell my family and friends.

♥ **Divide and conquer.** Picture a three-compartment plate. Use one of the small sections for meat/chicken/fish and the other small section for potato/rice/pasta. The big section? Fill it with vegetables. People who eat the greatest variety of vegetables are leaner than the straight meat-and-potatoes crowd. So pile 'em on!

♥ **Enjoy every morsel.** You'll be eating less food, so enjoy it more. Slow down. Drink a glass of water before you dig in. Put your fork down between bites. Chew until your mouth is empty. Concentrate on the flavor of your food instead of watching TV. All of this will give your brain time to register that you've eaten enough—before you overdo it.

♥ **Milk it for all it's worth.** Have three low-fat dairy foods every day. Men and women and children of all ages who sport milk mustaches wear 11 fewer pounds of body fat than those who avoid dairy products but otherwise eat the same amount of food. Amazing! Pore over chapters 6 and 15 for milky ways to do your body good.

♥ **Mini-mize it.** Let's face it, super-sizing has gotten us into a ton of trouble. Over the past 30 years, a single serving of fries has tripled in size and now delivers one-third of a day's worth of calories. Fight back! At fast-food places and other popular restaurants, order the smallest of everything, whether it's a hamburger, a soft drink, an ice cream cone, or popcorn. Then super-size the salad.

♥ **Dine on the half shell.** Dining out? Order any entrée you want, but eat only half. Of course, take the other half home for a (free!) second meal. You'll make all of the wonderful flavor, the calories, and your money go twice as far. And naturally, you'll share dessert. The more forks, the merrier.

Okay, sounds like a plan!

Now let's get cooking!

The Chicken and the Egg Drop Soup

Egg drop soup is filling but light. It's a quick lunch that won't weigh you down all afternoon. Add some carrot sticks and a piece of fruit, and you're good to go.

1 cup fat-free chicken broth
1 large egg
2 ounces diced cooked chicken breast
1/2 cup cooked yellow corn
Freshly ground black pepper to taste
1 tablespoon sliced green onions

> **The Inside Skinny:**
> Blood levels of choline can drop as much as 40% after hard exercise. We need this B vitamin to help with memory storage and muscle control. Eggs are tops for filling up on choline.

In a small saucepan over medium heat, bring the broth just to a simmer.

Meanwhile, break the egg into a cup and scramble vigorously with a fork. Gradually drizzle into the simmering broth, allowing it to cook into "threads." When all the egg is cooked, stir in the chicken and corn and cook gently, just until heated through. Ladle into a lotus bowl and garnish with the pepper and onions.

Yield: 1 serving

Nutritional data per serving: Calories, 252; protein, 27 g; carbohydrate, 19 g; dietary fiber, 3 g; total fat, 8 g; saturated fat, 2 g; cholesterol, 256 mg; sodium, 746 mg; vitamin A, 11% of Daily Value; vitamin C, 9%; calcium, 3%; iron, 9%; vitamin D, 8%; vitamin E, 4%; folate, 12%; potassium, 11%; zinc, 11%.

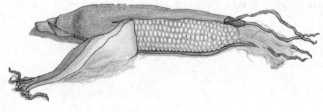

Alpha Chicken Soup

When I've been working or playing hard and need to recover fast, I need carbs, sodium, and fluids to refill my muscles' energy stores and rehydrate my body. This soup is one of my favorite refuelers.

2 teaspoons chicken bouillon granules
1/2 cup grated carrots
1/2 cup alphabet pasta
1/8 teaspoon garlic powder
1 teaspoon parsley flakes
Freshly ground black pepper to taste

Bring 3 cups water to a boil in a medium saucepan. Stir in the bouillon, carrots, pasta, garlic, parsley, and pepper. Return to a boil. Reduce the heat to medium and simmer for 8 to 9 minutes, or until the pasta is done. Ladle into a serving bowl. Enjoy with some whole grain bread, a glass of milk, and a piece of fresh fruit.

Yield: 1 serving

Nutritional data per serving: Calories, 294; protein, 12 g; carbohydrate, 56 g; dietary fiber, 3 g; total fat, 3 g; saturated fat, <1 g; cholesterol, 1 mg; sodium, 1,864 mg; vitamin A, 3% of Daily Value; vitamin C, 1%; calcium, 4%; iron, 15%; vitamin B_1 (thiamin), 44%; vitamin B_2 (riboflavin), 20%; vitamin B_3 (niacin), 24%; folate, 38%; potassium, 5%.

QUICK TRICK: If you're planning to do a lot of gardening or heavy outdoor work tomorrow, before you go to bed, fill a water bottle half-full of red Gatorade. Cap it and freeze it. In the morning, fill the rest of the bottle with yellow Gatorade. You'll have a cold "sunrise" that will help keep you energized all morning.

Split Pea and Ham Soup

1 cup diced onions
1 cup thinly sliced carrots
1 clove garlic, minced
1 tablespoon olive oil
1 pound split green peas
8 cups fat-free chicken broth
4 ounces lean ham, diced

In a soup pot or Dutch oven over medium heat, sauté the onions, carrots, and garlic in the oil for about 5 minutes, until beginning to soften.

Meanwhile, rinse the peas and remove any foreign matter. Set aside.

Stir the broth into the vegetables and add the peas and ham. Bring to a boil. Reduce the heat, cover, and simmer for 60 to 90 minutes, or until the peas are soft. Ladle into soup bowls.

Yield: 10 servings

Nutritional data per serving: Calories, 161; protein, 12 g; carbohydrate, 23 g; dietary fiber, 9 g; total fat, 2 g; saturated fat, 0 g; cholesterol, 4 mg; sodium, 509 mg; vitamin A, 36% of Daily Value; vitamin C, 5%; calcium, 2%; iron, 8%; vitamin B$_1$ (thiamin), 20%; folate, 17%; vitamin K, 24%; copper, 10%; magnesium, 10%; potassium, 13%; zinc, 8%.

Lovely Leftovers

Create cream soup by stirring ⅓ cup nonfat dry milk into each cup of hot soup.

Udon Noodle Bowl

When you're feeling just like a limp noodle, this may be exactly the right dish for you! A high-carbohydrate treat, this soup is a great recovery food after any kind of exercise.

1 cup udon noodles* or thick
    spaghetti
1 cup fat-free chicken broth
2 ounces diced cooked lean pork or
    chicken breast
1/4 cup thinly sliced carrots
1/4 cup thinly sliced celery
1/4 cup sliced shiitake mushrooms
1 tablespoon sliced green onions

DOUBLE DUTY

Besides delivering protein, lean pork is a super source of B vitamins that help turn your food into energy.

Fill a medium saucepan with water and bring to a boil. Add the noodles or spaghetti. Reduce the heat to medium and cook for 8 minutes, or according to package directions.

Meanwhile, in a medium saucepan, combine the broth, pork or chicken, carrots, celery, and mushrooms. Bring to a boil. Reduce the heat and simmer until the noodles are done. Drain the noodles, ladle into a soup bowl, and add the soup. Garnish with the onions.

Yield: 1 serving

Nutritional data per serving: Calories, 376; protein, 29 g; carbohydrate; 50 g; dietary fiber, 6 g; total fat, 6 g; saturated fat, 2 g; cholesterol, 53 mg; sodium, 719 mg; vitamin A, 97% of Daily Value; vitamin C, 8%; calcium, 6%; iron, 18%; vitamin B_1 (thiamin), 55%; vitamin B_2 (riboflavin), 21%; vitamin B_3 (niacin), 27%; vitamin B_6, 24%; vitamin D, 27%; potassium, 18%.

*Available at Trader Joe's and other international foods stores.

Waffles with Autumn Sauce

When I'm trying to get more carbs, I pile on the fruits, vegetables, and whole grains and ease up on the fat. This spicy breakfast really gets the job done.

2 medium apples, cored and coarsely chopped
¼ cup dark seedless raisins
½ cup ruby red grapefruit blend with calcium
½ teaspoon pumpkin pie spice
1 teaspoon molasses
4 frozen whole grain waffles
2 tablespoons sunflower seeds

In a medium saucepan, combine the apples, raisins, grapefruit juice, spice, and molasses. Bring to a boil. Reduce the heat and simmer, uncovered, for 10 minutes, or until the apples are tender and the sauce is thick. Toast the waffles and place two on each of two large plates. Ladle one-fourth of the sauce onto each waffle and garnish each with sunflower seeds. Serve with glasses of cold milk.

Yield: 2 servings

Nutritional data per serving: Calories, 381; protein, 9 g; carbohydrate, 77 g; dietary fiber, 9 g; total fat, 8 g; saturated fat, 1 g; cholesterol, 5 mg; sodium, 740 mg; vitamin A, 1% of Daily Value; vitamin C, 42%; calcium, 29%; iron, 43%; vitamin B$_6$, 44%; vitamin E, 18%; potassium, 19%.

SUPER SUB

Replacing typical pancake syrup with this fruit sauce more than doubles your breakfast fiber.

1 cup

Breakfast of Champions Spinner

Cars can't run on empty, and neither can you. When you have no time to sit down to breakfast, throw together this blender "spinner" to sip on your way to work.

1 cup fat-free milk
1 cup Wheaties cereal
1 cup sliced fresh strawberries
1/2 teaspoon vanilla extract
1 teaspoon honey

In a blender, combine the milk, cereal, strawberries, vanilla, and honey. Blend until smooth. Pour into your favorite travel mug and eat like a champion!

Yield: 1 serving

Nutritional data per serving: Calories, 269; protein, 13 g; carbohydrate, 53 g; dietary fiber, 6 g; total fat, 2 g; saturated fat, <1 g; cholesterol, 4 mg; sodium, 343 mg; vitamin A, 37% of Daily Value; vitamin C, 185%; calcium, 38%; iron, 48%; vitamin B_2 (riboflavin), 51%; folate, 35%; magnesium, 19%; potassium, 23%.

The Inside Skinny: This lively little cupful is jam-packed with more than 1/3 of your daily requirement of vitamin A, calcium, iron, vitamin B_2, and folate, plus almost 2 days' worth of vitamin C. Powerful!

String Cheese Tortilla

Flavor galore and gooey cheese. What could be better?

1/4 cup fat-free refried beans
1 tablespoon chopped green chile peppers
2 tablespoons chopped black olives
2 small corn tortillas
2 pieces reduced-fat string cheese

Preheat the toaster oven to 500°F.

In a small bowl, combine the beans, peppers, and olives. Stir until well mixed. Place the tortillas on the toaster-oven tray and spread half of the bean mixture on each. Add a piece of string cheese in the center. Bake for 5 minutes, or until the cheese begins to melt. Let cool slightly, then roll the tortilla around the cheese and eat.

Yield: 1 serving

Nutritional data per serving: Calories, 355; protein, 25 g; carbohydrate, 46 g; dietary fiber, 9 g; total fat, 8 g; saturated fat, 2 g; cholesterol, 10 mg; sodium, 1,276 mg; vitamin A, 12% of Daily Value; vitamin C, 10%; calcium, 53%; iron, 14%; folate, 15%; magnesium, 9%.

> **QUICK TRICK:** Use canned chopped chile peppers and olives.

White Bean and Garlic Pizza

Pizza doesn't need meat to be savory. Garlic, herbs, and spices help keep fat down so carbs can fuel your afternoon.

1 individual pizza crust
1 teaspoon Oven-Roasted Garlic (page 319) or 2 teaspoons
    minced garlic (from a jar)
1/2 cup rinsed and drained canned cannellini beans
4 thin slices tomato
Dash of dried oregano
Freshly ground black pepper to taste
1 ounce shredded reduced-fat mozzarella cheese

Preheat the toaster oven to 450°F.

Lightly mist the crust with olive oil spray and spread the garlic on top. Place the beans on top, then mash lightly and spread to cover the crust to within 1/4 inch of the edge. Overlap the tomato slices to cover most of the beans. Sprinkle with the oregano and pepper and mist with olive oil spray. Top with the cheese. Place on the oven rack. Bake for 5 to 7 minutes, or until the cheese is melted and beginning to brown. Let cool slightly before eating.

Yield: 1 serving

Nutritional data per serving: Calories, 440; protein, 24 g; carbohydrate, 69 g; dietary fiber, 8 g; total fat, 8 g; saturated fat, 3 g; cholesterol, 14 mg; sodium, 566 mg; vitamin A, 10% of Daily Value; vitamin C, 27%; calcium, 41%; iron, 34%; folate, 24%; copper, 19%; magnesium, 21%; potassium, 22%; zinc, 18%.

SUPER SUB

1 CUP

On this little pizza, the beans provide 10 grams of protein—as much as 1 1/2 ounces of meat—with virtually no fat.

Habanero Flatbread Wrap

Boosting carbs? Make the bread bigger and more important than the filling by using intensely flavored ingredients, but fewer of them. Here's a sample.

$^{1}/_{2}$ ounce shredded habanero Jack cheese
1 tablespoon sliced black olives
$^{1}/_{4}$ cup shredded romaine lettuce
$^{1}/_{4}$ cup diced tomatoes
1 tablespoon fat-free ranch dressing
1 whole wheat Mediterranean-style
  flatbread (7 inches)

In a small bowl, combine the cheese, olives, lettuce, tomatoes, and dressing. Toss until well blended. Pile the mixture in the center of the flatbread, roll it up, and eat.

Yield: 1 serving

Nutritional data per serving: Calories, 340; protein, 11 g; carbohydrate, 44 g; dietary fiber, 3 g; total fat, 14 g; saturated fat, 4 g; cholesterol, 15 mg; sodium, 730 mg; vitamin A, 11% of Daily Value; vitamin C, 25%; calcium, 22%; iron, 19%; folate, 6%.

 The P·E·R·F·E·C·T Companion
Refuel your muscles by mixing 1 cup pineapple juice with 1 cup grape juice.

Kid-Stuff Ravioli

Got tiny athletes to feed? These mini ravioli are just right for little mouths, and the sauce is simplicity itself. That means you'll have more time to play with your sweet babies.

1 can (14½ ounces) zucchini with Italian-style
    tomato sauce
Dash of dried basil
7 ounces Buitoni mini three-cheese ravioli
¼ cup grated Parmesan cheese

In a medium serving bowl, roughly chop the zucchini into smaller pieces. Stir in the basil. Cover and microwave on high for 4 minutes, stirring once after 2 minutes.

Meanwhile, in a large saucepan, bring 3 quarts water to a boil, Add the ravioli and cook for 3 to 5 minutes, or until tender. Drain and stir into the zucchini. Sprinkle with the cheese.

Yield: 4 servings

Nutritional data per serving: Calories, 184; protein, 9 g; carbohydrate, 27 g; dietary fiber, 2 g; total fat, 4 g; saturated fat, 2 g; cholesterol, 20 mg; sodium, 663 mg; vitamin A, 9% of Daily Value; vitamin C, 8%; calcium, 16%; iron, 16%; zinc, 4%.

 **The
P·E·R·F·E·C·T
Companion**

Stir 2 teaspoons Hershey's chocolate syrup into 1 cup fat-free milk. Kids will drink chocolate milk with anything!

Creste di Gallo Pasta with Fresh Tomato Sauce

I was thinking outside the spaghetti box when I came upon this bag of amazing pasta. Shaped like rooster combs, they're red, yellow, gold, brown, green, black, and white. Gorgeous—and perfectly delicious with this simple little sauce that you can toss with any pasta, even when you're whipped after a tough day.

4 ounces Creste di Gallo pasta
2 large tomatoes, diced
6 large leaves fresh basil, slivered
1 clove garlic, minced
1 tablespoon olive oil
1/4 teaspoon salt
Freshly ground black pepper to taste
1/2 cup freshly grated pecorino
   Romano cheese

> **DOUBLE DUTY**
>
> Here, the cheese provides both calcium and protein—no need for meat!

In a large saucepan, bring 4 quarts water to a boil. Add the pasta and cook for 10 to 11 minutes, or until al dente.

Meanwhile, in a medium bowl, combine the tomatoes, basil, garlic, oil, salt, pepper, and 1/4 cup of the cheese. Toss until well mixed. Drain the pasta and toss with the tomato mixture. Divide evenly between two pasta bowls and sprinkle with the remaining 1/4 cup cheese. Serve with crusty bread and red wine.

Yield: 2 servings

Nutritional data per serving: Calories, 400; protein, 17 g; carbohydrate, 52 g; dietary fiber, 4 g; total fat, 15 g; saturated fat, 5 g; cholesterol, 26 mg; sodium, 327 mg; vitamin A, 15% of Daily Value; vitamin C, 59%; calcium, 30%; iron, 16%; vitamin E, 9%; folate, 43%; potassium, 13%.

Barley Corn Chili

Try a little barley with your chili for a whole different grain sensation and plenty of long-lasting energy. Not hot enough for you? Toss in a can of chopped green chile peppers. Scorching!

1 cup coarsely chopped onions
1 large green bell pepper, diced
4 cloves garlic, minced
2 tablespoons olive oil
6 cups water
1 cup pearled barley, rinsed
1/2 teaspoon salt
1 jar (15 ounces) medium salsa
1 can (15 1/2 ounces) red kidney beans, rinsed
    and drained
1 package (10 ounces) frozen yellow corn

In a large, deep saucepan or Dutch oven over medium-high heat, sauté the onions, pepper, and garlic in the oil for about 5 minutes, until soft. Stir in the water, barley, and salt. Cover and bring to a boil. Reduce the heat and simmer for 50 minutes. Stir in the salsa, beans, and corn and heat through. Serve with chopped onions and shredded reduced-fat cheese as toppings.

Yield: 10 servings

Nutritional data per serving: Calories, 211; protein, 8 g; carbohydrate, 39 g; dietary fiber, 10 g; total fat, 3 g; saturated fat, 0 g; cholesterol, 0 mg; sodium, 377 mg; vitamin A, 1% of Daily Value; vitamin C, 30%; calcium, 1%; iron, 4%; folate, 14%; magnesium, 11%; omega-3 fatty acids, 11%.

Seafoam Artichoke Pesto

Here's a pretty pesto sauce that provides more carbohydrate and less fat than traditional pesto.

1 pound spiral pasta
1/4 cup almond oil
2 cloves garlic
1/2 cup shelled salted pistachios
1/4 cup packed fresh basil
1/2 cup fat-free chicken broth
1/2 teaspoon salt
Freshly ground black pepper to taste
1 pound frozen artichoke hearts

Bring a large saucepan of water to a boil. Add the pasta and cook according to package directions.

Meanwhile, pour the oil into a food processor and begin to blend on high. Gradually add the garlic, pistachios, and basil, dropping them through the feeder tube. Add the broth, salt, and pepper. Process until smooth. Drop in the artichokes a few at a time and process until coarsely chopped. Drain the pasta and place in a serving bowl. Stir in the sauce and serve immediately.

Yield: 8 servings

Nutritional data per serving: Calories, 331; protein, 11 g; carbohydrate, 48 g; dietary fiber, 5 g; total fat, 12 g; saturated fat, 1 g; cholesterol, 0 mg; sodium, 203 mg; vitamin A, 2% of Daily Value; vitamin C, 6%; calcium, 3%; iron, 13%; vitamin B_1 (thiamin), 40%; vitamin B_3 (niacin), 20%; vitamin E, 16%; folate, 22%.

Sports-Night Casserole

Mindy Hermann's twin sons are now 12 years old and involved in tons of activities. On nights when they have a game or practice, Mindy assembles this casserole in advance, then pops it into the oven when they get home. By the time they've washed their hands and changed their clothes, dinner is served!

8 corn tortillas
1 can (15½ ounces) fat-free refried beans
1 can (15½ ounces) chopped tomatoes, drained
1 jar (16 ounces) mild salsa
8 ounces grated low-fat Monterey Jack cheese

In a baking dish, arrange four of the tortillas so they cover the bottom. Top with the beans, then the tomatoes. Cover with the remaining four tortillas, the salsa, and the cheese. Refrigerate until dinnertime, then bake at 375°F for about 15 minutes, or until the cheese is melted. No game tonight? Go directly to the oven without stopping at the refrigerator.

Yield: 4 servings

Nutritional data per serving: Calories, 420; protein, 29 g; carbohydrate, 52 g; dietary fiber, 12 g; total fat, 12 g; saturated fat, 7 g; cholesterol, 40 mg; sodium, 1,508 mg; vitamin A, 29% of Daily Value; vitamin C, 39%; calcium, 68%; iron, 21%; folate, 19%; potassium, 10%.

SUPER SUB

Corn tortillas boost bones with three times as much calcium as flour tortillas.

Red Chile Penne with Black Beans

For providing sustained levels of energy, these beans are black magic!

4 ounces red chile pepper and garlic penne pasta
2 tablespoons Garlic Aioli (page 320)
2 medium tomatoes, diced
1 cup rinsed and drained canned black beans
1 tablespoon chopped fresh cilantro or 1 teaspoon
    dried cilantro
Dash of dried oregano
1/4 teaspoon salt
Freshly ground black pepper to taste

Bring a medium saucepan of water to a boil. Add the pasta and cook for 9 minutes, or according to package directions. Drain and return to the pan. Add the aioli and stir until the pasta is well coated. Add the beans, cilantro, oregano, salt, and pepper. Toss until well blended. Divide evenly between two pasta bowls and serve with hearty bread and a glass of red wine.

Yield: 2 servings

Nutritional data per serving: Calories, 462; protein, 16 g; carbohydrate, 73 g; dietary fiber, 12 g; total fat, 13 g; saturated fat, 1.5 g; cholesterol, 24 mg; sodium, 909 mg; vitamin A, 13% of Daily Value; vitamin C, 65%; calcium, 6%; iron, 28%; vitamin B_1 (thiamin), 54%; vitamin B_2 (riboflavin), 30%; vitamin B_3 (niacin), 30%; vitamin E, 19%; folate, 56%; potassium, 23%.

> **QUICK TRICK:** Can't find red chile penne? Use regular penne and add a pinch of ground red pepper when you toss it with the sauce.

Herb-Grilled Potatoes

*What a delicious way to add more fiber to your diet! Keeping
"regular," as they say, keeps you feeling frisky.*

2 medium red-skin potatoes, scrubbed
2 teaspoons olive oil
1/2 teaspoon garlic powder
1/4 teaspoon salt
Freshly ground black pepper to taste
2 tablespoons chopped fresh herbs (such as chives, basil,
    and thyme) or 3/4 teaspoon dried herbs

Thinly slice the potatoes into a medium bowl. Stir in the oil,
garlic powder, salt, and pepper. Toss until the potatoes are well
coated. Make two squares of heavy-duty foil and pile half of the
potatoes in the center of each. Top each with 1 tablespoon of the
herbs and seal the packets. Grill over medium heat for 15 to 20
minutes, turning every 5 minutes. Serve with grilled chicken or
pork.

Yield: 2 servings

*Nutritional data per serving: Calories, 171; protein, 3 g; carbohydrate,
30 g; dietary fiber, 3 g; total fat, 5 g; saturated fat, <1 g; cholesterol, 0 mg;
sodium, 301 mg; vitamin A, 1% of Daily Value; vitamin C, 33%; calcium,
2%; iron, 9%; vitamin B_1 (thiamin), 10%; vitamin B_3 (niacin), 11%; vitamin
B_6, 22%; potassium, 16%.*

QUICK TRICK: For thin-slicing vegetables, nothing
beats a mandolin (available at kitchen specialty stores and
by mail order). Watch your fingers, though—that baby is
sharp! Always use the guard when slicing.

Butter Pecan Rice

If you're browsing through the many-splendored rice offerings at your supermarket, you may come across wild pecan rice. It contains neither wild rice nor pecans. It's just nutty-flavored, chewy rice grown in southern Louisiana. It's tasty on its own, but adding your own pecans sure makes it special.

½ teaspoon salt
1 package (7 ounces) Konriko wild pecan rice
1 tablespoon parsley flakes
1 tablespoon butter
¼ cup coarsely chopped toasted pecans

In a large saucepan, bring 2 cups water and the salt to a boil. Stir in the rice, parsley, and butter. Reduce the heat, cover, and simmer for 20 minutes, or until the water is absorbed. Remove from the heat, stir in the pecans, and fluff the rice. Serve piping hot.

Yield: 6 servings

Nutritional data per serving: Calories, 169; protein, 3 g; carbohydrate, 26 g; dietary fiber, 1 g; total fat, 6 g; saturated fat, 1.5 g; cholesterol, 5 mg; sodium, 221 mg; vitamin A, 2% of Daily Value; vitamin C, 1%; calcium, 1%; iron, 3%.

Lovely Leftovers Stir cold rice into French vanilla instant pudding to make butter pecan pudding. Carbs galore!

Wild Porcini Rice

When I was a kid, we ate beef for dinner almost every night. Now it's more of a special treat, so I want a fancy side dish to go with it. This dark, rich, earthy rice blend is the perfect complement.

1 cup red wine
1/2 ounce dried porcini mushrooms
1 clove garlic, minced
3/4 cup chopped red bell peppers
1 tablespoon butter
1 1/2 cups water
1 cup Lundberg wild blend rice
1 tablespoon parsley flakes
2 beef bouillon cubes

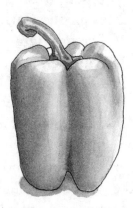

In a small saucepan over high heat, bring the wine to a boil. Remove from the heat, stir in the mushrooms, and let stand for 10 minutes, or until rehydrated.

Meanwhile, in a medium saucepan over medium heat, sauté the garlic and peppers in the butter for about 5 minutes, or until the peppers are soft. Stir in the water, rice, parsley, bouillon, and the mushrooms and wine. Bring to a boil. Reduce the heat, cover, and simmer for 45 to 50 minutes, or until the liquid is absorbed.

Yield: 6 servings

Nutritional data per serving: Calories, 174; protein, 5 g; carbohydrate, 28 g; dietary fiber, 3 g; total fat, 3 g; saturated fat, 1 g; cholesterol, 5 mg; sodium, 409 mg; vitamin A, 8% of Daily Value; vitamin C, 31%; calcium, 1%; iron, 9%; potassium, 2%.

Green Beans with Garlic Croutons

This is my personal, healthier (and tastier!) twist on the old version with buttered bread crumbs.

1/2 pound fresh green beans, washed and trimmed
2 teaspoons Garlic Aioli (page 320)
1 slice multigrain or whole wheat bread
1/8 teaspoon salt
Freshly ground black pepper to taste

Insert a steamer basket in a large saucepan with about 1 inch of water. Cut the beans diagonally into 1-inch pieces and add to the basket. Cover and bring to a boil. Reduce the heat to medium and cook for 5 minutes, or until crisp-tender.

Meanwhile, spread the aioli on one side of the bread. In toaster oven, toast the bread garlic side up until the bottom is crisp and the aioli is melted. Let cool and cut into tiny cubes. Place the beans in a serving bowl and sprinkle with the salt and pepper. Add the croutons and toss. Serve piping hot.

Yield: 2 servings

Nutritional data per serving: Calories, 113; protein, 3 g; carbohydrate, 15 g; dietary fiber, 5 g; total fat, 4 g; saturated fat, <1 g; cholesterol, 8 mg; sodium, 143 mg; vitamin A, 3% of Daily Value; vitamin C, 14%; calcium, 7%; iron, 5%; vitamin E, 4%; potassium, 8%.

> **QUICK TRICK:** Out of aioli? Mix light mayo, a few drops of lemon juice, and chopped garlic from a jar and spread it on the bread.

Ragin' Cajun Roasted Potatoes

I've been hooked on spuds since I was a little kid. And that's a good thing, because they're fabulous for restoring your energy when you're just beat.

3 pounds tiny red-skin potatoes, washed and halved
4 teaspoons garlic powder
1 teaspoon onion powder
1/2 teaspoon ground red pepper
1 teaspoon dried thyme
1/4 teaspoon freshly ground black pepper
1/2 teaspoon salt
1/2 teaspoon toasted cumin seeds

> ## DOUBLE DUTY
>
> While potatoes are supplying plenty of carbs to fuel your body, they're also delivering a super dose of minerals, such as copper, iron, magnesium, and potassium. These are needed for building bones and blood and keeping blood pressure under control.

In a deep saucepan with just enough water to cover, bring the potatoes to a boil. Cook for 10 minutes, then drain.

Meanwhile, in a small bowl, combine the garlic powder, onion powder, red pepper, thyme, black pepper, salt, and cumin. Stir until blended. Set aside. Lightly mist a baking sheet with olive oil spray. Arrange the potatoes cut side up on the baking sheet and mist lightly. Sprinkle with the seasoning mixture. Broil for about 5 minutes, or until brown and crisp.

Yield: 10 servings

Nutritional data per serving: Calories, 115; protein, 4 g; carbohydrate, 24 g; dietary fiber, 5 g; total fat, <1 g; saturated fat, 0 g; cholesterol, 0 mg; sodium, 457 mg; vitamin A, 0% of Daily Value; vitamin C, 12%; calcium, 7%; iron, 47%; vitamin B$_6$, 18%; copper, 60%; magnesium, 10%; potassium, 16%.

Instant Energy Banan-za

A yogurt-fruit combo like this one is digested quickly, so it delivers plenty of energy on short order.

1 cup fat-free plain yogurt
1 tablespoon apricot preserves
1 medium slightly green banana
Dash of ground cinnamon

In a cereal bowl, combine the yogurt and preserves. Stir until well blended. Peel the banana, split lengthwise, and cut into bite-size pieces. Swirl into the yogurt mixture and sprinkle with the cinnamon. Spoon it up!

Yield: 1 serving

Nutritional data per serving: Calories, 294; protein, 15 g; carbohydrate, 59 g; dietary fiber, 3 g; total fat, 1 g; saturated fat, <1 g; cholesterol, 4 mg; sodium, 197 mg; vitamin A, 2% of Daily Value; vitamin C, 24%; calcium, 50%; iron, 4%; vitamin B_2 (riboflavin), 41%; vitamin B_6, 41%; folate, 15%; potassium, 32%.

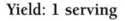

DOUBLE DUTY

The creamy banana delivers lots of easy-energy carbohydrate and $1/3$ of your day's potassium, too. It's a positively powerful mineral that fights high blood pressure.

Banana Spooner

There was a little place called Sander's Corner where we'd end up looking for ice cream after a Saturday run. My favorite was their homemade banana, but sadly, they no longer make their own ice cream. Although my heart is spared all that saturated fat, my taste buds still crave the flavor. Surprise! This comes very close.

2 tablespoons cold fat-free evaporated milk
1 cold medium banana
1/4 cup cold reduced-fat ricotta cheese
Dash of ground nutmeg

In a blender, combine the milk, banana, and ricotta. Blend on high until creamy and smooth. Scrape into a tall glass and dust with the nutmeg. Eat with an iced-tea spoon.

Yield: 1 serving

Nutritional data per serving: Calories, 218; protein, 11 g; carbohydrate, 34 g; dietary fiber, 3 g; total fat, 6 g; saturated fat, 3 g; cholesterol, 20 mg; sodium, 115 mg; vitamin A, 12% of Daily Value; vitamin C, 19%; calcium, 27%; iron, 4%; vitamin B_6, 36%; potassium, 19%.

SUPER SUB

Replacing ice cream with ricotta cheese boosts protein and calcium and knocks off about 200 calories and 20 grams of fat!

1 CUP

Super Banana Shake

Turn an overripe banana into a fatigue-fighting beverage with just a little help from your blender. The potassium in the fruit keeps your muscles humming.

1 very ripe banana
1 cup fat-free plain yogurt
1/2 cup fat-free milk
1 tablespoon vanilla extract
1 tablespoon honey
1 tablespoon toasted wheat germ
Dash of ground cinnamon

In a blender, combine the banana, yogurt, milk, vanilla, honey, and wheat germ. Blend on high until creamy and smooth. Pour into a tall glass and dust with the cinnamon.

Yield: 1 serving

Nutritional data per serving: Calories, 440; protein, 21 g; carbohydrate, 74 g; dietary fiber, 4 g; total fat, 6 g; saturated fat, 3 g; cholesterol, 30 mg; sodium, 227 mg; vitamin A, 12% of Daily Value; vitamin C, 23%; calcium, 56%; iron, 7%; vitamin B_1 (thiamin), 23%; vitamin B_2 (riboflavin), 55%; vitamin B_6, 45%; vitamin E, 9%; folate, 14%; potassium, 36%.

DOUBLE DUTY

This shake serves up more than 1/3 of your potassium and 1/2 of your calcium for the day.

Ginger-Mint Pear Smoothie

When you're in a slump, the jazzy taste of this refreshing drink will put you back on your feet.

1 cup fat-free plain yogurt
2 pieces candied ginger (about 1 inch square each), minced
1 tablespoon mint jelly
1 large Bartlett pear, cored and cut into eighths

In a blender, combine the yogurt, ginger, and jelly. Blend on high. Remove the feeder cap and drop in the pear slices one by one. Process until smooth and creamy. Pour into a 12-ounce glass and serve with a straw.

Yield: 1 serving

Nutritional data per serving: Calories, 306; protein, 11 g; carbohydrate, 70 g; dietary fiber, 5 g; total fat, <1 g; saturated fat, 0 g; cholesterol, 5 mg; sodium, 147 mg; vitamin A, 2% of Daily Value; vitamin C, 14%; calcium, 33%; iron, 4%; vitamin E, 5%; copper, 12%; potassium, 8%.

> **QUICK TRICK:** Use 3 well-drained canned pear halves instead of a fresh pear.

Baked Spiced Pears

I found these enormous red pears at the store the other day. I ate one plain. Yum! Then I decided to turn the other one into dessert for two. Even better.

1 large red Bartlett pear, halved
  and cored
2 tablespoons water
1 tablespoon chopped pecans
1 tablespoon dried cranberries
1 teaspoon brown sugar
1/4 teaspoon ground cinnamon
2 tablespoons frozen cranberry juice
  cocktail, thawed
1/2 teaspoon cinnamon sugar

> ### The
> ### P·E·R·F·E·C·T
> ### Companion
>
> Place an Earl Grey tea bag in each of 2 tall mugs and fill with boiling water, Steep for 5 minutes, then remove the tea bags. Sweeten each with 1 teaspoon sugar and 1/4 cup fat-free milk.

Preheat the oven to 350°F. In a 3-cup baking dish, arrange the pears cut side up and add the water.

In a small bowl, stir together the pecans, cranberries, brown sugar, and cinnamon. Divide evenly and spoon onto the pears. Drizzle 1 tablespoon of the cranberry juice over each half. Cover and bake for 30 minutes, or until the pears are very tender. Place each in a small dessert dish. Pour half of the baking liquid over each and dust with the cinnamon sugar.

Yield: 2 servings

Nutritional data per serving: Calories, 150; protein, 1 g; carbohydrate, 32 g; dietary fiber, 3 g; total fat, 3 g; saturated fat, 0 g; cholesterol, 0 mg; sodium, 2 mg; vitamin A, 0% of Daily Value; vitamin C, 21%; calcium, 2%; iron, 3%; vitamin E, 3%; potassium, 5%.

Mini Banana Split

Nothing speaks to me of utter indulgence like a banana split. But who can take all those calories? Here's my mini version, with all the fabulous flavors packed into one small serving.

1 finger banana
1/2 cup fat-free vanilla frozen yogurt
2 fresh strawberries, thinly sliced
2 tablespoons fresh pineapple
1 tablespoon Hershey's chocolate syrup
1 tablespoon toasted chopped walnuts
1 tablespoon whipped cream

Peel the banana, halve lengthwise, and arrange in a large dessert dish. Scoop the frozen yogurt between the halves. Surround with the strawberries and pineapple and drizzle the chocolate syrup over everything. Garnish with the walnuts and whipped cream.

Yield: 1 serving

Nutritional data per serving: Calories, 272; protein, 6 g; carbohydrate, 50 g; dietary fiber, 4 g; total fat, 6 g; saturated fat, 1 g; cholesterol, 3 mg; sodium, 61 mg; vitamin A, 1% of Daily Value; vitamin C, 64%; calcium, 33%; iron, 5%; vitamin B_6, 19%; folate, 7%; magnesium, 9%; potassium, 10%; omega-3 fatty acids, 76%.

> **The Inside Skinny:** An average banana split weighs in at over 1,000 calories!

Fuel Up for Sport

Healthy meals and regular exercise team up for plenty of feel-good energy, whether you're a daily walker or a world-class athlete. But some folks don't quite get the connection.

An Olympic triathlete dropped in to see me, wondering if what she ate might affect her performance. She had the best exercise equipment, a personal trainer, and a highly touted triathlon coach, but eating for peak performance had, for the first time, just crossed her mind. So I gave her this short course in sports nutrition.

It's the key to peak performance for child or teenage athletes, college scholarship jocks, weekend warriors, and elite Olympic or professional competitors—male or female. What's best is that it will work for nonathletes, too. Apply these basics to your own diet, and you'll find that your feet have wings during your daily walk!

♥ **Training meals**, day in and day out, should provide 60 percent of calories from high-carbohydrate foods such as whole grain breads, crackers, and cereals; pasta; rice; potatoes and sweet potatoes; starchy vegetables such as corn, lima beans, and peas; other vegetables; and fruit—along with adequate protein and some healthy fat.

♥ **Drinking plenty of fluids** is crucial for training and performance. The fluids cool your body through sweat and keep you well-coordinated. Drink before you're thirsty to give your body time to absorb and use them. What you drink early is far more important than what you drink late.

♥ **Pregame and preworkout meals** should be low in fat and high in carbohydrates that deliver a steady supply of energy. Include items such as low-fat yogurt and frozen yogurt; fat-free milk; oranges and orange juice; apples; pears; grapes; fruit smoothies; plums; peaches; multigrain waffles, bread, or cereal; pasta; rice, beans; sweet potatoes; granola; bran muffins; and energy bars and sports drinks.

♥ **Postgame and postworkout recovery meals** should be high in easily absorbed carbohydrates to refuel your muscles for tomorrow's activity. Top picks include any bread or bagel with lean beef, turkey, or ham; pretzels; cereal; pasta; potatoes and sweet potatoes; carrots; green peas; corn; bananas; smoothies; and some sports drinks.

♥ **Sports drinks such as Gatorade** help during events that last more than 60 to 90 minutes by fueling your brain to keep you well-coordinated, providing salt to make you thirsty so you'll drink more, and delivering easily absorbed fluids.

♥ **A balanced diet** of whole grains, fruits, vegetables, lean protein, dairy foods, and healthy fats will help keep your immune system going full blast and help you deal with the stress of heavy training so you don't get sick when you should be at your best.

Whether you're a daily walker or an endurance athlete, a body builder (yes, you need carbs. too!) or a baseball player, there are no magic foods—just darned good diets that can give you the edge in making the most of what you have in both talent and training. The meals, drinks, and snacks on pages 381–405 will maximize the athlete in you and deliver plenty of energy for the rest of the day. You'll discover that you can shine at your job, play with your kids, and have energy to spare.

CHAPTER 14

ENJOY BEING
A GIRL

CALM THOSE TURBULENT HORMONES

I HATE TO WHINE, BUT BEING A WOMAN AND SUBJECT TO estrogen's whims does have its drawbacks. Fortunately, we know now that diet can turn down the volume on our hormone-related gripes. So let's skip the whining and just pour a cup of tea, grab a chunk of chocolate, and talk about the food facts of a woman's life.

♥ **Feeling tired and run down?** Iron deficiency is the bane of a young woman's existence, whether she's menstruating (and losing iron-rich red blood cells monthly) or pregnant (and creating iron-rich new blood cells for baby daily). If that's you, drag your bod over to chapters 1 and 3 to learn about the benefits of eating lean red meat, chicken, and fish. They'll pump up your diet with double-acting heme iron, which is easily absorbed and boosts iron

uptake from plant foods such as beans, vegetables, and bread. Vegetarian? Pair beans and bread with foods high in vitamin C from chapter 12 to increase iron absorption.

♥ **Hoping to get pregnant?** *Before* you conceive, boost the amount of folate (the natural form of folic acid) in your diet to protect against birth defects such as spina bifida and anencephaly. These problems develop during the first 28 days after conception, so by the time you've done your early pregnancy test, it's too late. Start now. We'll cook up a mess of beans, a top-notch source of this B vitamin. And be sure to enjoy plenty of dark green, leafy vegetables and citrus fruit, too (see chapters 7 and 12).

♥ **Already pregnant?** Have some eggs! Okay, I admit there were a couple of months when the very smell of eggs sent me into spasms of morning sickness, but after that, I was fine. Eggs are packed with choline, a B vitamin that boosts a baby's brain development. Milk is loaded with it, too. And don't forget fish. Its fancy fats are crucial for a baby's brain and vision, so drop a line into chapter 3.

♥ **Distressed by PMS?** If you want to minimize mood swings, fluid retention, food cravings, cramps, backache, headache, insomnia, breast tenderness, and even crying spells, get 1200 milligrams of calcium daily. It's true! A wonderful study of women with severe PMS showed that just three

Double Up on Folic Acid

Folic acid is so important for preventing birth defects that any woman who can become pregnant should get 400 micrograms of folate from food and 400 micrograms of folic acid daily from a supplement or a fortified food, according to the Centers for Disease Control and Prevention.

months on a high-calcium diet cut symptoms in half. And since the same high calcium intake has been shown to help ban body fat and boost bones, this is really quite a deal. Check out recipes using dairy foods in chapters 6 and 15.

While we're talking about moods, review chapter 13 for delicious recipes rich in soothing high-carbohydrate foods such as bananas, pasta, and potatoes, which help raise brain serotonin levels so you'll feel just a little happier.

And let's do chocolate. It's packed with antioxidants that fend off heart disease and cancer. So what if researchers can't figure out exactly why it works? (Personally, I think it's magic.) Studies do show that chocolate won't raise your cholesterol, and it serves you as many antioxidants as a glass of red wine, so just enjoy. If you're concerned about calories, consider this: Women burn an extra 200 to 500 calories daily during the 3 to 5 days before their periods start. That's enough to allow for a few chocolate kisses or a nice little bar. So indulge!

♥ **Coping with nagging urinary tract infections?** Cranberries, blueberries, purple grapes, and their juices are awash in condensed tannins that will float your troubles away. That's because the bacteria that cause UTIs come with little hooks that grab onto the walls of your urinary tract, so it's hard to get rid of them. Condensed tannins relax the hooks, and swoosh, away go the bacteria! If you want relief, latch on to chapter 10.

♥ **Going through menopause?** That's when estrogen plummets and health risks rise. But you can outsmart "The Change" with beans and soy—and go on to enjoy a healthy, happy second half of your life! Sound too good to be true? Get this: Beans beat heart disease with soluble fiber that lowers cholesterol and folate that keeps homocysteine (a potential mischief maker) in check. Their soluble fiber also helps stabilize blood sugar levels to deter diabetes. And research suggests soy's protein and isoflavones work in tandem to strengthen bones, lower cholesterol, control diabetes, manage weight, and fend off cancer. Shazam! That is powerful stuff! Will soy cool your hot flashes? The jury is still out on that one. Soy milk cooled me off, but you'll have to check it out for yourself.

Okay, I know beans and soy don't qualify as "fast food," but they're a lot easier to make into a meal than you might imagine. And if you're thinking, "Yuck, tofu," you've got a big surprise in store. I can hardly wait to see the look on your face when you taste the goodies in the next few pages! Each recipe is guaranteed to keep one of the girl problems above far away!

Skip the Soy Supplements

Resist this shortcut. Soy's protein and isoflavones occur together in food and are powerful natural partners. Neither works as well when it tries to stand alone in a supplement. Besides, overdosing on supplements may raise breast cancer risks in postmenopausal women.

baked beans

Slurp-It-Up Edamame

My kids keep trying to educate me on the joys of sushi, and slowly but surely, I'm starting to like some of it...mostly when it's cooked. But here's what I love. In many sushi restaurants, you can get this wonderful, soybean-in-the-pod appetizer. Don't choke when you find out how easy it is to make at home! (You can find frozen edamame in natural food stores and many large supermarkets.)

2 cups frozen edamame
¹/₂ teaspoon salt (optional)

Bring 2 quarts water to a boil in a 4-quart saucepan over high heat. Add the edamame and the salt, if desired, and return to a boil. Reduce the heat and simmer for 5 minutes. Pour off the boiling water, then rinse with cold water. Divide the pods between two bowls. One by one, gently squeeze the pods and slurp the soybeans right into your mouth. It's both fun and delicious!

> **The P·E·R·F·E·C·T Companion**
>
> Even at home, you must do green tea with this appetizer. Put 4 tea bags in a pot with an Asian design. Add boiling water and steep for 3 to 5 minutes, then remove the tea bags. It's best served plain, without sweetener or milk.

Yield: 2 servings

Nutritional data per serving: Calories, 100; protein, 8 g; carbohydrate, 9 g; dietary fiber, 4 g; total fat, 3 g; saturated fat, 0 g; cholesterol, 0 mg; sodium, 30 mg; vitamin A, 9% of Daily Value; vitamin C, 9%; calcium, 5%; iron, 9%.

Rainy Day Bean Soup

The truth is, it's pouring outside and I wanted to go out, so I'm feeling cranky and out of sorts. I need soothing soup without a lot of hassle. Help is at hand.

1 can (11½ ounces) can Campbell's Healthy Request bean
    with ham and bacon soup
1 cup fat-free milk
½ teaspoon dried cilantro
Dash of ground cumin

Empty the soup into a medium saucepan. Use a wire whisk to gradually stir in the milk, cilantro, and cumin. Cook, stirring, over medium heat until just beginning to boil. Ladle into a large soup bowl, spoon up, and enjoy.

Yield: 1 serving

Nutritional data per serving: Calories, 468; protein, 26 g; carbohydrate, 78 g; dietary fiber, 18 g; total fat, 6 g; saturated fat, 3 g; cholesterol, 17 mg; sodium, 1,349 mg; vitamin A, 40% of Daily Value; vitamin C, 4%; calcium, 46%; iron, 26%; folate, 23%; vitamin E, 9%; magnesium, 33%; zinc, 37%; potassium, 39%.

SUPER SUB

1 CUP

When used in place of meat, beans zap cholesterol with 18 grams of fiber and boost bones with lots of calcium, magnesium, potassium, and zinc.

Spiral Pasta and Bean Soup

When I want a quick but hearty supper, I can whip up a pot of soup in almost no time. Then all I need is a slice of chewy whole grain bread, and I'm a happy woman!

4 cups fat-free chicken broth
1 cup frozen mixed vegetables
2 ounces spiral pasta
1 tablespoon garlic (from a jar)
1 teaspoon dried basil
1/8 teaspoon dried oregano
Freshly ground black pepper to taste
1 cup rinsed and drained canned cranberry beans*
2 ounces shredded Asiago cheese

The Inside Skinny: Canned cranberry beans (and great Northern beans) are tops in folate, providing 50% of the Daily Value per cup.

In a large saucepan over high heat, bring the broth to a rolling boil. Stir in the vegetables, pasta, garlic, basil, oregano, and pepper. Return to a boil. Reduce the heat to medium and cook for 9 minutes, or until the pasta is tender. Stir in the beans and cook for 1 to 2 minutes, or until heated through. Ladle into two soup bowls and sprinkle each serving with 1 ounce of the cheese.

Yield: 2 servings

Nutritional data per serving: Calories, 386; protein, 25 g; carbohydrate, 52 g; dietary fiber, 13 g; total fat, 9 g; saturated fat, 5 g; cholesterol, 26 mg; sodium, 1,438 mg; vitamin A, 47% of Daily Value; vitamin C, 7%; calcium, 36%; iron, 22%; vitamin B$_6$, 10%; folate, 42%; magnesium, 21%; potassium, 16%; zinc, 20%.

*These are small red Italian beans available in natural foods stores.

Molé Bean Soup

Not only does my friend Edee Hogan share my birthday, she also shares my preference for good food that's fast! She taught me to make this simple soup that tastes as if it took hours. Her secret? A little cocoa, the key to classic molé.

2 cans (15½ ounces each) black beans
2 teaspoons unsweetened cocoa powder
Dash of ground cinnamon
1 can (14½ ounces) fat-free chicken broth
1 cup chopped onions
½ cup sour cream

In a medium saucepan, use a wooden spoon or potato masher to roughly mash the beans (with liquid). Stir in the cocoa and cinnamon, then gradually add the broth. Stir until well mixed. Cover and cook over medium heat until the soup reaches serving temperature. Ladle into four bowls. Top each serving with equal portions of the onions and sour cream.

Yield: 4 servings

Nutritional data per serving: Calories, 283; protein, 16 g; carbohydrate, 42 g; dietary fiber, 16 g; total fat, 7 g; saturated fat, 4 g; cholesterol, 13 mg; sodium, 1,078 mg; vitamin A, 6% of Daily Value; vitamin C, 15%; calcium, 12%; iron, 24%; folate, 36%; potassium, 24%.

DOUBLE DUTY

Beans deliver a whopping dose of folate to protect against birth defects when you're young and fend off heart disease as you get older.

Four-Bean Tossed Greens

Some of my girlfriends are lax about getting their folate. When they come for lunch, I give 'em a secret boost with a salad like this. Shhh…don't tell.

1 cup rinsed and drained canned red kidney beans
1 cup rinsed and drained canned chickpeas
1 cup rinsed and drained canned soybeans
1 cup rinsed and drained canned black beans
1 cup canned or frozen yellow corn
2 tablespoons light ranch dressing
1/2 cup sliced celery
1/2 cup diced red bell peppers
4 cups mixed salad greens
2 tablespoons light vinaigrette dressing

In a medium bowl, combine the kidney beans, chickpeas, soybeans, black beans, corn, and ranch dressing. Stir until well mixed. Set aside.

In another medium bowl, combine the celery, peppers, greens, and vinaigrette dressing. Toss until well coated. Divide the salad mixture among four luncheon plates. Pile equal portions of the beans on top of the greens. Serve with hot rolls and cold white wine.

Yield: 4 servings

Nutritional data per serving: Calories, 356; protein, 20 g; carbohydrate, 50 g; dietary fiber, 14 g; total fat, 10 g; saturated fat, 1 g; cholesterol, 2 mg; sodium, 1,022 mg; vitamin A, 27% of Daily Value; vitamin C, 87%; calcium, 15%; iron, 33%; folate, 54%; potassium, 28%.

Salad without an Egg to Stand On

I got this idea for eggless egg salad from Morinaga Nutritional Foods, the folks who make Mori-Nu silken tofu—and I'm amazed! Firm, silken tofu has the same texture as cooked egg white, so it makes a pretty cool egg salad look-alike. I like mine with lots of extra vegetables. Want to give it a try?

2 tablespoons light ranch dressing
Freshly ground black pepper to taste
¹/₄ teaspoon turmeric
¹/₄ cup diced celery
¹/₂ cup diced peeled cucumbers
¹/₄ cup grated carrots
6 ounces (¹/₂ package) Mori-Nu silken lite firm tofu, diced
1 small whole wheat pita pocket

In a small bowl, combine the dressing, pepper, and turmeric. Stir until well blended. Add the celery, cucumbers, and carrots. Stir until well coated. Gently fold in the tofu until well mixed. Toast the pita until puffed. Split one side halfway through and stuff with salad.

Yield: 1 serving

Nutritional data per serving: Calories, 357; protein, 17 g; carbohydrate, 48 g; dietary fiber, 7 g; total fat, 11 g; saturated fat, 2 g; cholesterol, 5 mg; sodium, 758 mg; vitamin A, 78% of Daily Value; vitamin C, 11%; calcium, 8%; iron, 22%; vitamin E, 4%; folate, 11%; vitamin K, 50%; potassium, 11%.

Soy Nut Butter and Apricot English Muffin

Roasted soy nut butter is tasty stuff, but mixing it with fresh fruit fires up the flavor and makes it even better.

1 whole grain English muffin
2 small fresh apricots
2 tablespoons roasted soy nut
   butter
1/8 teaspoon ground cinnamon

Split and toast the English muffin. Pit and dice the apricots. In a small bowl, combine the apricots, soy nut butter, and cinnamon. Stir until well blended. Spread on the muffin.

Yield: 1 serving

Nutritional data per serving: Calories, 338; protein, 13 g; carbohydrate, 45 g; dietary fiber, 7 g; total fat, 13 g; saturated fat, 2 g; cholesterol, 0 mg; sodium, 379 mg; vitamin A, 18% of Daily Value; vitamin C, 12%; calcium, 10%; iron, 18%; potassium, 10%.

 **The
P·E·R·F·E·C·T
Companion**

Stir 1 teaspoon almond extract into a glass of cold fat-free milk for an amazing flavor match.

Soy Nut Oatmeal with Oranges

Want a double serving of soy? Lots of flavor, too? Start your day right with a bubbling-hot bowl of oatmeal. You'll load up on those isoflavones that protect your health.

½ cup old-fashioned oats
1 cup fat-free calcium-added vanilla soy milk
1 tablespoon soy nut butter
½ cup undrained canned mandarin oranges
Dash of ground cinnamon

In a microwave-safe cereal bowl, combine the oats and soy milk. Stir until well mixed. Microwave on high for 4 to 5 minutes, stirring once after 2 minutes. Add the soy nut butter and stir until melted and well blended. Stir in the oranges and cinnamon.

Yield: 1 serving

Nutritional data per serving: Calories, 392; protein, 15 g; carbohydrate, 66 g; dietary fiber, 6 g; total fat, 9 g; saturated fat, 1 g; cholesterol, 0 mg; sodium, 142 mg; vitamin A, 9% of Daily Value; vitamin C, 53%; calcium, 43%; iron, 23%; vitamin D, 24%; magnesium, 27%; potassium, 7%.

SUPER SUB

Canned mandarin oranges are actually mini-tangerines (clementines) that deliver half your vitamin C for the day.

Cranberry-Cottage Cheese Roller

Do you ever wonder why we eat cranberry sauce only at Thanksgiving and Christmas? Well, UTIs don't wait until the holidays, and neither should you.

¹/₂ cup high-calcium cottage cheese
¹/₄ cup whole-berry cranberry sauce
1 large leaf red leaf lettuce
1 tablespoon chopped toasted walnuts

In a small bowl, combine the cottage cheese and cranberry sauce. Stir until well blended. Pile on the lettuce leaf and sprinkle with the walnuts. Roll up the lettuce and eat this little treat like a taco.

Yield: 1 serving

Nutritional data per serving: Calories, 252; protein, 17 g; carbohydrate, 31 g; dietary fiber, 2 g; total fat, 7 g; saturated fat, 2 g; cholesterol, 9 mg; sodium, 475 mg; vitamin A, 4% of Daily Value; vitamin C, 3%; calcium, 20%; iron, 3%; vitamin B₂ (riboflavin), 13%; folate, 7%; vitamin K, 26%.

♥ **The**
P·E·R·F·E·C·T
Companion ♥

Stir ¹/₄ teaspoon pumpkin pie spice into a cup of Lipton tea. Sweeten with 1 tablespoon orange juice.

Tijuana Tofu Soft Taco

Tofu is so accommodating, it will take on just about any flavor you can throw at it. This time, it's wearing a sombrero.

1 red chile tortilla
2 ounces White Wave Mexican-style baked tofu*
1 slice Lite and Less low-fat veggie
  singles*
1/2 cup romaine lettuce
1 small Roma (plum) tomato, sliced
1 tablespoon chopped black olives
1 1/2 teaspoons light ranch dressing

> **The Inside Skinny:**
> Buying soy cheese? Check the Nutrition Facts label to be sure each slice contains at least 20% calcium.

On a paper plate, microwave the tortilla on high for 20 to 30 seconds, or until warm. Slice the tofu into 1/2-inch strips, place on a paper plate, and microwave for 45 to 60 seconds, or until heated through. Place the veggie cheese on the tortilla and top with the hot tofu to melt the cheese.

In a small bowl, combine the lettuce, tomato, olives, and dressing. Stir until well mixed. Pile on top of the tofu, then wrap and roll the tortilla. It'll be just a tad spicy, but not too hot for even a sensitive palate.

Yield: 1 serving

Nutritional data per serving: Calories, 440; protein, 25 g; carbohydrate, 45 g; dietary fiber, 5 g; total fat, 19 g; saturated fat, 2 g; cholesterol, 2 mg; sodium, 1,132 mg; vitamin A, 63% of Daily Value; vitamin C, 33%; calcium, 28%; iron, 16%; vitamin E, 12%; folate, 12%.

*Available in natural foods stores and the vegetarian foods section of many large supermarkets.

Pocket Veggie Burger

You can turn a veggie burger into a walk-away meal in a flash. Watch how easy it is, then try it yourself. This one has a little bit of just about anything a girl could want.

1 cup chopped spinach
**1 ounce shredded reduced-fat cheddar
  cheese**
1 tablespoon light ranch dressing
1 small pita pocket
1 frozen soy veggie burger

In a small bowl, combine the spinach, cheese, and dressing. Toss well. Toast the pita until puffed, then split halfway. Meanwhile, microwave the burger according to package directions. Stuff into the pita, then fill with the spinach mixture.

Yield: 1 serving

Nutritional data per serving: Calories, 450; protein, 24 g; carbohydrate, 59 g; dietary fiber, 8 g; total fat, 13 g; saturated fat, 5 g; cholesterol, 38 mg; vitamin A, 30% of Daily Value; vitamin C, 15%; calcium, 45%; iron, 13%; vitamin B_1 (thiamin), 34%; vitamin B_2 (riboflavin), 34%; vitamin B_3 (niacin), 21%; folate, 32%; vitamin K, 150%; magnesium, 19%; potassium, 15%; zinc, 20%.

The Inside Skinny: Although a whole wheat pita provides a richer array of vitamins and minerals, a white pita made with enriched flour offers a girl added folate.

Soy Nut Trail Mix

All right, it's that time of month again. You're craving salt. You're craving chocolate. And you're really in no mood for healthy cooking or eating. Don't fret. Just grab a handful of this tasty mix and meet all of your body's needs.

1 cup salted roasted soy nuts
1 cup semisweet chocolate bits
2 cups Total cereal
½ cup dark seedless raisins
½ cup golden seedless raisins
½ cup craisins (dried cranberries)
1 cup salted mixed nuts

The Inside Skinny:
Although salted nuts satisfy your craving for that salty taste, they don't pack nearly as much sodium as processed foods such as canned soup.

In a large resealable plastic bag, combine the soy nuts, chocolate, cereal, dark and golden raisins, craisins, and mixed nuts. Shake until well mixed. Measure ¾ cup into a small resealable bag to take for lunch. Also take a piece of string cheese to be sure you get enough calcium.

Yield: 9 servings

Nutritional data per serving: Calories, 328; protein, 9 g; carbohydrate, 44 g; dietary fiber, 6 g; total fat, 16 g; saturated fat, 5 g; cholesterol, 0 mg; vitamin A, 11% of Daily Value; vitamin C, 31%; calcium, 13%; iron, 40%; vitamin B$_6$, 34%; folate, 33%; vitamin E, 41%; potassium, 9%; zinc, 37%.

"Listen Up" Pasta Salad

When I was a kid, nobody used the word pasta. *There was* spaghetti, *and then there was elbow macaroni. Now we have a wonderful wide world of pasta to play with, and it's so much fun! I especially like orichetti, or "little ears," in this recipe because they're so good for scooping up the dressing.*

2 cups cooked orichetti pasta
1/2 cup rinsed and drained canned red kidney beans
4 ounces cooked chicken breast, cut into chunks
1/2 cup diced green bell peppers
1/2 cup thinly sliced yellow squash
2 tablespoons Italian dressing
2 cups mesclun or field greens
1 tablespoon sliced black olives

In a large bowl, combine the pasta, beans, chicken, peppers, squash, and dressing. Toss until well coated. Line two luncheon plates with the greens and top each with half the salad. Garnish with the olives. Serve with hot dinner rolls.

Yield: 2 servings

Nutritional data per serving: Calories, 429; protein, 29 g; carbohydrate, 53 g; dietary fiber, 10 g; total fat, 11 g; saturated fat, 2 g; cholesterol, 48 mg; sodium, 210 mg; vitamin A, 19% of Daily Value; vitamin C, 78%; calcium, 6%; iron, 19%; vitamin B$_3$ (niacin), 54%; vitamin E, 12%; folate, 50%; magnesium, 20%; potassium, 14%; omega-3 fatty acids, 66%.

DOUBLE DUTY

Green peppers provide "crunch" and nearly a full day's supply of vitamin C.

Lady-in-Waiting Egg Sandwich

Remember all that stuff you learned about hanging around with the wrong crowd? Eggs are like that. Wrap them in bacon, cheese, and butter, and there's trouble in River City. But serve them up with whole grain bread, fruits, and veggies, and they'll help you (and your baby-to-be) remember all of life's important lessons—because they're among Mother Nature's best sources of memory-building choline.

2 slices whole wheat toast
1 tablespoon reduced-fat mayonnaise
1 hard-boiled egg, sliced
½ dill pickle, sliced
1 thick slice large tomato
1 leaf romaine lettuce
Freshly ground black pepper to taste

Spread one slice of the toast with the mayonnaise. Arrange the egg on top. Add the pickle, tomato, lettuce, and pepper. Top with the second slice of toast and cut in half diagonally. Cuddle up with your sandwich and the baby name book.

Yield: 1 serving

Nutritional data per serving: Calories, 257; protein, 12 g; carbohydrate, 34 g; dietary fiber, 5 g; total fat, 9 g; saturated fat, 2 g; cholesterol, 212 mg; sodium, 919 mg; vitamin A, 15% of Daily Value; vitamin C, 22%; calcium, 7%; iron, 16%; vitamin D, 8%; vitamin E, 7%; folate, 15%; potassium, 10%; omega-3 fatty acids, 9%.

Soy Fun Pepperoni Pizza

If you love Italian food, you'll love this soy-full pizza.

1 California-style pizza bread (16 ounces) or
　　other pizza crust
1 cup tomato-basil pasta sauce
4 ounces Smart Deli meatless pepperoni
8 slices soy cheese

Preheat the oven to 450°F. Place the crust on a pizza pan and spread the sauce evenly on top. Arrange the pepperoni on the sauce, then cover with the cheese. Bake for 8 to 10 minutes, or until the cheese bubbles and begins to melt. Let cool slightly. Use a pizza cutter or a large, heavy knife to cut into eight pieces. Serve with crisp green salad and ice-cold light beer.

Yield: 8 servings

SUPER SUB

Replacing regular pepperoni with the soy version eliminates saturated fat and cholesterol and provides isoflavones that help lower cholesterol.

Nutritional data per serving: Calories, 270; protein, 14 g; carbohydrate, 43 g; dietary fiber, 2 g; total fat, 5 g; saturated fat, 0 g; cholesterol, 0 mg; sodium, 734 mg; vitamin A, 12% of Daily Value; vitamin C, 1%; calcium, 22%; iron, 7%; vitamin E, 10%; potassium, 8%.

Kitchen Cabinet Soybeans and Rice

I love cooking from scratch, but there are days when ingredients straight from the pantry really come in handy.

1 cup Uncle Ben's instant brown rice
1 teaspoon butter
1 teaspoon dehydrated onions
1/8 teaspoon garlic powder
1 tablespoon parsley flakes
1/2 teaspoon salt
1 cup rinsed and drained canned organic soybeans

Bring 1¼ cups water to a boil in a medium saucepan. Stir in the rice, butter, onions, garlic powder, parsley, and salt. Reduce the heat, cover, and simmer for 4 minutes. Stir in the soybeans and cook for 1 minute. Serve piping hot. A crisp green bagged salad completes the meal.

Yield: 3 servings

Nutritional data per serving: Calories, 227; protein, 11 g; carbohydrate, 31 g; dietary fiber, 4 g; total fat, 7 g; saturated fat, 1.5 g; cholesterol, 3 mg; sodium, 503 mg; vitamin A, 2% of Daily Value; vitamin C, 4%; calcium, 7%; iron, 24%.

> **The Inside Skinny:** Soybeans are a rich, plant-based source of iron, which women need during their childbearing years.

Caribbean Tofu with Tropical Fruit

One bite of this tropical treat erased every bad thought I ever had about tofu. But a word of warning: This tofu is plenty hot!

2 teaspoons peanut oil
2 ounces Soy Boy Caribbean tofu,* cut into 4 thin slices
1 red banana or ¹/₂ medium yellow banana, halved
   lengthwise
1 teaspoon chunky peanut butter
¹/₄ cup reserved fruit salad liquid
¹/₂ cup drained canned tropical fruit salad in light syrup

In a heavy nonstick skillet over high heat, warm the oil. Arrange the tofu in a single layer in the center of the skillet. Add the banana cut side down beside the tofu. Cook for about 3 minutes, or until beginning to crisp and brown. Gently turn and cook for 1 to 2 minutes, or until crisp. Arrange on a dinner plate.

Reduce the heat to low and add the peanut butter to the skillet. Heat for about 30 seconds, then stir in the fruit liquid. Stir until well mixed. Add the fruit, cover, and cook for 1 minute, or until heated through. Spoon over the banana, then drizzle the sauce over the tofu. Serve with rice.

Yield: 1 serving

Nutritional data per serving: Calories, 423; protein, 13 g; carbohydrate, 59 g; dietary fiber, 4 g; total fat, 17 g; saturated fat, 3 g; cholesterol, 0 mg; sodium, 281 mg; vitamin A, 4% of Daily Value; vitamin C, 135%; calcium, 13%; iron, 11%; vitamin E, 9%; potassium, 13%.

*Available in natural foods stores and the vegetarian foods section of many large supermarkets.

Soy Ravioli with Roma Tomatoes

This sauce is as fresh as a summer breeze...and it makes you feel like a natural woman (or man).

1 package (13 ounces) frozen soy-filled ravioli
6 Roma (plum) tomatoes, chopped
2 tablespoons olive oil
1 clove garlic, minced
2 tablespoons slivered fresh basil
1/4 teaspoon dried oregano
1/4 teaspoon salt

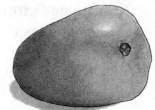

Bring 3 quarts water to a boil in a large saucepan. Reduce the heat and add the ravioli. Simmer gently, stirring occasionally, for 4 to 6 minutes, or until the ravioli float. Drain in a colander and return to the pan. Add the tomatoes, oil, garlic, basil, oregano, and salt and toss.

Yield: 2 servings

Nutritional data per serving: Calories, 434; protein, 20 g; carbohydrate, 66 g; dietary fiber, 2 g; total fat, 13 g; saturated fat, 2 g; cholesterol, 0 mg; sodium, 557 mg; vitamin A, 13% of Daily Value; vitamin C, 61%; calcium, 17%; iron, 24%; potassium, 12%.

SUPER SUB

Surprise! Enriched white pasta delivers 1/4 of your baby-protecting folate for the day. Whole wheat pasta contains very little.

Turkey-Pasta Toss

Ground turkey breast does a great job of creating a "meaty" pasta sauce, and few will ever notice that they're not eating ground beef.

4 ounces wagon-wheel pasta
1/2 pound ground turkey breast
2 teaspoons olive oil
1 small onion, chopped
1 baby zucchini, quartered and sliced
4 large radishes, halved and sliced
1 1/2 cups Healthy Choice chunky vegetable pasta sauce
1/4 cup grated Parmesan cheese

Bring 4 quarts water to a boil in a large saucepan. Add the pasta and cook for about 10 minutes, or according to package directions.

Meanwhile, in a medium saucepan over medium-high heat, brown the turkey in the oil. Reduce the heat to medium and stir in the onion, zucchini, and radishes. Cook, stirring often, until soft but not brown. Stir in the sauce, cover, and cook for about 3 minutes, or until heated through. Drain the pasta and divide between two plates or individual serving dishes. Top each with half of the sauce, then toss to combine. Sprinkle each with half of the cheese.

Yield: 2 servings

Nutritional data per serving: Calories, 454; protein, 33 g; carbohydrate, 57 g; dietary fiber, 5 g; total fat, 10 g; saturated fat, 3 g; cholesterol, 57 mg; sodium, 852 mg; vitamin A, 14% of Daily Value; vitamin C, 23%; calcium, 26%; iron, 23%; vitamin B_3 (niacin), 34%; vitamin B_6, 22%; folate, 28%; magnesium, 14%; zinc, 15%.

Lightning-Fast Pasta with Soy Crumbles

My daughter Bobbi serves this "beef look-alike" pasta to her husband, Paul, and his friends, and not one of them has ever noticed that the "beef" is soy crumbles. And besides, she says, most of those guys don't eat nearly enough vegetables, so this is a neat way to sneak a healthy meal to the whole crew!

10 ounces fresh pasta
1 jar (24 ounces) Healthy Choice garlic and sun-dried
   tomato pasta sauce
1 package (12 ounces) Morningstar Farms burger-style
   soy crumbles
3 ounces grated Parmesan cheese

Bring a large pot of water to a boil, add the pasta, and cook for about 3 minutes, or according to package directions.

Meanwhile, in a large skillet over medium heat, combine the sauce and soy crumbles. Cover and simmer until the pasta is done. Drain the pasta and place in a large serving bowl. Top with the sauce and sprinkle with the cheese.

Yield: 6 servings

Nutritional data per serving: Calories, 477; protein, 29 g; carbohydrate, 61 g; dietary fiber, 9 g; total fat, 13 g; saturated fat, 5 g; cholesterol, 73 mg; sodium, 912 mg; vitamin A, 4% of Daily Value; vitamin C, 10%; calcium, 27%; iron, 39%; vitamin B$_1$ (thiamin), 381%; folate, 38%; zinc, 16%.

DOUBLE DUTY

Soy is good for boys, too. It protects them against prostate cancer and heart disease.

Grilled Asparagus with Avocado

It was raining cats and dogs tonight, but I wanted grilled asparagus. So I cranked up my George Foreman grill and got the job done inside. The cat and dog joined us by the fire while my husband and I had a cozy dinner.

10 thick spears asparagus
¹/₂ avocado, diced
1 tablespoon fresh lime juice
¹/₈ teaspoon salt
Freshly ground multicolor pepper to taste

Preheat the grill for 5 minutes.

Wash the asparagus, pat dry, and break off the tough stems. Place vertically on the grill, close the lid, and cook for 10 minutes, or until crisp-tender. Cut into 1-inch pieces. In a medium bowl, combine the asparagus and avocado. Sprinkle with the lime juice, salt, and pepper. Toss until well blended. Serve cold or at room temperature.

Yield: 2 servings

Nutritional data per serving: Calories, 101; protein, 3 g; carbohydrate, 8 g; dietary fiber, 4 g; total fat, 8 g; saturated fat, 1 g; cholesterol, 0 mg; sodium, 152 mg; vitamin A, 8% of Daily Value; vitamin C, 28%; calcium, 2%; iron, 7%; vitamin E, 11%; folate, 34%; copper, 14%; potassium, 15%.

Lovely Leftovers Stuff some into a pita pocket with a couple of slices of turkey for an out-of-this-world lunch.

Peanut Butter Snack Shake

Snacking is fun, fun, fun, especially when the food is good and good for you. Whip up this soothing treat when your hormones are out of control.

¾ cup chocolate soy milk
1 tablespoon creamy peanut butter
½ cup frozen mixed tropical fruit

In a blender, combine the soy milk, peanut butter, and fruit. Blend until thick and creamy.

Yield: 1 serving

Nutritional data per serving: Calories, 369; protein, 11 g; carbohydrate, 60 g; dietary fiber, 4 g; total fat, 11 g; saturated fat, 2 g; cholesterol, 0 mg; sodium, 194 mg; vitamin A, 11% of Daily Value; vitamin C, 156%; calcium, 23%; iron, 11%; vitamin E, 30%; potassium, 15%.

DOUBLE DUTY

Yummy peanut butter provides just the right kind of heart-smart fat, and it keeps you from getting hungry again too soon.

Lemon-Berry Soy Swirl

Imagine a delicious drink that can protect your bones, lower your cholesterol, and help ward off cancer. This is it!

6 ounces vanilla Silk cultured soy yogurt
1 teaspoon fresh lemon juice
Dash of grated lemon peel
1 cup sliced fresh strawberries
1 tablespoon seedless black raspberry preserves

In a blender, combine the yogurt, lemon juice, lemon peel, strawberries, and preserves. Blend until smooth and creamy. Pour into a 12-ounce glass and sip through a straw.

Yield: 1 serving

Nutritional data per serving: Calories, 267; protein, 5 g; carbohydrate, 57 g; dietary fiber, 5 g; total fat, 3 g; saturated fat, 0 g; cholesterol, 0 mg; sodium, 28 mg; vitamin A, 1% of Daily Value; vitamin C, 164%; calcium, 53%; iron, 4%; folate, 9%; vitamin K, 29% potassium, 8%.

QUICK TRICK: Use frozen berries instead of fresh. Change flavors by using different berries.

Chocolate-Strawberry Soy Shake

When you're feeling moody and blue, soothe yourself with this lovely shake.

1 cup cold calcium-fortified chocolate soy milk
1 small banana
1 cup sliced fresh strawberries

In a blender, combine the soy milk, banana, and strawberries. Blend until smooth. A little too thick? Add a tablespoon or two of water and blend again. Pour into a tall glass and sip through a straw.

Yield: 1 serving

Nutritional data per serving: Calories, 344; protein, 9 g; carbohydrate, 71 g; dietary fiber, 7 g; total fat, 4 g; saturated fat, <1 g; cholesterol, 0 mg; sodium, 156 mg; vitamin A, 11% of Daily Value; vitamin C, 172%; calcium, 32%; iron, 15%; vitamin B_6, 40%; vitamin D, 24%; vitamin E, 27%; folate, 12%; vitamin K, 30%; potassium, 29%.

DOUBLE DUTY

While you're building muscles with soy's protein power, you can also cash in on its isoflavones, which can help lower your cholesterol.

Melon Cooler with Champion Chocolate Sauce

What looks like an ice cream sundae and tastes like an ice cream sundae, but delivers a lot more nutrition for a lot fewer calories? Check this out.

2 cups cold watermelon cubes
2 cups cold honeydew melon cubes
1/4 cup fat-free plain yogurt
2 tablespoons Hershey's chocolate syrup
4 sprigs mint

In a large bowl, combine the watermelon and honeydew. Stir until well mixed. Spoon into four pretty dessert dishes.

In a small bowl, combine the yogurt and chocolate syrup. Stir until well mixed. Drizzle one-fourth of the sauce over each fruit bowl and garnish with a mint sprig.

Yield: 4 servings

Nutritional data per serving: Calories, 86; protein, 2 g; carbohydrate, 20 g; dietary fiber, 1 g; total fat, <1 g; saturated fat, 0 g; cholesterol, 0 mg; sodium, 23 mg; vitamin A, 3% of Daily Value; vitamin C, 47%; calcium, 3%; iron, 2%; vitamin B$_1$ (thiamin), 8%; potassium, 9%.

> **QUICK TRICK:** Use frozen melon balls instead of fresh. Defrost them in the microwave.

Cinnamon-Chocolate Fruit Dip

I'm especially fond of "social" food, the kind that has everybody digging into the same big dish. The setting generates good conversation.

¹/₄ cup semisweet or bitter chocolate bits
1 tablespoon 2% milk
¹/₄ teaspoon ground cinnamon
1 banana, cut into 8 pieces
2 fresh apricots, pitted and quartered
1 fresh peach, pitted and cut into 16 slivers
8 large strawberries, with caps, washed and patted dry

In a small microwave-safe dish, microwave the chocolate and milk on high for 20 to 30 seconds, or until the chocolate begins to soften and the milk bubbles around the edges. Add the cinnamon and stir constantly for about 1 minute, or until smooth and creamy. Place in the center of a dinner plate. Surround with the banana, apricots, peach, and strawberries. Set out a shot glass filled with toothpicks so everyone can spear the fruit and dip it in the sauce.

Yield: 4 servings

Nutritional data per serving: Calories, 138; protein, 2 g; carbohydrate, 25 g; dietary fiber, 4 g; total fat, 4 g; saturated fat, 2 g; cholesterol, <1 mg; sodium, 3 mg; vitamin A, 7% of Daily Value; vitamin C, 46%; calcium, 2%; iron, 4%; vitamin B_6, 11%; folate, 5%; potassium, 10%.

The Inside Skinny:
Even though chocolate contains saturated fat, studies show it's the kind that doesn't raise your cholesterol.

Almond Butter Pudding

Looking for comfort food? You could eat this luscious, gooey treat for breakfast, lunch, an afternoon snack, dinner, or dessert. Believe me, I have!

2 tablespoons almond butter
1 cup fat-free plain yogurt
1 small banana, sliced
Dash of ground nutmeg

In a microwave-safe dessert dish, microwave the almond butter on high for about 1 minute, or until melted. Quickly stir in the yogurt. Top with the banana and dust with the nutmeg. Mmmmmm, good!

Yield: 1 serving

Nutritional data per serving: Calories, 432; protein, 20 g; carbohydrate, 49 g; dietary fiber, 4 g; total fat, 20 g; saturated fat, 2 g; cholesterol, 4 mg; sodium, 192 mg; vitamin A, 1% of Daily Value; vitamin C, 19%; calcium, 58%; iron, 10%; vitamin B_2 (riboflavin), 51%; vitamin B_6, 37%; vitamin E, 34%; folate, 28%; potassium, 36%; zinc, 23%.

DOUBLE DUTY

This simple, power-packed combo delivers more than half your calcium and 1/3 of your vitamin E for the day. Happy bones, happy heart!

Cherry-Chocolate Freeze

Researchers have tried in vain to explain why American women crave chocolate, especially at "that time of the month." Here's what we know: We don't really care why. Just give it to us!

1 cup fat-free chocolate milk
1 cup frozen pitted dark red cherries
1 cup ice cubes
2 tablespoons unsweetened cocoa powder

In a blender, combine the milk, cherries, ice, and cocoa. Blend on high until thick and smooth. Pour into a frosty glass and drink with a straw.

Yield: 2 servings

Nutritional data per serving: Calories, 134; protein, 6 g; carbohydrate, 24 g; dietary fiber, 3 g; total fat, 2 g; saturated fat, 1 g; vitamin A, 14% of Daily Value; vitamin C, 4%; calcium, 16%; iron, 16%; vitamin B₂ (riboflavin), 16%; potassium, 16%.

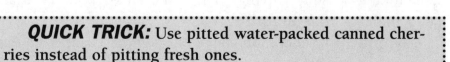

QUICK TRICK: Use pitted water-packed canned cherries instead of pitting fresh ones.

CHAPTER 15

TAKE CARE OF YOUR TUMMY

EASY WAYS TO HEAL THE HURTING

As FAR BACK AS I CAN REMEMBER, PEPPERMINT TEA HAS been my family's treatment of choice for soothing upset stomachs. For years, I thought it worked just because of the placebo effect. After all, who wouldn't feel better when someone makes you a cup of tea, carries it to the couch for you, fluffs your pillow, and coos, "Poor baby!"

Actually, though, the cure wasn't all in my head. It turns out that peppermint is bursting with menthol's natural oils, which can quell tummy spasms, help digestion, and even kill bacteria. That's enough to take your breath away!

No matter what condition your stomach is in, chances are that sooner or later, you are going to have a tummyache. They come in as many shapes and sizes as tummies do, and some need medical attention. But many digestive woes are temporary, and we can treat or prevent them by tweaking what and how we eat. Here's how you can find relief from some common discomforts.

♥ **Indigestion** comes from eating too much or too fast. Preventing the problem is as simple as this: Slow down and enjoy dinner with family and friends. Isn't that sweet medicine? And do try some peppermint tea. I'll show you how to make it, along with other tummy soothers such as chamomile, anise, caraway, coriander, and fennel.

♥ **Gas** is the most embarrassing tummy problem, of course, and you just have to hope your family will still love you until it's over! Try to track your trouble foods. Once you've identified them, eat them less often and in smaller portions. To help you recover, eat low-fiber foods for a day or two to rest your gut. This chapter is bursting with delicious, gentle recipes to tide you over.

♥ **Heartburn** happens when stomach acid washes up into your esophagus and burns the tender tissue there. Ouch! Coffee (even decaf), alcohol, peppermint, and chocolate often cause the back-check valve between your esophagus and stomach to relax on the job. Cutting way down on those foods will often get you off the hook.

♥ **Ulcers,** which are little holes in the lining of your stomach, are usually made by rude little bacteria called *Helicobacter pylori.* Thank goodness, antibiotics can wipe them out. But while you're healing, it's best to cut down on alcohol, coffee, and the size of your meals. Antioxidants from high-fiber fruits and vegetables (chapters 2, 7, 8, and 12) will also help heal an ulcer and prevent new ones. Flavonoids from onions (chapter 11), cranberries (chapter 10), and probiotic foods such as yogurt also appear to attack and kill *H. pylori.* So eat up.

♥ **Diarrhea** strikes for many reasons, so it's yogurt and other probiotics (kefir and acidophilus) to the rescue. They contain live, active cultures of good bacteria that live in your gut and work day and night. First, they get you back to normal, then they fend off future germ attacks. This chapter is loaded with luscious tips on how to use these cultured foods.

While you're in distress, drink plenty of fluids to avoid dehydration, and choose low-fiber, easily digestible foods such as bananas, white rice, applesauce, and white toast to give your bowels a rest. Don't frown. We'll make them tasty with fragrant cinnamon and other sweet spices that will help settle your stomach *and* fight bad bacteria.

♥ **Irritable bowel syndrome** happens in fits and starts. When your bowels are okay, go with plenty of fiber. In troubled times, you'll need soothing food, so rely on white bread; Cream of Wheat; applesauce; other low-fiber foods such as white rice, noodles, and ground meats; and even canned fruits and vegetables. Plus, of course, bananas and yogurt. This chapter is packed with high-nutrition foods with a tummy-soothing attitude.

♥ **Diverticulosis** is still a medical mystery, but it seems to be payback for skipping your whole grains, fruits and vegetables, and lean meats. Some used to think that nuts and seeds triggered diverticulosis, but that theory has gone out the window. It's never too late to take some positive action against this problem: Drink lots of water, get some exercise, and eat a little better. Hopefully, these steps will prevent intestinal inflammations (diverticulitis).

Okay, poor baby, are you ready for some tender tummy treats? We'll skip the onions, garlic, chile peppers, and fiber, and I'll show you how to make some easy, soothing food that will keep your energy and nutrition up and your tummy rumbles down.

Kinder, Gentler Hummus

Usually when I make hummus, I pour on the garlic and spices and serve it with whole wheat pita. It's potent stuff! But when my tummy needs more TLC, I switch to this kinder, gentler version.

1 can (15½ ounces) chickpeas, drained and liquid reserved
2 tablespoons olive oil
2 teaspoons sesame oil
2 teaspoons bottled lemon juice
1 tablespoon parsley flakes
½ teaspoon salt

In a blender, combine the chickpeas, olive oil, sesame oil, lemon juice, parsley, and salt. Pulse on high several times. Add 3 tablespoons of the reserved chickpea liquid, 1 tablespoon at a time, pulsing after each addition, until the hummus reaches the desired consistency. Serve with Carr's Water Crackers or saltines.

Yield: 20 servings

Nutritional data per serving: Calories, 35; protein, 1 g; carbohydrate, 3 g; dietary fiber, 1 g; total fat, 2 g; saturated fat, 0 g; cholesterol, 0 mg; sodium, 181 mg; vitamin A, 0% of Daily Value; vitamin C, 0%; calcium, 1%; iron, 1%; vitamin E, 1%.

♥ **The P·E·R·F·E·C·T Companion** ♥

Place a black cherry berry tea bag in a large mug and cover with boiling water. Steep for 3 to 5 minutes and remove the tea bag. Sweeten with a cinnamon honey straw.

Easy, Breezy Squash Soup

This practically instant soup is simple, soothing, and sweet. Oh, I almost forgot—it's nutritionally loaded, too!

1 package (14 ounces) frozen yellow
   squash, thawed
1/4 teaspoon turmeric
1/4 teaspoon salt
1 teaspoon olive oil
1 cup fat-free evaporated milk

In a medium saucepan over medium-high heat, bring the squash to a boil. Stir in the turmeric, salt, and oil. Use a wire whisk to gradually stir in the milk. Heat just to boiling. Ladle into a soup bowl.

Yield: 1 serving

Nutritional data per serving: Calories, 466; protein, 26 g; carbohydrate, 86 g; dietary fiber, 5 g; total fat, 5 g; saturated fat, 1 g; cholesterol, 9 mg; sodium, 884 mg; vitamin A, 220% of Daily Value; vitamin C, 46%; calcium, 86%; iron, 24%; vitamin B$_2$ (riboflavin), 60%; vitamin D, 51%; folate, 29%; potassium, 48%.

  **The
P·E·R·F·E·C·T
Companion**

Need a cool drink? Drop a Lemon Ice cold-brew tea bag into 8 ounces of cold water in a 12-ounce glass. Steep for 5 minutes and remove the tea bag. Fill the glass with ice. Sweeten with canned pineapple juice.

Huggable Chicken Soup

Just snuggle down with a bowl of tummy-soothing soup. It feels kind of like a warm hug.

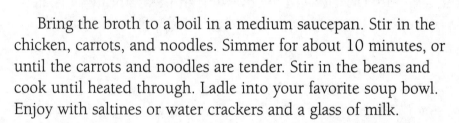

2 cups fat-free chicken broth
2 ounces frozen unbreaded chicken
    tenders, thawed and cut into
    1/2-inch-thick slices
5 baby carrots, quartered
    lengthwise
1/2 cup egg noodles
1 cup drained canned green beans

Bring the broth to a boil in a medium saucepan. Stir in the chicken, carrots, and noodles. Simmer for about 10 minutes, or until the carrots and noodles are tender. Stir in the beans and cook until heated through. Ladle into your favorite soup bowl. Enjoy with saltines or water crackers and a glass of milk.

Yield: 1 serving

Nutritional data per serving: Calories, 224; protein, 25 g; carbohydrate, 24 g; dietary fiber, 4 g; total fat, 3 g; saturated fat, <1 g; cholesterol, 62 mg; sodium, 1,310 mg; vitamin A, 80% of Daily Value; vitamin C, 18%; calcium, 6%; iron, 16%; vitamin B_3 (niacin), 35%; vitamin B_6, 18%; folate, 26%; vitamin K, 64%; potassium, 12%.

Instant Comfort:
Tummy still a mess? Place 1 teaspoon crushed caraway seeds in a mug and cover with boiling water. Steep for 15 minutes, then strain into a cozy cup. Sweeten with confectioners' sugar, then sip.

Melt-in-Your-Mouth Salad

I'm hooked on green, but sometimes I need it soft. That's when I reach for the butterhead lettuce. It's as delicate as cotton candy.

2 cups butterhead lettuce, washed, spun dry, and torn
1 cup drained canned whole green beans
8 canned quartered artichoke hearts
¹/₂ avocado, cut into chunks
2 tablespoons light Catalina dressing
¹/₄ teaspoon dried basil

In a medium bowl, combine the lettuce, beans, artichokes, and avocado. Drizzle with the dressing and toss until well coated. Divide evenly between two individual salad bowls and garnish with the basil.

Yield: 2 servings

Nutritional data per serving: Calories, 164; protein, 5 g; carbohydrate, 20 g; dietary fiber, 5 g; total fat, 8 g; saturated fat, 1 g; cholesterol, 0 mg; sodium, 631 mg; vitamin A, 20% of Daily Value; vitamin C, 27%; calcium, 4%; iron, 15%; vitamin B₆, 10%; folate, 23%; vitamin K, 43%; potassium, 16%.

 **The
P·E·R·F·E·C·T
Companion**

Place 2 Cozy Chamomile tea bags and a cinnamon stick in a teapot and fill with boiling water. Steep for 5 minutes and remove the tea bags. Pour into 2 delicate cups. Sweeten with stevia (a natural herbal sweetener).

Mandarin Orange and Red Banana Cup

This salad is perfect for times when you're yearning for a crunchy, cold salad, but you don't dare eat one.

1 large leaf butterhead lettuce
1 small red banana
1 cup well-drained canned mandarin oranges
$\frac{1}{2}$ cup Stonyfield fat-free apricot-mango yogurt
Grated peel of 1 lime
Dash of ground cinnamon

Place the lettuce on a salad plate and slice the banana into the "cup" formed by the leaf. Arrange the oranges on top of the banana. In a small bowl, combine the yogurt and lime peel. Drizzle over the fruit and dust with the cinnamon.

Yield: 1 serving

Nutritional data per serving: Calories, 228; protein, 5 g; carbohydrate, 54 g; dietary fiber, 3 g; total fat, <1 g; saturated fat, 0 g; cholesterol, 0 mg; sodium, 71 mg; vitamin A, 12% of Daily Value; vitamin C, 57%; calcium, 24%; iron, 5%; folate, 6%; potassium, 12%.

Instant Comfort: Do you get carsick? To fend off the nausea, a half-hour before you leave, eat a couple of 1-inch-square pieces of crystallized ginger. And take some along for the ride. If you notice symptoms, say in about 3 hours, have another piece to settle things again.

Tummy-Tamer Cream of Wheat

Sweet, smooth, soothing...this is my breakfast of choice when my tummy is rumbling.

3 tablespoons instant Cream of Wheat cereal
1 cup fat-free milk
1 teaspoon honey
1 teaspoon butter
1 small ripe banana, diced

In a microwave-safe cereal bowl, combine the Cream of Wheat and milk. Microwave on high for 2 to 3 minutes, stirring once each minute, until most of the milk is absorbed. Stir in the honey, butter, and banana. Spoon it down, and feel your tummy smile.

Yield: 1 serving

Nutritional data per serving: Calories, 356; protein, 13 g; carbohydrate, 67 g; dietary fiber, 5 g; total fat, 5 g; saturated fat, 3 g; cholesterol, 15 mg; sodium, 172 mg; vitamin A, 19% of Daily Value; vitamin C, 19%; calcium, 36%; iron, 56%; vitamin D, 25%; folate, 38%; potassium, 24%.

The
 P·E·R·F·E·C·T
Companion

Snuggle into your softest bathrobe and brew yourself a cup of Cozy Chamomile tea. Pour boiling water over a tea bag in your favorite mug. Steep for 3 to 5 minutes and remove the tea bag. Sweeten with cinnamon honey.

Apple Pie Cream of Rice

I don't mind being under the weather quite as much if I can find something good to eat. This simple treat reminds me of my mother's apple pie.

¹/₄ cup Cream of Rice cereal
1 cup fat-free milk
Dash of salt
1 teaspoon butter
2 teaspoons dark brown sugar
¹/₄ teaspoon pumpkin pie spice
¹/₂ cup applesauce

> **Instant Comfort:**
> Settle your tummy with a cup of fennel tea. In a small bowl, pour 1 cup boiling water over 1 teaspoon crushed fennel seeds. Steep for 15 minutes and strain into a heated mug.

In a microwave-safe cereal bowl, combine the cereal, milk, and salt. Microwave on high for 2 to 4 minutes, stirring once each minute, until the milk is absorbed. Add the butter, brown sugar, and spice. Stir until melted and well blended. Add the applesauce. Inhale. Enjoy.

Yield: 1 serving

Nutritional data per serving: Calories, 412; protein, 11 g; carbohydrate, 82 g; dietary fiber, 2 g; total fat, 5 g; saturated fat, 3 g; cholesterol, 15 mg; sodium, 207 mg; vitamin A, 19% of Daily Value; vitamin C, 8%; calcium, 33%; iron, 8%; vitamin B₂ (riboflavin); 25%; folate, 7%; potassium, 17%; zinc, 10%.

Honey-Banana Oatmeal

When your innards are grouching and grumbling, soothe them with this delicious, nutritious breakfast.

1 packet plain instant oatmeal
1 cup fat-free milk
1 medium banana, diced
1 tablespoon honey
Dash of ground cinnamon

In a microwave-safe cereal bowl, combine the oatmeal and milk. Microwave on high for 2 to 3 minutes, or according to package directions. Stir in the banana and honey and dust with the cinnamon.

Yield: 1 serving

Nutritional data per serving: Calories, 365; protein, 14 g; carbohydrate, 75 g; dietary fiber, 6 g; total fat, 3 g; saturated fat, <1 g; cholesterol, 4 mg; sodium, 413 mg; vitamin A, 61% of Daily Value; vitamin C, 22%; calcium, 48%; iron, 38%; folate, 33%; magnesium, 26%; potassium, 28%.

SUPER SUB

Instant oats pack all the same nutrients as old-fashioned oats. They're sliced thinner so they cook more quickly and digest faster. Just what the doctor ordered!

Mint Condition Cream of Wheat

I remember when I actually had to cook cereal on the stove—the messy pot, yucky spoon, and drips all over the range top. Don't you just love microwave cereal?

3 tablespoons instant Cream of Wheat cereal
3/4 cup fat-free milk
2 tablespoons mint jelly

In a microwave-safe cereal bowl, combine the cereal and milk. Microwave on high for 3 to 4 minutes, stirring once each minute, until thickened. Stir in the jelly. Relax and enjoy.

Yield: 1 serving

Nutritional data per serving: Calories, 306; protein, 10 g; carbohydrate, 62 g; dietary fiber, 1 g; total fat, <1 g; saturated fat, 0 g; cholesterol, 3 mg; sodium, 120 mg; vitamin A, 11% of Daily Value; vitamin C, 3%; calcium, 27%; iron, 53%; folate, 32%; potassium, 11%.

 The P·E·R·F·E·C·T Companion

Place an Almond Sunshine tea bag in a cup and cover with boiling water. Steep for 3 to 5 minutes and remove the tea bag. Sweeten with honey.

On-Hand Sandwich

Pita pockets made with enriched white flour keep very well in the freezer. Keep some on hand for when you're feeling funky, along with some turkey.

> 1 small enriched white-flour pita pocket
> 2 ounces Spam oven-roasted turkey
> ½ cup drained canned French-cut green beans
> 2 tablespoons light French dressing
> ⅛ teaspoon dried basil

Lightly toast the pita until puffed, then split to form a pocket. Dice the turkey. In a small bowl, combine the turkey, beans, dressing, and basil. Toss until well mixed and stuff into the pita. Enjoy with a glass of fat-free milk and some canned fruit cocktail.

Yield: 1 serving

Nutritional data per serving: Calories, 282; protein, 17 g; carbohydrate, 42 g; dietary fiber, 3 g; total fat, 5 g; saturated fat, 1 g; cholesterol, 30 mg; sodium, 1,216 mg; vitamin A, 8% of Daily Value; vitamin C, 6%; calcium, 8%; iron, 13%; vitamin B_1 (thiamin), 24%; vitamin B_2 (riboflavin), 12%; vitamin B_3 (niacin), 14%; folate, 14%.

Instant Comfort: Constipated? Have a glass of prune juice with a squeeze of fresh lemon juice. Prune juice packs sorbitol, a natural laxative that will get you going quick as a wink.

Delicate Tuna Tortilla

Okay, so I'm off the jalapeños, garlic, and onions. I can still put a flour tortilla to good use. Just don't call me late for lunch!

3 ounces drained water-packed white albacore tuna
1 tablespoon light canola oil mayonnaise*
1 teaspoon parsley flakes
4 canned quartered artichoke hearts
1 tablespoon chopped black olives
1 large flour tortilla
½ cup shredded iceberg lettuce

In a small bowl, combine the tuna, mayonnaise, parsley, artichokes, and olives. Stir until well mixed. Pile in the center of the tortilla and top with the lettuce. Wrap and roll.

Yield: 1 Serving

Nutritional data per serving: Calories, 431; protein, 29 g; carbohydrate, 49 g; dietary fiber, 4 g; total fat, 13 g; saturated fat, 2 g; cholesterol, 36 mg; sodium, 356 mg; vitamin A, 2% of Daily Value; vitamin C, 9%; calcium, 11%; iron, 27%; vitamin B$_1$ (thiamin), 27%; vitamin B$_2$ (riboflavin), 15%; vitamin B$_3$ (niacin), 38%; vitamin B$_6$, 12%; vitamin D, 34%; vitamin E, 10%; folate, 27%; potassium, 10%.

*Available in natural foods stores and some large supermarkets.

SUPER SUB

While it's true that iceberg lettuce can't hold a candle to romaine in the nutrition department, it does deliver more magnesium than romaine—a bit of a bonus when your tummy is temperamental.

Taste of Thanksgiving Turkey

Without going to all that trouble (not to mention the ton of calo-ries), you can capture some of the distinctive tastes of Thanksgiving in just a few minutes.

**1 medium sweet potato, scrubbed
and pierced
3 ounces ground turkey
¹⁄₄ teaspoon salt
1 tablespoon jellied cranberry sauce**

Microwave the sweet potato for 8 to 10 minutes on high, turn-ing once, or until cooked through and tender.

Meanwhile, in a small nonstick skillet over medium heat, brown the turkey. On a plate, cut the potato halfway through, first lengthwise, then crosswise. Squeeze the sides to open. Fill with the turkey, sprinkle with the salt, and garnish with the cranberry sauce. Instant lunch!

Yield: 1 serving

Nutritional data per serving: Calories, 327; protein, 23 g; carbohydrate, 34 g; dietary fiber, 4 g; total fat, 10 g; saturated fat, 3 g; cholesterol, 80 mg; sodium, 681 mg; vitamin A, 249% of Daily Value; vitamin C, 47%; calcium, 5%; iron, 11%; vitamin B₆, 29%; folate, 8%; copper, 16%; magnesium, 11%; potassium, 17%; zinc, 17%.

> **The Inside Skinny:** The potato skin makes a great container for this happy meal, but if your tum's on the bum, just leave the skin behind.

Pork and Artichoke Gemelli

Even if I'm eating bland, I still want a little color in my life. I rely on V8 vegetable juice to make a very gentle pasta sauce.

2 ounces pork tenderloin, cut into matchsticks
1 teaspoon olive oil
1 teaspoon cornstarch
½ cup vitamin-rich V8 vegetable juice
1 can (14 ounces) quartered artichoke hearts
1 cup cooked gemelli or other spiral pasta

In a medium saucepan over medium-high heat, gently sauté the pork in the oil just until cooked through.

Meanwhile, in a small dish, combine the cornstarch and V8 and stir until dissolved. Stir into the pork and simmer for 4 to 5 minutes, or until thickened. Add the artichokes. Cover and simmer for 5 to 10 minutes. Place the pasta in a bowl and pour on the sauce.

Yield: 1 serving

Nutritional data per serving: Calories, 439; protein, 29 g; carbohydrate, 58 g; dietary fiber, 5 g; total fat, 10 g; saturated fat, 2 g; cholesterol, 53 mg; sodium, 963 mg; vitamin A, 50% of Daily Value; vitamin C, 79%; calcium, 3%; iron, 33%; vitamin E, 54%; folate, 21%; potassium, 18%.

Instant Comfort:

Need tummy help? In a small bowl, pour 1 cup boiling water over 1 teaspoon crushed coriander seeds. Steep for 15 minutes and strain into your favorite teacup. Sweeten with a drop of honey.

Tenderloin Chicken in Olive Leaves

I was browsing through the gourmet pasta at my local store last night and found this wonderful shape called Foglie D'Olivia made by Castellana. It's colored green with spinach and shaped like the leaves on an olive tree. I could hardly wait to cook up a batch. What a pretty dish!

1$\frac{1}{2}$ cups fat-free chicken broth
3 ounces unbreaded chicken tenders, cut into
$\frac{1}{2}$-inch pieces
2 ounces olive leaf–shaped pasta or other spinach pasta
2 teaspoons olive oil

In a medium saucepan over high heat, bring the broth and chicken to a boil. Stir in the pasta and oil. Return to a boil, then reduce the heat and simmer for 9 minutes, or according to package directions. Ladle into a pasta bowl and enjoy!

Yield: 1 serving

Nutritional data per serving: Calories, 461; protein, 24 g; carbohydrate, 56 g; dietary fiber, 3 g; total fat, 16 g; saturated fat, 3 g; cholesterol, 34 mg; sodium, 1,080 mg; vitamin A, 0% of Daily Value; vitamin C, 0%; calcium, 0%; iron, 12%; vitamin B$_1$ (thiamin), 35%; vitamin B$_2$ (riboflavin), 15%; vitamin B$_3$ (niacin), 20%; folate, 35%.

> **The P·E·R·F·E·C·T Companion**
>
> Put an Emperor's Choice red tea bag in a large cup and fill with boiling water. Steep for 3 to 5 minutes and remove the tea bag. Sweeten with a brown sugar cube.

Turkey Cuddled in Cream Sauce

Gentle, gentle, gentle—but packed with flavor and nutrition.

2 medium baked or microwaved potatoes
8 ounces ground turkey
¼ teaspoon dried basil
1 tablespoon butter
1 tablespoon flour
1 cup fat-free milk
1 teaspoon chicken
  bouillon granules

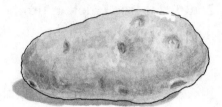

Place the potatoes on two plates. Cut each halfway through, first lengthwise, then crosswise. Squeeze the sides to open. Set aside.

Lightly coat a small nonstick skillet with nonstick spray. Crumble in the turkey and top with the basil. Sauté over medium-high heat until well done and beginning to brown. Stuff into the potatoes. Set aside.

Melt the butter in a small saucepan over medium heat. Add the flour and stir until a thick paste forms. Use a wire whisk to gradually stir in the milk. Cook, stirring, until just beginning to boil and thicken. Add the bouillon and stir until well blended. Spoon half of the sauce over each potato.

Yield: 2 servings

Nutritional data per serving: Calories, 368; protein, 31 g; carbohydrate, 38 g; dietary fiber, 2 g; total fat, 10 g; saturated fat, 5 g; cholesterol, 87 mg; sodium, 571 mg; vitamin A, 13% of Daily Value; vitamin C, 28%; calcium, 18%; iron, 14%; copper, 14%; magnesium, 12%; potassium, 20%; zinc, 6%.

Stewed Chicken and Orzo

This lovely little dinner is packed with protein and carbohydrate. It's quick, easy, and gentle. Delicious, too!

2 cups fat-free chicken broth
3 ounces cooked chicken breast, diced
2 ounces orzo

In a medium saucepan, bring the broth and chicken to a boil. Stir in the orzo. Return to a boil, then reduce the heat and simmer for 9 minutes, or until the orzo is tender. Ladle into a soup bowl.

Yield: 1 serving

Nutritional data per serving: Calories, 316; protein, 31 g; carbohydrate, 38 g; dietary fiber, 2 g; total fat, 3 g; saturated fat, <1 g; cholesterol, 55 mg; sodium, 946 mg; vitamin A, 0% of Daily Value; vitamin C, 0%; calcium, 2%; iron, 14%; vitamin B$_1$ (thiamin), 20%; vitamin B$_2$ (riboflavin), 13%; vitamin B$_3$ (niacin), 41%; vitamin B$_6$, 14%; zinc, 9%.

DOUBLE DUTY

Chicken's protein is easy to digest, and it delivers plenty of B vitamins to fuel your immune system.

Tender Beef with Vegetables

Now here's where ground beef comes in handy. I like to brown it thoroughly, rinse off the fat, and pat it dry. Then I know I have the taste of beef that I love with very little saturated fat—and a complete skillet meal in a matter of minutes. What could be better?

1 pound extra-lean ground beef
1 tablespoon cornstarch
2 cups fat-free beef broth
1/2 teaspoon dried basil
1 can (14 1/2 ounces) sliced carrots, drained
1 can (15 1/2 ounces) cut green beans, drained
1 can (15 ounces) small whole potatoes, drained

In a large, deep skillet over medium heat, brown the beef. Drain off the fat and rinse the beef in a strainer under hot running water. Return to the skillet.

In a small bowl, combine the cornstarch with 1/4 cup of the broth and stir until dissolved. Add to the beef. Add the basil and the remaining 1 3/4 cups broth. Cook, stirring, over medium heat until thickened. Stir in the carrots, beans, and potatoes. Cover and simmer for about 5 minutes, or until heated through. Serve immediately.

Yield: 4 servings

Nutritional data per serving: Calories, 278; protein, 27 g; carbohydrate, 23 g; dietary fiber, 5 g; total fat, 5 g; saturated fat, 2 g; cholesterol, 60 mg; sodium, 865 mg; vitamin A, 104% of Daily Value; vitamin C, 17%; calcium, 4%; iron, 33%; vitamin B$_6$, 17%; potassium, 12%.

Golden Glow Potatoes

I hate to admit this, but I just love canned potatoes. I know, their texture is waxy, but that's why they're so cool. It takes very little butter to make them tasty. Now let's mix and match them with another easy favorite.

1 can (15 ounces) sliced white potatoes, well drained
1 can (15 ounces) sweet potatoes in light syrup,
    well drained
1 tablespoon bread crumbs
1 tablespoon butter
1/2 teaspoon pumpkin pie spice

Lightly coat a 1½-quart baking dish with nonstick spray. Arrange the sliced potatoes to cover the bottom. Top with the sweet potatoes (you may need to cut them a bit to get even coverage). Sprinkle with the bread crumbs, dot with the butter, and dust with the spice. Bake at 450°F for 15 minutes, or until heated through.

Yield: 5 servings

Nutritional data per serving: Calories, 134; protein, 2 g; carbohydrate, 26 g; dietary fiber, 3 g; total fat, 3 g; saturated fat, 1.5 g; cholesterol, 6 mg; sodium, 235 mg; vitamin A, 55% of Daily Value; vitamin C, 20%; calcium, 3%; iron, 5%; copper, 6%.

Lovely Leftovers
Mash extra potatoes with a fork, then brown them in a nonstick pan coated with nonstick spray.

Carrots in Honey-Ginger Sauce

Raw baby carrots are my constant companions. But when I'm feeling less than great, canned carrots come to the rescue!

1 can (14½ ounces) sliced carrots,
    drained and liquid reserved
2 teaspoons cornstarch
½ teaspoon ground ginger
2 tablespoons honey

In a medium saucepan over medium heat, combine the reserved carrot liquid, cornstarch, and ginger. Stir until dissolved. Bring to a boil, stir in the honey, and cook until thickened. Add the carrots and bring to a boil. Reduce the heat, cover, and simmer for about 10 minutes. Serve with chicken or fish.

Yield: 3 servings

Nutritional data per serving: Calories, 84; protein, 1 g; carbohydrate, 21 g; dietary fiber, 3 g; total fat, 0 g; saturated fat, 0 g; cholesterol, 0 mg; sodium, 345 mg; vitamin A, 139% of Daily Value; vitamin C, 5%; calcium, 5%; iron, 5%; vitamin B$_6$, 8%; potassium, 7%.

Lovely Leftovers

Use that third serving as topping on a baked potato for tomorrow's lunch.

Ginger-Peachy Yogurt Smoothie

You may not be feeling great, but you still have work to do. This soothing smoothie will fuel you for hours.

1 cup Stonyfield fat-free plain yogurt
1 cup juice-packed canned peaches
1 tablespoon peach preserves
¹/₈ teaspoon ground ginger

In a blender, combine the yogurt, peaches (with juice), preserves, and ginger. Blend on high until smooth. Pour into a 12-ounce glass and sip through a big, fat straw.

Yield: 1 serving

Nutritional data per serving: Calories, 259; protein, 10 g; carbohydrate, 43 g; dietary fiber, 3 g; total fat, 0 g; saturated fat, 0 g; cholesterol, 0 mg; sodium, 145 mg; vitamin A, 9% of Daily Value; vitamin C, 23%; calcium, 46%; iron, 6%; vitamin E, 19%; potassium, 9%.

DOUBLE DUTY

True, peaches build your beta-carotene reserves. And surprise— they're also a very good source of vitamin E.

Caramel Freeze

Sometimes we buy too many bananas, and I'll bet you can guess what happens. They get too ripe and Ted just won't eat them. So I peel them and freeze them on a baking sheet. When they're solid, I wrap them individually and bag them. They're ready when I am!

1 cup Stonyfield plain yogurt
1 frozen peeled banana
2 tablespoons caramel ice cream topping
2 cherries

Place the yogurt in a blender. On a cutting board, use a sharp knife to cut the banana into 1-inch pieces. With the blender running on high, remove the feeder cap and drop in the banana pieces. Blend until smooth. Add the caramel sauce and blend for 1 minute. Divide between two glasses and stick a straw and a spoon in each. Top with a cherry.

Yield: 2 servings

Nutritional data per serving: Calories, 186; protein, 5 g; carbohydrate, 43 g; dietary fiber, 2 g; total fat, 0 g; saturated fat, 0 g; cholesterol, 0 mg; sodium, 135 mg; vitamin A, 1% of Daily Value; vitamin C, 12%; calcium, 24%; iron, 2%; vitamin B_6, 17%; potassium, 7%.

> **The Inside Skinny:** Refrigerate bananas to slow ripening. The skins may darken, but the bananas are fine!

Nouriche Me Tropical

Got a burning yearning for fruit? Try a canned tropical fruit mix. The island taste is there, without the digestive hassles.

1 bottle (11 ounces) Yoplait Nouriche tropical flavor smoothie
1 cup drained canned tropical fruit in light syrup
1 tablespoon wheat germ
Dash of ground cinnamon

In a blender, combine the smoothie, fruit, and wheat germ. Blend on high until smooth. Pour into a tall glass and dust with the cinnamon.

Yield: 1 serving

Nutritional data per serving: Calories, 238; protein, 6 g; carbohydrate, 152 g; dietary fiber, 4 g; total fat, 0 g; saturated fat, 0 g; cholesterol, 2 mg; sodium, 155 mg; vitamin A, 15% of Daily Value; vitamin C, 93%; calcium, 15%; iron, 11%; vitamin D, 13%; vitamin E, 16%; folate, 16%; zinc, 11%.

The Inside Skinny: Nouriche contains probiotics—live, active cultures of good bacteria that take care of your tummy. It also packs inulin, a nutrient that probiotics feed on so they can multiply.

Apple Pie Sipper

Mmmmm...smell the cinnamon. Yum. It's enough to tempt even the crankiest tummy into enjoying a little liquid refreshment.

> 1 cup Stonyfield fat-free plain yogurt
> 1 cup natural berry-flavored applesauce
> 2 tablespoons apple jelly
> ½ teaspoon ground cinnamon

In a blender, combine the yogurt, applesauce, jelly, and cinnamon. Blend on high for about 1 minute, or until well blended. Pour into a 16-ounce glass and sip through a straw.

Yield: 1 serving

Nutritional data per serving: Calories, 328; protein, 8 g; carbohydrate, 56 g; dietary fiber, 3 g; total fat, 0 g; saturated fat, 0 g; cholesterol, 0 mg; sodium, 150 mg; vitamin A, 1% of Daily Value; vitamin C, 92%; calcium, 47%; iron, 4%; potassium, 6%.

DOUBLE DUTY

The insoluble fiber in applesauce helps lower your cholesterol and tames your tummy as well.

Calming Mint Smoothie

When you're feeling a little hungry, but your digestive tract still needs a rest, slowly sip this refreshing drink.

1 cup Stonyfield fat-free plain yogurt
3 tablespoons mint jelly

In a blender, combine the yogurt and jelly. Blend on high until creamy. Pour into a 10-ounce glass and sip with a straw.

Yield: 1 serving

Nutritional data per serving: Calories, 280; protein, 8 g; carbohydrate, 52 g; dietary fiber, 0 g; total fat, 0 g; saturated fat, 0 g; cholesterol, 0 mg; sodium, 155 mg; vitamin A, 0% of Daily Value; vitamin C, 6%; calcium, 45%; iron, 2%.

SUPER SUB

Stonyfield packs more kinds of tummy-taming live, active cultures into their yogurt than any other brand.

Banana-Cinnamon Wafers

A cookie is a good thing, even under the worst of circumstances. When my tummy's tumbling, I often want a sweet treat. These cookies fill the bill.

1 ripe banana, quartered and sliced
¼ cup reduced-fat ricotta cheese
1 teaspoon cinnamon sugar
12 vanilla wafers

In a small bowl, use a fork to thoroughly mash the banana. Add the ricotta and cinnamon sugar and stir until well blended. Spread 1 teaspoon on each cookie. Enjoy!

Yield: 4 servings

Nutritional data per serving: Calories, 105; protein, 2 g; carbohydrate, 18 g; dietary fiber, 1 g; total fat, 3 g; saturated fat, 1 g; cholesterol, 5 mg; sodium, 57 mg; vitamin A, 2% of Daily Value; vitamin C, 4%; calcium, 5%; iron, 3%; vitamin B$_6$, 9%; folate, 2%; potassium, 4%.

 ## The P·E·R·F·E·C·T Companion

Place 2 cinnamon-apple spice tea bags in a teapot and fill with boiling water. Steep for 3 to 5 minutes and remove the tea bags. Pour into pretty cups and flavor with honey and milk.

Paradise Pudding Pears

Quick as a wink, this creamy dessert can be yours. Chill during dinner for a really cool treat.

1 can (15 ounces) sliced pears in light syrup
1¼ cups 2% milk
1 package (3.4 ounces) French vanilla instant pudding mix
Dash of ground cinnamon

Drain the pear syrup into a 4-cup measuring cup and add enough milk to make 2 cups. Set aside.

Place the pears in a 1½-quart baking dish and chop coarsely. Set aside.

Add the pudding mix to the milk mixture. Use a wire whisk to stir for about 2 minutes, or until well blended and beginning to thicken. Pour over the pears and sprinkle with the cinnamon. Let stand for 5 minutes and serve, or refrigerate until later. The pudding mixture will remain soft and creamy and is best served in small dessert dishes

Yield: 6 servings

Nutritional data per serving: Calories, 126; protein, 2 g; carbohydrate, 29 g; dietary fiber, 1 g; total fat, 1 g; saturated fat, <1 g; cholesterol, 4 mg; sodium, 267 mg; vitamin A, 3% of Daily Value; vitamin C, 2%; calcium, 7%; iron, 1%; potassium, 4%.

The P·E·R·F·E·C·T Companion

Place 2 mandarin orange spice tea bags in a teapot and fill with boiling water. Steep for 3 to 5 minutes and remove the tea bags. Pour into small cups and sweeten with honey.

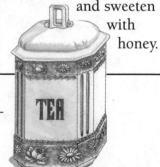

Black Raspberry Crispies

Rice Krispies treats have been around for so long, it's hard to imagine life without them. This purple version is now my friends' football favorite, since we're all fans of the Baltimore Ravens. (Yes, that purple stadium is ours!)

3 tablespoons butter
9 ounces mini-marshmallows
6 cups Rice Krispies cereal
1/4 cup seedless black raspberry preserves

> **Instant Comfort:**
> Try this tummy soother. In a small bowl, pour 1 cup boiling water over 1 teaspoon crushed aniseeds. Steep for 15 minutes and strain into a teacup. Sweeten with a little honey or sugar, if desired.

Lightly coat a 9-inch by 12-inch baking pan with cooking spray.

Melt the butter in a very large saucepan over medium heat. Add the marshmallows and cook, stirring, until melted. Add the preserves and cook, stirring, until the mixture is completely purple. Add the cereal and stir until well mixed. Spoon into the prepared pan and use a flat spatula coated with nonstick spray to spread the mixture evenly. Let cool and cut into 24 squares or oblongs.

Yield: 24 servings

Nutritional data per serving: Calories, 81; protein, 1 g; carbohydrate, 17 g; dietary fiber, 0 g; total fat, 1.5 g; saturated fat, <1 g; cholesterol, 4 mg; sodium, 91 mg; vitamin A, 6% of Daily Value; vitamin C, 6%; calcium, 0%; iron, 2%; folate, 6%.

THE

HEALTH FINDER

Throughout this book are more than 415 recipes that we've developed to help keep you and your family in perfect health. In the lists on the following pages, they are organized according to the diseases and conditions most likely to threaten your health.

If you'd like to keep any one of those ills at bay, just skim down the columns until you reach a disease or condition in which you're interested and look over the amazing recipes listed under it. Then think about including those dishes in your diet on a regular basis. Just keep in mind that no one food or meal will ever prevent or relieve a condition on its own—but a healthy, balanced diet that includes the recipes in this book can be a big help.

Diabetes

Digestive Problems

Fatigue

White Bean and Garlic Pizza, 387
Wild Porcini Rice, 397

High Blood Pressure

Almond Butter and Banana
    Sandwich, 44
Asian Fruit Salad, 60
Autumn Harvest Applesauce, 57
Casaba Melon with Raspberry Sorbet, 59
Celery Cabbage with Cashews, 41
Chayote Squash with Cinnamon, 50
Chinese Celery Cabbage Stir-Fry, 46
Confetti Spaghetti Squash, 53
Dad's Cucumber Salad, 39
Dilled French Green Beans, 49
Garlic Mashed Potatoes with Olive
    Oil, 51
Garlic Potato Crisps, 54
Jicama Fiesta Salad, 38
Long Beans Amandine, 47
Marinated Vegetable Antipasto, 34
Mindy's Mom's Pureed Vegetable
    Soup, 37
Mixed-Message Mushrooms, 52
Nutty Fruit Plate, 61
Portobello-Onion Burger, 43
Rainbow Salsa Salad, 40
Salsa-Salmon Baked Potato, 45
Shoppers' Minestrone, 35
Snow Peas with Shiitake Mushrooms, 48
Springtime Vegetable Soup, 36
Sugar Snap Peas and Baby Carrots, 55

Super K Smoothie, 56
Traffic Light Parfait, 58
Yogurt-Lime Dressing, 42

High Cholesterol/Heart Disease

Asparagus Mousse Soup, 100
Bean Burrito with Avocado, 12
Beef Stew Sauvignon, 24
Buckwheat Breakfast Pancakes, 105
Cashew Butter and Jam Sandwich, 107
Chicken and Black Olive Wrap, 13
Chicken Winter Waldorf Salad, 8
Curried Hummus Spread, 5
Fantastico Olive Oil Dip, 99
Friday Night Sausage Bowl, 21
Garden Pizza, 110
Ginger-Sesame Dressing, 103
Green Chicken Chili, 34
Ham and Chutney Sandwich, 19
Italian Sausage Sandwich with Peppers
    and Onions, 17
Lemon-Hazelnut Mayonnaise, 104
Meat and Mushroom Pasta Sauce, 28
Mighty Minestrone, 7
Mom's Oven-Fried Chicken, 29
(Not) Your Mother's Meat Loaf, 25
Olive Array Appetizer, 97
Olive Orange, 109
Passionate Chicken, 10
Peanut Butter Oatmeal, 108
Pepper Steak with Tomatoes and
    Onions, 26

Pizza Muffin, 14
Pork Loin Chops with Mangoes and
    Lemon Curd, 22
Pumpkin-Seed Salad, 101
Romanian Sausage Bake, 20
Sausage-Stuffed Mushroom Caps, 4
Sicilian Tapenade, 98
Snow Soup, 6
Take-Flight Buffalo Salad, 11
Talkin' Turkey Tacos, 18
Three-Pound Goulash, 23
Turkey-in-the-Straw Mushrooms, 9
Turkey Pesto Wrap, 15
Walnut Buckwheat Muffins, 106
"Wing It" Buffalo Burger, 16
Your Goose Is Cooked, 27
Zucchini-Basil Salad, 102

Memory Problems

Baked Black Plums, 309
"Be an Angel" Cherry-Frosted Cake, 311
Beets with Risotto, 297
Berry Memorable Spinach, 300
Blueberry-Basil Smoothie, 304
Blue Moon Fruit Sauce with Frozen
    Yogurt, 308
Cherry Vanilla Pudding, 312
Chilled Blueberry Soup, 286
Chipotle Ranch Salad, 287
Chocolate-Raspberry Pancakes, 292
"Color Purple" Salad, The, 290
Cranberry Beet Greens, 299
Cranberry-Grape Relish, 301

Cuppa Red Pasta Sauce, 295
Deep Purple Plums, 306
Double Berry Decadence, 307
Double Grape Crush, 305
Flaming Wasabi Salad, 289
Grilled Tuna Cobb Salad, 294
Lemon-Blueberry Muffins, 302
Oven-Roasted Beets, 298
Peanut Butter and Jelly Sipper, 303
Pink Sunset Parfait, 310
Roasted-Pepper and Green Olive
    Spread, 285
Romanian Red Slaw, 296
Spicy Hot Fruit Compote, 291
Sweet Beet Salad, 288
Whole Grain Waffles with Hot Raisin
    Syrup, 293

Osteoporosis

Apricot Sunset, 180
Banana-Coconut Shake, 179
Beans 'n Greens Tomato Soup, 161
Bella Bella Pocket Salad, 164
Cheddar Cheese Sauce, 177
Cherry-Chocolate Hazelnut Cup, 182
Clip 'n Snip Summer Vegetable Dip, 159
Creamy Broccoli Soup, 160
Figs, Feta, and Field Greens, 162
Fresh Strawberries and Frozen
    Yogurt, 184
Fresh Strawberry Cream Dip, 158
"Goddess" Wild Mushroom Pasta, 169
Gouda Mac, 173

Stroke

INDEX